Philosophy in a Feminist Voice

Philosophy in a Feminist Voice

CRITIQUES AND

RECONSTRUCTIONS

JANET A. KOURANY, EDITOR

PRINCETON UNIVERSITY PRESS

PRINCETON, NEW JERSEY

Library of Congress Cataloging-in-Publication Data

Philosophy in a feminist voice : critiques and reconstructions / Janet A. Kourany, editor.
p. cm.
Includes bibliographical references and index.
ISBN 0-691-03313-7 (alk. paper) — 0-691-01936-3 (pbk. : alk. paper)
1. Feminist theory. 2. Feminist criticism. 3. Feminism—Philosophy. I. Kourany, Janet A.
HQ1190.P53 1997   97-22817   305.42—dc21   CIP

This book has been composed in Sabon

Princeton University Press books are printed on acid-free paper and meet the guidelines for
permanence and durability of the Committee on Production Guidelines for Book
Longevity of the Council on Library Resources

http://pup.princeton.edu

Printed in the United States of America

1 2 3 4 5 6 7 8 9 10

1 2 3 4 5 6 7 8 9 10
(pbk)

CONTENTS

PREFACE

THIS BOOK has grown out of a number of concerns: that philosophy as we know it today in the West is largely the product of the work of misogynist men of the past, men who were either unresponsive to the needs and interests of women, or whose ideas were downright antithetical to those needs and interests; that feminist philosophy, which *is* responsive to the needs and interests of women, has been largely ignored by this same philosophical tradition; that the same kind of feminist critical and reconstructive work that has been largely ignored by philosophy in recent times has been transformative of other fields (like history and theology and biology and psychology and English literature); that these other fields attract large—and, indeed, ever growing—numbers of women to them; and that philosophy, by contrast, has yet to attract significant numbers of women to it

Our aim, of course, is to change all this. To that end we offer a clear understanding, free of jargon or specialized presuppositions, of what feminist philosophy is about, why it is important, and what it offers to philosophy. More specifically, we offer a comprehensive feminist critique of most of the major areas of philosophy, written by distinguished contributors to these areas, together with a sketch of some of the new directions in which work is proceeding in these areas, and also some of the new directions in which philosophical work can and ought to proceed. We hope thereby to promote informed dialogue between so-called feminist philosophers and mainstream philosophers, and thereby bring about much-needed change in philosophy.

Many people have added immeasurably to this project, whether with suggestions, advice, or encouragement. Foremost among them are Sandra Bartky, Paddy Blanchette, Phil Quinn, and especially Jim Sterba, to whom the book is dedicated. Ann Wald, Helen Hsu, and Karen Verde of Princeton University Press showed immense patience and fortitude through an avalanche of problems and delays. Finally, my daughter, Sonya, contributed the love and support needed to see the project through to its completion.

LOUISE M. ANTONY is Associate Professor of Philosophy at the University of North Carolina at Chapel Hill, where she teaches courses in the philosophy of language, the philosophy of mind, and feminist theory. She is author of numerous essays in these areas, and is coeditor, with Charlotte Witt, of *A Mind of One's Own: Feminist Essays on Reason and Objectivity* (1993).

SUSAN BORDO is Professor of Philosophy and holds the Singletary Chair of Humanities at the University of Kentucky. She is the author of *The Flight to Objectivity: Essays on Cartesianism and Culture* (1987) and *Unbearable Weight: Feminism, Western Culture, and the Body* (1993). Her forthcoming books are *Twilight Zones: The Hidden Life of Cultural Images from Plato to O.J.* (1997) and *My Father's Body and Other Unexplored Regions of Sex, Masculinity, and the Male Body* (Farrar, Straus & Giroux).

LORRAINE CODE is Distinguished Research Professor in the Department of Philosophy at York University in Toronto, Canada. In addition to numerous articles in epistemology and feminist theory, she is the author of *What Can She Know? Feminist Theory and the Construction of Knowledge* (1991) and *Rhetorical Spaces: Essays on (Gendered) Locations* (1995). She is working on a book on ecology, responsibility, and the politics of knowledge, and is general editor of an encyclopedia of feminist theories, forthcoming from Routledge, UK.

NANCY FRANKENBERRY is Stone Professor of Intellectual and Moral Philosophy and Professor of Religion at Dartmouth College. She currently chairs the Department of Religion and has chaired the Women's Studies Program. Her writings cover topics in philosophy of religion, American religious thought, and, most recently, pragmatism.

VIRGINIA HELD is Distinguished Professor of Philosophy at Hunter College and the Graduate School of the City University of New York. Among her books are *Justice and Care: Essential Reading in Feminist Ethics* (editor, 1995); *Feminist Morality: Transforming Culture, Society, and Politics* (1993); *Rights and Goods: Justifying Social Action* (1984, 1989); and *The Public Interest and Individual Interests* (1970).

CAROLYN KORSMEYER is Professor of Philosophy at the State University of New York at Buffalo. She is coeditor with Hilde Hein of *Aesthetics in Feminist Perspective* (1993), and with Peg Brand she coedited *Feminism and Tradition in Aesthetics* (1995). At present she is working on a study of the sense of taste.

JANET A. KOURANY is editor of *Scientific Knowledge* (1987, 1998) and coeditor, with James Sterba and Rosemarie Tong, of *Feminist Philosophies* (1992, 1998). Among her forthcoming works are *The Gender of Science*

(1998) and *Feminism and Its Critics* (Rowman and Littlefield). She teaches courses in the philosophy of science and feminist theory at the University of Notre Dame, where she is also a Fellow of the Reilly Center for Science, Technology, and Values.

ANDREA NYE is the author of a number of books exploring the relation between philosophy and feminist theory, the latest of which is *Philosophy and Feminism: at the Border* (1995). She is also the author of *Words of Power: A Feminist Reading of the History of Logic* (1990). She is Professor of Philosophy at the University of Wisconsin—Whitewater.

SUSAN MOLLER OKIN is the author of *Women in Western Political Thought* (1979, 1992) and *Justice, Gender, and the Family* (1991). She is the Marta Sutton Weeks Professor of Ethics in Society and a member of the Political Science Department at Stanford University, where she teaches political theory. She is currently working on a project about feminism and cultural differences.

EILEEN O'NEILL is Associate Professor at the University of Massachusetts—Amherst. She has published on feminist aesthetics, on seventeenth-century metaphysics, and on women's contributions to early modern philosophy. She is currently completing the two-volume *Women Philosophers of the Seventeenth and Eighteenth Centuries: A Collection of Primary Sources* for Oxford University Press.

Philosophy in a Feminist Voice

Philosophy in a *Feminist Voice*?

JANET A. KOURANY

WHAT IS philosophy good for? Why do we do it, and why do we teach it and study it? Does it provide us with a deeper understanding of knowledge and reality, justice and virtue "than that somewhat chaotic view which everyone by nature carries about with him under his hat"?[1] Does it enable us to enlighten and empower artists and scientists and theologians and jurists with special insights into their fields? Does it enable us to live more satisfying lives? Exactly what does philosophy accomplish?

Make the question more focused and concrete. We tell our students philosophy will do valuable things for them: teach them how to think and express themselves clearly, make them more critical of customary beliefs and assumptions, give them a general framework to help them make sense of their experiences, give them guidance in everyday life, and the like. Does the philosophy we teach actually deliver on these promises?

It is the message of this book that much of the philosophy most Western philosophers engage in and teach and study is significantly flawed in what it delivers. Indeed, this philosophy often provides outlooks and ways of thinking unhelpful to everyone, but especially unhelpful to women. Far from functioning as the proverbial gadfly that rouses everyone from complacency on every question, this philosophy tends to ignore women even while it reflects and reinforces or in other ways perpetuates some of the most deeply entrenched and abusive biases against women in our society. The essays that follow, in fact, provide examples of such neglect and such biases, and philosophy's role in their perpetuation, for most of the major areas of Western philosophy.

The message of the book is not only a pessimistic one, however. It is also an optimistic one: that the philosophy we engage in and teach and study *can be* a powerful force for change, and that some of it currently is. Indeed, the essays that follow also outline some of the new directions in which work is proceeding in the various areas of philosophy, and also some of the new directions in which philosophical work can and ought to proceed. In contrast to the overwhelmingly male-dominated philosophical enterprise that most Western philosophers engage in and teach and study, all of this new work—these new directions in philosophy, as well as the critiques that have motivated them—aim in one way or another to make visible and improve women's situation. And, again in contrast to the male-dominated philosophical enterprise, almost all of this new work is being done by women. It is thus appropriate to speak of this book and the work it deals with as philosophy in a different voice—indeed, philosophy in a *feminist* voice. But the new work this book deals with is relevant and helpful to men as well as women, and in fact promises to more adequately fulfill the aims that philosophers espouse for themselves than the philosophical enterprise that most Western philosophers now engage in. To motivate men as well as women philosophers to pursue this new work, or at least to give it a serious hearing, is the foremost objective of *Philosophy in a Feminist Voice*. It signals the different voice—the full and diverse chorus of voices—*Philosophy in a Feminist Voice* ultimately hopes to call forth.

THE VOICE OF THE WESTERN PHILOSOPHICAL TRADITION

What is this philosophical enterprise most Western philosophers engage in and teach and study? Despite its diversity of methods and goals, contributors and viewpoints and styles, it is characterized by a number of features that are of special concern to the authors of this book. The Western philosophical enterprise is, first of all, one from which, until quite recently, women's voices have been removed. In "Disappearing Ink: Early Modern Women Philosophers and Their Fate in History," Eileen O'Neill illuminates both the dimensions of this loss and the process by which it came about. Focusing on the early modern period, O'Neill provides an overview of the published work of seventeenth- and eighteenth-century women philosophers from England, France, Belgium, Germany, Italy, Mexico, Switzerland, and Russia. These women addressed a wide range of questions current in the philosophical circles of their day, questions that were the historical predecessors of contemporary topics in metaphysics, epistemology, moral theory, social and political philosophy, aesthetics, philosophical theology, philosophy of science, and philosophy of education. And their work was well acknowledged by their contemporaries, as evidenced, for example, by its representation in the scholarly journals of the period and by its numerous editions and translations that continued to appear into the nineteenth century. Yet few philosophers today are familiar with these women's work, or even with their names. This is not, O'Neill suggests, because of well-justified criteria of selection that ultimately demanded the exclusion of the women from our histories of Western philosophy. Rather, it is because of a group of related, though mostly external, factors—the socially encouraged practice of anonymous authorship for women; the late eighteenth- and nineteenth-century "purification" of Western philosophy from topics that formed the subject matter of much of the women's work, topics such as woman's nature and role in society; the growing perception in the nineteenth century that women's contributions to philosophy were "feminine" (that is, degenerate, not serious, philosophy); the growing acceptance, at the same time, of the view that women were incapable of doing philosophy; and the growing threat that women authors in general, and women philosophers in particular, posed to the maintenance of a patriarchal social order in the midst of a newly democratic political order.

But whatever the reasons for the disappearance of women's voices from within our Western philosophical tradition, what have been the consequences? This is a second concern of the authors of this book. If women's voices have been silenced, what of the men's voices that can still be heard? In " 'Human Nature' and Its Role in Feminist Theory," Louise Antony answers that the men's voices that can still be heard philosophizing about human nature have, by and large, been those of a highly privileged group of men. As a result, there has been much room for bias in their philosophizing—because these men have theorized about a very large and diverse group, the whole human race, from the vantage point of their rather small and homogeneous group, because these men have come to their theories, and justified them, on the basis of an aprioristic method of reflection and introspection that makes it easy to generalize their own characteristics and concerns in at least a normative way to all others, and because these men have had strong motives for devising theories of human nature that justify their own dominant social position. There has been much room for bias in the Western tradition's philosophy of persons, then, and Antony tells us that there *has* been much bias. For example, there has been bias in the field's emphasis on the mind and "reason" in its characterization of human nature (both associated with privileged masculinity) and in its de-emphasis and devaluation of the bodily and physical (both associated with femininity). There has been bias in the kind of activity it has chosen to canonize as "reason." And there has been bias in the field's exclusion of women from the group of full and proper exemplars of this human nature. All this has reflected the situation, needs, and values of privileged men who are (and who want to continue to be) relatively free of mundane cares and responsibilities.

The field of ethics presents at least as unfortunate a story. Indeed, Virginia Held tells us in "Feminist Reconceptualizations in Ethics" that the great theorists within ethics have been not only privileged men but (quoting Annette Baier) "men who had minimal adult dealings with (and so were then minimally influenced by) women"—"clerics, misogynists, and puritan bachelors." As a result, Held suggests, the history of ethics has been constructed from distinctively male points of view to at least as great an extent as the history of philosophy of persons. Thus, ethics has concerned itself throughout its history only with the world of men and their activities—with the so-called public world. The world of the home and women's traditional activities—the so-called private world—has been portrayed, on the other hand, as a "natural" and "instinctive" and "biological" world, and hence as outside the domain of moral theory. For example, a mother's sacrifice for her child has traditionally been seen as outside morality, in the sphere of "natural relationships." Relatedly, the self that moral theory has tended to deal with in the history of ethics is an egoistic, isolated, individualistic self whose needs must be reconciled with those of the universal "all others"—a quite masculine self. And the self that moral theory has tended *not* to deal with is a self constituted at least in part by family relations and relations of friendship, group ties, and neighborhood concerns—a more feminine self. Finally, the way the self has been instructed to deal with moral problems in the history of ethics is through reason rather than emotion, where reason and emotion have been represented as antithetical to each other. Think, for example, of the endless search within moral theory for very general, very abstract, universal moral principles like Kant's Categorical Imperative or the Utilitarians' Principle of Utility that promise to solve all moral problems on the basis of reason alone. But, of course, this instruction has been directed at men, since women have been held in this tradition (and out of it!) to be deficient in reason, though well equipped with emotion. In all these ways, Held suggests, masculinity has been inscribed within the history of ethics, while femininity has been excluded.

Much the same can be said of the history of political philosophy. In "Feminism and Political Theory," Susan Okin surveys the now vast literature showing that the history of political philosophy has also been constructed from male points of view—has also been "a tradition of theorizing created by, for, and about men." To be sure, the basic concepts of political theory, concepts like *human nature, autonomy, freedom* and *individualism, contract, consent, power, justice,* and *democracy,* have been designed to fit men and their experiences, not women. For example, the characteristics—like rationality, aggressiveness, and competitiveness—that have been put forward as definitive of *human nature* in this tradition and linked up to other fundamental concepts turn out to express the tradition's concept of male human nature, since female human nature is defined very differently. Indeed, female human nature has been defined in the tradition in terms of such characteristics as emotionality, passivity, subservience, enslavement to passions, incapacity for rational, universalistic, or principled thinking, and the like, just the antithesis of the tradition's *human nature.* And this disparity is significant, since the tradition's conception of female human nature has been used to justify women's inferior social status, which has then been used as a disqualification for any other status. Again, the various notions of *freedom* within the tradition have been rooted in a freedom *from* the body and its demands, a freedom *from* necessity in general. But again, this concept has been designed for men, not women, with their reproductive and other labors.

Conceptual exclusion, Okin points out, is not the only problem for women within the history of political philosophy. Indeed, fundamental issues that have been questioned or argued about for men have simply been assumed for women. For example, the subordination of women to men has often been assumed, unlike the inequalities among men. Again, household tasks have simply been assumed to be women's, not men's, responsibility; as a result women, unlike men, have been regarded as unsuited for, or at least unavailable for, participation in political life. And with the exclusion of women from the political realm has gone the exclusion of the domestic, familial, private, personal, and sexual, even though power resides in these areas as well, and even though the distribution of power in these areas is closely connected with the distribution of power in the political realm. Finally, great value has been placed on the things traditionally associated with men (reason, individualism, aggressiveness, competition) and little value has been placed on the things traditionally associated with women (concern with physical needs and the family, nurturance, emotionality, cooperation both with other people and with nature) even though the latter are at least as important for human survival.

Masculinity is inscribed in similar ways in the history of aesthetics as well, Carolyn Korsmeyer reports. In "Perceptions, Pleasures, Arts: Considering Aesthetics," she explains that, just as the history of ethics and the history of political philosophy have dealt only with the public world of men, so too the history of aesthetics has recognized aesthetic value only in "public" objects like paintings and statues and symphonies, typically produced by men, not in domestic decorations or clothing or utensils, personal letters or diaries, or any of the other objects typically produced by women and embedded in women's "private" daily activities. And just as the history of ethics and the history of political philosophy have dealt with their subject matters on a very general, very abstract, universal plane, detached from the concrete and the practical, so, too, the history of aesthetics has sought to establish abstract principles of taste that are universal, on a foundation provided by the "aesthetic"/"cognitive" senses of sight and hearing. These "higher" senses, distinguished from the "lower," "bodily" senses of taste, touch, and smell, have traditionally been held to be more allied with reason, more "distant" from our physical being. And just as the history of ethics and the history of political philosophy have required control of emotion for reliable moral and political judgments to be possible, so, too, the history of aesthetics has required control of emotion—"disinterested" responses—for reliable aesthetic judgments to be possible, so that once again women have been considered less able than men to make such judgments. Of course women—along with paintings, sculptures, and scenery—have been considered appropriate *objects* of aesthetic judgments within the history of aesthetics even when they have not been considered appropriate *subjects* of such judgments, thereby assigning women the role of (passive) objects for the delectation of (male) perceivers. And relatedly, Korsmeyer adds, women have been considered appropriate subjects of paintings and sculptures and other works of art within the history of aesthetics, though they have been considered incapable

of being artists themselves, much less artists of genius. In short, the field of
aesthetics, too, has been very much a masculine terrain.

So, too, the field of philosophy of religion. Though one might expect issues surrounding the divine to transcend issues of gender, Nancy Frankenberry tells us in "Philosophy of Religion in Different Voices" that within the
philosophy of religion the divine has traditionally been conceived of in masculine terms and within hierarchical patterns of relations—as, for example,
"Father," "King," "Lord," "Bridegroom," "Husband," and "God-He." Indeed, the concept of the divine has functioned within and drawn meaning
from a comprehensive scheme of interrelated hierarchical oppositions like
God/world, sacred/profane, heaven/earth, mind/body, subject/object, rea-
son/passion, activity/passivity, all related to masculine/feminine. What's
more, this masculine gendering of the divine has deeply affected the basic
issues of traditional philosophy of religion. For example, none of the divine
attributes receives more attention in the literature than "omnipotence," by
which is meant some version of "perfect power," where the kind of power
in question is one of domination, or power-over. But possessing this kind of
power is one of the characteristics associated with ideal masculinity (as is
true, of course, with other characteristics attributed to the divine, like self-
sufficiency and independence of the will). Again, the main question of theodicy—How can an *all-powerful* God *permit* evil?—bespeaks the very same
concept of masculine power. (Needless to say, misogyny, rape, and other ills
inflicted on women by men rarely make the list of evils discussed in standard
treatments of theodicy.)

But exclusion of the feminine from the terrain of philosophy of religion is
not the only kind of exclusion operating there. Frankenberry also details
how traditional philosophy of religion has been a philosophy not so much
of *religion* as of the *Christian* (and particularly the *Protestant*) religion, and
even then has been oblivious to culturally diverse (in terms of race, class,
geographic region, and the like) expressions of Christianity. What's more, it
has focused on the single category of "belief" abstracted from all the most
concrete aspects of religious life. In short, traditional philosophy of religion
has been a rather parochial as well as patriarchal enterprise.

Epistemology, involved as it is with issues concerning reason and knowledge, is another field one might expect to transcend issues of gender. Lorraine Code, however, assures us in "Voice and Voicelessness: A Modest Proposal?" that such transcendence is not to be found in epistemology either.
Indeed, throughout the history of Western philosophy at least since Plato,
and despite changing understandings of reason and knowledge, the
knower—the "man of reason"—has been characterized using whatever
symbols and metaphors have been used to characterize ideal masculinity,
and excluding whatever has been taken to be characteristic of the feminine.
In the modern era he has been thought of as like a practitioner of one of the
"hard" (i.e., masculine) sciences, regulating his behavior according to the

ideals of such sciences. Thus, he is said to base his views, his "knowledge," on "the facts," represented as neutrally there, found not made, and he is held accountable only to those facts. His motives for acquiring this knowledge, and the uses to which it will be put once acquired, on the other hand, are deemed irrelevant—external to the knowledge-seeking process—as are his personal characteristics and circumstances. He functions, in fact, like a detached, disinterested, and solitary observer and searcher after truth, just like any other observer and searcher after truth, and, in fact, interchangeable with them, and therein lies his objectivity. Such is the quite masculine conception of the knower and knowledge that underlies modern epistemology, and it continues to shape the problems and puzzles in the field. As a result, it makes sense to speak abstractly of the necessary and sufficient conditions for "S knows that p," and to focus attention almost entirely on this issue rather than on, for example, what is involved in knowing other persons, knowing how to do things, establishing, conferring, and withholding epistemic authority, and the like. But once we recognize that the production of knowledge is a social enterprise involving negotiation among variously empowered and disempowered individuals, and constrained by social institutions and social structures, as well as by what is given in nature, and once we recognize that our knowledge has political and social implications, not the least of which has been the subordination of women, we also recognize that the masculine conception of knowledge is completely unacceptable, if not downright dangerous.

Underlying the masculine terrain of epistemology is the masculine terrain of philosophy of science. Indeed, in "A New Program for Philosophy of Science, in Many Voices," I sketch out some of the modern pictures of science furnished by the philosophy of science that support the masculine conception of knowledge of modern epistemology. The central problem with philosophy of science, however, I argue, is not that its pictures of science deal with the modern "man of reason" or the public world of men scientists but that its pictures of science *hide* the fact that they do. To be sure, modern Western science has been masculine right from the start—in the way it has aimed to dominate a nature conceived of as feminine, with a method characterized by disinterestedness and emotional detachment, aggression and competitiveness, in the way men have controlled it right from the start, in the way it has tended to leave women largely invisible in its knowledge and research, and in the way it has often portrayed women, and things feminine, in negative terms when it *has* considered us. And this masculinity of science has had damaging effects on all of us, but especially on women. But the comprehensive pictures of science produced by philosophy of science hide this masculinity. For example, they portray ("good," "normal," "rational") science as entirely determined by observation and logic (logical empiricism), or by paradigms or research programmes or research traditions or scientific domains (the "new" philosophy of science), and thus as entirely indepen-

dent of the social and its economic/political/cultural—including gender—
and other modes of influence. Moreover, they provide conceptual structures
(e.g., the empiricist criterion of meaning) that safeguard science and its masculinity from social critique, including gender critique. Operating from such
pictures, philosophy of science has helped keep the masculinity of science
and its damaging effects invisible and intact.

But science is not the only masculine institution in need of exposure and
change. Modern society furnishes examples of many others, not the least of
which is language itself. To be sure, Andrea Nye points out in "Semantics in
a New Key," gender hierarchy is embedded in language in a variety of ways.
In English, for example, generic masculine forms (like the noun "man" and
the pronoun "he") code onto grammar the equivalence of humanity with
masculinity and the anomalous and inferior status of femininity, pairs of
words are asymmetrically coded so that feminine counterparts are always of
lesser power and, relatedly, are frequently sexualized (as in "master/mis-
tress"), diminutive endings mark the inferior status of feminine counterparts
(as in "poet/poetess"), women's identities are determined through their relations with men (as in the titles Miss/Mrs.) and the like. What's more, empirical studies have disclosed differences in women's and men's conversational
and writing styles (women do not innovate in language, they produce half-
finished sentences, they use fewer clauses and logical connectives, etc.), and
have even disclosed the institutionalization of such differences in some cultures, or else the use of different dialects or phonetics by women. Of course,
the achievement of equality between women and men depends upon getting
rid of such language-related inequalities, but how? Feminist activists have
drawn help in recent years from such fields as linguistics, literary criticism,
and continental philosophy, fields that have dealt with issues related to gender and language both descriptively and critically. But feminist activists have
steered clear of Anglo-American philosophy of language, a field that has
shown no interest in these issues. Meanwhile, Anglo-American philosophy
of language has concerned itself with such issues as the possibility of alternative and incommensurable conceptual schemes, the possibility of "radical"
translation from one language community to another, the difficulty of establishing singular reference across "different worlds," and the like, but with
virtually no reference to actual failures of communication or problems of
gender inequality. Nye's aim is thus to initiate a dialogue between feminists
and philosophers of language on issues of mutual concern, such as the relation between beliefs and attitudes and the structure of vocabularies and syntax, and the nature of meaning and reference and the definition of truth—
issues on which the prospects for feminist reform of language and a widely
based feminist movement depend. Such a dialogue not only would promise
feminists the theoretically adequate conceptions needed for feminist practice, but also would promise philosophers of language the contact with human experience and human problems that could enrich and revitalize the
sometimes sterile formalisms of philosophy of language.

PHILOSOPHY IN A FEMINIST VOICE

What is the upshot? We tell our students philosophy will do valuable things for them: teach them how to think and express themselves clearly, make them more critical of customary beliefs and assumptions, give them a general framework to help them make sense of their experiences, give them guidance in everyday life, and the like. And we tell ourselves much the same thing—that philosophy will help us live more intelligent, more useful, more satisfying lives. This promise of philosophy is especially valuable to women. For the message is there in children's stories and textbooks (where women are the nurses, the mothers, the farmers' wives, but never the farmers, or where women are simply invisible), in advertising (where women are depicted as completely absorbed by the appearance of their nails or the appearance of their bathroom bowls), in the positions of greatest authority and status and power in society (all occupied by men), and even in our language (where *he* constitutes humanity, and *she* constitutes his little helpmate). Women and men are *still* raised in our society to see women as less capable and less valuable than men, intellectually, physically, and frequently even morally. And women must deal with that message of inferiority, and combat it, in ourselves as well as in those who underpay us, fail to employ or promote us, sexually harass or rape us, and patronize and belittle us. But the Western philosophical tradition does not give women the wherewithal to do this. Indeed, far from pointing women toward a more adequate set of conceptions, this tradition tends to ignore women even while it reflects and reinforces or in other ways perpetuates the same message of women's inferiority. At least, as we have seen, the men's voices in most of the major areas of Western philosophy—nearly the only voices we ever hear—seem to teach women anew that we lack the capacities of men (e.g., emotional control and rationality) and that these capacities in turn define human excellence and even human nature itself. As a result, women are left to see ourselves, our activities, and our achievements as having no real value—no moral value, no political value, no epistemic value, no aesthetic value, no spiritual value.

Well, what can we do? If we are going to keep on telling our students and ourselves how enriching and valuable philosophy is for *everyone*, both women and men, then our philosophy is going to have to deal with women and our experiences and concerns as fairly and comprehensively as it deals with men and theirs. The authors of the following essays suggest ways to move in this direction. Thus, Louise Antony tells us that there is increasing empirical evidence for the existence of a human cognitive nature—for the existence of a universal capacity in humans for language acquisition and, with it, a universal capacity for abstract thought and rationally directed action, for linguistic communication, social affiliation, and cultural creation. Such a human nature, Antony continues, can begin to provide us with a conception of what Aristotle calls "human flourishing," a conception that, unlike Aristotle's, is both nonarbitrary and equally applicable to women and men. And such a human nature, along with its attendent conception of human flourishing, is a central part of any genuinely universal and comprehensive philosophy. For example, notions of human nature and human flourishing are needed to articulate and defend feminism's protests against the systematic *dehumanization* of women in our society—the treatment of women in ways that prevent or impede the full development of our *human* capacities.

A genuinely universal and comprehensive philosophy, then, will deal with persons who share a common human nature. But these persons will not be the abstract intellects—the masculine individuals—of traditional Western philosophy. Indeed, they will have, in addition to their common human nature, all the traits that have been traditionally disparaged and ignored and, in effect, denied persons because associated with women. Thus, they will be *embodied* persons: racially, culturally, and historically specific gendered individuals. And they will be thoroughly *social* persons, associating in families and communities, as well as in the "public" world. And they will be *emotional* as well as intellectual persons. What changes in philosophy will the addition of such traits produce? Consider a few examples.

If the persons philosophy deals with are *embodied*, then, Nancy Frankenberry suggests, philosophy of religion has to deal with such issues as the relation of embodied persons to God (e.g., the dilemmas posed to masculinity when men worship a male God in a culture based on heterosexual complementarity) or the relation of embodied persons to religious experience (e.g., the role of sexuality in mystical experience, and how it affects the symbols or concepts involved). Moreover, if the embodied persons philosophy deals with are differently situated, culturally and racially and economically, then philosophy of religion has to deal with a plurality of religious traditions, for the sake of creating a truly cross-cultural philosophy of *religions* rather than a philosophy of one version of the Christian religion. And this requires the elaboration of new models of interpretation, a broader theory of evidence, a cross-culturally adequate conception of human rationality, and a more complex appraisal of the norms applicable to cases of rival religious claims and disagreements. Similarly, Carolyn Korsmeyer suggests, aesthetics has to allow for and illuminate the diversity of aesthetic response that emerges from differences among people, while at the same time being prepared to fulfill a critical function with respect to such differences—that is, being prepared not to perpetuate a cultural status quo. Moreover, if the embodied persons philosophy deals with are women as well as men, then aesthetics has to deal with more than the public world of men. It must include consideration of works produced in private contexts where the majority of women have spent their time, so that it has the chance of including in its purview artistic traditions where women have been the principal practitioners, as well as the canonical artistic traditions where women have been largely excluded. This provides opportunities not only to supplement conventional notions of art but also to appreciate the aesthetic dimensions of daily life. And, I suggest, philosophy of science has to investigate the work of women scientists as well as men, especially extraordinary women scientists and women scientists who have been relatively free of men scientists' domination. Investigating such work, along with the work of the men scientists that is regularly investigated by philosophers of science, may provide examples of different ways of doing science, and will have the added benefit of helping us to see science as a possible and appropriate activity for women as well as men, one to which women have already made significant contributions. Finally, Susan Okin suggests, if the embodied persons philosophy deals with are women as well as men, then political philosophy has to redefine its most basic concepts to apply to women as well as men, the private as well as the public. At the same time it has to rethink the public-private distinction itself, to bring into focus the political dimensions of the "private."

So much for the *embodied* nature of philosophy's subjects. If the persons philosophy deals with are thoroughly *social* as well, then, Virginia Held suggests, ethics has to develop a new conception of autonomy, one that avoids positing self-sufficient (and thus highly artificial) individuals—one that recognizes that social relations are a large part of what we are. And ethics has to take account of such things as actual relationships between persons and what those relationships require. For example, it has to take account of bringing up children, of what the relevant norms and practices ought to be, and of how the institutions and arrangements throughout society and the world ought to be structured to facilitate the right kinds of development of the best kinds of new persons. Moreover, Lorraine Code suggests, epistemology has to acknowledge that the knowledge production engaged in by such persons is a social affair whose products bear the marks of their makers and whose stories, therefore, need to be told. Epistemology has then to take empirical account of how such persons come to know—the desires and interests that motivate their cognitive projects, the cooperative or other relations among them, the helps or hindrances provided by their situations, the nature of the public to whom their knowledge is presented and the way it is presented, the uses to which their knowledge is put, and the like—and must critically reflect on the results of these investigations. Similarly, I suggest, philosophy of science has to acknowledge that social values, including gender-related values, shape scientific research and its results. As a consequence, philosophers of science who seek to analyze, say, the structure and functions of scientific theories, or their validation, have to deal with the analysis and justification of such values, including their origins and consequences in the society in which the science is pursued. And philosophers of science who seek to make epistemological sense of actual episodes in the history of science have to situate those episodes in their social settings as an essential part of the analysis. At the same time, Andrea Nye adds, philosophy of language must acknowledge that its subject matter is the linguistic process of speaking together about objects of common interest, not, or not only, language as a code for internal events (as in cognitive or empiricist theories of language), or as a system of classification (as in structuralism), or as an adaptation of logical form (as in truth-theoretic semantics). It is also about what language can and should be if it is to produce understanding and knowledge, knowledge that serves all people of all races and cultures, women as well as men.

Finally, if the embodied and social persons philosophy deals with have emotions as well as intellects, then, Virginia Held suggests, ethics has to include a reevaluation of the place of emotion in morality—the emphasis in traditional theories on rational control over the emotions (e.g., rage) rather than on the cultivation of desirable forms of emotion (e.g., love for children). Indeed, ethics must include feelings of empathy and caring and other emotions, as well as abstract rules of justice, as guides to action. And, I suggest, philosophy of science has to include a reevaluation of the place of emotion in science—for example, recognizing and investigating the fact that scientists sometimes form close emotional ties to the objects of their research that facilitate every stage of that research, from the kinds of questions they ask of those objects to the theories that form answers and the observations that support such theories. And, Carolyn Korsmeyer adds, aesthetics has to take advantage of current analyses of emotion to elucidate the important role of emotion in aesthetic judgment, as well as to investigate the light these analyses can shed on long-standing questions in aesthetics.

Thus, if the persons philosophy deals with share a common human nature but are embodied in racial-, cultural-, class-, and gender-specific ways, if they are thoroughly social, and if they have emotions as well as intellects—if, that is to say, they are *real* persons like ourselves—then Western philosophy will need to make many and varied changes in all its major areas. Such changes, as we have seen, will help to ensure that Western philosophy no longer ignores women or perpetuates its traditional biases against women. But such changes will also help to ensure that Western philosophy does full justice to *men* as well as women, since men as well as women are embodied in specific ways, are social, and have emotions as well as intellects. If all these changes are instances of philosophy in a feminist voice, then we can see that ours is no small undertaking. Fortunately, it does not begin from scratch. Indeed, as Eileen O'Neill makes clear, philosophers in the past, especially women philosophers, were at least sometimes engaged in it, though most of us are now completely ignorant of their contributions. To profit from their contributions it is necessary to redo the history of philosophy so as to make them visible. O'Neill provides two possible strategies for doing this. The first involves including in our histories a detailed account of the interrelations among our foremothers' (and, in some cases, forefathers') contributions and those of their philosophical predecessors, contemporaries, and successors, showing the place of these contributions within the ongoing dialectic of philosophy. For example, we might expand our histories to include an account of early modern women philosophers' views of woman's nature, showing how these views were related to broader metaphysical, social, political, and epistemological issues, and how they had wide-ranging implications for such areas as the philosophy of education. This would allow us to chronicle how the early modern women philosophers were of philosophical importance in their time—how their contributions raised the level of discussion about a whole variety of issues. The second strategy involves providing historical narratives that make clear why forgotten philosophers of the past should *now* count as major or minor figures in philosophy. The narratives' plots would consist, in part, in showing that these philosophers contributed to ongoing debates of the time that are of enduring philosophical interest. For example, we might provide historical narratives that show that early modern women philosophers were major contributors to the debates regarding the role that sentiment and emotion ought to play in moral deliberations, that this was a major philosophical issue in the eighteenth century, and that it is still of pressing concern today.

Philosophy in a feminist voice, then, includes some of women's (and men's) forgotten philosophical contributions of the past, as well as the contemporary philosophical contributions that the authors of this book survey and provide and suggest, and it includes, as well, the rewriting of the history of philosophy. Philosophy in a feminist voice represents, moreover, some very wholesome and long-overdue changes in the Western philosophical tradition, changes that will enable that tradition to deal adequately and helpfully with women as well as men, women and men of various races, classes, and cultural locations. It therefore deserves a fair hearing—from men as well as women. But thus far it has *not* received a fair hearing—as Susan Bordo makes abundantly clear in her postscript essay "The Feminist as Other." On the contrary, Bordo contends, the critical and reconstructive projects of philosophy in a feminist voice have been perceived as narrowly concerned with "women's" issues as opposed to "universal" and "human" (i.e., men's) issues, or as concerned simply with "gender" critique as opposed to "culture" critique (which is presumed gender-free), and these projects have been perceived as merely concerned with the "practical" as opposed to the "theoretical" (i.e., that which is abstract and largely free of practical consequence, and hence more impressive). As a result, philosophy in a feminist voice has been treated as something that can legitimately be left to "others" (i.e., ignored), and its achievements have been either minimized or credited to the philosophical mainstream. But this neglect of the critical and reconstructive work of philosophy in a feminist voice, Bordo suggests, is of a piece with the neglect of the work of women philosophers within the Western philosophical tradition, and also is of a piece with the neglect of women within the philosophies of this tradition, and like them can no longer be tolerated. Change is thus needed. It is the foremost objective of *Philosophy in a Feminist Voice* to help bring about this change.

NOTE

    1. William James, "The Sentiment of Rationality," in *Essays on Faith and Morals* (Cleveland, Ohio: World Publishing, 1968), p. 63.

Disappearing Ink:
Early Modern Women Philosophers and
Their Fate in History

EILEEN O'NEILL

> Even if forgetfulness affects the life of the dead in the Lower World,
> yet even there, I would be able to remember Hypatia.
>
> —*Synesius,* Letters *(fifth century* A.D.*)*[1]

WOMEN ARE not included in the standard nineteenth- and twentieth-century histories of European philosophy as significant, original contributors to the discipline's past. Indeed, only a few women's names even survive in the footnotes of these histories; by the twentieth century, most had disappeared entirely from our historical memory. But recent research, influenced by feminist theory and a renewed interest in the history of philosophy, has uncovered numerous women who contributed to philosophy over the centuries.

Ancient Women Philosophers 600 B.C.–500 A.D., the first volume of Mary Ellen Waithe's *History of Women Philosophers*, has provided a detailed discussion of the following Greco-Roman figures: Themistoclea, Theano I and II, Arignote, Myia, Damo, Aesara of Lucania, Phintys of Sparta, Perictione I and II, Aspasia of Miletus, Julia Domna, Makrina, Hypatia of Alexandria, Arete of Cyrene, Asclepigenia of Athens, Axiothea of Philesia, Cleobulina of Rhodes, Hipparchia the Cynic, and Lasthenia of Mantinea.[2] In addition to the medieval and Renaissance philosophers discussed in the second volume of Waithe's *History* (Hildegard of Bingen, Heloise, Herrad of Hohenbourg, Beatrice of Nazareth, Mechtild of Magdeburg, Hadewych of Antwerp, Birgitta of Sweden, Julian of Norwich, Catherine of Siena, Oliva Sabuco de Nantes Barrera, Roswitha of Gandersheim, Christine de Pisan, Margaret More Roper, and Teresa of Avila), such humanist and Reformation figures as Isotta Nogarola, Laura Cereta, Cassandra Fidele, Olimpia Morata, and Caritas Pickheimer have been the focus of attention by scholars like Paul O. Kristeller and Margaret King.[3] The present essay, however, focuses on early modern women's published philosophical contributions, the recognition of this work in the seventeenth and

eighteenth centuries, and the subsequent disappearance of any mention of
these contributions from the history of philosophy.

Perhaps it is wise to begin a discussion of women's inclusion in early
modern philosophy with some reminders about women scholars' entrance
into the academic institutions of Europe during this period. This material
should prepare us for some of the upshots of this paper: women's scholarly
contributions, especially in philosophy, have frequently been considered as-
tounding feats, accomplished by "exceptional women," which, while of significant interest at the time of the circulation or publication of a text, have
been taken to be of marginal value given "the long view" of history.

During the Middle Ages there had been a tradition of allowing a few
women to attend or give lectures at the University of Bologna. And, in the
early seventeenth century, Anna Maria van Schurman had attended (albeit
behind a curtain) the lectures of the theologian Gisbertus Voetius at the University of Utrecht. But it was not until 1678 that the first woman received a
university degree when the University of Padua conferred a doctorate of
philosophy on Elena Cornaro Piscopia of Venice.[4] It is difficult to overestimate the excitement that this produced; some twenty thousand spectators
gathered to see the event. Immediately afterward, the university agreed to
admit no more women.

On April 17, 1732, Laura Bassi defended forty-nine theses in natural philosophy in a public disputation with five professors of the University of Bologna. On the basis of this defense she was awarded a doctorate on May 12;
on October 29 the senate decided to award her a university chair "on the
condition, however, that she should not read in the public schools except on
those occasions when her Superiors commanded her, because of [her] Sex."[5]
It had taken Herculean political efforts for Bassi to become the first woman
to receive an official teaching position at a European university. Yet despite
these efforts, and the academic privileges and channels of influence allowed
Bassi, she held her lectureship at the university's Studium only in the capacity of a supernumerary. No other early modern woman would be granted
such institutional power ever again in the sphere of scholarship. In 1750,
when Maria de Agnesi of Milan, already a member of the Academy of the
Institute for Sciences at Bologna, was awarded a position in mathematics at
the University of Bologna, it was only an honorary chair.

While France could boast, at this same time, of such important natural
philosophers as Émilie du Châtelet, women there were excluded from the
universities and scholarly institutions, like the Académie Royale des Sciences
or the Académie Française. It was, rather, the Academy of the Institute for
Sciences at Bologna that admitted du Châtelet in 1746. Similarly, in the
seventeenth century, Madeleine de Scudéry and Anne Dacier were nomi-
nated, but rejected, for election to the Académie Française, though both
were accepted by the Accademia de' Ricovrati in Padua.[6] With respect to
university positions in France, it is noteworthy that the first woman to hold
a chair at the Sorbonne was Marie Curie in the twentieth century.[7]

In England, in 1667, Margaret Cavendish became the first woman to visit the Royal Society of London, in order to see some of Robert Boyle's experiments. Her visit caused enormous controversy. Not only was she not permitted to join the society, despite the fact that she had published numerous books on natural philosophy, but no other woman became a full member until 1945.[8] During the whole of the eighteenth century, to my knowledge, no university degrees were awarded to women in either England or France.[9] This occurred only in Italy, as we have seen, and also in Germany. At the University of Halle, in 1754, Dorothea Erxleben became the first woman to receive a medical degree in Germany. The first doctor of philosophy awarded to a woman in Germany went to the mineralogist Dorothea Schlözer in 1787.[10] But throughout the eighteenth and nineteenth centuries, such women were unable to establish precedents for the regular admission of women to universities.

Given the extremely limited access of early modern women to universities and other institutional spheres of scholarly activity, we might be led to think that these women could not have contributed to philosophy in any significant way. But this would be to forget the blossoming of philosophical activity outside of the schools since the Renaissance. Philosophy was being done in convents, religious retreats for laypersons, the courts of Europe, and the salons; philosophical networks, which stretched throughout Europe, communicated via letters, published pamphlets and treatises, and scholarly journals. What is surprising is the disappearance from our historical memory, until quite recently, of almost all trace of women's published contributions to early modern theoretical knowledge. Why do we no longer know *any* of the once praised, reprinted, translated, and commented upon books of philosophy by seventeenth- and eighteenth-century women? How is it that when Dorothea Erxleben wrote a defense of women's right to education in 1742, the preface noted that although Anna Maria van Schurman had published a book on this topic a century earlier, "it was not to be had"? Why, fifty years later, did Amalia Holst note in her book on this topic that Erxleben's text was "no longer available"?[11]

Why were women's printed books treated as if written in disappearing ink—extant yet lost to sight? How many such books were there? Who were the early modern women philosophers? Why is it that, at best, we know no more of them than we do of Hypatia and Laura Bassi: their names and reputation, not their thought or works?

This paper will begin, to quote from French philosopher Michèle Le Doeuff's important 1977 article, "Women and Philosophy," "by recalling some women who have approached philosophy. Their very existence shows that the non-exclusion (a relative non-exclusion) of women is nothing new."[12] In the first section I provide an overview of the published philosophical writings by female authors from England, France, Belgium, Germany, Italy, Mexico, and Switzerland. It will be shown that these women addressed a wide range of issues in metaphysics, epistemology, moral theory, social and political philosophy, philosophical theology, natural philosophy, and philosophy of education. While many of these issues, hotly debated in the philosophical circles of their day, are now largely of historical interest only, some are the philosophical predecessors of topics of current interest. I also suggest that the relative nonexclusion of these women has sometimes been reflected in histories of philosophy, for a number of early modern historians were keenly interested in chronicling women's role in philosophy.

In the second section I discuss "the problem of disappearing ink": Why have these philosophers' writings become lost to sight? In addition to the problems generated by the standard practice of anonymous authorship for women, I argue that many of the broader theoretical frameworks in which women's philosophical views had a place, and some of the major motivations for their philosophical arguments, were relegated to the status of nonphilosophy by the nineteenth century. I try to show that the feminine gender has traditionally been aligned with philosophical positions, with styles of philosophizing, and, indeed, with underlying forms of episteme, that were not to "win out" in the history of philosophy. This factor, together with slippage between gendered styles of philosophy and the sex of those doing the philosophizing, accounts for a good deal of the disappearance of the women's writing. But I also stress that perhaps the most significant reasons for the erasure of women's philosophical publications from the historical record were the social and political events surrounding the French Revolution.

Finally, I suggest that philosophers, however important their contributions are to contemporary philosophical concerns, not only must produce followers and critics but also must find a place in an influential history of philosophy, if they are to remain in the discipline's memory. To my knowledge, no one has yet written a general history of early modern philosophy in which it is argued that some women deserve preeminent places either because of the important role they played in past debates or because their work, in part, has moved thought along to the place where we now are. In the final section, I turn to the issue of the revision of the history of philosophy. After briefly outlining some historiographical methods, I suggest that given some of our current philosophical interests, and given the recent recovery of women's philosophical contributions to the debates of the seventeenth and eighteenth centuries, it would seem to be high time that women be given their rightful places in the histories of our discipline.

THE INCLUSION OF WOMEN IN EARLY MODERN PHILOSOPHY

Voltaire, in a dedicatory epistle to Madame du Châtelet, wrote: "I dare say that we live in an era when a poet ought to be a philosopher and when a woman can boldly [*hardiment*] be one."[13] The seventeenth century already found women, throughout Europe and the New World, replacing the humanist formulas for texts addressing the *querelle des femmes*, or woman question, with philosophical argumentation. Thus, in *The Equality of Men and Women* (1622), Marie de Gournay, the adopted daughter of Montaigne, replaced the exaggerated claims about women's superiority to men, and persuasive force based on example, with the use of skepticism as a philosophical method.[14] Later in the seventeenth century, Anna Maria van Schurman, the "Star of Utrecht," and Sor Juana Inés de la Cruz of Mexico discussed woman's nature and argued for her fitness for learning. Schurman, in *Whether a Maid may be a Scholar? A Logick Exercise . . .* (1659),[15] presented fifteen syllogistic arguments, which drew on Aristotelian views and responded to the woman question in the moralistic writings of the period. In an attempt to defend her own scholarly activity from the criticism of the Inquisition, Sor Juana, in "Response to Sor Filotea de la Cruz" (1691; published posthumously in 1700), offered theological and political defenses of women's natural inclination and suitableness for learning.[16] Her discussion drew on Scholastic, as well as Neoplatonic hermetic sources. By 1673, when Bathsua Makin published *An Essay to Revive the Antient Education of Gentlewomen*, an unbroken line of influence, explicitly acknowledged in the texts, ran from Lucrezia Marinelli's *The Nobility and Excellence of Women* (1600), through Gournay and Schurman, to Makin.[17] Interest in woman's nature, her place in society, and her fitness for education led women in the second half of the century to proffer large-scale views about the relation of education to religion and to society. Detailed accounts of how girls should be educated appeared. Noteworthy among such philosophies of education are the *Rule for the Children of Port Royal* (1665) by the Port Royal educator Sister Jacqueline Pascal,[18] and the letters and conversations on education of Madame de Maintenon.[19]

In the second half of the Age of Reason, women also produced a number of works on morals and the passions. For example, we have the maxims of Marguerite de la Sablière, the marquise de Sablé, and the comtesse de Maure, two series of maxims by Queen Christina of Sweden, and the latter's "Remarks on the Moral Reflections of La Rochefoucauld."[20] But perhaps the most well known seventeenth-century woman writer of moral psychology is the *précieuse*, Madeleine de Scudéry. Leibniz, in discussing a debate on the nature of divine love, said "Of all of the matters of theology, there aren't any of which women are more in the right to judge, since it concerns the nature of love. But . . . I would like [women] who resemble Mlle de Scudéry, who has clarified the temperaments and the passions in her novels and conversations on morals. . . ."[21] In her two sets of conversations (1680; 1684), her two sets of moral conversations (1686; 1688), and her *Talks Concerning Morals* (1692), Scudéry discusses such issues as "Uncertainty," "Of the Knowledge of Others and of Ourselves," and "The Passions That Men Have Invented." Her style of philosophizing is quite different from that of the maxim writers or of the earlier moral didactic writers. Closer to the dialectical strategies of Montaigne, Scudéry presents vignettes to make certain points and adduces arguments for the possible positions, but she draws no explicit conclusion. The reader must make up her own mind about the issue. Her works were discussed in Le Clerc's *Bibliothèque universelle et historique* (1699) and in the *Mercure* (1731), mentioned in Bayles's *Dictionary*, and reprinted and translated until the end of the eighteenth century.

Another type of philosophical writing by women begins to appear after 1660, to wit, the treatment of natural philosophy. In Paris, sometime after 1680, Jeanne Dumée published *A Discussion of the Opinion of Copernicus Concerning the Mobility of the Earth* . . . , in which she explains in detail the three motions attributed to the earth and provides the arguments that support and those that militate against Copernicus's system. The English playwright and fiction writer Aphra Behn translated Fontenelle's popularization of Cartesian philosophy, *A Discovery of New Worlds*, in 1688. In her preface she discusses Copernicus's system and argues that it "saves the phaenomena" better than Ptolemy's system; the only serious challenges to Copernicus's picture, she claims, are the arguments that attempt to show that it is inconsistent with Holy Scripture. Behn gives the details of these arguments and charges that, given the best contemporary biblical exegesis, Holy Scripture is as compatible with Copernicus's view as with Ptolemy's. She concludes by noting that Scripture was never meant to teach us astronomy, geometry, or chronology.[22]

But by far the most prolific female writer of natural philosophy was Margaret Cavendish, duchess of Newcastle. The earliest influence on her ideas seems to have come from Hobbes, tutor to her husband's family. She became a member of the "Newcastle Circle," which included Hobbes, Charleton, and Digby. This group of philosophers had a strong interest in materialism and had been influenced by contact with Gassendi and Mersenne during the English civil war years. While exiled in Paris and Antwerp, Cavendish met Descartes and Roberval. From 1653 to 1671, she published numerous books that dealt in some way with natural philosophy. In her first work, *Poems and Fancies* (1653), Cavendish presented a fanciful atomism in rhymed verses. It appears that it was this book, along with her other early works, namely, *Philosophical Fancies* (1653), *The World's Olio* (1655), the first edition of *The Philosophical and Physical Opinions* (1655), and *Nature's Pictures Drawn by Fancie's Pencil to the Life* (1656), on which most of Cavendish's critics based their responses. The responses themselves were frequently full of invective and wildly contradicted each other. For example, her friend the Epicurean Walter Charleton told her that her imaginative atomism proceeded from an "Enthusiasm" which scorned "the control of reason"; on the other hand, a number of critics argued that her work must have been plagiarized since no lady could understand so many "hard termes." In consequence, Cavendish's husband felt compelled to defend his wife's authorship in an opening "Epistle" to her *Philosophical and Physical Opinions*. Either way, the upshot was that no one took the duchess seriously as an aspiring philosopher. Thus, the Cambridge Platonist Henry More wrote to the philosopher Anne Conway (who will be discussed shortly) of his amusement at hearing that in *The Philosophical Letters* (1664) Cavendish had attempted to confute Hobbes, Descartes, van Helmont, and More himself. Later More accurately predicted to Conway: "She [the duchess] is affrayed some man should quitt his breeches and putt on a petticoat to answer her in that disguize. . . . She expresses this jealousie in her book, but I believe she may be secure from any one giving her the trouble of a reply."[23] Cavendish makes clear, in the preface to her *Philosophical Letters,* that she had written her responses to some famous philosophers in the form of letters and "by so doing, I have done that, which I would have done unto me." Her letters are written to a fictitious noblewoman. There are few moments in the history of women philosophers more poignant than in the letter on identity and the Trinity, where Cavendish writes to her imaginary noblewoman about another philosophical friend, Lady N. M., and concludes: "I wish with all my heart, Madam, you were so near as to be here at the same time, that we three might make a Triumvirate in discourse as well as we do in friendship."[24] Lady N. M. may well be Lady Newcastle, Margaret. Cavendish may have been aware that by 1664 she was reduced to writing philosophy for the trinity of her own personas.

This is particularly unfortunate since, as I hope to show in a future essay, Cavendish's *Philosophical Letters* and *Grounds of Natural Philosophy* (1668) constitute extremely interesting philosophical contributions. In these works she abandons her earlier commitment to atomistic materialism and embraces a possibly Stoic-inspired materialist organicism. On this view, matter intrinsically possesses some degree of vital force, sense, and intellect. The view is organicist in that causation is understood through the vital affinity one part of matter has for another, rather than via a mechanical model. Some of Cavendish's major criticisms of Descartes and Hobbes turn on showing how the mechanical philosophers have failed to provide a satisfactory model of causation. According to Cavendish, the mechanists' talk of the translation of motion, or of the imprinting of an image in perception, can only be interpreted in terms of a transfer model. Such a causal model, she argues, is far too crude to account for sensation and memory, and is inconsistent with a substance/accident ontology.

Another English philosopher, Viscountess Anne Conway, wrote *The Principles of the Most Ancient and Modern Philosophy*, which was published posthumously in Latin in 1690 by the cabalist "scholar Gypsy," Francis Mercurius van Helmont and was translated into English in 1692. In this metaphysical treatise, Conway argues against Cartesian dualism, Spinoza's pantheistic monism, and Hobbes's materialism in favor of a Neoplatonic triad of substances: God, Christ, and creatures. In her analysis of creaturely substance, Conway argues that what many philosophers take to be distinct essences (e.g., Descartes's mind and body, or Aristotelian natural kinds) are just accidental properties of a single substance; they differ from

one another only in terms of degree, not essentially. As for creaturely substance, she holds that all of its species are gradations from active spirit to
vital matter. Thus, in opposition to the view of certain Cambridge Platonists, the active principle is not a separate incorporeal substance pervading
inert matter. Conway agrees with Descartes that "all natural motions proceed according to rules and laws mechanical." But she charges that nature is
"a living body, having life and sense, which body is far more sublime than
a mere mechanism, or mechanical motion."[25]

On the Continent, Princess Elisabeth of Bohemia, whose letters to Descartes had exposed the weakness of the latter's published views on mind-
body interaction and free will, discussed Conway's views with her Quaker
correspondent, Robert Barclay.[26] Leibniz and the Electress Sophie of Hanover were introduced to Conway's *Principles* by van Helmont, sometime
around 1696. The following year, Leibniz wrote to Thomas Burnet:

> My views in philosophy approach somewhat closely those of the late Countess of
> Conway, and hold a middle position between Plato and Democritus, since I be-
> lieve that everything happens mechanically as Democritus and Descartes main-
> tain, against the opinion of Monsieur More and his like, and I believe that never-
> theless everything also happens vitally and according to final causes; everything is
> replete with life and perceptions contrary to the opinion of the followers of
> Democritus.[27]

Unfortunately, as Carolyn Merchant has argued, Heinrich Ritter, the nineteenth-century historian of philosophy, incorrectly attributed the *Principles*
to van Helmont. In consequence, later scholars like Ludwig Stein, who argued that Leibniz's concept of the monad owed much to the *Principles*, took
it that van Helmont was the one who had influenced Leibniz. Because of this
historical error, neither the late-nineteenth-century revival of interest in
Leibniz nor the twentieth-century interest in essentialist metaphysics has,
until quite recently, given Conway's philosophy the attention it deserves.[28]

Turn-of-the-century England produced Mary Astell, who in the *Letters
Concerning the Love of God between the Author of the Proposal to the
Ladies and Mr. John Norris* (1695) discussed Norris's Malebranchean view
that God alone is the cause of all things, including all of our pleasant sensations. Norris concluded from this that God should be the sole object of our
love. Astell argued against Norris's occasionalism and maintained that sensation is directly caused by the interaction of mind and body, and indirectly
and mediately caused by God. So far, the account is basically Cartesian. But
Astell further suggests that something like More's "plastic part of the soul"
might be used to explain the agreement between external objects and sensations. This Neoplatonic plastic spirit was traditionally a third substance—
according to More both immaterial yet extended—that mediated between
inert matter and the rational soul. Thus, like the early More, Astell here
proffers an amalgam of Cartesian and Neoplatonic metaphysics.

In *A Serious Proposal to the Ladies, Part II. Wherein a Method is offer'd for the Improvement of their Minds* (1697), Astell realized that her 1694 proposal for founding a women's college would not be realized. She offered women, in this second part, a manual for improving their powers of reasoning, which drew on Lockean and Cartesian views about knowledge, Cartesian "method," and insights from the Cartesian-inspired Port Royal textbook, *La Logique, ou l'art de penser [The Logic, or The Art of Thinking]* (1662), penned by Nicole and Arnauld. By this stage of her philosophical development, Astell had emerged as more solidly Cartesian, as evidenced by her endorsement of clarity and distinctness as the mark of indubitable propositions, mechanism as the model for purely bodily change, dualism, and Cartesian views on sense perception and judgment.[29]

Lady Damaris Cudworth Masham also argued against Norris's occasionalism in *A Discourse Concerning the Love of God* (1696). There she criticized the Malebranchean picture of seeing all things in God not on the basis of *purely* metaphysical considerations but because she saw this as an unsatisfactory grounding for the Christian faith—which was part of Norris's motivation for appropriating occasionalism. In 1693, while living with Masham and her family, Locke himself had written *An Examination of P. Malebranche's Opinion of Seeing all Things In God* and *Remarks upon Some of Mr. Norris' Books, wherein he asserts P. Malebranche's opinion of our seeing all things in God.*

In 1705, Astell responded to both Locke and Masham with *The Christian Religion as Profess'd by a Daughter of the Church* (1705). She argued that the highest purpose of thought was to contemplate abstract ideas that would bring the mind in contact with the Good, which was immaterial and not sensory. Locke, in his *Reasonableness of Christianity*, had rejected abstract thought as necessary for understanding Christianity. Astell also discussed Locke's treatment—in both his *Essay* and the *Correspondence with Stillingfleet*—of the possibility of "thinking matter," arguing that there was a tension between his two accounts.

Several months after Astell's *The Christian Religion* came out, Masham published her own account of Christian theology for women: *Occasional Thoughts in Reference to a Vertuous or Christian Life* (1705). She argued for the importance of education for women and set into relief the difficulties facing a woman who educated herself about Christian theology. She also defended a number of Lockean views on knowledge, education, and the relative merits of reason and revelation. Concerning the popular topic of the basis for moral virtue, Masham argued that since our passions frequently blind us to the light of nature, the latter is an insufficient foundation for morality. What is needed is reason assisted by revelation.

Masham also conducted an intellectual correspondence with Locke, wrote to Leibniz on a number of metaphysical issues, and sent both Leibniz and Jean Le Clerc a defense of Cudworth's views against Bayle's criticisms.[30]

She wrote an essay on Locke for the *Great Historical Dictionary*, and we have her biography of Locke in manuscript.[31] Finally, her work received critical notice in such scholarly journals as the *Bibliothèque Choisie*.[32]

Yet despite this scholarly career, Masham stood in need of defense against Thomas Burnett's charge that her arguments addressed to Leibniz seemed to have come from a hand other than her own.[33] It was the philosopher Catharine Trotter Cockburn who came to her defense. Trotter Cockburn published a number of philosophical works, including *A Defence of Mr. Locke's Essay of Human Understanding* (1702), which was praised by Toland, Tyrell, Leibniz, and Norris, as well as by Locke himself. Her *Remarks upon some Writers in the Controversy concerning the Foundation of Moral Virtue and Moral Obligation* . . . (1743) argued in support of a theistic, though nonvoluntarist, theory of the grounds of moral goodness and obligation. Her final philosophical work was a defense of Clarke's moral views entitled *Remarks upon the Principles and Reasonings of Dr. Rutherford's Essay* . . . (1747).[34]

Locke also influenced Judith Drake, who, in *An Essay in Defence of the Female Sex* (1696), used a number of his epistemological principles to argue that women's intellectual inferiority resulted from their lack of education and intellectual experience rather than from a lack of intellectual powers.[35] The views of Locke, as well as those of Descartes and Malebranche, are also drawn upon by Lady Mary Chudleigh in her discussions of knowledge, education, and the passions in *Essays upon Several Subjects in Prose and Verse* (1710).[36] Chudleigh corresponded with John Norris, Mary Astell, and Leibniz's philosophical interlocutor, Electress Sophie of Hanover.[37]

In France, in the final years of the seventeenth century, Gabrielle Suchon published an ambitious philosophical text, *Treatise of Morals and of Politics*, containing three book-length parts devoted, respectively, to a treatment of "liberty," "learning," and "authority."[38] In this work Suchon argues that although women are in fact deprived of access to all three, they are, by nature, qualifed to have access to them. Her arguments display an understanding of the views of the ancient Stoics, Cynics, and Skeptics, and of Scholastics, like St. Thomas and St. John of the Cross. She also responds to arguments found in the highly influential feminist treatise *Of the Equality of the Two Sexes* (1673) by the Cartesian François Poulain de la Barre. Excerpts of the *Treatise* appeared in the influential *Journal des Savants* (1694); excerpts from a second work by Suchon, *Treatise of the Willing Single Person*, appeared in the equally influential *Nouvelles de la Republic des Lettres* (1700). Unfortunately, since the *Treatise of Morals and of Politics* was published under the pseudonym "G. S. Aristophile," Suchon fell into oblivion by the late eighteenth century.[39]

My overview of women's philosophical publications in the seventeenth century would be incomplete if I did not say something about those women who constituted the bulk of women writers in the second half of the century, namely, the women prophets and preachers. In England alone, during the tumultuous civil war years, there are publications by, or accounts of, over three hundred women prophets from the radical religious sects, of which some two hundred were Quakers.[40] While the pure description of visions by such popular mystics as Jane Lead are philosophically barren, religious spokeswomen like the Quaker Margaret Fell Fox, in her *Women's Speaking Justified* (1666), provided a series of arguments for women's right to take part in public discussions of religious matters.[41] On the Continent, the quietism of Jeanne-Marie Guyon's philosophical theology and the Pietism of Anna Maria van Schurman's theological writings, after her conversion to Labadism, won both the label of "mystic" by their contemporaries.[42] I want to emphasize here that, in the seventeenth century, mystical theology was considered a part of philosophy. But the supporters and followers of these women, and indeed *the women themselves*, justified both the truth of their views and their right to speak on the following claim: the women were mere instruments through which God *directly* spoke.[43] The upshot was that the women's writings did not issue from their intellects. In sum, in the seventeenth century, mystical writings were considered to be "real" philosophy, but they were not "really" written by women. (Ironically, as we shall see in a moment, by the time freethinking historians acknowledged these women as the true authors of the mystical works, such material would no longer be deemed "philosophical.")

Given the number of female contributors to philosophy in the seventeenth century and the scope of their works, the eighteenth century has often been seen as something of a disappointment. For example, the nineteenth-century historian of philosophy Victor Cousin said that the women writers of the French Enlightenment knew a little math and physics, and had some wit, but had "no genius, no soul, and no conviction."[44] In mid-eighteenth-century England, the rather conservative Bluestockings who included Hester Chapone, Elisabeth Montagu, Hannah More, and Elizabeth Carter, were the women who dominated the philosophical scene, producing a number of moral and religious works, as well as treatises on the need for women to be educated.[45] While it must be admitted that the philosophical content of the writings of the Bluestockings was a bit thin, this was more than made up for by the surge of philosophical writing by women in England during the second half of the eighteenth century.

In 1767, Catharine Macaulay's pamphlet entitled *Loose Remarks on . . . Hobbes' Philosophical Rudiments of Government and Society* was published. Here Macaulay challenged a purely contractarian picture of the emergence of civil society, a purely rationalist grounding of parental rights, and arguments in support of absolute monarchy. This text was followed by several political pamphlets, an eight-volume history of England (which won the admiration of such figures as Madame Roland), and her philosophical magnum opus, *Letters on Education, with Observations on Religious and Metaphysical Subjects* (1790). In the tradition of Locke, this work treats education as the major test case for one's views about epistemology, metaphysics, and morals. After a detailed exposition of her theory of education, Macaulay turns, in part 2, to a historical and theoretical account of the effects of education on manners, morals, and culture in various civilizations. Part 3 contains her sustained discussion of the metaphysical and moral views that underlie her theory of education: views on the origin of evil, free will and necessity, and the role of revelation in the grounding of moral duty. In the course of her discussion, Macaulay critically evaluates Bolingbroke's moral theory and that of the ancient Stoics.[46]

Mary Wollstonecraft's early *Thoughts on the Education of Daughters* (1787) was strongly influenced by Macaulay's work. In her *Vindication of the Rights of Woman* (1792), Wollstonecraft argues against Rousseau's views about women's nature, their role in society, and how they should be educated; she criticizes Madame Genlis's *Adele and Theodore, or Letters on Education* (1782) and finds only portions of Hester Chapone's *Letters on the Improvement of the Mind* . . . (1773) helpful. But she acknowledges that her opinions on education so coincide with those of Catharine Macaulay that she will simply refer the reader to her work rather than quote her at length. A review of Macaulay's *Letters on Education* . . . by Wollstonecraft appeared in the journal *Analytical Review*.[47]

Mary Hays echoed the feminist social and political concerns of both Macaulay and Wollstonecraft in her *Letters and Essays Moral and Miscellaneous* (1793) and the *Appeal to the Men of Great Britain in Behalf of Women* (1798). Her discussion of the works of Mary Astell, in her six-volume *Female Biography* . . . (1803), demonstrated that by the end of the eighteenth century English women were beginning to trace a history of feminist social and political philosophy that reached back about one hundred years.[48]

With the growing professionalization of philosophy, and the placement of it over against the belles lettres and religion, we also find for the first time in England "pure" philosophical writing by women. That is, we find philosophy stripped of its moorings within discussions of the woman question and theology, expressed in technical language, and written in a journalistic style. In short, we find a corpus like that of Lady Mary Shepherd, which includes *An Essay upon the Relation of Cause and Effect, controverting the Doctrine of Mr. Hume* . . . (1824); a discussion of Berkeley, among other topics, in *Essays on the Perception of an External Universe* . . . (1827); a review of John Fearn's book on epistemology; and an article summarizing her metaphysics for *Fraser's Magazine*. Interestingly enough, these significant contributions to professional philosophy have disappeared from historical accounts of early modern philosophy even more completely than some of the mystical, feminist, or largely literary endeavors of some of Shepherd's predecessors. I shall briefly explore why this is so in what follows.[49]

Eighteenth-century France provides us with an equally impressive group of women philosophers. Anne Lefèvre Dacier, a classicist by training, was regarded in the eighteenth century as one of the most learned women in Europe. In 1691 she and her husband translated the writings of Marcus Aurelius, with Madame Dacier supplying a commentary called "Remarks on the Meditations of Marcus Aurelius." In this commentary, she criticizes, albeit sympathetically, the writings of the ancient Stoics from the point of view of her own Christian Stoicism. Dacier actively participated in the salon of Madame de Lambert and thus was exposed to the great intellectual controversies of her day. In 1714, in response to an attack on Homer, Dacier entered the debate between the ancients and moderns; in her book *The Causes of the Corruption of Taste*, she argued in favor of the values of the ancients. So closely was the name "Dacier" associated with ancient thought, and with Stoicism in particular, that the earliest history of women philosophers produced in the modern era was dedicated to her—namely, the history of Gilles Ménage.[50]

Dacier's friend the renowned salonist Anne Thérèse, marquise de Lambert, published a number of works on education and morals, which reflect the style of addressing such philosophical issues that prevailed in her salon—a salon frequented by such figures as Madame Dacier, Fontenelle, Mairan, Montesquieu, Marivaux, and La Motte. Hers is the art of persuasion and suggestion, enlivened by wit, which eschews all pedantry and dogmatism. Like her predecessors Montaigne and Gournay, she rejected idle metaphysical speculation in favor of "the fields of study useful to our perfection and our happiness." And yet in the debate between the ancients and moderns on the question of taste, Lambert was clearly on the side of the moderns. She attempted to show that taste is much more a matter of sentiment than of reason. And her style was decidedly modern: refined, but concise, and not averse to novelty. Indeed, Sainte-Beuve saw her as an intermediate figure between the Age of Reason and the Enlightenment: "She is midway between them and is already turning her eyes in the direction of the more modern."[51] *Letters on True Education* (1728/1729), much praised by Fénelon, shows the influence of Locke on Lambert's views on education. It also exemplifies her reliance on secular morality, which she saw as a substitute for the no longer effective traditional piety. *New Reflections on Women* (1727), arguably her most important work, also appeared under the title *Metaphysics of Love*. In this influential protofeminist text, which was read with interest by Montesquieu, Lambert discusses the ways social customs and institutions, including the educational and legal systems, and heterosexual love, are designed to maintain male hegemony. She rejects what she takes to be the male-centered construction of heterosexual love in her time and offers an alternative conception, which she deems more favorable to women. Finally, Lambert also wrote moral treatises, including *Treatise on Friendship* (1732) and *Treatise on Old Age* (1732).[52] These works exemplify early-eighteenth-century France's interest in blending a Cartesian theoretical paradigm with a provisional morality based on readings of the Stoics, Plato, Cicero, and other ancient authors. Some of Lambert's works continued to be published a century after their original publication and went into as many as fifteen editions.[53]

In eighteenth-century France, the old *querelle des femmes*, which had questioned woman's moral and intellectual faculties, and which debated *whether* she should be educated, was replaced by a new set of issues on the "woman question." Now, not woman's soul but the relative inputs of nature and nurture were examined in relation to woman's character. It was *assumed* that women should receive *some* education. But woman's role in society needed to be debated since this would determine the *type* of education that she should receive.

In 1772, Antoine Thomas published his *Essay on the Character, Morals and Mind of Woman in Different Centuries*. Diderot responded in his *On Women*, and Louise d'Épinay registered her reactions to Thomas in her letter to the Abbé Galiani in the same year. D'Épinay was a member of philosophical networks that included such figures as Hume, D'Holbach, Diderot, and Rousseau. Her most important philosophical contribution was her treatment of woman's nature and education, *The Conversations of Émilie* (1774), which, like the work of Madame Panckoucke, was a response to Rousseau.[54] Numerous treatises on education were written by women in Enlightenment France.[55] Of special note is Stéphanie Félicité de Genlis's *Adèle et Théodore* (1782), which provided a Rousseau-inspired philosophy of education for girls. Genlis, however, models the education of a girl more on Rousseau's program for Émile than for Sophie.[56] In addition to an essay on education, Louise-Marie Dupin left an extensive manuscript, *Observations on the Equality of the Sexes and of Their Difference*, which she dictated to her secretary, Jean-Jacques Rousseau.[57]

The period of the French Revolution spawned numerous works, now not only on woman's character and social duties but on her rights as a citizen as well. This genre includes Olympe de Gouges's *Declaration of the Rights of Woman* (1791) and Fanny Raoul's *Opinion of One Woman on Women* (1801).[58]

While Madame Roland, the Girondist friend of Wollstonecraft and admirer of Macaulay, did not publish works on women, her early philosophical essays "On the Soul," "On Liberty," "On Luxury," and on "Morality and Religion" were published in the nineteenth century.[59]

In the area of natural philosophy, there is no question but that Émilie du Châtelet deserves recognition as an important figure of the eighteenth century. Du Châtelet's philosophical erudition, as well as her training in mathematics—received in part from Maupertuis—enabled her to make interesting contributions to the contemporary debates: force and its metaphysical status, and the precise formulations of the laws of motion and gravity. In *Institutions of Physics* (1740), she sides with the Newtonians on some of the details of the laws of nature but attempts to provide a metaphysical foundation for Newtonianism. Thus, her position can be seen as an attempt to reconcile what she takes to be most useful in Newtonian mechanics and Leibnizian philosophy. The 1742 edition of the *Institutions* also included a text on the *vis viva*, or active force controversy, which she wrote in response to the philosopher Jean Jacques Dortous de Mairan. This was followed, in 1744, by her essay *On the Nature and Propagation of Fire*, and at the end of her life she produced the translation of Newton's *Principia* (with commentary) that remains the standard French edition of his work. Besides her writings in natural philosophy, du Châtelet also published an expansive *Reflections on Happiness* (1796), and her essays on such topics as the existence of God, the formation of color, and grammatical structure were published posthumously.[60]

The anatomist and author of an empirical study of putrefaction, Marie Thiroux d'Arconville, left us no texts on natural philosophy, but she did publish texts on moral psychology such as *On Friendship* (1761), *Of the Passions* (1764), and *Moral Thoughts and Reflections* (1775).[61]

And Sophie de Grouchy, the marquise de Condorcet, having first produced translations of Adam Smith's *Theory of the Moral Sentiments* and *Dissertation on the Origin of Languages*, went on to write her own blend of rationalist and moral sentiment ethics in her *Letters on Sympathy* (1798).[62]

By the end of the eighteenth century, French women were producing broad critiques of culture and the arts, as is evidenced in the mathematician Sophie Germain's *General Considerations on the State of the Sciences and Letters . . .* (1833).[63] In this text, much praised by Auguste Comte, Germain argues that there is no essential difference between the arts and sciences. But perhaps the most influential of the French cultural critics was Anne Louise Germaine Necker, baronne de Staël-Holstein, who published a number of works about the interrelations among politics, morals, and the arts in the new republican era, including *On the Influence of the Passions on the Happiness of Individuals and Nations* (1796) and *On Literature Considered in Relation to Social Institutions* (1800). Her first published work was *Letters on the Character and Writings of Jean-Jacques Rousseau* (1788).[64]

Eighteenth-century Germany spawned a number of critical treatments of Kant's views on women, including one by an unidentified "Henriette" and a second by Amalia Holst—both published in 1802.[65]

The Swiss Isabelle de Charrière also criticized Kant's moral views in some of her novels and published a *Discourse in Honor of Jean-Jacques Rousseau . . .* (1797).[66] Marie Huber, also of Switzerland, published three Enlightenment texts in which she added her voice to the contemporary debates concerning the principles of natural religion, the controversies over disembodied souls, whether eternal damnation is compatible with God's goodness, and the relation of science to faith. These texts are *The World Unmasked* (1731), *System of . . . the Soul Separated from Their Bodies* (1733), and *Letters on the Religion Essential to Man* (1738).[67]

Finally, eighteenth-century Italy was the home of a number of women natural philosophers, including Laura Bassi of Milan, who was mentioned earlier. Her forty-nine published theses (1732), which she debated for her doctorate at the University of Bologna, and her published theses concerning the nature of water (1732) can be found in the Bibliothèque Nationale, Paris. Four papers in natural philosophy were published in the *Commentaries of the Bologna Academy and Institute of Arts and Sciences*.[68] The mathematician Maria Gaetana de Agnesi discussed topics in logic, metaphysics, and Cartesian physics in her treatise *Philosophical Propositions* (1738).[69] In 1722, Giuseppa-Eleonora Barbapiccola, friend of the daughter of the Cartesian critic Giovanni Battista Vico, published a translation and critical introduction for Descartes's *Principles of Philosophy*. In her introduction, Barbapiccola examined the relation of Descartes's views, particularly on motion and form, to those of Aristotle.[70]

EXCLUSION: THE REPRESENTATION OF WOMEN PHILOSOPHERS IN MODERN HISTORIES OF PHILOSOPHY

Why have I presented this somewhat interesting but nonetheless exhausting bibliographic and doxographic overview of seventeenth- and eighteenth-century women philosophers? Quite simply, to overwhelm you with the presence of women in early modern philosophy. It is only in this way that the problem of women's virtually complete absence in contemporary histories of philosophy becomes pressing, mind-boggling, possibly scandalous. So far, my presentation has attempted to indicate the quantity and scope of women's published philosophical writing. It has also been suggested that an acknowledgment of their contributions is evidenced by the representation of their work in the scholarly journals of the period and by the numerous editions and translations of their texts that continued to appear into the nineteenth century. But what about the status of these women in the histories of philosophy? Have they ever been well represented within the pre-twentieth-century histories?

A quick look at some of the standard histories indicates a lively interest in the topic of women philosophers in France in the late seventeenth century. In 1690 Gilles Ménage wrote *The History of Women Philosophers*, which he dedicated to Madame Dacier. It was a doxography of some seventy women philosophers of the classical period.[71] And the most widely read history of philosophy in the seventeenth century, Thomas Stanley's, contains a brief discussion of some twenty-four women philosophers of the ancient world.[72] With respect to the "moderns," in 1663, Jean de La Forge produced *The Circle of Women Scholars*, and five years later Marguerite Buffet published her *New Observations on the French Language . . . with the Elogies of Illustrious Women Scholars Ancient as Well as Modern*.[73] And this is just the tip of the iceberg; numerous compendia of *femmes savantes* appeared at this time. But this long list of women philosophers gets narrowed to the mention of a handful by the nineteenth century. Most of the standard eighteenth- and nineteenth-century histories mention Queen Christina of Sweden as the patroness of Descartes. She is not, however, described as a philosopher, and no reference is made to her writings. Tennemann's eighteenth-century history mentions the English mystic Jane Lead; Hegel tells us that Leibniz dedicated his *Theodicy* to Sophie Charlotte; and Renouvier, in the nineteenth century, quotes at length from the correspondence of Descartes and Princess Elisabeth of Bohemia.[74] Victor Cousin, in his nineteenth-century *Course of the History of Modern Philosophy*, discusses four women: the mystic Madam Guyon, Damaris Masham, Jacqueline Pascal, and finally the one woman who appears in a number of the standard histories of philosophy and who is now known to almost no one: Antoinette Bourignon.[75] The Belgian Bourignon was a seventeenth-century itinerant writer of theology whose career Leibniz and Trotter Cockburn followed with interest. She produced a large corpus, parts of which she disseminated to her followers by means of a printing press that she carried with her. A Cartesian, Pierre Poiret, renounced his former philosophical commitments, became her disciple, and published her collected works in nineteen volumes after her death. Bourignon discusses such issues as free will and predestination, and the nature of divine cooperation with respect to secondary causes, with the result that Trotter Cockburn's friend Thomas Burnet attributed to her "solid judgment (in the greatest matters of theology oftentimes)."[76] But Bourignon's unorthodox quietism, as well as much of her rhetoric, got her labeled, even in her own time, as a mystic first and foremost.

So it was a handful of women—largely mystics—who figure in the eighteenth- and nineteenth-century histories of philosophy. Let me stress that this absence of women in the histories is not due to ignorance about the existence of the women. In the nineteenth century, Lescure published *The Women Philosophers* (1881), in which chapters were devoted to such eighteenth-century figures as Mesdames du Châtelet, de Lambert, d'Épinay, and de Staël.[77] Foucher de Careil wrote books on Descartes's relationships with Princess Elisabeth and Queen Christina, and on Leibniz's relationships with Electress Sophie and Sophie Charlotte.[78] Cousin even wrote books on Scudéry and Sablé, yet he failed to mention them in his own history of philosophy.[79] Why? What were the factors that led to the ink of these women's published texts disappearing in the nineteenth century? Why was any mention of these women's important contributions omitted from the general histories of the discipline?

To begin with, the socially encouraged practice of anonymous authorship for women clearly did not help to put them on the map of philosophy. Instead, it frequently led to misattributions (Conway), charges of plagiarism (Cavendish), charges that the woman philosopher had been "helped" by a prominent male philosopher (du Châtelet), or, most commonly, neglect pure and simple. But this cannot account for our almost complete ignorance of the large number of published texts that bore the women philosophers' names and were evaluated in contemporary journals.

Other factors that must be considered are those that might be termed
"internal to philosophy as a scholarly enterprise," like the effects of the late
eighteenth and nineteenth centuries' "purification" of philosophy. As I indicated earlier, either the bulk of early modern women's philosophical writing
directly addressed such topics as faith and revelation, and "the woman question," or these topics were addressed within a larger philosophical context.
But by the nineteenth century, philosophy had "confined theology to its own
domain," as Cousin put it.[80] Indeed, the story of the purification of philosophy from the taint of religion is an interesting and complex one, which goes
far beyond the limits of this essay. Suffice it to note that Tennemann's *Manual of the History of Philosophy* (1832) contains a classification called "su-
pernaturalists and mystics."[81] Included under this head are not only true
mystics like Jane Lead, who simply wrote of her visions and attempted no
philosophical speculation or analysis, but scholars who were once taken to
be major *philosophical* thinkers, like More and Cudworth. By allying philosophy motivated by religious concerns with an unreflective mysticism,
eighteenth-century historians excised whole philosophical schools, and the
work of many women, from philosophy proper. In addition, German historians, taking Kantianism as the culmination of early modern philosophy and
as providing the project for future philosophical inquiry, viewed treatments
of "the woman question" as precritical work, of purely anthropological interest. In sum, by the nineteenth century, much of the published material by
women, once deemed philosophical, no longer seemed so.

But what about those texts that were solidly philosophical from the post-
eighteenth-century vantage point? Here we have to admit that a number of
the women's works have dropped out of sight simply because their views or
underlying *episteme* were ones that simply did not "win out." Thus, the
writings of Schurman and Suchon, because of the Scholastic exposition, or
of Scudéry and Conway, with their underlying Neoplatonic *episteme*, may
seem too removed from our present philosophical concerns to gain a position in our histories. Notice that such a decision assumes that our histories
of philosophy take present philosophical concerns as their main point of
departure in reconstructing philosophy's past. I will return to methodology
in the history of philosophy in a moment, but first I want to point out an odd
feature of "philosophical views that did not win out," namely, that they
have frequently been characterized as "feminine." For example, as Benjamin
Farrington has shown, Francis Bacon's description of ancient—particularly
Aristotelian—philosophy as "feminine" is meant to convey that it is weak
and passive as opposed to the active, potent experimental philosophy that
Bacon introduces.[82] I have tried to show elsewhere that the Neoplatonism of
the seventeenth-century French salonists and of the Cambridge Platonists, as
well as of the Hermeticists, came to be regarded, at the end of the seventeenth century, as "feminine."[83] Here again, the point was not that it was the
philosophy of women but rather that it was a degenerate philosophy of both

men and women, which was on its way out. But given that one meaning of "feminine" is "that which befits a woman," will there not be some slippage between "feminine" (i.e., outdated) philosophy, which perhaps "deserves" to be left out of the canon, and philosophy written by women? Might there not be an unarticulated presumption that women's philosophical work is "feminine" philosophy par excellence, and thus worthy of forgetting? I think my speculation may be supported by an examination of yet another factor, namely, philosophical form or style.

Londa Schiebinger, in her illuminating study *The Mind Has No Sex? Women in the Origins of Modern Science,* has recently shown that "poetic" style in the eighteenth century was identified with the feminine, at the same time that it was being ushered out of the domains of philosophy and science. So, for example, in the middle of the eighteenth century, the natural historian Buffon was hailed as combining the rigors of mathematics with rhetorical and poetic style. But by the end of the century, Madame d'Épinay expressed the general consensus that Buffon's work was more "poetic" than "true."[84] By the end of the century, the salonists would be seen as literary figures and, by that very fact, not philosophers. It would seem, then, that feminine style could be had by men or women, and that it once again signaled an exclusion from the sphere of the philosophical. But Rousseau's attack on the scholarly style issuing from the French salons, in his "Letter to M. d'Alembert on the Theater" (1758), raises my earlier concerns. For it is not feminine style per se that he attacks but the influence of women on style. He charges that the decadence of arts and letters in France is due to men's practice of "lowering their ideas to the range of women," since "everywhere that women dominate, their taste must also dominate; this is what determines the taste of our age."[85] At the end of the century, Louis Sébastien Mercier will make the point explicitly with respect to philosophy: "What claim to fame has the woman who suddenly decides to make her entrance into the sanctuary of the muses and philosophy? She has ogled, bantered, simpered, made silk knots and little nothings."[86] It would seem that the end of the eighteenth century in France not only marked the end of the feminine poetic style in philosophy but also signaled a material change in women's acceptance into philosophy's domain. In her *New Reflections on Women,* Madame de Lambert lamented: "There were, in an earlier time, houses where [women] were allowed to talk and think, where the muses joined the society of the graces. The Hôtel de Rambouillet, greatly honored in the past century, has become the ridicule of ours."[87] In short, Lambert no longer lived in that era in which women could boldly be philosophers.

In Germany, which was to become arguably the hub of philosophy by the nineteenth century, the historian of philosophy Karl Joël described the French Enlightenment as a time when "woman was philosophical and philosophy was womanly."[88] He viewed this period as an interregnum between the "manly" philosophy of the English Enlightenment and the "masculine

epoch" of the German philosophy introduced by Kant. Notice that Joël jux-
taposes and possibly elides feminine philosophy and women's presence in
philosophy. When Kant himself describes the masculine character of the
profundity of philosophy, he refers not to gendered systems or styles but to
sexual difference: "A woman who has a head full of Greek, like Madame
Dacier, or one who engages in debate about the intricacies of mechanics, like
the Marquise du Châtelet, might just as well have a beard; for that expresses
in a more recognizable form the profundity for which she strives."[89]

Let me sum up the hypothesis I have presented so far about the absence of
women in the history of philosophy. In the transition from the eighteenth to
the nineteenth century, there were a number of developments, internal to
philosophy, regarding what constituted the main philosophical problems,
the proper method of inquiry, and the appropriate style of exposition. In
consequence of these developments, numerous men, as well as women, came
to disappear from our historical memory. But the alignment of the feminine
gender with the issues, methods, and styles that "lost out," together with a
good deal of slippage between gender and sex, and the scholarly practice of
anonymous authorship for women, led to the almost complete disappearance of women from the history of early modern philosophy.

But there would also seem to be another factor that plays some role in
accounting for the absence of any mention of early modern women philosophers' published texts in the general histories of philosophy. I shall call it the
"oxymoron problem": early modern European thought has generally presupposed that a woman philosopher is something barely possible and always unnatural. As Bathsua Makin, in her *An Essay to Revive the Antient
Education of Gentlewomen*, observed in the seventeenth century: "The Bar-
barous custom to breed Women low, is grown general amongst us, and hath
prevailed so far, that it is verily believed . . . that women are not endued with
such Reason, as Men; nor capable of improvement by Education as they are.
It is lookt upon as a monstrous thing; to pretend the contrary. A Learned
Woman is thought to be a Comet, that bodes Mischief, when ever it appears."[90] A full century later, Samuel Johnson, who in fact did much to
encourage the writing of the Bluestocking philosophers, commented that "a
woman's preaching is like a dog's walking on his hind legs. . . . you are
surprised to find it done at all."[91] By the nineteenth century, Proudhon
would pithily state: "The woman author does not exist; she is a contradiction. . . . [A] woman's book . . . is . . . philosophy on nothing."[92] Because
philosophy written by a woman has been so difficult for early modern culture to conceive of as possible—and thus because the reality of it has always
come as something of a shock—history has deemed it sufficient to note that
it has been done by some "Tenth Muse," some time ago. Thus, Hypatia and
a few other Titans get mentioned. These exceptional authors need not be
read; it is enough that philosophy was ever done by a woman at all. In this
way, the inclusion in the standard histories of philosophy of one or two
women of mythic proportions acts as a strategem of exclusion.

But the account I have given so far still does not explain the extent of the disappearance of women's published contributions from the histories of philosophy. My hypothesis, about the alignment of the feminine gender (and women) with ultimately unsuccessful philosophical topics and methods, applies equally well to the erasure of some women from seventeenth-century histories as it does to the more extensive disappearance of women philosophers in subsequent centuries. And while my focus on the rise of Kantian critical thought and the "purification" of philosophy does identify the nineteenth century as the pivotal era of disappearance, it is unable to explain why virtually *all* women's philosophical contributions are lost to sight at this point. In short, I have not yet explained what happened in the nineteenth century. Why did this century not produce texts like Stanley's seventeenth-century history, which included numerous female contributors to the discipline?

To satisfactorily answer these questions I believe we must look far beyond developments internal to philosophy proper. In addition, such a factor as the "oxymoron problem" itself requires an explanation, pointing beyond the dialectics internal to Enlightenment arts and letters more generally. The dramatic disappearance of women from the histories of philosophy in the nineteenth century can be fully understood only against the political backdrop of the aftermath of the French Revolution.[93]

It is difficult to overestimate the perceived social and political threat that the woman author—particularly the female *theoretical* author, and most particularly the female *philosophical* author—represented for Western culture at the very commencement of modern democracy. Here I can give only a cursory sketch of the thesis artfully defended by the philosopher Geneviève Fraisse in *Reason's Muse: Sexual Difference and the Birth of Democracy.* Fraisse demonstrates, through an analysis of a wide range of late-eighteenth-century and early-nineteenth-century French texts, the crisis of culture at that time: How to embrace the ideals of a common humanity and egalitarian social order while at the same time preserving a system of sexual difference that underpins masculine hegemony? Since reason was the property essential to human nature, and since it was the sole requirement needed by a man to be admitted as citizen, the texts of this period are filled with debates about the precise character of woman's exercise of reason, and thus her rightful role as citizen. A few voices, like those of the marquis de Condorcet, Madame Clément-Hémery, and Charles Fourier, would argue for women's rights as citizens—particularly their right to education. Their arguments were based on the demonstrated reason and accomplishments of women who had been given the requisite opportunities. But the majority of voices would argue either for the limited participation of women in public life based on social utility, as did Madame Gacon Dufour, or, as in the case of Sylvain Maréchal, for the radical exclusion of women from the public sphere. Culture's anxiety was focused on whether women's limited entrance into the newly democratized public sphere would lead to women's equal participation in civic, economic, and political power. Thus, even such figures as Constance de Salm and Madame de Staël, who boldly entered this public sphere via their writings and salons, and who advocated the education of women, would retain assumptions about sexual difference entailing that any claim to such power for women be rejected. Madame de Staël would write: "It is right to exclude women from political and civic affairs. Nothing is more opposed to their natural vocation than those things that would set up a rivalry with men; and for a woman, fame itself can only be a source of grief bursting forth in the form of happiness."[94] And Stendahl, the Enlightenment defender of women's education, added that only the economic necessity of having to support a family could provide a justification for a woman to be an author.[95] As Fraisse argues, by 1800, the woman author came to epitomize a new phenomenon: all women's increasing access to "individual autonomy and economic independence." The woman author thus became an "emblem of social transformation."[96] She symbolized the possibility of dismantling the patriarchal order.

It is not surprising, then, that the nineteenth century is filled with invective against the female author. Fraisse's analysis helps us to make sense of the seemingly bizarre text of Maréchal, *The Proposed Law Prohibiting Women from Learning to Read* (1801). Why would one want to prevent women from learning to read? Because "reason does not desire, any more than French grammar, that a woman be an author" and "reading is extremely contagious; as soon as a woman opens a book, she believes she can write one."[97] We are also in a better position to understand what is motivating the earlier quotation from Proudhon about the woman author as a contradiction. I would add that while women authors in general were scoffed at, female theoretical authors—especially philosophers—received a particularly nasty reception in the nineteenth century. The following remark by Proudhon is indicative of the level of invective I have in mind: "It may be affirmed without fear of calumny, that the woman who dabbles with philosophy and writing destroys her progeny by the labor of her brain and her kisses which savor of man; the safest and most honorable way for her is to renounce home life and maternity; destiny has branded her on the forehead; made only for love, the title of concubine if not of courtesan suffices her."[98] The woman philosopher, by the nineteenth century, is to be compared to the courtesan, for the latter is one of the few classical roles open to women in the sphere of the polis.

In the nineteenth century, philosophy was still considered the pinnacle of theoretical knowledge; it was seen to have the power to demarcate and distinguish all the other branches of knowledge, to decide the value of alternative avenues of inquiry and methodology. To be admitted into the sphere of philosophy, publicly via published texts, was to partake of a singular form of public power: to be a philosopher was to be a shaper of culture. But what if the sphere of philosophy became democratized? What if, for example, "philosopher queens" ruled in the polis? To imagine such a dismantling of male hegemony at the birth of modern democracy was more than even Condorcet, its staunchest supporter, could manage. Even he claimed that while women had displayed "genius" in a number of fields, so far none had done so in philosophy.[99] He says this, while also citing Catharine Macaulay, Marie de Gournay, Madame du Châtelet, and Madame de Lambert as examples of women lacking "neither force of character nor strength of mind."[100]

My examination of the reasons for the absence of women in modern histories of philosophy has moved us from a consideration of reasons internal to philosophy's own development to reasons ultimately rooted in the emerging democratic political order. In part, my aim has been to show that while *explanations* are readily available for the disappearance of women from our histories, only rarely are there *justifications* for the exclusion of specific women. And, as we might have expected, *no* justification exists for the wholesale exclusion of women philosophers from the history of our discipline. Perhaps all of this should make us suspicious about our histories; about the implicit claim that our criteria of selection justify our inclusion of philosophers as major, minor, or well-forgotten figures; about our ranking of issues and argumentative strategies as central, groundbreaking, useful, or misguided. The historiography of philosophy is an important and thorny subject, which I cannot hope to tackle here. But I do wish to conclude this essay with some notes on the subject, in relation to the project of making women's philosophical contributions visible once more in history.[101]

THE RECOVERY OF WOMEN'S CONTRIBUTIONS AND THE REWRITING OF HISTORY

In this section I sketch three models for the historiography of early modern philosophy. Two of these models are useful ideals, a mixture of which usually underlies any given attempt at doing such history—or so I shall suggest. But the third model will not be particularly attractive to a philosopher who is doing the history of philosophical thought.

Let me begin with the latter model, which I shall term the "pure history" model. According to this historiographical method, *evaluations* of philosophical arguments and projects, while crucial to philosophy, are irrelevant to the history of philosophy. Scholars who use this model, like the nineteenth-century historian of ancient philosophy Eduard Zeller, see the history of philosophy as a dispassionate *chronicling* of every move in the dialectic of philosophy. Of course, for all their attempts at writing the "pure history" of philosophy, even the followers of Zeller omitted the women, who were seen as significant contributors to the field in their own time. This suggests that the particular interests and blind spots of the historian, and of the era in which the historian lives, will come into play—come what may. But, of course, the real issue is not what the history of philosophy is like, come what may, but which methodology we ought to take as our ideal—even if this ideal is never achieved. Still, it is not entirely clear what the point would be of chronicling *every* position in the endless dialectic (*per impossible*), in accordance with this first method. For this model might be characterized, as Walter Benjamin noted, as one "which despairs of grasping and holding the genuine historical image as it flares up briefly. Among medieval theologians it was regarded as the root cause of sadness."[102] Perhaps a philosopher might think that, with this detailed "pure history" of philosophy before her, she would be in the best position to evaluate philosophical arguments and projects, for she then would be able to judge which were the most innovative, strategically useful, and elegant moves in the game called "philosophy." But, of course, this historical narrative itself never attains closure; it must be revised as philosophy itself changes its rules and even, perhaps, the very goals of the game. The evaluation of moves in the game, thus, cannot be made after the detailed history is completed; the evaluations must be made as we go along rewriting the history of the discipline—as we "brush history against the grain."[103] So, what might look like a philosophical interest in having a "pure history" of philosophy turns out to be a nonstarter.

Suppose, then, that we are interested from the start in a "philosophical history" of philosophy, one that attempts to justify the merits of both the larger philosophical projects in which arguments are embedded and the methodological strategies relative to the philosophical goals. There are at least two models of the history of philosophy that attempt such justifications. The "internal history" model would offer a detailed historical account of the interrelations among the arguments of the women philosophers and those of their philosophical predecessors, contemporaries, and successors.[104] It would attempt to provide the philosophical source of the women's views by discovering their place within an ongoing dialectic internal to philosophy. Notice how different this is from the first model: we are not dispassionately chronicling philosophical views, without regard to the truth of the views or the validity of the arguments. This is also a different matter from simply providing "historical reconstructions" of philosophical views, as Richard Rorty has termed it. For here we are not attempting to make philosophical views (which we might take to be false) intelligible, by placing them in the context of the less enlightened times in which they were produced. To the contrary, this second method of historiography attempts to make past views intelligible by painstakingly piecing together the rational grounds for them. A Rortyean historical reconstruction of, say, texts about the *querelles des femmes* might situate these views about woman's nature in the context of the quaint medical and religious debates of the early modern period. But the "internal history" model of historiography would be at pains to show that discussions about woman's nature were of central *philosophical* concern—interrelated as they were to broader metaphysical, social and political, and epistemological issues. By chronicling how the women's contributions increasingly raised the level of intelligibility about these issues, and by showing the wide-ranging philosophical implications of their views for such areas as the philosophy of education, a case could begin to be made for the inclusion of these women authors in the history of philosophy.

The third type of history of philosophy is what Richard Rorty, taking Hegel as a master of the genre, has termed *Geistesgeschichte*. This genre of history of philosophy

> works at the level of problematics rather than of solutions to problems. It spends more of its time asking "Why should anyone have made the question of ———— central to his thought?" . . . rather than on asking in what respect the great dead philosopher's answer or solution accords with that of contemporary philosophers. . . . It wants to justify the historian and his friends in having the sort of philosophical concerns they have—in taking philosophy to be what they take it to be.[105]

Historians of philosophy frequently have seen their role as that of reformers and revisionists. Influential historians, like Tiedemann and Tennemann, each rewrote the history of philosophy, raising up certain figures and quickly passing over others. And typically they constructed their histories so that they conveniently "led up to" their pet philosophical projects, be it "Lockean sensualism," "Kantian idealism," or some other view. Indeed, most of the great philosophers themselves included elements of *Geistesgeschichte* in their own philosophical works, as a method of tying their arguments to the philosophical past. Consider Descartes's treatment of the Scholastics or Kant's depiction of himself as the synthesis of what is true in Leibniz's "noologism" (or, to transform the Greek into Latin, "rationalism") and in Locke's "empiricism." Philosophers sometimes called for a new *Geistesgeschichte* to be written, as a justification for a newly emerging philosophical canon. The historian Victor Cousin, in his 1828 Paris lectures to a crowd of two thousand gentlemen, said:

> Let us hope that France, . . . which has already produced Descartes, will enter in her turn upon . . . the history of philosophy. . . . Every great speculative movement contains in itself, and sooner or later produces necessarily, its history of philosophy, and even a history of philosophy which is conformed to it; for it is only under the point of view of our ideas that we represent to ourselves the ideas of others.[106]

This passage is interesting in what it suggests about the role that gender, class, ethnicity, and nationalism may have played in the actual constructions of modern histories of philosophy. But it may also lead us to wonder why we should not just abandon sweeping narratives that lead up to a particular set of contemporary interests. Critics have argued that it is misguided to turn to the philosophy of the past as a way of justifying one's present philosophical concerns, since past philosophers cannot do a better job than we at solving our current problems. And they argue that it is a mistake to construct history with an eye to the *present*, since this simply distorts the history of philosophy. To borrow the beautiful image from Walter Benjamin, the Angel of History is propelled backward into the future, ever keeping its gaze on the *past*.[107]

If we historians of philosophy do go the way of *Geistesgeschichte*, what we need is a narrative that makes clear why some of the women discussed in this paper should figure as major or minor figures. The plot will consist, in part, in the giving of reasons for the decision to count certain questions or argumentational strategies as central. The *Geistesgeschichte* that goes along with the "relative non-exclusion" of women, which currently exists, is one in which some token women are allowed to play *extremely* marginal roles. The story goes that these women *did* contribute to ongoing philosophical debates of the time but that the debates are no longer of philosophical interest, or that the women simply added flourishes to the philosophical programs of major male philosophers. But, to take one example, it now seems clear—largely because of the work of "internal history" scholars—that the role that sentiment and emotion ought to play in moral deliberations was a central philosophical issue in the eighteenth century, and that women were major contributors to these debates. Writers of a new *Geistesgeschichte* can point out that descendants of this philosophical topic are of pressing concern to many philosophers today. The model of "internal history" saves our endeavors from turning into potty history; *Geistesgeschichte* draws the attention of philosophers to philosophy's past, so that it is not just those with purely antiquarian interests who will want to know about early modern women philosophers.

As a last example, let us take the research for the present essay. I began by using the method of "internal history" to locate those women who were contributing to the philosophical debates of the seventeenth and eighteenth centuries. But it was the method of *Geistesgeschichte* that got me to wondering if anything like our present feminist philosophical concerns had ancestors in the philosophical writings of early modern women. These present feminist concerns helped to open up the past for me; I started to notice that early modern women frequently addressed issues dealing with the relation of gender to traditional philosophical topics. The philosophical interest I now have in the past motivated me to use "internal history" to discover the ways that the early modern "woman question" is continuous with, and the ways it sharply departs from, twentieth-century feminist concerns. But it was surely *Geistesgeschichte* that initially motivated me to make the discovery that the "woman question" constituted a major set of philosophical issues in the early modern period and that women made, perhaps, the most outstanding contributions of anyone to these debates.

It appears, then, that we are at a point, both philosophically and in terms of our knowledge of philosophy's internal history, where a rewriting of the narrative of philosophy is called for—one in which a number of the women cited here, and some of the forgotten men, will emerge as significant figures.[108] Contemporary feminist philosophers have already begun to turn to the women philosophers of the past in the attempt to trace a history of feminist thought. In some sense, Michèle Le Doeuff's work is precisely the attempt to provide a *Geistesgeschichte* that will make women visible once again in the history of philosophy.[109] A number of philosophers have also begun the detailed work of reconstructing women's contributions to the complex internal history of philosophy.[110] By showing both how women's contributions to early modern philosophy are relevant to our present philosophical concerns and how their contributions are a vital part of the internal dialectics of philosophy, women may escape being footnotes and flourishes to the history of philosophy—makers of nothing more than silk knots and little nothings.

ACKNOWLEDGMENTS

Initial stages of research were supported by a grant from the Research Foundation of the City University of New York, an NEH Travel to Collections Grant, a Queens College Faculty in Residence Award, and a University of Pennsylvania Mellon Fellowship in the Humanities. For helpful comments on earlier versions of this paper, I thank the audiences at the University of Massachusetts—Amherst, The Graduate Center of CUNY, Harvard Graduate School of Education, Barnard College, Columbia University, Princeton University, Haverford College, Girton College, the New York City Chapter of the Society for Women in Philosophy, and the 1990 and 1991 Eastern Division Meetings of the APA, especially Madonna Adams, Lanier Anderson, Martha Bolton, Alan Gabbey, Gary Hatfield, Eva Kittay, Areyeh Kosman, Stephen Menn, Christia Mercer, Robert Nozick, Mary Ellen Waithe, and Sue Weinberg. I am grateful to Susan Bordo, Richard Foley, Daniel Garber, Janet Kourany, Richard Popkin, James Ross, Robert Sleigh, and Margaret Wilson; the encouragement I have received from them over the years has meant more to me than I can neatly put into words. I am indebted to Sarah Hutton and Susan James for organizing the conference on "Women and the History of Philosophy" at Girton College, Cambridge. Thanks also go to the participants in my 1991 Harvard seminar, "Women Philosophers of the Early Modern Period," whose suggestions and criticisms helped to sharpen my understanding of the texts of Gournay, Schurman, Sor Juana, Cavendish, Astell, Masham, Elisabeth of Bohemia, Conway, Trotter Cockburn, Macaulay, and Scudéry. I am especially grateful to Gary Ostertag and Wolfgang Mann, my interlocutors on the historiography of philosophy. Finally, I want to thank Jonathan Rée, whose comments on an earlier draft, and whose own illuminating work, forced me to think more critically about canon formation than I had previously. This paper is dedicated to the women philosophers with whom I have had the privilege to study: Leigh Cauman, Sue Larson, Mary Mothersill, Onora O'Neill, and Margaret Wilson.

Notes

1. Cited in Gilles Ménage, *The History of Women Philosophers*, trans. Beatrice Zedler (Lanham, Md.: University Press of America, 1984), p. 27.

2. This text and others, to which I shall frequently refer, and their abbreviations are as follows:

BTS *Beyond Their Sex: Learned Women of the European Past*, ed. Patricia La-balme (New York: New York University Press, 1980).

FS   *Female Scholars: A Tradition of Learned Women before 1800*, ed. J. R. Brink (Montreal: Eden Press, 1980).

FW   *French Women and the Age of Enlightenment*, ed. Samia Spencer (Blooming-ton/Indianapolis: Indiana University Press, 1984).

H   *Hypatia: A Journal of Feminist Philosophy*, Special Issue: The History of Women in Philosophy, 4, no.1 (Spring 1989).

HD   *Hypatia's Daughters: Fifteen Hundred Years of Women Philosophers*, ed. Linda Lopez McAlister (Bloomington/Indianapolis: Indiana University Press, 1996).

HWP *A History of Women Philosophers*, ed. Mary Ellen Waithe, 4 vols. (Dor-drecht/Boston/London: Kluwer Academic Publishers, 1987–95).

WS   *Woman and Society in Eighteenth-Century France: Essays in Honor of John Stephenson Spink*, ed. Eva Jacobs, W. H. Barber, Jean H. Bloch, F. W. Leakey, and Eileen Le Breton (London: Athlone Press, 1979).

WW   *Women Writers of the Seventeenth Century*, ed. Katharina Wilson and Frank Warnke (Athens: University of Georgia Press, 1989).

Whenever possible, the primary sources cited in this paper will be the original-language first editions. (I shall provide translations of foreign language titles in the main body of the paper.) In some cases, where a modern edition of a text is currently available, I shall also cite this. Unfortunately, few of the texts cited in this paper are currently in print. A recent anthology and a forthcoming two-volume work will begin to remedy this situation. Margaret Atherton's *Women Philosophers of the Early Modern Period* (Indianapolis: Hackett Press, 1994) contains excerpts from texts by six English women philosophers and reproduces John Blom's translation of two French letters from Elisabeth of Bohemia to Descartes. Eileen O'Neill's *Women Philosophers of the Seventeenth and Eighteenth Centuries: A Collection of Primary Sources*, 2 vols. (Oxford/New York: Oxford University Press, forthcoming), will contain selections from some forty women philosophers, including translations from Latin, Spanish, French, German, and Italian texts.

Selected secondary sources, relevant to the work of individual women philosophers, will be cited as each figure is discussed. For a thumbnail sketch of women's contributions to philosophy, see Eileen O'Neill, "Women in the History of Philosophy," *The Encyclopedia of Philosophy*, Supplement, ed. Donald Borchert (New York: Simon and Schuster/Macmillan, 1996). While the number of relevant reference works is quite large, I do want to recommend the following list of modern secondary sources, which treat early modern women scholars and the intellectual, social, and political context in which they were situated. In what follows, they will be cited by author's name.

INTELLECTUAL AND SOCIAL HISTORY

Roland Bainton, *Women of the Reformation*, Vol. 1, *Germany and Italy* (1971); Vol. 2, *France and England* (1973); Vol. 3, *Spain and Scandinavia* (1977) (Minneapolis: Augsburg).

Carol Blum, *Rousseau and the Republic of Virtue* (Ithaca, N.Y./London: Cornell University Press, 1986).

Natalie Zemon Davis and Arlette Farge, eds., *A History of Women in the West: III. Renaissance and Enlightenment Paradoxes* (Cambridge: Belknap/Harvard University Press, 1993).

Geneviève Fraisse, *Muse de la raison: La démocratie exclusive et la différence des sexes* (Aix-en-Provence: Editions Alinéa, 1989); English translation: *Reason's Muse: Sexual Difference and the Birth of Democracy*, trans. Jane Marie Todd (Chicago/London: University of Chicago Press, 1994).

Antonia Fraser, *The Weaker Vessel* (New York: Knopf, 1984).

Wendy Gibson, *Women in Seventeenth-Century France* (London: Macmillan, 1989).

Octave Gréard, *L'Education des femmes par les femmes* (Paris: Hachette, 1907).

Joan Kelly, *Women, History, and Theory: The Essays of Joan Kelly* (Chicago/London: University of Chicago Press, 1984).

Joan Landes, *Women and the Public Sphere in the Age of the French Revolution* (Ithaca, N.Y./London: Cornell University Press, 1988).

Vera Lee, *The Reign of Women in Eighteenth-Century France* (Cambridge: Schenkman, 1976).

Gerda Lerner, *The Creation of Feminist Consciousness: From the Middle Ages to Eighteen-Seventy* (Oxford: Oxford University Press, 1993).

Carolyn C. Lougee, *Le Paradis des Femmes: Women, Salons, and Social Stratification in Seventeenth-Century France* (Princeton, N.J.: Princeton University Press, 1976).

Myra Reynolds, *The Learned Lady in England: 1650–1760* (Boston: Houghton Mifflin, 1920).

Gustave Reynier, *La Femme au XVII siècle, ses ennemies et ses defenseurs* (Paris: Editions J. Tallendier, 1929).

Katharine M. Rogers, *Feminism in Eighteenth-Century England* (Urbana: University of Illinois Press, 1982).

Jeannette Rosso, *Etudes sur la féminité aux XVIIᵉ et XVIIIᵉ siècles* (Pisa: Libreria Goldiardics, 1984).

Hilda Smith, *Reason's Disciples* (Urbana: University of Illinois Press, 1982).

Dale Spender, *Women of Ideas and What Men Have Done to Them: From Aphra Behn to Adrienne Rich* (London: Routledge and Kegan Paul, 1982).

Doris Stenton, *The English Woman in History* (London: Routledge and Kegan Paul, 1957).

LITERARY STUDIES

Antoine Adam, *Histoire de la littérature française au XVIIᵉ siècle*, 5 vols. (Paris: del Duca, 1962).

George Ballard, *Memoirs of Several Ladies of Great Britain* . . . (Oxford, 1752; new edition by Ruth Perry, Detroit: Wayne State University Press, 1985).

Margaret Ezell, *Writing Women's Literary History* (Baltimore, Md./London: Johns Hopkins University Press, 1993).

Erica Harth, *Cartesian Women: Versions and Subversions of Rational Discourse in the Old Regime* (Ithaca, N.Y./London: Cornell University Press, 1992).

Elaine Hobby, *Virtue of Necessity: English Women's Writing 1649–88* (Ann Arbor: University of Michigan Press, 1992).

Ian Maclean, *Woman Triumphant: Feminism in French Literature: 1610–1652* (Oxford: Clarendon Press, 1977).

Sylvia Harcstark Myers, *The Bluestocking Circle: Women, Friendship, and the Life of the Mind in Eighteenth-Century England* (Oxford: Clarendon Press, 1990).

Roger Picard, *Les Salons littéraires et la société française 1610–1789* (New York: Brentano's, 1943).

HISTORY OF SCIENCE

Margaret Alic, *Hypatia's Heritage: A History of Women in Science from Antiquity through the Nineteenth Century* (Boston: Beacon Press, 1986).

Robert Hugh Kargon, *Atomism in England from Hariot to Newton* (Oxford: Clarendon Press, 1966).

Evelyn Fox Keller, *Reflections on Gender and Science* (New Haven, Conn./London: Yale Unversity Press, 1985).

Carolyn Merchant, *The Death of Nature: Women, Ecology, and the Scientific Revolution* (San Francisco: Harper and Row, 1980).

Gerald Dennis Meyer, *The Scientific Lady in England 1650–1760: An Account of Her Rise with Emphasis on the Major Roles of the Telescope and Microscope* (Berkeley and Los Angeles: University of California Press, 1955).

H. J. Mozans, *Women in Science* (1913; reprint, Notre Dame: University of Notre Dame Press, 1991).

Marilyn Bailey Ogilvie, *Women in Science: Antiquity through the Nineteenth Century* (Cambridge, Mass.: MIT Press, 1988).

Londa Schiebinger, *The Mind Has No Sex? Women in the Origins of Modern Science* (Cambridge, Mass.: Harvard University Press, 1989).

3. Margaret L. King, *Women of the Renaissance* (Chicago/London: University of Chicago Press, 1991); *Her Immaculate Hand: Selected Works By and About the Women Humanists of Quattrocento Italy*, ed. Margaret King and Albert Rabil (Binghamton, N.Y.: Center for Medieval and Early Renaissance Studies, 1983); Paul O. Kristeller, "Learned Women of Early Modern Italy: Humanists and University Scholars," in *BTS; Women Writers of the Renaissance and Reformation*, ed. Katharina Wilson (Athens: University of Georgia Press, 1987). On medieval women philosophers see Peter Dronke, *Women Writers of the Middle Ages* (Cambridge: Cambridge University Press, 1984); Elizabeth Petroff, *Medieval Women's Visionary Literature* (New York: C. Bynum, 1986); *Women Mystics In Medieval Europe*, ed. Emilie Zum Brunn and Georgette Epiney-Burgard, trans. Sheila Hughes (New York: Paragon House, 1989); *Medieval Women Writers*, ed. Katharina Wilson (Athens: University of Georgia Press, 1984); Joan Ferrante, "The Education of Women in the Middle Ages in Theory, Fact and Fantasy," in *BTS*.

Letizia Panizza discusses Modesta Pozzo (1555–92) in her paper "Do Women Have Rational Souls?: 16th- and 17th-Century Italian Debates from Baldassare Castiglione to Elena Tarabotti" (paper presented at the British Society for the History of Philosophy conference on "Women and the History of Philosophy," 1992).

4. *Helenae Lucretiae (Quae & Scholastica) Corneliae Piscopiae, Virginis Pietate, & Eruditione admirabilis; Ordini D. Benedicti Privatis votis adscriptae Opera quae quidem haberi potuerunt*, ed. Bacchini (Parma,1688). Secondary sources include Massimilliano Deza, *Vita di Helena Lucretia Cornara Piscopia* (Venice, 1686), Monsignor Nicola Fusco, P.A., *Elena Lucrezia Cornaro Piscopia (1646–1684)* (Pittsburgh: U.S. Committee for the Elena Lucrezia Piscopia Tercentenary, 1975); Francesco Ludovico Maschietto, *Elena Lucrezia Cornaro Piscopia (1646–1684)*, *prima donna laureata nel mundo* (Padua: Editrice Antenore, 1978); Paul O. Kristeller, "Learned Women of Early Modern Italy: Humanists and University Scholars," in *BTS*; Patricia Labalme, "Women's Roles in Early Modern Venice: An Exceptional Case," in *BTS*; Margaret King, *Women of the Renaissance* (Chicago/London: University of Chicago Press, 1991); *HWP*, vol. 3.

For a detailed study of early modern women in Italy's universities and academies, see Paula Findlen, "Science as a Career in Enlightenment Italy: The Strategies of Laura Bassi," *ISIS* 84 (1993): 441–69.

5. Translation is from Findlen, "Science as a Career," p. 450; see note 4.

6. In 1980, Marguerite Yourcenar became the first woman to be elected to the Académie Française.

7. See *The International Dictionary of Women's Biography*, ed. Jennifer Uglow (New York: Continuum, 1985).

8. See Schiebinger, pp. 26, 284 n. 47.

9. Ibid., p. 246. As Schiebinger points out, Sophie Germain did attempt to pursue studies at the Ecole Polytechique in the 1790s.

10. On Erxleben and Schlözer, see ibid., pp. 250–60.

11. Dorothea [Erxleben] Leporinin, *Gründliche Untersuchung der Ursachen, die das weibliche Geschlecht vom Studieren abhalten* (Berlin, 1742); Amalia Holst, *Über die Bestimmung des Weibes zur höhern Geistesbildung* (Berlin, 1802). This observation about Erxleben and Holst is in Schiebinger, p. 270.

12. Michèle Le Doeuff, "Women and Philosophy," *Radical Philosophy* 17 (Summer 1977): 2–11.

13. François-Marie Arouet de Voltaire, "Épitre à Madame Du Châtelet," *Alzire*, in *Oeuvres Complètes de Voltaire*, ed. M. Léon Thiessé (Paris, 1831), vol. 3, p. 457.

14. Marie le Jars de Gournay, *L'Egalité des hommes et des femmes* (Paris, 1622); the modern edition of this work appears in Mario Schiff, *La Fille d'alliance de Montaigne, Marie de Gournay* (Paris: Librarie Honoré Champion, 1910), pp. 61–86. An English translation, by Eileen O'Neill, appears in *Social and Political Philosophy in Perspective: Classical Western Texts in a Feminist and Multicultural Perspective*, ed. James Sterba (Belmont, Calif.: Wadsworth, 1994). In addition to Schiff, secondary sources on Gournay include S. A. Richards, "Feminist Writers of the Seventeenth Century" (M.A. thesis, University of London, 1914); Lula McDowell Richardson, *The Forerunners of Feminism in French Literature from Christine of Pisa to Marie de Gournay* (Baltimore, Md.: Johns Hopkins University Press, 1929); Marjorie H. Ilsley, *A Daughter of the Renaissance: Marie le Jars de Gournay, Her Life and Works* (The Hague: Mouton, 1963); Maja Bijvoet, "Editor of Montaigne: Marie de Gournay," in *WW*; Beatrice Zedler, "Marie le Jars de Gournay," in *HWP*, vol. 2; Eileen

O'Neill, "Marie le Jars de Gournay," *The Encyclopedia of Philosophy,* Supplement, ed. Donald Borchert (New York: Simon and Schuster/Macmillan, 1996). For useful overviews of the texts of the *querelle des femmes* tradition, to which Gournay is responding, see Maclean and Kelly.

   15. This is the English translation of Anna Maria van Schurman, *Amica dissertatio inter nobilissimam virginem Annam Mariam a Schurman et Andream Rivetum de ingenii muliebris ad scientias et meliores literas capacitate* (Paris, 1638), which also appeared in her collected works, *Nobiliss. Virginis Annae Mariae à Schurman. Opuscula, hebraea, graeca, latina, gallica, Prosaica et metrica* (Leiden, 1648). Secondary sources on Schurman include Una Birch (Pope-Hennessy), *Anna Maria van Schurman: Artist, Scholar, Saint* (London: Longmans, Green, 1909); Joyce L. Irwin, "Anna Maria van Schurman: The Star of Utrecht," in *FS*; Joyce L. Irwin, "Learned Woman of Utrecht: Anna Maria van Schurman," in *WW*; Cornelia N. Moore, "Anna Maria van Schurman," *Women Writing in Dutch*, ed. Kristina Aercke (New York/London: Garland Publishing, 1994); Eileen O'Neill, "Anna Maria van Schurman, " *The Routledge Encyclopedia of Philosophy*, ed. Edward Craig (London/New York: Routledge, forthcoming).

   16. Juana Inés de la Cruz, *Fama, Y Obras Posthumas Del fenix De Mexico, Decima Musa, Poetisa Americana . . .*, ed. Juan Ignacio Castorena y Ursúla (Madrid, 1700). English translations include *A Sor Juana Anthology*, trans. Allan S. Trueblood (Cambridge, Mass.: Harvard University Press, 1988) and *The Answer/La Repuesta Including a Selection of Poems*, critical edition and translation by Electa Arenal and Amanda Powell (New York: Feminist Press at CUNY, 1994). The standard edition of her work is *Obras completas*, 4 vols., ed. A. Méndez Plancarte [A. Salceda] (Mexico: Fondo de Cultúra Económica, 1951–57). Secondary sources include Gerard Flynn, *Sor Juana Inez de la Cruz* (New York: Twayne, 1971); Octavio Paz, *Sor Juana or, The Traps of Faith* (Cambridge, Mass.: Harvard University Press, 1988); *Feminist Perspectives on Sor Juana Inés de la Cruz*, ed. Stephanie Merrim (Detroit: Wayne State University Press, 1991); Mary Christine Morkovsky, CDP, "Sor Juana Inés de la Cruz," in *HWP*, vol. 3; Donald Beggs, "Sor Juana's Feminism," in *HD*.

   17. Bathsua Makin, *An Essay to Revive the Antient Education of Gentlewomen, in religion, manners, arts and tongues with an Answer to the Objections against this Way of Education* (London, 1673). Secondary source material on Makin includes J. R. Brink, "Bathsua Makin: Educator and Linguist (1608?-1675?)," in *FS*; *First Feminists: British Women Writers 1578–1799*, ed. Moira Ferguson (Bloomington: Indiana University Press, 1985); Frances Teague, "Bathsua Makin: Woman of Learning," in *WW*; *HWP*, vol. 3; and Smith.

   Lucrezia Marinelli, *La nobiltà, et l'eccellenza delle donne, co' difetti e mancamenti de gli huomini* (Venice, 1600). Among the secondary sources is Ginevra Conti Oderisio, *Donne e società nel Seicento: Lucrezia Marinelli e Arcangela Tarabotti* (Rome: Bulzoni, 1979).

   18. In *Lettres, opuscules et mémoires de Madame Perier et de Jacqueline, soeurs de Pascal et de Marguerite Perier, sa nièce par M. P. Faugère* (Paris, 1845). Secondary sources include Victor Cousin, *Jacqueline Pascal: Premières études sur les femmes illustres et la société du XVIIᵉ siècle* (Paris, 1844); S. W. Weitzel, *Sister and Saint: A Sketch of the Life of Jacqueline Pascal* (New York, 1880).

   19. *Oeuvres de Mme de Maintenon, publiées pour la première fois d'après les manuscrits et copies authentiques . . .*, ed. Théophile Lavallée (Paris, 1854–57). Sec-

ondary sources include Paul le duc de Noailles, *Histoire de Madame de Maintenon et des principaux événements du règne de Louis XIV*, 4 vols. (Paris, 1849–58); Théophile Lavallée, *Histoire de la Maison Royale de St. Cyr* (Paris, 1853); Louis Chabaud, *Mesdames de Maintenon, de Genlis et Campan, leur rôle dans l'éducation chrétienne de la femme* (Paris: Librairie Plon,1901); and Gréard.

20. *Réflexions ou sentences et maximes morales de Monsieur de la Rochefoucauld, maximes de Madame la marquise de Sablé. Pensées diverses de M. L.D. et les maximes chrétiennes de M***** [Mme de La Sablière] (Amsterdam, 1705); *Maximes de Madame la Marquise de Sablé et Pensées diverses de M.L.D.* (Paris, 1678); *Madame La Comtesse de Maure, Sa Vie et sa Correpondance suivies des Maximes de Madame De Sablé*, ed. Edouard de Barthelemy (Paris, 1863). Secondary sources include Victor Cousin, *Madame de Sablé: Nouvelles études sur la société et les femmes illustres du dix-septième siècle* (Paris, 1854); Vicomte S. Menjot-d'Elbenne, *Mme de la Sablière, ses pensées chrétiennes et ses lettres a l'abbé de Rancé* (Paris: Plon, 1923); N. Ivanoff, *La Marquise de Sablé et son salon* (Paris: Presses Modernes, 1927); Reynier.

Christina's two series of maxims, *"Ouvrage de Loisir"* and *"Sentimens,"* together with *Réfléxions diverses sur la Vie et sur les Actions du Grand Alexandre*, "Réfléxions sur la Vie et les Actions du César," a sampling of her correspondence, and unfinished autobiography, *La Vie de la Reine Christine faite par Elle-même, dédiée à Dieu*, are published in *Mémoires concernant Christine, reine de Suède pour servir d'éclaircissement à l'histoire de son regne et principalment de sa vie privée, et aux evenements de son tems civile et literaire*, ed. Johan Archenholtz, 4 vols. (Leipzig/Amsterdam, 1751–60); an early English translation of some maxims is *The Works of Christina Queen of Sweden . . .* (London, 1753). A secretarial draft of the maxims, existing in manuscript at the Royal Library, Stockholm, is considered the most authoritative version; it was published in Sven Stolpe, *Drottning Kristina Maximer—Les Sentiments Heroiques, Acta Academiae Catholicae Suecanae I* (Stockholm: Bonniers, 1959). Susanna Åkerman, however, has recently discovered a completed, unaltered, late edition of the maxims (ca. 1683) in the Herzog August Bibliotek, Wolfenbüttel, that may supersede all others. Christina's notes on the maxims of La Rochefoucauld have been published in *La Rochefoucauld—Maximes suivés par des réfléxions diverses, du portrait de la Rochefoucauld par lui-même et des remarques de Christine de Suède sur les maximes*, ed. J. Truchet (Paris: Garnier, 1967). Secondary sources include Galeazzo Gualdo Priorato, *The History of the Sacred and Royal Majesty of Christina Alessandra queen of Swedland . . .* (London, 1658); Ernst Cassirer, *Descartes: Lehre—Persönlichkeit—Wirkung* (Stockholm: Bermann-Fischer Verlag, 1939); Sven Stolpe, *Queen Christina*, trans. R. M. Bethel (London: Burns and Oates,1966); Susanna Åkerman, *Queen Christina of Sweden and Her Circle: The Transformation of a Seventeenth-Century Philosophical Libertine* (Leiden/New York: E. J. Brill, 1991).

21. From a letter of Leibniz to the Electress Sophie of Hanover, first published by Louis Foucher de Careil, *Lettres et opuscules inédits de Leibniz* (Paris, 1854), p. 254. Scudéry's work includes *Conversations sur divers sujets*, 2 vols. (Paris, 1680), English translation: *Conversations upon Several Subjects*, 2 vols., trans. F. Spence (London, 1683); *Conversations nouvelles sur divers sujets*, 2 vols. (Paris,1684); *Conversations morale* (Amsterdam, 1686); *Nouvelles Conversations de morale* (The Hague, 1688); *Entretiens de morale*, 2 vols. (Paris, 1692). Secondary sources include Reynier; Émile Magne, *Le Salon de Mlle de Scudéry ou Le Royaume de Tendre*

(Monaco: Société des Conférences, 1927); Georges Mongrédien, *Madeleine de Scudéry et son salon* (Paris: Tallandier, 1946); Alain Niderst, *Madeleine de Scudéry, Paul Pellisson et leur monde* (Paris: Presses Universitaires de France, 1976); Nicole Aronson, *Mademoiselle de Scudéry* (Boston: Twayne, 1978); and Harth.

For a discussion of Scudéry's philosophical method and her feminism, see my "Women Cartesians, 'Feminine Philosophy,' and Historical Exclusion," in *Feminist Interpretations of Descartes*, ed. Susan Bordo (University Park: Pennsylvania State University Press, forthcoming).

22. Jeanne Dumée, *Entretien sur l'opinion de Copernic touchant la mobilité de la terre* (Paris, n.d.), ms. ca. 1680, Bibliothèque Nationale, Fonds français 19941. Aphra Behn, "The Translator's Preface" in Bernard le Bovier de Fontenelle, *A Discovery of New Worlds*, trans. Aphra Behn (London, 1688).

23. *The Conway Letters: The Correspondence of Anne, Viscountess Conway, Henry More, and Their Friends, 1642–1684*, ed. Marjorie Hope Nicholson, rev. ed. by Sarah Hutton (Oxford: Clarendon Press, 1992), p. 237.

24. Margaret Cavendish, duchess of Newcastle, *Philosophical Letters: Or Modest Reflections upon Some Opinions in Natural Philosophy, Maintained by Several Famous and Learned Authors of this Age, Expressed by Way of Letters* (London, 1664), pp. 494–95, selections from which appear in Margaret Atherton's *Women Philosophers of the Early Modern Period* (Indianapolis: Hackett, 1994). Her other mature works of natural philosophy include *Grounds of Natural Philosophy* (London, 1668) and *Observations upon Experimental Philosophy. To which is added, The Description of a New World Called the Blazing World* (London, 1666.). A modern edition of *The Description of a New World . . .* is in Margaret Cavendish, *The Blazing World and Other Writings*, ed. Kate Lilley (New York/London: Penguin Classics, 1994). Secondary sources include Virginia Woolf, "The Duchess of Newcastle," *The Common Reader* (London: Hogarth Press, 1925); Douglas Grant, *Margaret the First: A Biography of Margaret Cavendish, Duchess of Newcastle, 1623–1673* (London: University of Toronto Press, 1957); Lisa Sarasohn, "A Science Turned Upside Down: Feminism and the Natural Philosophy of Margaret Cavendish," *Huntington Library Quarterly* 47, no. 4 (1984): 299–307; Silvia Bowerbank, "The Spider's Delight: Margaret Cavendish and the 'Female Imagination,' " *Women in the Renaissance: Selections from English Literary Renaissance*, ed. Kirby Farrell, Elizabeth Hageman and Arthur Kinney (Amherst: University of Massachusetts Press, 1991); Londa Schiebinger, "Margaret Cavendish, Duchess of Newcastle," in *HWP*, vol. 3; Kargon; Merchant; Meyer; Eileen O'Neill, "Margaret Lucas Cavendish," *The Routledge Encyclopedia of Philosophy*, ed. Edward Craig (London/New York: Routledge, forthcoming).

25. Anne Conway, *The Principles of the Most Ancient and Modern Philosophy*, ed. Peter Loptson (The Hague: Martinus Nijhoff, 1982), p. 221. This edition includes the 1692 London text, as well as *Principia philosophiae antiquissimae et recentissimae de Deo, Christo et creatura, id est de spiritu et materia in genere* (Amsterdam, 1690). A new translation of the Latin text, with a useful historical introduction, is Anne Conway, *The Principles of the Most Ancient and Modern Philosophy*, trans. and ed. Allison P. Coudert and Taylor Corse (Cambridge: Cambridge University Press, 1996). See also Alan Gabbey, "Anne Conway et Henry More," *Archives de Philosophie* 40 (1977): 379–404 and *The Conway Letters* (cited in note 23). Secondary sources include Joseph Politella, "Platonism, Aristotelianism, and Cabalism in the Philosophy of Leibniz" (Ph.D. diss., University of Pennsylvania, 1938); Carolyn

Merchant, "The Vitalism of Anne Conway: Its Impact on Leibniz's Conception of the Monad," *Journal of the History of Philosophy* 17, no. 3 (1979): 255–69; Merchant; Jane Duran, "Anne Viscountess Conway: A Seventeenth Century Rationalist," in *H* and reprinted in *HD*; Richard Popkin, "The Spiritualistic Cosmologies of Henry More and Anne Conway," *Henry More (1614–1687): Tercentenary Studies*, ed. Sarah Hutton (Dordrecht: Kluwer Academic Publishers, 1990); Lois Frankel, "Anne Finch, Viscountess Conway," in *HWP*, vol. 3; Sarah Hutton, "Anne Conway," *The Routledge Encyclopedia of Philosophy*, ed. Edward Craig (London/New York: Routledge, forthcoming); Sarah Hutton, "Anne Conway: critique de Henry More," *Archives de Philosophie*, forthcoming.

    26. *Oeuvres de Descartes*, 11 vols., ed. C. Adam and P. Tannery (Paris: Vrin, 1964–74); *Reliquiae Barclaianae: Correspondence of Colonel Barclay and Robert Barclay of Urie and his son Robert, including Letters from Princess Elizabeth of the Rhine* . . . (London, 1870). Secondary sources include A. Foucher de Careil, *Descartes et la Princesse Palatine, ou de l'influence du cartésianisme sur les femmes au XVIIᵉ siècle* (Paris, 1862) and his *Descartes, la princesse Elisabeth et la reine Christine* . . . (Paris: Germer-Bailliere, 1879); Charles Adam, *Descartes, ses amitiés féminines* (Paris: Boivin, 1917); Elizabeth Godfrey [Jessie Bedford, pseud.], *A Sister of Prince Rupert: Elizabeth Princess Palatine and Abbess of Herford* (London: John Lane, 1909); Marguerite Néel, *Descartes et la princesse Elisabeth* (Paris: Editions Elzévir, 1946); Daniel Garber, "Understanding Interaction: What Descartes Should Have Told Elisabeth," *Southern Journal of Philosophy* 21, suppl. (1983): 15–32; Janna Thompson, "Women and the High Priests of Reason," *Radical Philosophy* 34 (1983): 10–14; Beatrice Zedler, "The Three Princesses," in *H*; Harth; Eileen O'Neill, "Elisabeth of Bohemia," *The Routledge Encyclopedia of Philosophy*, ed. Edward Craig (London/New York: Routledge, forthcoming); *Feminist Interpretations of Descartes*, ed. Susan Bordo (University Park: Pennsylvania State University Press, forthcoming).

    27. Gottfried Wilhelm Leibniz, *Die Philosophischen Schriften von Gottfried Wilhelm Leibniz*, 7 vols., ed. C. J. Gerhardt (Hildesheim: Georg Olms,1960), vol. 3, p. 217.

    28. Notice, for example, that Victor Cousin attributes the *Principles* to van Helmont in the former's *Course of the History of Philosophy* (New York: D. Appleton, 1872), p. 114. See Merchant, ch. 11. See also Stuart Brown, "Leibniz and More's Cabalistic Circle," *Henry More (1614–1687) Tercentenary Studies*, ed. Sarah Hutton (Dordrecht: Kluwer Academic Publishers, 1990).

    29. Mary Astell, *Letters Concerning the Love of God, Between the Author of the Proposal to the Ladies and Mr. John Norris* . . . (London, 1695); *A Serious Proposal to the Ladies, Part II: Wherein a Method Is Offer'd for the Improvement of Their Minds* (London, 1697), a modern edition of which is in *A Serious Proposal to the Ladies Parts I and II, by Mary Astell*, ed. Patricia Springborg (Brookfield, Vt.: Pickering and Chatto, 1996); *The Christian Religion as Profess'd by a Daughter of the Church of England* (London, 1705). Secondary sources include Florence Smith, *Mary Astell* (New York: Columbia University Press, 1916); Joan Kinnaird, "Mary Astell and the Conservative Contribution to English Feminism," *Journal of British Studies* 19, no. 1 (Fall 1979): 53–75; Smith; Ruth Perry, *The Celebrated Mary Astell: An Early English Feminist* (Chicago: University of Chicago Press, 1986); Kathleen Squadrito, "Mary Astell's Critique of Locke's View of Thinking Matter," *Journal of the History of Philosophy* 25, no. 3 (July 1987): 434–39, and her "Mary Astell," in

HWP, vol. 3; Margaret Atherton, "Cartesian Reason and Gendered Reason," in *A Mind of One's Own: Feminist Essays on Reason and Objectivity*, ed. Louise M. Antony and Charlotte Witt (Denver: Westview Press, 1992); Eileen O'Neill, "Mary Astell," *The Routledge Encyclopedia of Philosophy*, ed. Edward Craig (London/ New York: Routledge, forthcoming), and " Women Cartesians, 'Feminine Philosophy,' and Historical Exclusion," see note 21.

30. Damaris Masham, *A Discourse Concerning the Love of God* (London, 1696) and *Occasional Thoughts in Reference to a Vertuous or Christian Life* (London, 1705); her letters to Locke are in *The Correspondence of John Locke*, ed. E. S. de Beer (Oxford: Clarendon Press, 1976); her letters to Leibniz are in *Die Philosophischen Schriften von Leibniz*, 7 vols., ed. C. J. Gerhardt (Hildesheim: Georg Olms, 1960), vol. 3. Secondary sources include Lois Frankel, "Damaris Cudworth Masham," in *HWP*, vol. 3 and reprinted in *HD*; Margaret Atherton, see note 29; Sarah Hutton, "Damaris Cudworth, Lady Masham: Between Platonism and Enlightenment," *British Journal for the History of Philosophy* 1, no. 1 (Spring 1993): 29–54.

31. Universitiets-Bibliotheek Amsterdam Remonstrants' MSS. J. 57a, according to Ethel M. Kersey, *Women Philosophers: A Bio-Critical Source Book* (New York: Greenwood Press, 1989), p. 155.

32. *Bibliothèque Choisie* 7 (1705): 383–90.

33. I want to thank Sarah Hutton and Martha Bolton for identifying the Burnet in question.

34. These works, along with *A Guide to Controversies*, some letters, and a play, appeared in *The Works of Mrs. Catharine Cockburn, Theological, Moral, Dramatic, and Poetical*, ed. Thomas Birch, 2 vols. (London, 1751). An excerpt from *A Defence of Mr. Locke's Essay of Human Understanding* appears in Margaret Atherton's *Women Philosophers of the Early Modern Period* (Indianapolis: Hackett, 1994). Selected secondary sources include Mary Ellen Waithe, "Catharine Trotter Cockburn," in *HWP*, vol. 3; Martha Brandt Bolton, "Some Aspects of the Philosophy of Catharine Trotter," *Journal of the History of Philosophy* 31, no. 4 (October 1993): 565–88, reprinted in *HD*. I thank Martha Bolton and Margaret Atherton for bringing Catharine Trotter Cockburn's name to my attention.

35. Anon. [Judith Drake], *An Essay in Defence of the Female Sex . . .* (London, 1696; reprinted, New York, 1970). For a discussion of problems regarding the attribution, see *First Feminists: British Women Writers 1578–1799*, ed. Moira Ferguson (Bloomington: Indiana University Press, 1985), pp. 201–2; Florence Smith, citation in note 29. See also Reynolds and Smith.

36. Lady [Mary] Chudleigh, *Essays upon Several Subjects in Prose and Verse* (London, 1710). A modern edition is available in *The Poems and Prose of Mary, Lady Chudleigh*, ed. Margaret J. M. Ezell (Oxford/New York: Oxford University Press, 1993). Secondary sources include Ballard and Smith.

37. *Correspondance de Leibniz avec l'électrice Sophie de Brunswick-Lunebourg*, 3 vols., ed. O. Klopp (Hanover, 1874); *Briefwechsel der Kurfürstin Sophie von Hanover* (Berlin/Leipzig: K. J. Koehler, 1927). Secondary sources include A. Foucher de Careil, *Leibniz et les deux Sophies* (Paris, 1876); Beatrice Zedler, "The Three Princesses," in *H*.

38. Gabrielle Suchon, *Traité de la morale et de la politique, divisé en trois parties, savoir: la liberté, la science et l'autorité où l'on voit que les personnes du Sexe, pour en être privées, ne laissent pas d'avoir une capacité naturelle qui les en peut rendre*

participantes. Avec un petit traité de la foiblesse, de la legereté et de l'inconstance qu'on leur attribuë mal à propos (Lyon, 1693) of which part 1 was published in *Traité de la morale et de la politique 1663: La liberté,* ed. Séverine Auffret (Paris: Des femmes, 1988); *[Traité] Du célibat volontaire, ou la vie sans engagement, par Demoiselle Suchon* (Paris, 1700). Secondary sources include S. A. Richard, *Feminist Writers of the Seventeenth Century* (London: David Nutt, 1914); Paul Hoffman, "Le Féminisme spirituel de Gabrielle Suchon," *XVIIe siècle* 121 (1978): 269–76; Michèle Le Doeuff, *Hipparchia's Choice,* trans. T. Selous (Oxford/Cambridge, Mass.: Basil Blackwell, 1991); Pierre Ronzeaud, "La Femme au pouvoir ou le monde à l'envers," *XVIIe siècle* 108 (1975): 9–34.

39. For example, S. A. Richard, in *Feminist Writers of the Seventeenth Century* (see note 38), discusses the *Treatise of Morals and of Politics* and characterizes it as a "serious" feminist text in the tradition of the work of Poulain de la Barre. However, he attributes it to "Damoiselle G. S. Aristophile."

40. See Phyllis Mack, "Women as Prophets during the English Civil War, *Feminist Studies* 8, no. 1 (1982): 19–45.

41. Margaret Fell [Fox], *Women's Speaking Justified, Proved and Allowed of by the Scriptures, all such as speak by the Spirit and Power of the Lord Jesus . . .* (London,1666); *A Brief Collection of Remarkable Passages and Occurrences relating to the Birth, Education, Life, of the Eminent and Faithful Servent of the Lord, Margaret Fell, but by her Second Marriage, Margaret Fox, together with Sundry of Her Epistles, Books and Christian Testimonies to Friends and Others* (London, 1710). Secondary sources include Isabel Ross, *Margaret Fell, Mother of Quakerism,* (London: Routledge and Kegan Paul, 1949); Patricia Crawford, *Women and Religion in England 1500–1720* (London/New York: Routledge, 1993); Smith; Ezell.

42. *Oeuvres complètes de Mme. Guyon,* 40 vols. ed. J.-P. Dutoit (Lausanne, 1767–91). There is no standard edition. Secondary sources include T. Upham, *Life and Religious Opinions of Madame Guyon, together with some account of the personal history and religious opinions of Fénelon, Archbishop of Cambray,* 2 vols. (New York, 1847); Louis Guerrier, *Madame Guyon, sa vie, sa doctrine et son influence* (Orleans, 1881; reprinted, Geneva: Slatkine Reprints, 1971); Adam; Ernest Antoine Aimé Leon, Baron Seillère, *Mme Guyon et Fénelon: Precurseurs de Rousseau* (Paris: Alcan, 1918) (see note 75).

Anna Maria van Schurman, *EYKΛHPIA: seu melioris partis electio . . .* [Eukleria: Or the Choice of the Better Part, As Presenting a Brief Sketch of Her Religion and Life] (Altona,1673; Dutch translation, Amsterdam, 1684); *Korte Onderrichtinge . . .* [Short Instruction Concerning the State and Way of Life of Those Persons Whom God Gathers and Has United in His service through the Actions of His Faithful Servant Jean de Labadie and His Brothers and Fellow-Workers Pierre Yvon and Pierre Dulignon]* (Amsterdam, 1675); *EYKΛHPIA II* (Amsterdam, 1684). See Joyce Irwin, "Anna Maria van Schurman: From Feminism to Pietism," *Church History* 46 (1977): 46–62.

43. See Mack, "Women as Prophets," where this is argued for persuasively (see note 40).

44. Victor Cousin, *Jacqueline Pascal: Premières études sur les femmes illustres et la société du XVIIe Siècle* (Paris, 1844), p. 20.

45. Their works include Hester Chapone's *Letters on the Improvement of the Mind: Addressed to a Young Lady,* 2 vols. (London, 1773) and *The Works of Mrs. Hester Chapone . . . ,* 4 vols. (London, 1807); Elisabeth Montagu's dialogues in

Dialogues of the Dead, ed. George Lyttelton (London, 1760), pp. 291–320; Hannah More's *Essays on Various Subjects, Principally designed for Young Ladies* (London, 1777) and *Strictures on the Modern System of Female Education* . . . , 2 vols. (London, 1799; reprinted by Gina Luria, New York: Garland, 1974). The foremost intellectual of this circle was Elizabeth Carter, who had studied classics, Hebrew, Italian, French, history, math, and astronomy. She brought this scholarship to bear on her translations of the works of Epictetus (1758) and of Algorotti's *Explanation of Newton's Philosophy for the Use of the Ladies* (1739). Her "Notes on the Bible and Answers to Objections Concerning the Christian Religion" were published posthumously in *Memoirs of the Life of Mrs. Elizabeth Carter, with a New Edition of her Poems*, 2 vols., ed. Montagu Pennington (London, 1808).

46. Catharine Macaulay, *Loose Remarks on Certain Positions to be found in Mr. Hobbes' Philosophical Rudiments of Government and Society, with a Short Sketch of a Democratic form of Government in a Letter to Signior Paoli* (London, 1767) and her *Letters on Education with Observations on Religious and Metaphysical Subjects* (London, 1790; reprinted by Gina Luria, New York: Garland, 1974). In addition to her philosophical works, Macaulay also published an eight-volume history of England and a number of political pamphlets, including *Observations on a Pamphlet entitled "Thoughts on the Cause of the Present Discontents"* (London, 1770); *A Modest Plea for the Property of Copyright* (Bath, 1774); *An Address to the People of England, Scotland and Ireland on the Present Important Crisis of Affairs* (Bath, 1775); *Observations on the Reflections of the Rt. Hon. Edmund Burke, on the Revolution in France* (London, 1790). Secondary sources include Bridget Hill, *The Republican Virago: The Life and Times of Catharine Macaulay* (Oxford: Clarendon Press, 1992); Florence Boos, "Catharine Macaulay's *Letters on Education* (1790): An Early Feminist Polemic," *University of Michigan Papers in Women's Studies* 2, no. 2 (1976): 64–78; Patricia Ward Scaltsas, "Catharine Macaulay: A Woman of the Enlightenment" (paper presented at the British Society for the History of Philosophy conference on "Women and the History of Philosophy," 1992); Spender; and *HWP*, vol. 3.

47. Mary Wollstonecraft, *Thoughts on the Education of Daughters: with Reflections on Female Conduct, in the more Important Duties of Life* (London, 1787); *A Vindication of the Rights of Men, in a Letter to the Right Honourable Edmund Burke* (London, 1790); *A Vindication of the Rights of Woman, with Strictures on Political and Moral Subjects* (London, 1792); review of Catharine Macaulay's *Letters on Education, Analytical Review* (November 1790). Wollstonecraft's writings have finally been assembled in a critical edition: *The Works of Mary Wollstonecraft*, 7 vols., ed. Janet Todd and Marilyn Butler (Bloomington/Indianapolis: Indiana University Press, 1989). Secondary sources here are numerous, but see especially George Eliot, "Margaret Fuller and Mary Wollstonecraft" (1855), in *Essays of George Eliot*, ed. Thomas Pinney (London: Routledge and Kegan Paul, 1963); Regina M. Janes, "Mary, Mary, Quite Contrary, or Mary Astell and Mary Wollstonecraft Compared," *Studies in Eighteenth-Century Culture* 5 (1975): 121–39; Carolyn Korsmeyer, "Reason and Morals in the Early Feminist Movement: Mary Wollstonecraft," *Women and Philosophy*, ed. Carol Gould and Marx Wartofsky (New York: Putnam, 1976); Jane R. Martin, *Reclaiming the Conversation: The Ideal of the Educated Woman* (New Haven, Conn.: Yale University Press, 1985); Jean Grimshaw, "Mary Wollstonecraft and the Tensions in Feminist Philosophy," *Radical Philosophy* 52 (Summer 1989): 11–17; Kate Lindemann, "Mary Wollstonecraft," in *HWP*,

vol. 3; Virginia Shapiro, *A Vindication of Political Virtue: The Political Theory of Mary Wollstonecraft* (Chicago/London: University of Chicago Press, 1992); Spender.

48. Mary Hays, *Letters and Essays Moral and Miscellaneous* (London, 1793; reprinted by Gina Luria, New York: Garland, 1974); *Appeal to the Men of Great Britain in Behalf of Women* (London, 1798; reprinted by Gina Luria, New York: Garland, 1974); *Female Biography, or Memoirs of Illustrious and Celebrated Women of All Ages and Countries, Alphabetically Arranged*, 6 vols. (London, 1803); *Monthly Magazine*, July 2, 1796; March 2, 1797. Secondary sources include Joyce Marjorie Sanxter Tompkins, "Mary Hays, Philosophess," *The Polite Marriage* (Cambridge: Cambridge University Press, 1938); Gina Luria, "Mary Hays's Letters and Manuscripts," *Signs: Journal of Women in Culture and Society* 3, no. 2 (Winter 1977): 524–30; Spender.

49. Lady Mary Shepherd, *An Essay upon the Relation of Cause and Effect, controverting the Doctrine of Mr. Hume, concerning the Nature of that Relation; with Observations upon the Opinions of Dr. Brown and Mr. Lawrence, connected with the same subject* (London, 1824); *Essays on the Perception of an External Universe and other Subjects Connected with the Doctrine of Causation* (London, 1827), excerpts from which appear in Margaret Atherton's *Women Philosophers of the Early Modern Period* (Indianapolis: Hackett, 1994); *An Essay on the Academical or Sceptical Philosophy, as Applied by Mr. Hume to the Perception of External Existence; with several shorter Essays, upon subjects relating to the Doctrine of Causation* (London, 1827); "Observations of Lady Mary Shepherd on the 'First Lines of the Human Mind,'" *Parriana: or Notices of the Rev. Samuel Parr. LL.D., collected from various sources, printed and manuscript and in part written by E. H. Barker, esq.* (London, 1828–29); "Lady Mary Shepherd's Metaphysics," *Fraser's Magazine for Town and Country* 5, no. 30 (July 1832): 697–708. Shepherd's views are discussed by John Fearn in his reply to her review in the same volume of *Parriana*. See also Samuel Allibone, *A Critical Dictionary of English Literature and British and American Authors* (Philadelphia, 1858–71; reprinted Detroit: Gale Research, 1965); Ethel Kersey, *Women Philosophers*. I thank Margaret Atherton for bringing Shepherd's 1824 publication to my attention.

50. Anne Lefèvre Dacier, *Réflexions morales de l'empereur Marc Antonin . . .* (Paris, 1690–91; English translation, London, 1692); *Des Causes de la corruption du goût* (Paris, 1714). Secondary sources include Fern Farnham, *Madame Dacier: Scholar and Humanist* (Monterey: Angel, 1976); *FW*; Gibson; Schiebinger.

51. Charles Augustin Sainte-Beuve, *Portraits of the Eighteenth Century: Historic and Literary*, trans. Kathleen Wormeley (New York/London: Putnam, 1905), Part II p. 57. Sainte-Beuve actually places Lambert between representative salons of the respective centuries: that of Mme de Rambouillet and that of Mme Necker, mother of Mme de Staël.

52. Anne Thérèse de Lambert, *Réflexions nouvelles sur les femmes, par une dame de la cour de France* (Paris, 1727); *Lettres sur la véritable éducation* (Amsterdam, 1729)—first published as *Avis d'une mère à son Fils et à sa Fille* (Paris, 1728); *Traité de l'amitié, Traité de la vieillesse, Réflexions sur les femmes, sur le goût, sur les richesses* (Amsterdam, 1732) are all contained in *Oeuvres complètes, précédées d'une notice, suivies de ses lettres à plusieurs personnages célèbres* (Paris, 1808). In addition to Sainte-Beuve (see note 51), secondary sources include M. de Lescure, *Les Femmes philosophes* (Paris, 1881); J.-P. Zimmermann, "La Morale laïque au

commencement du XVIIIᵉ siècle: Madame de Lambert," *Revue d'Histoire Littéraire de la France* 24 (1917): 42–64, 440–66; Ellen M. Hine, "Madame de Lambert, Her Sources and Her Circle: On the Threshold of a New Age," *Studies on Voltaire* 102 (1973): 173–91; Robert Granderoute, "De L'Éducation des filles aux Avis d'une mère à sa fille: Fénelon et Madame de Lambert," *Revue d'Histoire Littéraire de la France* 87 (1987): 15–30; Picard; Rosso; Gréard; *FW*; *WS*.

53. For example, *Avis d'une mère à sa fille* saw fifteen editions between 1732 and 1828. See the preface by Milagros Palma to Anne Thérèse de Lambert, *Réflexions nouvelles sur les femmes* (Paris: Côté-femmes éditions, 1989).

54. Louise d'Épinay, *Les Conversations d'Émilie* (Leipzig, 1774/Paris, 1781); Mme Panckoucke, *Sentiments de reconnaissance d'une mère addressés à l'ombre de J. J. Rousseau*, in Rousseau, *Oeuvres*, vol. 10 (Neuchâtel, 1779). Secondary sources include Élisabeth Badinter, *Émilie, Émilie ou l'ambition féminine au XVIIᵉ siècle* (Paris: Flammarion, 1983); Francis Steegmuller, *A Woman, a Man and Two Kingdoms: The Story of Madame D'Épinay and the Abbé Galiani* (Princeton, N.J.: Princeton University Press, 1991); Samia Spencer, "Women and Education," in *FW*; Gréard.

55. For example, see Mlle d'Espinassy, *Essai sur l'éducation des demoiselles* (Paris, 1764); Marie Leprince De Beaumont, *Instructions pour les jeunes qui entrent dans le monde . . .* , 3 vols. (London, 1764); Charlotte Chaumet d'Ormoy, *Les Malheurs de la Jeune Émilie, pour servir d'instruction aux âmes vertueuses et sensibles*, 2 vols. (Paris, 1777); Marie Joséphine Monbart, *Sophie: ou de l'éducation des filles* (Berlin, 1777); Anne d'Aubourg de la Bove, comtesse de Miremont, *Traité de l'éducation des femmes, et cours complet d'instruction*, 7 vols. (Paris, 1779–89); Jeanne Louisa Campan, *De l'Éducation*, 3 vols. (Paris, 1824); Elizabeth Guizot, *Essai sur l'homme, les moeurs, les caractères, le monde, les femmes, l'éducation* (Paris, 1828). Secondary sources include Paul Hoffman, *La Femme dans la pensée des Lumières* (Paris: Éditions Orphrys, 1977); Paul Rousselot, *Histoire de l'éducation des femmes en France*, 2 vols. (Paris: Librairie académique Didier, 1883); Léon Abensour, *La Femme et le féminisme avant la révolution* (Paris: Ernest Leroux, 1923); Lougee; Samia Spencer, "Women and Educations," in *FW*.

56. Stéphanie Felicité Du Crest de Saint-Aubin, comtesse de Genlis, *Adèle et Théodore ou lettres sur l'éducation* (Paris, 1782; English translation, London, 1783); *Discours sur la suppression des couvents de religieuses et l'éducation publique des femmes* (Paris, 1790). Secondary sources include Charles Augustin Sainte-Beuve, *Nouvelle Galerie de femmes célèbres* (Paris, 1865); Louis Chabaud, *Mesdames de Maintenon, de Genlis et Campan, leur rôle dans l'éducation chrétienne de la femme* (Paris: Librairie Plon,1901); Gabriel de Broglie, *Madame de Genlis* (Paris: Perrin, 1985); Madeleine Raaphorst, "Adele Versus Sophie: The Well Educated Woman of Mme de Genlis," *Rice University Studies* 64, no. 1 (1978): 41–50; P. D. Jimack,"The Paradox of Sophie and Julie: Contemporary Response to Rousseau's Ideal Wife and Ideal Mother," in *WS*.

57. Louise-Marie Dupin, "Idées sur l'éducation," published posthumously in *Le Portefeuille de Madame Dupin, dame de Chenonceaux*, ed. le comte Gaston de Villeneuve-Guibert (Paris, 1884). According to Lee, Dupin's manuscript was sold at an auction in the 1970s and was being prepared for publication by Professor Leland Thielemann.

58. Olympe de Gouges [Marie Gouze], *Les Droits de la femme. A la Reine* (n.p., n.d. [1791]); *Oeuvres*, ed. Benoîte Groult (Paris: Mercure de France, 1986). Second-

ary sources include Olivier Blanc, *Olympe de Gouges* (Paris: Syros, 1981); Marie Cerati, *Le Club des citoyennes républicaines révolutionnaires* (Paris, Editions Sociales, 1966); Léopold Lacour, *Les Origines du féminisme contemporain, Trois femmes de la Révolution: Olympe de Gouges, Théroigne de Méricourt, Rose Lacombe* (Paris: Plon, 1900); Jules Michelet, *Les Femmes de la Révolution française* (Paris, 1854).

Fanny Raoul, *Opinion d'une femme sur les femmes, par F.R.**** [Fanny Raoul], ed. Princesse de Salm (Paris, 1801), reproduced with published texts by Marie-Armande-Jeanne Gacon-Dufour and Albertine Clément-Hémery in *Opinions de femmes: De la veille au Lendemain de la Révolution Française* (Paris: Côte-femmes éditions, 1989). Secondary sources include Fraisse.

59. Jeanne-Marie [Manon] Phlipon Roland, *Oeuvres de Jeanne-Marie Phlipon Roland, femme de l'ex-ministre del'Intérieur*, 3 vols., ed. L.-A. Champagneux (Paris, 1800); *The Works (never before published) of Jeanne-Marie Phlipon Roland . . .* (London, 1800). Secondary sources include Gita May, "Rousseau's 'Antifeminism' Reconsidered," in *FW*, and her *Madame Roland and the Age of Revolution* (New York/London: Columbia University Press, 1970); Edith Bernadin, *Les Idées religieuses de Madame Roland* (Paris: Les Belles Lettres, 1933); Théodore Gosselin Lenôtre (pseud.), "The Salon of Madame Roland," in *Paris in the French Revolution*, trans. H. N. Williams (London: Hutchinson, 1925); Una (Pope-Hennessy) Birch, *Madame Roland* (New York: Dodd, Mead, 1918); Blum.

60. [Gabrielle-Émilie Le Tonnelier De Breteuil, marquise du Châtelet-Lomont], *Institutions de physique* (Paris, 1740); *Réponse de Madame**** [du Châtelet] *à la lettre que M. de Mairan . . . lui a écrite le 18 février sur la question des forces vives* (Brussels, 1741); *Dissertation sur la nature et la propagation du feu* (limited edition by Académie des Sciences, 1739/Paris, 1744); *Principes mathématiques de la philosophie naturelle*, 2 vols. (Paris, 1756; first complete edition 1759; reprinted Paris: A. Blanchard, 1966); *Réflexions sur le Bonheur* in *Opuscules philosophiques et littéraires, la plupart posthumes ou inédits* (Paris, 1796); essays in Ira O. Wade, *Studies on Voltaire with Some Unpublished Papers of Mme du Châtelet* (Princeton, N.J.: Princeton University Press, 1947). Secondary sources include Ira O. Wade, *Voltaire and Mme du Châtelet: An Essay on the Intellectual Activity at Cirey* (Princeton, N.J.: Princeton University Press, 1941); William H. Barber, "Madame du Châtelet and Leibnizianism: The genesis of the *Institutions de Physique*," *The Age of Enlightenment*, ed. W. H. Barber et al. (Edinburgh/London: Oliver and Boyd, 1967); Carolyn Iltis [Merchant], "Madame du Châtelet's Metaphysics and Mechanics," *Studies in History and Philosophy of Science* 8, no. 1 (1977): 29–48; Linda Gardiner Janik, "Searching for the Metaphysics of Science: The Structure and Composition of Mme du Châtelet's *Institutions de physique*, 1737–40," *Studies on Voltaire and the Eighteenth Century* 201 (1982): 85–113; Élisabeth Badinter, *Émilie, Émilie ou l'ambition féminine au XVIIe siècle* (Paris: Flammarion, 1983); Alic; Merchant (1980); Ogilvie; Mozans; Schiebinger; Harth; *FW*.

61. Marie Thiroux D'Arconville, *Mélanges de littérature, de morale et de physique*, 7 vols., ed. Rossel (Amsterdam, 1775). In addition, she published translations of English scientific works and of Lord Halifax; her *Vie du Cardinal d'Ossat* was reviewed by Diderot. Her circle included Voltaire and Lavoisier. Secondary sources include Schiebinger and Alic.

62. *Théorie des Sentimens Moraux . . . par Adam Smith; Traduit de l'Anglais . . . par S. Grouchy Ve. Condorcet. Elle y a join huit Lettres sur le Sympathie* (Paris, 1798). Secondary sources include Jules Michelet, *Les Femmes de la Révolution*

française (Paris, 1854); Antoine Guillois, *La Marquise de Condorcet* (Paris, 1897); Thierry Boissel, *Sophie de Condorcet* (Paris: Presses de la Renaissance, 1988); Barbara Brookes, "The Feminism of Condorcet and Sophie de Grouchy," *Studies on Voltaire and the Eighteenth Century* 189 (1980): 297–361.

63. Sophie Germaine, *Considérations générales sur l'état des sciences et des lettres aux différentes époques de leur culture*, ed. Armand-Jacques Lherbette (Paris,1833); *Oeuvres philosophiques de Sophie Germain, suivies de pensées et de lettres inédites et précédées d'une notice sur sa vie et ses oeuvres par Hippolyte Stupuy* (Paris,1879). Secondary sources include Lynn M. Osen, *Women in Mathematics* (Cambridge, Mass.: MIT Press, 1974); Mozans; Ogilvie; Schiebinger.

64. Anne Louise Germaine Necker, baronne de Staël-Holstein, *Lettres sur le caractère et les écrits de Jean-Jacques Rousseau* (1788); *De l'Influence des passions sur le bonheur des individus et des nations* (1796); *De Littérature considérée dans ses rapports avec les institutions sociales* (1800). All appear in *Oeuvres Complètes de Madame la Baronne de Staël-Holstein*, ed. Auguste de Staël (1820; reprinted, Geneva: Slatkine Reprints, 1967). Secondary sources include Amelia Gere Mason, *The Women of the French Salons* (New York, 1891); Charles Augustin Sainte-Beuve, *Nouvelle galerie de femmes célèbres* (Paris, 1865); Fraisse, *FW*.

65. [Henriette], *Philosophie der Weiber* (Leipzig, 1802); Amalia Holst, *Über die Bestimmung des Weibes zur höhern Geistesbildung* (Berlin, 1802). Secondary sources include Schiebinger; I am indebted to this source for these references.

66. Isabelle de Charrière, *Eloge de Jean-Jacques Rousseau, qui a concouru pour le prix de l'Académie française* (Paris, 1797); *Oeuvres complètes*, 10 vols., ed. Jean-Daniel Canadaux et al. (Amsterdam: van Oorschot, 1979–84). I am indebted to Gina Fisch-Freedman for bringing Charrière to my attention. The citation of the text on Rousseau appears in Blum. Secondary sources include Phillipe Godet, *Madame de Charrière et ses amis* (Geneva: Julien, 1906); Rolf Winiker, *Madame de Charrière: Essai d'un itinéraire spirituel* (Lausanne: Editions l'Age d'homme, 1971).

67. Marie Huber, *Le Monde fou préféré au monde sage* (Amsterdam, 1731); *Le Système des anciens et des modernes, . . . sur le etát des âmes séparées des corps . . .* (London, 1731) both in English translation as *The World Unmask'd, or the Philosopher the greatest Cheat in Twenty Four Dialogues . . . To which is added, The State of Souls Separated from their Bodies . . . In Answer to a Treatise entitled, An Enquiry into Origenism* (London,1736); *Lettres sur la religion essentielle à l'homme, distinguée de ce qui n'en est que l'accessoire* (Amsterdam,1738; English translation 1738). Secondary sources include Gustave A. Metzger, *Marie Huber. Sa vie, ses oeuvres, sa théologie* (Geneva, 1887); E. R. Briggs, "Marie Huber and the Campaign against Eternal Hell Torments," in *WS*.

68. Laura Maria Caterina Bassi [Veratti], *Philosophica Studia . . .* [forty-nine theses disputed for the doctorate] (Bologna, 1732); *De acqua corpore naturali elemento aliorum corporum parte universi* [theses for a disputation] (Bologna,1732); the following appear in *De Bononiensi Scientiarum et Artium Instituto atque Academia Commentarii*: *De aeris compressione* (1745); *De problemate quodam hydrometrico* (1757); *De problemate quodam mechanico* (1757); *De immixto fluidis aere* (1792). Secondary sources include Marta Cavazza, "L' 'aurata luce settemplice': Algarotti, Laura Bassi e Newton," in her *Settecento inquieto: Alle origini dell'Istituto delle Scienze di Bologna* (Bologna: Mulino, 1990); Alberto Elena,"'In lode della filosofessa di Bologna': An Introduction to Laura Bassi," *Isis* 82 (1991): 510–18; Paula Findlen, "Science as a Career" (see note 4); Schiebinger; Alic; Mozans; Ogilvie.

69. Maria Gaetana Agnesi, *Propositiones Philosophicae* (Milan, 1738). Agnesi's important contribution in calculus was translated into English as *Analytical Institutions*, trans. John Colson (London, 1801). Secondary sources include Lynn M. Osen, *Women in Mathematics* (Cambridge, Mass.: MIT Press, 1974); Giovanna Tilche, *Maria Gaetana Agnesi: La scienziata santa del '700* (Milan: Rizzoli, 1984); Carla Vettori Sandor, "L'opera scientifica ed umanitaria di Maria Gaetana Agnesi," in *Alma mater studiorum: La presenza femminile dal XVIII al XX secolo* (Bologna: CLUEB, 1988), pp. 105–18; Schiebinger; Alic; Mozans; Ogilvie.

70. *I principi della filosofia di Renato Des-cartes tradotti . . . da Giuseppa-Eleonora Barbapiccola . . .* (Turin, 1722). Secondary sources include Mozans; Ogilvie.

71. Gilles Ménage, *Historia mulierum philosopharum . . .* (Lyon, 1690; English translation, 1702); a recent English translation is cited in note 1.

72. Thomas Stanley, *A History of Philosophy . . .*, 3 vols. (London, 1687).

73. Jean de La Forge, *Le Cercle des femmes sçavantes . . .* (Paris, 1663). Marguerite Buffet, *Nouvelles observations sur la langue françoise . . . Avec les éloges de illustres sçavantes tant anciennes que modernes* (Paris, 1668).

74. Wilhelm Gottlieb Tennemann, *Geschichte der Philosophie*, 11 vols. (Leipzig, 1798–1819); Georg Wilhelm Friedrich Hegel, *Vorlesungen über die Geschichte der Philosophie* (Berlin, 1833–36), English translation: *History of Philosophy*, trans. Haldane (London, 1892); Charles Renouvier, *Manuel de Philosophie Moderne* (Paris, 1842).

Sophie Charlotte, who became the first queen of Prussia, was the daughter of the Electress Sophie of Hanover and niece of Elisabeth of Bohemia. She corresponded with Leibniz and John Toland, among others. Secondary sources include Louis Foucher de Careil, *Leibniz et les deux Sophies* (Paris, 1876); Merchant; Beatrice H. Zedler, "The Three Princesses," in *H*.

75. Victor Cousin, *Cours de Philosophie* (Paris, 1828), English translation: *Course of the History of Modern Philosophy*, New York, 1872).

Jeanne-Marie Bouvier de La Motte Guyon attempted to convince her readers of the doctrines of Catholic quietism, including the importance of achieving indifference and passivity of the soul, in works such as *Moyen court et très-facile pour l'oraison . . .* (Grenoble, 1685) and *Les Torrents spirituels* (Amsterdam, 1704.) She was imprisoned several times for her allegedly heretical published views, which included, among other things, disparaging ceremonial devotion and claiming that in the soul's union with God the soul is beyond good and evil (see note 42).

Antoinette Bourignon's complete works appear in *Toutes les oeuvres de Mlle Antoinette Bourignon*, 19 vols. (Amsterdam, 1686). English translations of her writings include *The Light of the World* (London, 1696) and *The Academy of Learned Divines* (London, 1708). Secondary sources include A. R. Macewen, *Antoinette Bourignon, Quietist* (London: Hodder and Stoughton, 1910); M. Van der Does, *Antoinette Bourignon, 1616–1689: La vie et l'oeuvre d'une mystique chrétienne* (Amsterdam: Holland University Press, 1974).

I wish to thank Richard Popkin for invaluable information about women preachers, prophets, and mystics in the seventeenth and early eighteenth centuries, especially about figures like Guyon and Bourignon. I am particularly indebted to him for bringing Margaret Fell Fox to my attention.

76. Catherine Trotter Cockburn, *Works*, vol. 2, part 1, p. 202 (see note 34).

77. M. [Mathurin] de Lescure, *Les Femmes philosophes* (Paris, 1881).

78. A. Foucher de Careil, *Descartes et la Princesse Palatine, ou de l'influence du cartésianisme sur les femmes au XVIIe siècle* (Paris, 1862); *Descartes, la princesse Elisabeth et la reine Christine* . . . (Paris: Felix Alcan, 1909); *Leibniz et les deux Sophies* (Paris, 1876).

79. Victor Cousin, *Madame de Sablé: Études sur les femmes illustres et la société du XVIIe siècle* (Paris, 1854); *La Société Française au XVIIe Siècle d'après Le Grand Cyrus de Mlle de Scudéry*, 2 vols. (Paris, 1858).

80. Cousin, *Course of the History of Modern Philosophy*, vol. 1, p. 316 (see note 28).

81. Wilhelm Gottlieb Tennemann, *Grundriss der Geschichte der Philosophie für den akademischen Unterricht* (1812), which was an abridgement of his *Geschichte der Philosophie* (see note 74), appeared in English as *Manual of the History of Philosophy*, trans. Rev. Arthur Johnson (Oxford, 1832).

82. Benjamin Farrington, "Temporis Partus Masculus: An Untranslated Writing of Francis Bacon," *Centaurus* 1 (1951): 193–205; I am indebted to Schiebinger for this reference.

83. Eileen O'Neill, "Women Cartesians, 'Feminine Philosophy,' and Historical Exclusion" (see note 21).

84. Schiebinger, pp. 153–54.

85. Translation in ibid., p. 156.

86. Louis Sébastien Mercier, *Tableau de Paris* (Amsterdam, 1782–88), pp. 295–96; translation in Lee, pp. 76–77.

87. Translation in Schiebinger, p. 110.

88. Karl Joël, *Die Frauen in der Philosophie* (Hamburg, 1896), pp. 44, 48; translation in Schiebinger, p. 152.

89. Immanuel Kant, *Beobachtungen über das Gefühl des Schönen und Erhabenen* (Köningsberg, 1764); translation in Schiebinger, p. 146.

90. Makin, *An Essay to Revive the Antient Education of Gentlewomen* . . . , p. 3 (see note 17).

91. Samuel Johnson quoted in Virgina Woolf, *A Room of One's Own* (New York: Harcourt, Brace and World, 1957), p. 56.

92. Pierre Joseph Proudhon, quoted in Jenny d'Hericourt, *A Woman's Philosophy of Woman; or Woman Affranchised* (New York: Carleton, 1864), p. 73.

93. I am indebted to Burton Dreben for suggesting that I examine more closely the relation of the French Revolution to the disappearance of women from the philosophical sphere—that is, for suggesting that factors "external to philosophy proper" might turn out to be quite illuminating here. It is not at all clear that Dreben would accept my interpretation of the import of these political factors.

94. Anne Louise Germaine Necker, baronne de Staël-Holstein, *De l'Allemagne* (1810) in *Oeuvres complètes* . . . (1820–21, 1861 edition reprinted Geneva: Slatkine Reprints, 1967); translation in Fraisse, p. 118.

95. Stendahl [Henri Beyle], *De l'amour* (Paris, 1822), cited in Fraisse, p. 69.

96. Ibid.

97. Sylvain Maréchal, *Projet d'une loi portant défense d'apprendre à lire aux femmes* (Paris: Massé, 1801); translation in Fraisse, p. 11.

98. Proudhon, as cited in d'Hericourt, *A Woman's Philosophy of Woman*, pp. 73–74 (see note 92). Cf. this report regarding Marie-Charlotte Corday in an official newsheet, as quoted in Linda Kelly, *Women of the French Revolution* (London:

Hamish Hamilton, 1987), p. 102: "She was a virago more brawny than fresh, graceless and dirty in her person as are almost all female philosophers. . . ."

99. Marie Jean Antoine Nicolas de Caritat, marquis de Condorcet, *Lettres d'un bourgeois de Newhaven à un citoyen de Virginie sur l'inutilité de partager le pouvoir législatif en plusieurs corps* (1788); cited in Fraisse, p. 52.

100. Marquis de Condorcet, "Sur l'admission des femmes au droit de cité," *Journal de la Société de 1789* 5 (3 July 1790), reprinted in *Paroles d'hommes (1790–1793)*, ed. Élisabeth Badinter (Paris: P.O.L., 1989).

101. The following papers on the historiography of philosophy are of particular interest: Jonathan Rée, "Philosophy and the History of Philosophy," in *Philosophy and Its Past*, ed. Jonathan Rée, Michael Ayers, and Adam Westoby (Brighton: Harvester, 1978); Richard Rorty, "The Historiography of Philosophy: Four Genres," in *Philosophy in History*, ed. Richard Rorty, J. B. Schneewind, and Quentin Skinner (Cambridge: Cambridge University Press, 1984); Michael Frede, "The History of Philosophy as a Discipline," *Journal of Philosophy* 85, no. 11 (November 1988): 666–72; Margaret D. Wilson, "History of Philosophy in Philosophy Today; and the Case of the Sensible Qualities," *Philosophical Review* 101 (January 1992): 191–243.

102. Walter Benjamin, *Illuminations: Essays and Reflections* (New York: Schocken Books, 1968), p. 256.

103. Ibid., p. 257.

104. For a clear exposition and defense of this form of historiography, see Wolfgang Mann, "The Origins of the Modern Historiography of Ancient Philosophy," *History and Theory* 35, no. 2 (1996): 165–95. It is not clear Mann would agree with my characterization of this form of historiography or with the use to which I would put it.

105. Rorty, "Historiography of Philosophy," p. 57 (see note 101).

106. Cousin, *Course of the History of Philosophy*, pp. 63–64, 230 (see note 28).

107. Benjamin, *Illuminations*, pp. 257–58 (see note 102).

108. Another way in which a narrative of the history of philosophy could be rewritten would be from a vantage point *external* to philosophical dialectic. One such narrative would be a postmodern intertextual one, in which women philosophers, together with forgotten female writers of fiction, autobiography, poetry, and so forth, would be portrayed as heroines and interwoven into the plot. Here the justification for the presence of women philosophers in an emerging new canon of Western thought would not make reference to any moves interpreted to be internal to philosophy. On this view there would be no such moves, since "moves purely internal to a discipline" would simply be taken to be illusions—as in Marxist historical materialism. But where historical materialism rejects any philosophical justification of the plot and ranking of figures in favor of a political/economic/social explanation, postmodernism gives up the privileging of any type of explanation: our canons are simply expressions of the sheer "pleasure of texts" and our delight in thinking through their interrelations. But philosophy, as we have known it in the West, takes justification as a constitutive ideal. It is what we have been aiming at, even if philosophy is a series of (occasionally somewhat brilliant) failures—even if we have never fully been able to justify a philosophical position. I do not have space here to argue for my view that postmodern intertextualism and Marxist historical materialism cannot provide satisfactory histories of philosophy, since they fail to value sufficiently this constitutive ideal of philosophy.

109. A bibliography, together with a useful discussion, of Michèle Le Doeuff's work to date can be found in Kerry Sanders, "Michèle Le Doeuff: Reconsidering Rationality," *Australasian Journal of Philosophy* 71, no. 4 (1993): 425–35.

110. See, for example, the papers that have been delivered at the APA meetings of the recently formed Society for the Study of Women Philosophers, and the articles in *HWP* and *HD*.

"Human Nature" and Its Role in Feminist Theory

LOUISE M. ANTONY

> A whistling woman and a crowing hen
> Will never come to a good end.
>
> —*Midwestern proverb*

PHILOSOPHICAL APPEALS TO "HUMAN NATURE"

Essentially positive conceptions of human nature have figured prominently in the normative theories of Western philosophers: Aristotle, Rousseau, Kant, and many others based their general ethical and political systems on substantive assumptions about the capacities and dispositions of human beings. Many of these views have been interpreted as affirming the inherent moral value and essential equality of all human beings, and a few have provided inspiration for emancipatory movements, including feminism.

Nonetheless, for anyone who would find in these theories a message of universal equality, there is one immediate difficulty: none of the major philosophers intended their claims about the natural entitlements of "man" to be applied to women.[1] Contrary to what's maintained by many contemporary exegetes, it's unlikely that the philosophers' use of masculine terms in the framing of their theories was a "mere linguistic convenience."[2] For if one looks at the (very few) places at which the major philosophers explicitly discuss women, one finds that women are expressly denied both the moral potentialities and the moral perquisites that are supposed to accrue to "man" in virtue of "his" nature.[3] If "man" is generic, and women are "men," then how could this be?

It's possible that the philosophers in question believed that men and women did not share a nature at all, in which case all their talk of "man" would be simply and literally talk of *men*. But this seems unlikely. Philosophers have not really wanted to claim that men and women are members of distinct *kinds*. Aristotle, Rousseau, and Kant, for example, who all made the possession of reason criterial of humanity, agreed that women could not plausibly be claimed to be utterly devoid of rationality.[4] Alternatively, then, the view must have been that men and women shared some sort of "human" nature, even while women differed from men in morally relevant respects.

On this view, it would not be the generic human nature per se that grounded the celebrated virtues and rights but rather something in the specifically male realization of that nature. If so, the distinction between a generic and a non-generic sense of "man" can be preserved; yet as long as "man's" virtues and rights still turn out to be identical with *men's*, it will be a distinction without a difference.[5]

In fact, the philosophers had a problem. They did not, as I said, wish to count women and men as distinct species. Still, if the differences between men and women were to rationalize differences in moral status, such differences would have to be, in some sense, matters of kind rather than of degree. For if mere quantitative differences could warrant assignments of different roles and virtues, then such distinctions would have to be made also among men, who differ from each other in quantitative ways.[6] The solution to this problem, independently embraced by Aristotle, Rousseau, and Kant, was to first affirm that women and men shared a nature but to then add the qualification that women were—by nature—unable to realize it fully.[7] Men thus became, by some kind of natural necessity, the only *proper* exemplars of "man." On this view, because women are still "men," the characteristics of "man" remain normative for women, despite their natural inability to instantiate them.

Aristotle, Rousseau, and Kant all made some effort to present the situation as one in which man and woman are separate but equal, with different but complementary roles, virtues, and forms of flourishing. But the not-so-benign reality is revealed in the fact that it is always *man's* nature alone, rather than some combination or disjunction of his nature with woman's, that is canonized as "human" nature. Furthermore, despite the fact that women's distinctive nature is supposed to yield a distinctive set of virtues, these virtues are clearly viewed as inferior to men's.[8] The upshot is that women can be good only insofar as they are considered *as women*; considered *as human* (i.e., according to the standards set by men), they are *necessarily* inferior. Women are human, but only in the way a broken wing is a wing; they are at best *defective* tokens of the human type.

It would be bad enough if all this signified nothing but the sexism of some of the Western world's greatest philosophers. But, unfortunately, it signifies much more. The theories and ideas articulated by these thinkers have had and continue to have a powerful influence on the lives of real women, by providing theoretical rationalization for the almost universal domination of women by men. While the nature of "man" has grounded lofty demands for moral equality or political independence, the particular nature of *woman* has grounded nothing but preemptory prohibitions and demeaning prescriptions. Leading philosophers agree: *because of their natures*, women should be denied serious educations and given only limited opportunities to develop physical strength. They should be barred from political or commercial activity and restricted entirely to the domestic sphere. They are not to aspire to any achievements—not even moral achievements—but what fit the character and scale of the domestic realm. In sum, *because of their natures*, women's entire lives are to be oriented toward pleasing and serving men.

What's gone wrong? Theories that seemed to promise a grounding for universal equality transmute before our eyes into rationalizations for the exploitation of women by men. In fact, there is nothing unusual here. Historically, it's been a standard strategy for explaining and justifying oppressive social hierarchies to appeal to alleged differences between the "natures" of oppressors and oppressed. The strategy is extraordinarily labile, exploiting in turn each of the various normative and modal connotations carried by the notion of "the natural," depending on the point that needs making. The trick is in picking the right stratagem at the right time.[9]

As a first move, it's best to try to represent the status quo as morally optimal. Thus counsels Rousseau: "If you want right guidance, always follow the leadings of nature. Everything that characterises sex should be respected as established by nature."[10] But should anyone be so bold as to disapprove of some aspect of nature's arrangements, the second stratagem can be brought into play: emphasize the futility of attempting to breach the laws of nature. Kant, for example, who can "hardly believe that the fair sex is capable of principle,"[11] warns that "whatever one does contrary to nature's will, one always does very poorly."[12] If it's pointed out that certain alleged laws have in fact been breached, the final stratagem must be deployed: show that success in some unnatural pursuit threatens one's wellbeing—even one's *identity*. Kant thus admonishes any would-be Elizabeths that "Laborious learning or painful pondering, even if a woman should greatly succeed in it, destroy [*sic*] the merits that are proper to her sex. . . . The fair can leave Descartes his vortices to whirl forever without troubling themselves about them."[13] Of course, this maneuver comports neatly with the notion that women have *distinctive* virtues and forms of flourishing.

The concession that it is *possible*, though not desirable, to alter or thwart the course of nature is necessitated by an internal tension in ideological appeals to natures. The problem is this: if nature is straightforwardly deterministic, if the social status quo is simply a neutral unfolding of the laws of nature, then why do we need prescriptions and warnings in order not to disturb it? As John Stuart Mill pointed out, there is no need to legislate against that which is anyway impossible, and no point in promoting what will happen all by itself.[14] If it's conceded, however, that the maintenance of the status quo *does* depend partly upon contingent human choices, an epistemological question arises: How do we know that the qualities we see displayed by men and women are due to differences in *natures*, rather than to the differences we engineer in their circumstances?[15] Furthermore, once it's granted that gender roles are not strictly determined by nature, the question of their justice can once again be opened, and must be otherwise forestalled. Hence the "normative determinism" exemplified in the quotations from

Kant: natures may not dictate what you *will* become, nor even what you will *want* to become, but they do dictate what will make you a *good* thing of your kind.

The same tensions emerge in the modern appeals to nature as in the classical ones: if women are naturally incapable of performing certain roles, why is it necessary to socially engineer against their attempting them? And given that the social engineering *is* necessary, how do we know that that is not what's responsible for the apparent differences in capacities? The answer, once again, is that such engineering is really a way of preserving a woman's own unique identity, of sparing her the frustration of her inevitable failure should she try to enter the world of men. The epistemology of such claims is left mysterious.

Consider, for example, Steven Goldberg, who contends that men's naturally higher levels of testosterone make them more aggressive, giving them a uniform competitive advantage over women. Goldberg has to confront the objection that girls appear to be less aggressive than boys even *before* puberty, when the relevant hormonal difference first appears. He admits that *this* difference must be attributable to different socialization but discounts the significance of this, arguing that it's rational and humane to train girls away from those highly valued activities where, in competition with boys, they'd certainly fail. How do we know they would certainly fail, given that we don't give them the opportunity to try? Because they're *naturally* less aggressive—aren't you paying attention?[16]

With eerie regularity, popular media in the United States trumpet "new" findings that purportedly establish completely biological—and hence "natural"—explanations for observed gender differences.[17] Paradoxically, though predictably, all this proof that gender roles are biologically mandated becomes the basis of support for discriminatory socialization, and for opposition to efforts to provide equality of opportunity. Here's John Stossel as the voice of reason on an ABC News special "Boys and Girls *Are* Different": "If we deny what science knows about human nature, how can we create sensible social policies? Isn't it better to act on the basis of what is true, rather than maintaining it has no right to be true?"[18]

Let us stop and take stock. Where does all this leave the feminist theorist with respect to the notion of human nature? One response to these difficulties would be to claim all and only the liberatory conceptions, and then insist on their proper extension to women and other denigrated groups. This strategy, favored by those feminists who see value in preserving what they see as the "humanism" at the core of liberal moral and political theory, strives to demonstrate the empirical falsity of negative claims that philosophers and others have made about the natures of women, and men of color, while leaving in place central assumptions about the theoretical and practical value of a substantive theory of human nature. Increasingly, however, feminist theorists are rejecting this line of response. Such theorists have come to the conclusion that careful analysis of the problems outlined here reveals that the notion of "human nature" is, from the theoretical point of view, conceptually bankrupt, and from the practical political point of view, inevitably pernicious. They argue, accordingly, that the long-standing philosophical project of characterizing "human nature" should not be refurbished, reformed, or revised but rather simply abandoned.

In the remainder of this essay, I would like to argue for a revival of the first strategy. I think that feminist theory needs an appeal to a universal human nature in order to articulate and defend its critical claims about the damage done to women under patriarchy, and also to ground its positive vision of equitable and sustaining human relationships.[19] Nonetheless, I accept the legitimacy of much of the recent feminist critique of appeals to "human nature" and of the philosophical strategies that prompt them. So in the next section, I'll explain the central elements of the critique that has emerged from feminist reflection on the problems cited earlier. In the third section, I'll try to demonstrate how the approach to the investigation of human nature that I favor takes account of the feminist critique. In the final section of the essay, I'll fill out and defend my claim that a theoretical appeal to a universal human nature is both possible and desirable as a grounding for feminist theory.

FEMINIST CRITIQUE

Leslie Stevenson, a philosopher at the University of St. Andrews, is the author of a book called *Seven Theories of Human Nature*[20] and editor of a collection of readings called *The Study of Human Nature*.[21] Both the monograph and the collection treat only the works of male theorists, and except for a few sentences here and there (a paragraph in an excerpt from Freud's *Question of Lay Analysis* in the collection, and a passing reference to Freud's theory of penis envy in the monograph), there is no discussion of women or girls in either book.[22] Neither one mentions, much less discusses, any of the problematic writings about women that we've been looking at. It is clear that Stevenson wishes his readers to form the impression that the theories he discusses are unproblematically applicable to women. Perhaps he even believes that their authors wished them to be so understood (although it should be clear that this is decidedly not so in at least three cases).

Stevenson appears to be genuinely sensitive to feminist criticism that his treatment of theories of *human* nature has ignored women. In the introduction to the second edition of the monograph, he comments perceptively on the use of "generic" language: "The use of the masculine word 'man' here is very convenient for brevity of question and statement, and . . . it has been very common practice. But straight away many of us will want to protest that what is involved is more than mere linguistic convenience, that some distinctive features and problems of women's nature have all too often been overlooked by the common assumption that the concept *man* can represent the whole human species."[23] But having evinced this much apprehension of the feminist critique, he reveals in his very next statement that he has, despite his good intentions, quite missed the point. "This book does not attempt any systematic discussion of feminist issues: it presents some rival theories of general *human* nature." Stevenson believes it possible that there exist "distinctive features and problems of women's nature," which "have all too often been overlooked," and yet he feels that such matters can be safely ignored within the context of a discussion of "*human* nature."[24] These are "feminist issues," matters of *special* interest to women and their champions, important but peripheral.[25]

Stevenson is certainly right that the character, cause, and significance of gender differences are matters of intense interest among feminist scholars and activists—necessarily so, since, as we saw in the last section, appeals to "women's nature" have been used to justify the subordination of women throughout Western history. But the issue feminists are trying to raise when we speak of philosophy's failure to "take account of gender" is independent of any of the detailed questions that can be raised about exactly how and why men and women are different, and it is more fundamental. The real issue concerns the *treatment of "difference"* itself.[26]

How is it, we ask, that someone like Stevenson can allow the possibility that women are importantly different from men and yet think that theorizing about "*human* nature" can proceed without attending to that fact? Why, indeed, is the situation conceptualized as one in which it is *women's* situation that bears "distinctive features and problems"? Are not men's situations equally "distinctive" relative to women's? The same questions arise, though more pointedly, for those philosophers we've been looking at who do explicitly discuss women: if women are supposed to have different properties than men, what then justifies the canonization of the distinctively *male* properties as the properties constitutive of full humanity? By what process of reasoning does a theorist who thinks that at least half the members of the species lack authoritative reason decide that it is precisely authoritative reason that is the distinctive mark of the species?

Ironically, questions of this sort arise even within feminist theory itself, for "mainstream" feminists (i.e., white, heterosexual, middle-class feminists) often canonize their own circumstances and concerns, while either ignoring or treating as peripheral the lives and problems of women who are "different." Liberal feminist discussion of liberation, marriage, motherhood, and work has been vigorously and properly criticized by black and Third World feminists, as well as by socialist feminists, for its failure to recognize both that the options middle-class women enjoy with respect to motherhood, domestic work, and paid employment are not available to most women and that the significance of these matters can vary enormously among women of different races, cultures, and sexual orientations.[27]

Similarly, radical feminists like Catherine MacKinnon, who make pornography and sexual violence the organizing points of their theories of oppression, have been criticized by black feminists like Angela Harris for ignoring the very different meanings such phenomena have for nonwhite and non-Western women.[28] Elizabeth Spelman emphasizes how even Simone de Beauvoir, who wrote so brilliantly about the process by which the dominant construct the subordinate as "the Other," failed to check the very same tendencies in her own theorizing, acknowledging the variety of women's circumstances on the one hand but then on the other making her own specific circumstances the basis of her analysis of women's oppression *as women*.[29]

Questions and observations like these have prompted many feminists to take a serious look at the circumstances in which philosophers have produced theories of "generic" human nature, at the methodologies they've employed, and at the background assumptions and values that have funded such projects. The regularity that emerges immediately is that the problematic treatments of difference always appear when individuals who are in some kind of *privileged* position undertake to theorize about some larger group of which they are the dominant members. This has led to speculation that the particular theories of human nature produced within Western philosophy, together, possibly, with the very idea that such a thing as human nature exists, reflect or express the privileged viewpoints of their authors.

Feminist elaborations of this idea have looked both at traditional philosophical method and at the specific content of theories of human nature. The methodological critiques begin by noting an important interaction between the aprioristic character of philosophical method and the privileged position of its most prominent practitioners. A method for discovering the qualities distinctive of humanity that depends heavily on reflection and introspection carries several inherent risks. One is that there will be a biased selection of traits—theorists may fasten on qualities that are particular to them rather than on qualities that are common to every member of humankind. A second danger is that the traits selected, whether or not they happen to be traits that all human beings possess, may nonetheless be traits that are not universally *valued*. Finally, theorists may mistake contingent properties for essential properties, treating as inherent qualities that are in fact the result of highly variable circumstances. Every one of these risks is increased when the theorists form a socially homogeneous group, since that makes it more likely that one theorist's hasty generalization will tend to confirm the others.'

So much follows just from familiar canons of empirical investigation. But many feminists, drawing on Marxist standpoint theory, have argued that the danger of distortion is further heightened when the homogeneous group of theorists is *privileged*. People in dominant social positions tend to be successful in limiting the range of views that are available for contention in the public domain, partly through their greater access to education and their monopoly over effective means of publication, and partly because of their ability to coerce at least the appearance of agreement among subordinates. Because consensus is often taken as a sign of objectivity, the absence of views that conflict with the theorist's own is taken, at least tacitly, as additional confirmation, and the absence of any stimulus to produce explicit defenses of the dominant view facilitates the illusion that the view is self-evident, enhancing the theorist's faith in the reliability of his own a priori method.[30]

Another aspect of traditional philosophical method that has provoked feminist criticism, and that interacts with the problems just described, is the emphasis on abstraction and idealization. Although any form of theoretical analysis is going to entail a certain amount of abstraction from the particular features of elements in the theoretical domain, the critical question is always *which* features are central to the phenomenon in question and which can be safely written off as theoretically insignificant. In the context of a theory of human nature, the very factors described previously that may lead to the inaccurate universalization of selected properties may also contribute to a skewed sense of what's *essential* to human existence.

Traditional philosophers have tended to take the official position that details of one's material circumstances—and indeed the very fact of embodiment—are all separable contingencies. But feminist theorists have argued that an abstraction that removes from one's essential nature such phenomenologically central properties as one's race and gender, and that idealizes away from all the facts about one's time, place, and experiences that give one a psychological and social identity, turns human beings into featureless, interchangeable, "pure" subjects. It may well be, feminists have argued, that the fact that we are embodied creatures is one of the defining constraints of the human condition; similarly, the fact that social interaction appears to be for us a practical necessity. If so, then of what conceivable use is a theory that posits immaterial, isolated "core" natures in our quest to understand ourselves?

Another potential problem besetting any form of idealization is the possibility that theory may separate and reify as independent parameters factors whose connection to each other actually constitutes the phenomenon. The ramifications of this insight for feminist theory have been profound: many feminist theorists have by now argued that race, gender, class, and sexual orientation are not theoretically separable from each other in the way that both traditional philosophy and even much feminist theory have assumed them to be. Audre Lorde, bell hooks, Angela Harris, Maria Lugones, and others have charged that attempts to treat oppression as a kind of interaction effect, involving separate gender, class, and racial "components," have obscured the sui generis forms of oppression suffered by women of color in American society.[31]

Elizabeth Spelman argues further that such approaches—which she calls "pop-bead" or "tootsie roll" theories—also encourage the ultimately dangerous thought that each of these components can be instantiated in more or less "pure" forms, and can be best understood in such instantiations: "gender," for example, when it is isolated from the effects of racial or class or heterosexist oppression, as it is in the lives of white, middle-class, heterosexual women. But, Spelman points out, the fact that certain women are not subject to oppression in virtue of their class or race or sexual orientation does not mean that the character of their oppression *as women* is any less affected by each of these factors than is the oppression of a lesbian or a woman of color. The idea that it's possible to observe "gender" in some unqualified form is really just another way of expressing the thought that privileged women are more *exemplary* women than their less privileged sisters, that they represent the "unmarked case" of *woman*. Pop-bead theorizing can also foster the illusion among privileged women that they are more *completely* women, that their femininity is not "diluted" or "compromised" by race, class, and so forth. Such women may believe, tacitly, that they do not even *possess* race or class, in the way American speakers of "standard English" consider that they do not possess "accents."[32]

This work of Spelman, Lorde, and others provides critical insight into the process documented in the first section of this essay, whereby counterexamples to one's general theory are *noticed* but are discounted as abnormalities. For it's clear that pop-bead theorizing can serve to vindicate the intuitions of the privileged that they are safe in generalizing their own characteristics and concerns to all members of their group, *in at least a normative way*. If I am the *archetype* of my kind, then my properties are the properties that are *normal* for my kind. Individuals may lack any of these properties and still be counted members of my kind, just as a dog continues to be a dog if it loses a leg. But then, like the crippled dog, these individuals' deviations from the normative standard mean that they must be viewed as *abnormal*, deficient.

Against this highly conceptual background, we must also remember the altogether mundane ways in which bias can operate. Remember that privileged individuals frequently have a stake in the outcome of theories of human nature. To the extent that his or her own position depends upon the exploitation or oppression of someone else, the theorist has a strong motive for discovering some way of justifying the status quo. As we have seen, theories that can trace inequalities within a society back to "natural" differences among its members have enormous ideological value, since they make social hierarchies seem at once fair, good, and inevitable. It is an empirical question whether or not any given philosopher was actually moved, consciously or unconsciously, by such venal considerations, but it cannot be denied that the risk is there.[33]

I have surveyed some of the mechanisms feminists have proposed by which theorizing about human nature *might* have been distorted by the conditions under which it has been conducted. Two questions remain, however: first, have any of these distortions actually occurred, and second, could such distortions be guarded against or corrected by changes in the way we conduct our theorizing? I'll review feminists' answers to these questions in turn.

Although feminists are divided on the first issue, many theorists, reflecting on the contents of the theories of "human" nature that philosophy has produced, believe that such distortions have occurred. Some theorists, particularly those working within ethical and political theory, believe that there are significant differences between the ways men and women think about themselves in relation to others, and that traditional normative theories have been based exclusively on the forms typical of men. The most famous of these theorists is probably Carol Gilligan,[34] who (in what always seems to me an eerie echo of Kant) holds that men are more likely to adopt the "perspective of justice" and women the "perspective of care." Traditional normative theories, she claims, have overvalued the former and ignored the latter. Virginia Held, Nell Noddings, and Sara Ruddick have argued, in a kind of ethical analogue to standpoint epistemology, that the biological and social roles occupied by women provide a better starting point than those of men for the development of normative theories.[35] Annette Baier thinks that traditional theories have ignored the moral significance of the emotions, the passions, and the affections, and have devalued them largely because of their association with femininity and the female.[36] Susan Okin has argued that liberal theory, in recognizing a public-private distinction that identifies the interests of an entire family with the interests of its "head," renders invisible the primary site of women's oppression.[37]

Other feminist theorists see the tradition's emphasis on "reason" and mentality, and its devaluation of the physical, as reflecting both the values and the situation of privileged individuals. Genevieve Lloyd has pointed out that the kind of mental activity canonized as "reason," and held to be most supremely human by Plato, Aristotle, Descartes, Kant, and others, is in fact a kind of activity that can be enjoyed on a regular basis only by those who are relatively free of mundane cares and responsibilities. Indeed, Lloyd contends, the very notion of "reason" has been constructed within theology and philosophy in explicit contrast to the properties displayed (or thought to be displayed) by the people to whom such responsibilities were standardly assigned: women, and men of lower class, caste, or race. The valuation of cognitive skills over manual skills may also be a reflection of class and gender privilege, since only those with material means can afford to neglect manual skills for the sake of pursuing the life of the mind.[38]

Alison Jaggar and Lorraine Code have argued that the highly abstract and individualistic character of the "person" that emerges from liberal political theory and traditional epistemology is ideologically useful in many ways: insofar as it elevates the mental over the physical, it rationalizes the lower status afforded to those who are symbolically or actually more concerned with the body, bodily functions, and the material side of day-to-day life. Also, in obscuring the specificity of each person's material and cultural location, abstract individualism encourages the fantasy that the knowing subject has a universal perspective, making it even less likely that theorists will come to attend to aspects of their own contingent circumstances that may in fact be producing bias.[39]

According to Evelyn Fox Keller, Naomi Scheman, and Susan Bordo, these efforts on the part of traditional philosophers to separate the "person" from the body reflect a very particular aspect of the male perspective. Drawing on

Nancy Chodorow's application of object-relations theory to the topics of mothering and gender identity, these theorists see the tradition's denigration of the bodily and of the female as expressive of distinctively male anxieties stemming from the process by which boys must construct their gender identity under conditions of patriarchy.[40]

Feminists' answers to the second of my two questions—whether some less distorted theory is possible—are much more difficult to discern. Many of the critiques outlined here are at least compatible with the idea that there exists some kind of universal "human" nature. Even those like Gilligan's and Chodorow's, which assume the existence of relatively stable gender differences, do not attribute these to differences in male and female *natures*, but rather to stable regularities in the social situations of males and females. Since the distortions that feminists have claimed to find are held to be artifacts of a situation we have independent reason to hope will change, perhaps there is at least the possibility of developing an *adequate* characterization of the basic nature that we all share, necessarily, as human beings.[41]

On the other hand, what positive reason is there to think that there *is* a "human nature" out there to be discovered? If there is any single point to emerge from all the critiques we have surveyed, it is this: differences among human beings, whatever their cause, are theoretically important for understanding ourselves and our relations with others. What reason, then, is there for assuming that if we abstract away from all those differences, there will be anything left? We should note, too, that such differences as *have* been noticed or posited have tended to be viewed as immutable *natural* differences rather than reflections of physical or social contingencies. Why, then, think that *any* of our properties are attributable to our *natures* rather than to the contingencies of our existence?

These two questions have led many feminists to suspect that the categories "human being" and "woman"—at least in the sense of these terms that's relevant for normative theory—are not *natural* categories at all but are, rather, "socially constructed." To say that a category is socially constructed is to say, first, that the existence of such a category is not determined by nature, and, second, that the criteria for membership in the category are sensitive to the interests and viewpoints of intentional beings. Since these interests and perspectives are not all identical, and since they tend to shift over time, the membership criteria for socially constructed categories may not be stable, and different things may be counted members at different times and places. Socially constructed categories may be thought of as similar to Lockean "nominal essences" in that they represent contingent, subjectively determined groupings that may or may not correspond to any "deeper" or more stable underlying commonality—in a sense, members of socially constructed kinds owe their membership to our agreement to call them all by the same name.

This does not mean that socially constructed categories are unreal, nor that the properties on which they are (contingently) based are without real causal power. And it does not mean that the categories are indefinable; at any given time, we may be perfectly able to identify the criteria determined by the relevant social and intentional activity. Catherine MacKinnon, for example, holds that "woman" is a socially constructed kind, but still is happy to give necessary and sufficient conditions. According to MacKinnon, one's status as a man or a woman is determined not by natural differences in reproductive capacities, but rather by one's location in a particular power hierarchy: one is a man if one is a sexual objectifier, and a woman if one is sexually objectified. There is nothing *natural* that women can be presumed to have in common with other women—a "woman" in MacKinnon's sense may even be biologically male, as she thinks is the case with certain male homosexuals—but there is nonetheless something very real that all women share.[42]

But as we've noted, MacKinnon's theory has been criticized on the grounds that it improperly universalizes an experience of sexuality that is typical of only a small group of women. Similar criticisms have been raised against Chodorow, Gilligan, Ruddick, and others who have offered general accounts of gender based on some presumably common feature of women's situations. Postmodernist feminists have argued that these theories all suffer from a common defect, which they share with the traditional theories of "human nature" they are meant to replace: they all yield to the impulse to "*essentialize.*" That is to say, as Nancy Fraser and Linda Nicholson put it, such theories "project onto all women and men qualities which develop under historically specific social conditions."[43] To avoid this defect, postmodernists argue, it's not enough to recognize that such categories as "man" and "woman" are not fixed by nature. It is necessary to go further and recognize that they are not fixed "*by anything*" at all.[44]

According to postmodernists, the very project of seeking a theory of gender, not to mention the project of seeking a theory of human nature, has at its core the dogmatic assumption that there is always some single thing—an essence, a definition, a nature—that can be found to underlie and explain observed diversity. As Iris Young explains it (borrowing a term from Adorno), this assumption reflects the "logic of identity": a mode of thought that attempts to impose a single static and abstract order onto the multiple and constantly shifting patterns of concrete events. Such thinking always leads to a pernicious normalization of the thinker's own characteristics, by the following process. It first denies difference, in its drive to reduce all diversity to an underlying unity; but then, ironically, difference is reintroduced in a new form: the normative dichotomy. "Since each particular entity . . . has both similarities and differences with other particular entities . . . , the urge to bring them into unity under a category or principle necessarily entails expelling some of the properties of the entities or situations. Because the totalizing movement always leaves a remainder, the project of reducing particulars to a unity must fail. Not satisfied then to admit defeat in the face of difference, the logic of identity shoves difference into dichotomous hierarchical oppositions."[45]

The postmodernist challenge, because it threatens not only the possibility of a theory of *human* nature but the possibility of a theory of (even socially constructed) *gender* as well, has generated enormous controversy among feminists. Many feminists feel that the availability of gender as an analytical category is vital to progress toward feminist goals, and they remain optimistic that there is some conception of "gender" that can survive the postmodernist challenge. Elizabeth Rapaport, defending Catherine MacKinnon, asserts the "utility of theoretical illuminations of aspects of women's common experience"[46] and argues that such a theory need not fall prey to the serious problems identified by Harris, Spelman, and others. Similarly, Susan Bordo, although very sympathetic to postmodernism overall, still worries that giving up "gender analytics" entails the loss of a powerful analytical tool, without which we may "cut ourselves off from the source of feminism's transformative possibilities."[47]

I want to say the same thing about "human nature."

Toward a New Understanding of "Natures"

Clearly some of the problems associated with normative appeals to "natures" stem from inequitable distributions of power and epistemic authority within the societies that produce them. But I believe that many of the problems that feminists have found with philosophical theories of "nature" and "essence" have a different source. Such problems stem, I believe, from particular difficulties that we face in conceptualizing the products of certain kinds of theoretical analyses. I'd like to suggest that the notion of a *disposition* may be of help both in outlining these difficulties, and in pointing a way to their solution.

Let's start by looking somewhat more closely at the notion of a "nature" or "essence." Contemporary philosophical conceptions of essence are informed by two central ideas. The first, deriving from Aristotle, is that natures should be, in some sense, "definitional"—a nature should be that which makes a thing the kind of thing it is; a specification of a nature should tell you what it is to be that thing. "Natures," then, are properties with certain modal features: at a minimum, any property that is part of an individual object's nature is a property that that object has *necessarily*, and any property that is part of the nature or essence of a kind is a property that is *necessary* for being an object of that kind. From Locke, we get the second idea of essence as an underlying explanatory structure: natures are, in this sense, *intrinsic* and *fundamental*. Locke contrasted these "*real* essences" with "nominal essences," which are simply any set of sensible qualities stably enough associated together to be given a name. Real essences were "hidden" structures, possibly unknowable, but nonetheless causally responsible for the object's observable properties and behavior.

On certain assumptions, these two notions of "nature" may appear to be in conflict: if we think of definitions as word meanings, and we think of meanings as introspectively available to competent speakers, then it would appear that essences could be discovered by a priori means. But Locke's essences were knowable, if at all, only by abductive inference from empirically determined regularities. If essences could be discovered through conceptual analysis, how could they yield empirical explanations? But if they could only be discovered through empirical investigation, how could they entail *necessities*? Work by Hilary Putnam and Saul Kripke in the 1970s suggested a resolution. Wittgenstein, Quine, and others had already challenged the model of language and linguistic knowledge implicit in the preceding assumptions about definitions; it remained for Putnam and Kripke to make a case for *a posteriori necessities*. They argued that our modal judgments about identity conditions for objects and natural kinds do not depend on their superficial qualities but, rather, on deeper structural or historical properties, properties that we assume to exist but may be unable to characterize in advance of scientific investigation. A thing's "definition," then, is not the dictionary "definition" associated with the thing's name but, rather, a theoretical specification of what, as a matter of empirical fact, the thing *is*.

Which of a thing's properties are candidates for being its essence? First, let's consider what *kinds* of properties there are. A standard distinction made in the philosophy of science is that made between "dispositional" properties and nondispositional, or what might be called "categorical," properties.[48] Roughly, a categorical property is a property attributable to an object in virtue of its current or actual state or behavior, whereas a dispositional property is a property attributable to an object in virtue of the state it *would* be in, or the behavior it *would* display under certain (typically nonactual) circumstances. For example, the salt currently in my saltshaker has the categorical property of solidity: it is right now in a solid state. At the same time, it has the dispositional property of solubility: it *would* dissolve *if* placed in water. The attribution of a dispositional property to an object is thus equivalent to the assertion of a certain conditional: *if* such and such circumstances obtain, *then* the object will display this or that categorical property. We can call the circumstances specified in the antecedent the "activating circumstances" and the categorical property cited in the consequent the "associated categorical." Now which, if any, of the salt's properties should be considered part of its essence? Clearly, many of the categorical properties of an object can change over time—the salt in my saltshaker is *now* solid, but I could easily change that by emptying the shaker into a pot of water. Solidity, therefore, cannot be part of the salt's essence; solidity is only the state that salt is in *under certain conditions*.

But what about the *dispositional* property of *solubility*? This seems more promising; it does seem to be a necessary feature of salt that it dissolves under certain conditions, and, indeed, that it remain solid under certain (different) conditions. But this can't be all there is to the story. Essences are supposed to be *explanatory* as well as definitive, and attributing solubility to salt seems to be just a way of saying *what* salt does rather than *why* it does it. What explains the disposition?

This is one of several good reasons for thinking that dispositional properties are always "grounded" in categorical properties.[49] Here's another: recall that a dispositional property can be correctly ascribed to an object even if the object is not, has never been, and will never be in the activating circumstances, and even if it does not, has never, and never will instantiate the associated categorical. But this then raises a question: What can or could be true of an object *now* that determines what it will or would do under nonactual conditions? This is a metaphysical, not an epistemological, matter, but the epistemology of dispositions points in the same direction. Our warrant for ascribing a dispositional property to one object is most often the observed behavior of objects we judge to be relevantly similar—this practice could only work if the objects we judge to have the same dispositions really do have something objectively in common.

Such a "grounding categorical," if it exists, would have a very good claim to being regarded as a nature or real essence. Since the advent of atomic theory and the reductionist paradigm in the physical sciences, it's been a working hypothesis that these real essences, at least in the case of physical objects, consist in quantitative and structural features of the objects' microstructures. The molecular structure of table salt explains not only its dispositional properties, like its solubility, but also many of its observable categorical properties: its solidity at room temperature and its crystalline structure when solid. It also expresses the objective feature that all salt has in common—it says "what it is to be" salt. Taking molecular structure to be the nature of salt, then, unifies the Lockean notion of real essence as hidden explanatory structure with the Aristotelian notion of essence as real definition.

This, then, is the general picture of "natures" that I wish to endorse: a nature is a (possibly hidden) categorical property that grounds dispositions and explains observable categorical properties. I do not mean to suggest that all natures are atomic or molecular structures—it's both possible and likely that different kinds of kinds will have different kinds of natures. The natures of biological kinds may consist in genomes; the nature of psychological kinds may consist in functional organizations. Nor do I wish to beg any questions against the social constructionists. It may turn out that some "kinds"—perhaps the kind "person" among them—have *no* natures in this sense at all and constitute groupings only because of features that are contingently of interest to some group at some time in some place. For all that, I do want to maintain that an inquiry that seeks a "human nature" in my sense will not be marred by the defects that have inspired feminist and progressive criticism of the traditional projects.

To see why this is so, I must point out two important features of this model of natures. The first thing to note is that when a real essence, in the sense of a grounding categorical, is found, it is always a *distinct property* from any of the categoricals associated with the dispositions it grounds. Thus, salt does not have a "dissolving nature"—rather, it has a nature *such that* it will, if placed in water, dissolve. "Natures" are thus *functional*, in the mathematical sense: they can be thought of as things that "yield" categorical properties *given* a specific set of circumstances. This fact about natures means that they are frequently difficult to characterize substantively—they are, in effect, hard to *name*. If and when there is developed a theoretical articulation of the grounding characteristics, natures can be named, but in advance of any such theory, it is difficult to conceptualize a nature, except by reference to one or more of the dispositions it grounds (consider the infamous *virtus dormitiva* possessed by Molière's secret sleeping preparation). These, in turn, tend to get conceptualized and named in terms of their associated categoricals: this is how a person who behaves aggressively in certain circumstances comes to have "an aggressive nature." I will call this difficulty in conceptualizing the grounding categoricals the "naming problem."

But, of course, even a person who is said to be "naturally aggressive" is not displaying aggression *all the time*. That brings us to the second important point: dispositional properties are only fully specified if the *activating circumstances* are fully specified. If they are not, then there is a danger either that the ascription of a disposition will be empty or ill defined, or else that it will be extremely apt to mislead. Often, the activating circumstances can be safely assumed to be understood, and needn't be explicitly mentioned. We all understand the term "soluble" to mean "soluble *in water*." Knowing this, we also know that if we want to say of something that it will dissolve in a fluid other than water, we must specify that fluid in the ascription: "soluble in alcohol."

Sometimes when the activating conditions are left unspecified, there's a presumption that they are simply the "normal" conditions. This is a much trickier assumption. Generally, the idea is that we are, in such cases, talking about "normalcy" in some flatly descriptive *statistical* sense—that is, the conditions that most frequently obtain. Sometimes the activating conditions are *so* prevalent that it's possible to forget that the instantiation of the associated categorical is *dependent* upon those conditions. We then stop bothering to express the dispositional property as such, and may even begin to conflate the property with its associated categorical. As noted earlier, many objects that we think of simply as "solid" or "liquid" are only contingently so—water is liquid *at some temperatures* but solid at others. In our standard characterizations of water and salt, we simply take for granted the presence of the activating conditions under which those substances appear in those states. Thus, the fact that the activating conditions for a dispositional property can be the (statistically) normally prevailing ones can effectively make us forget that many of the properties that we may think of as "belonging to the nature" of a thing—its apparent color, its shape, its physical state—are actually the result of an *interaction* of that thing's nature with the thing's environment.

This process partly accounts, I think, for the feeling many have that *any* attribution of "natures" is going to entail an unacceptable kind of determinism. When an associated categorical, like "aggression" or "intelligence," is treated not as the result of a certain nature in interaction with a particular environment but as itself part of the nature, it's easy to think that the aggression or intelligence is something that's there *all* the time, independently of circumstances. The *contingency* of the display of some particular categorical property becomes invisible—giving us, therefore, what I'll call the *problem of the invisibility of contingencies.*

This problem is exacerbated when the "normalcy" being presumed is not the relatively innocuous statistical sort of normalcy but is, rather, prescriptive—*ideal* or *optimal* conditions. There is nothing inherently wrong with the use, even the tacit use, of such a sense of normalcy. This is the use of "normal" in which it can make sense to say that some very large percentage of a population is above or below "normal"—we might, for example, document the extent of malnutrition in some war-torn region by pointing out that most of the children in the region are significantly below "normal" in height and weight. The "norm" appealed to here is obviously not merely the statistical average of the children's heights, nor even the average of their heights pooled with the heights of children elsewhere. Rather, it involves some notion of the *optimal* height and weight for human children of certain ages. Still, the introduction of an evaluative element into notions of normalcy is potentially problematic.

Sometimes there is and sometimes there is not a clear principle for the selection of "optimal" conditions. Height and weight norms, as I suggested, reflect assumptions about the *health* of the organism. Yet even this apparently clear and uncontroversial principle is not as straightforward as it might at first appear. Even if all our questions about empirical dependencies could be answered (At what weight is cardiovascular function most efficient? Does limiting fat in the diets of young children retard brain development?), there would still be difficult issues to resolve about what constitutes "good health": Is *length* of life the only determinant of the ultimate healthiness of the organism, or must length be weighed against *quality* of life? If so, who or what determines what counts as quality?

Sometimes all these issues are sidestepped by implicitly appealing to the status quo—that is, what is sometimes taken to be *normatively* normal is simply whatever we're used to. Because this assumption, when it's made, is generally implicit, the status quo is not frequently scrutinized in this context for either *desirability* or *mutability*. If, however, the presumption that the status quo is or ought to be stable *were* to be explicitly examined, it's likely that it would rarely hold up.

Note the *status quo* incorporates lots of differently caused regularities. Some of these, like the climate, are largely independent of human agency (which is, of course, not to say that human agency cannot largely mitigate the *effects* of climate). Other regularities, like war and poverty, are extremely sensitive to human agency. But the invisibility of contingencies can lead to the idea that natures that are expressed *one* way under the de facto prevailing conditions are *inevitably* expressed the same way, so that phenomena that are quite amenable to human control are written off as due to "laws of nature." (It may, in the end, be true that the poor will be with us always, but, if so, it will only be because those of us who aren't poor chose to do nothing about it.)

Another misconception that arises from the invisibility of contingencies is the completely unfounded idea that natures somehow set the "strength" of tendencies toward the display of some categorical property, even if they don't determine it, where strength is measured either in terms of the number of environments in which the categorical property will be expressed or in terms of the "difficulty" of suppressing the expression of the property. Thus, according to much current opinion, if intelligence is "natural," then it will shine through no matter how deprived the environment; and for "natural" stupidity, there is no environmental remedy.[50]

There is a concept from biology that can help dismantle this particular confusion—the concept of a "norm of reaction."[51] Remember that biologists distinguish the genotype of an organism from its phenotype. The *genotype* is the organism's particular genetic configuration; it is the biological analogue of molecular structure (or at least it can be so regarded for present purposes). The *phenotype* is the set of properties the organism actually displays: in general, the phenotype is a function of the genotype, the environment, and random factors. The genotype, then, can be regarded as the grounding categorical for the organism's disposition to display certain phenotypic properties in certain environments. My genotype, for example, makes me disposed to turn bright red if I'm exposed to an hour or more of direct sunlight.[52] Now it's possible, for some organisms, to chart, for a given genotype, the effects of the manipulation of a particular environmental variable on a particular phenotypic trait. Such a chart is called the "norm of reaction" (or "range of reaction") for that genotype.

In order to develop a norm of reaction for a genotype, several conditions must be satisfied: first, there must be available a large number of exemplars of the genotype; second, the environmental variable must be a factor that can be precisely quantified; and third, the phenotypic trait must also be a factor that can be precisely quantified. Because it is difficult to contrive (much less find) situations where all three conditions are satisfied, very few actual norms of reaction have been plotted. But we do know at least the following:

(i) One cannot in general extrapolate any one part of the norm of reaction from any other. Norms of reaction are not necessarily neat, and are rarely linear. It needn't be true even that a particular environmental factor that produces an increase in some phenotypic property for part of the range will continue to do so throughout the range. It is, in short, impossible to predict, just from the known parts of the norm of reaction, the phenotypic effects of a novel environmental alteration. (ii) The norm of reaction for *one* genotype cannot in general be used to predict the norm of reaction for another. The environment that produced optimal growth for one genotype may be stunting for another. Anything that is known about the *general* requirements or behavior of kinds of living things must be known either through old-fashioned empirical sampling and inductive generalization (with all the attendant risks) or through some abductive argument for a presumed universal (an example of which—the "poverty of the stimulus" argument—I'll discuss later). (iii) Difference in phenotypic properties does not entail difference in genotype, and similarity of phenotypic properties does not entail sameness of genotype.

This brings us to an extremely important point concerning the difference between *species* natures and *individual* natures. An individual nature can be thought of as a genotype grounding a norm of reaction. A species nature is then a generalization *over* genotypes. The first thing it's crucial to realize is that such a generalization is not the same as a generalization over observed phenotypic properties, nor as an abstraction from observed phenotypic differences. It is, rather, a generalization over *dispositions*. It is misleading to say that *language use* is part of the human essence. What's actually meant by such a claim is the empirical generalization that every human being is disposed to acquire language under an extremely large range of "normal" human environments. The same can be said for having two legs, ten toes, and so forth—our saying that such characteristics are determined by the human genome should be understood to mean "by almost every human genotype under the known range of environmental variation."

Frequently, the reliable generalizations that can be drawn from empirical observation concern extremes. We pretty much know the effects of both starvation and glutting on most animals, but we also know that, within a large range of "normal" consumption, the same number of calories consumed by different bodies (even different bodies within the same species) will have different effects on both size and health. We know a lot about the kinds of environments that produce various impairments and pathologies in human beings—we know that severe malnutrition produces mental retardation, for example, and we have evidence that extreme and sustained physical abuse produces dissociative personality disorders—but we don't have even the beginnings of serious theories about the role the environment plays in accounting for the variation we observe among people with "normal" personalities and intellects. We know that children who are completely deprived of social interaction with other human beings up until the age of puberty never acquire certain linguistic abilities; we know nothing, however, about the role of environmental variables—if there is one—in accounting for individual differences in normal linguistic development.

Altogether, what we know about norms of reaction tells us this: there are individual differences in *natures* (understood as genotypes) and also individual differences in phenotypes. But we cannot infer anything about the former directly from the latter. In carefully controlled conditions, where we have large numbers of genetically identical individuals and a precisely defined environmental variable that can be readily manipulated, it is possible to construct a norm of reaction for a single genotype. But outside such rare conditions, we are not entitled to assume that we know anything about any individual's *nature*.

In short, the very notion of a "nature/nurture" dichotomy is confused. It's considered good form in nature/nurture controversies, whichever side one is on, to concede that there might well be *some* natural/environmental "component" to whatever trait is being discussed. But such concessions miss the point. There is *always* a genetic "component" and always an environmental "component" in the genesis of a phenotypic trait, and there is no meaningful way to apportion *causal responsibility* between them. The genotype is just as "active" in an environment in which it produces one phenotype as it is in any other. What nongeneticists probably *mean* when they say things like "Eighty percent of intelligence is inherited" is probably something like this: changing the environment can only alter intelligence by about 20 percent— the genes are four times "stronger" than the environment. But *this* claim embodies another misconception.

As Richard Lewontin has explained, there is a huge difference between the *analysis of variance* and the *analysis of causes*.[53] We can explain the variance in phenotypic traits within a given population as being n percent due to genetic variation and m percent due to variations in the environment, but this is hardly the same as saying that n percent of the trait was caused by the individual's intrinsic nature while m percent was caused by the environment. Heritability estimates must always be relativized to populations and environments—that is why it is such a blatant fallacy to infer, as Herrnstein, Jensen, and Murray all do (despite persistent criticism on this point),[54] from the heritability of intelligence within one group to a genetic explanation of average differences in measured intelligence *between* groups.

Let me summarize, then, what all this tells us about the notion of *nature* and its use and abuse within both philosophy and science. I claim that the naming problem, which stems from the functional character of natures, together with the problem of the invisibility of contingencies, result in a problematic conflation of natures with particular categorical properties. When this conflation occurs against a background in which only privileged individuals are engaged in theorizing, we get the sorts of objectionable methods and results that feminist theorists have criticized: the activating circumstances that are tacitly privileged as "normal" become those that are typical of or are highly valued by the theorists themselves. The categorical properties that the theorists display in those circumstances then become the properties that are reified as "natures." Because the contingency of these circumstances is invisible, and because the conflation of the associated categorical with nature itself is wholly unnoticed, the absence of the selected categorical property in others is treated as a difference in *nature*.

Understanding that a nature does not determine a phenotypic property, but rather grounds a complex set of dispositions, can also help us to avoid problematic reifications of analytical parameters and to check the correlative tendency to think of some individuals in some circumstances as displaying "purer" expressions of these parameters than others. A nature, conceived as a grounding categorical, can *never* be expressed in some "pure" form: *any* expression of any genotype must be mediated by some environment. There may be some environments that are more *typical*, in the statistical sense, than others, and some that are more *optimal*, relative to some set of values, but there is no way to "factor out" the effects of "extrinsic" or "artificial" or "disturbing" influences so as to reveal nature in its pure form. (This also reveals the fundamental absurdity of the notion of "following the dictates of nature.") Furthermore, a category like "gender" can only refer to some genotypic parameter, some feature of the genotype. And individual parts of genotypes can no more receive "pure" expression than whole genotypes can.

A quick case study: let's analyze Stephen Goldberg's claim that men are "naturally" more aggressive than women, one of the most persistent claims about differences in the "natures" of men and women. We can see now that it's far from clear even what's meant by this: sometimes people seem to mean that there's some actual substance, "aggression," that men have more of than women (as some snakes store more venom than others); at other times they seem to mean that men are, given any particular situation, more likely to act aggressively than are women. The evidence cited for this claim (if indeed any evidence *is* cited) generally consists in facts about the relative number of aggressive acts committed by men and by women, or, as in Goldberg's case, about the connection between some biological factor presumed to be more prevalent in men (like testosterone) and the commission of aggressive acts.

But we can see now that none of this makes any sense. Let us grant that there is an observed regularity that men display more aggressive behavior than do women. That in itself tells us nothing about the underlying natures of men and women. It is, in fact, consistent with their having *identical* natures. What we would need to know in order to draw any conclusions about differences or similarities in natures is this: how men and women act when they grow up in the *same circumstances*, where this includes, crucially, being presented with the same set of behavioral options. The idea of an option is affected by *utility*—if women's and men's incentive structures are different, that's enough for their *options* to be different.[55]

The important lesson here is that regularities, even remarkably stable regularities in the observed behavior of the two genders, are not necessarily (and, given what we know, not even probably) evidence of a difference in natures. Neglect of this very important qualification in talk about men's "natural" aggression or women's "natural" tendency to nurture probably reflects either an indifference to, or approval of, whatever system of circumstances *produces* these regularities.[56]

THE NEED FOR NATURES

Perhaps if the foregoing is right, the notion of "nature" can be recovered and rendered innocuous. But why should we bother? Can this notion of nature do any of the work natures were supposed to do? And do we really want such work done anyway? There are really two aspects to the question of whether we "need" a notion of human nature. One aspect I take to be purely empirical: Are there, or are there not theoretically significant properties that all human beings share, that appear to be nearly invariantly expressed under a large range of circumstances? If there are such "universals," then whether we need it or not, there is such a thing as "human nature." I don't think that anyone has ever seriously doubted the existence of *biological* universals in this sense. The presence of one heart, two kidneys, two lungs, two arms with five digits each—though not absolutely universal—is taken, at least by biologists, to be *normal* and *natural* for human beings. I am not saying that such assumptions are wholly unproblematic: only that, properly understood, they seem to be *true*. And any problems that attend talk of "normalcy" and "naturalness" in this instance, I claim, stem from conflation of statistical and evaluative senses of these terms.

But in addition to biological natures, there is increasing evidence of the existence of a *cognitive* nature, of what Steven Pinker thinks of as a set of human *instincts*.[57] Instincts are not strict programs that determine behavior; they are, rather, programs that determine *dispositions*. The activating conditions for instincts can be quite specific or highly diverse; the associated categorical properties—overt behavior, in the case of these dispositions—can be quite rigid or highly plastic. The "language instinct" in humans, for example, is such that the child requires human social contact, and a modicum of linguistic input, but nothing in the way of explicit instruction in order for it to be triggered.[58] The "behavior" that's triggered is itself a grounding categorical (a grammar) for a highly complex disposition (a language). The general form of the grammar is dictated by the human genome, but within that form there is all the variation that can be found across human languages.

Thus, while we cannot say that *all* human beings, without exception, speak a language, and while there is no "universal language" spoken by all human beings, and while no one language can sensibly be thought closer to "natural" than any other,[59] it is still the case that there is, in the case of language, a genuine human universal. What's universal is a certain *capacity*: we are able to converge onto a grammar for any language that displays certain very abstract formal properties ("universal grammar") to which we are given a short exposure during a critical period of our youth. This means *any* human language is potentially acquirable by *any* human infant; in practical terms, it means that we can communicate a potential infinity of richly structured thoughts, and we can *intercommunicate*, at least potentially, with every other member of our species.

Surely this is a morally significant fact. The ability to communicate is *valuable*. It is not just *useful*—it is centrally connected to nearly everything human beings have ever claimed to value about themselves, everything from our capacity for abstract thought (so emphasized in the philosophical tradition) to our capacities for social affiliation and cultural creation. That we have language is, in short, a *good thing*. But if we can agree on this very minimal evaluative claim, then we are on our way to seeing how facts about *natures* can legitimately ground normative claims. Our capacity for language may in itself make us morally valuable creatures, as certain philosophers have claimed (though it surely would be only a sufficient and not a necessary condition). But even if that's not so, the fact that *language* is valuable, together with the fact that human beings have a capacity to acquire it, provides part of a nonarbitrary conception of what Aristotle called "human flourishing." If it's good for humans to develop and exercise their capacities for linguistic communication, then it counts as *damage* to human beings to impede or prevent this development.

I claim that some such conception of human flourishing, grounded in assumptions about a shared set of capacities, in fact lies behind feminism's protest against the treatment of women.[60] Feminists do not want to say *simply* that women are unhappy under patriarchy—for one thing, not all women are. Rather, I take it to be feminism's position that women under patriarchy are systematically *dehumanized*—treated in ways that prevent or impede the full development of their *human* capacities. Without a nonarbitrary background notion of human flourishing, the notion of *damage* makes no sense. And if feminists cannot make out the case that patriarchy *damages* women, then we are properly open to the charge, leveled at us often enough by our critics, that we are simply trying to impose on others our own parochial views of how life should be lived.

Notice that the need for appeal to *human* universals does not beg any questions against those who think that there are systematic differences between men and women. I have made no argument against this, although I think the considerations raised in the preceding section should make clear how hard it would be to properly justify any such claim. But consider what such a claim must mean once we understand natures properly as the grounds of complex dispositions. To say that boys "have better spatial abilities than girls" turns out to be many ways ambiguous. The (probably) intended meaning is that, in the standard curriculum, boys do better than girls. But suppose it so—it hardly follows that there are no curricula in which girls do as well as boys, or even better! And, of course, that environment could be provided to girls *without* disadvantaging boys: what is to prevent us as a society from providing girls with the environment that will permit *them* to flourish, and boys the environment that will permit *them* to flourish?

Nothing but *will*. This is already the scheme that's followed when the children in question are deemed truly valuable. In colleges and universities, in private elementary and secondary schools, and in the more affluent public schools, instructors labor mightily to provide "individualized instruction" to students with a variety of "special needs." Deficits in middle- and upper-class students are attributed to the environment; innate stupidity and laziness are found only in the poor. The idea that "natures" and "natural differences" are the only, or even *an important*, determinant of levels of human flourishing should be exposed for the self-serving nonsense that it is. It means nothing more or less than the patently abhorrent claim that the human flourishing of some individuals—men, white people, affluent people, English-speaking people, Christian people, straight people—is more valuable than that of others.

Questions of difference aside, however, there is a more fundamental point. As long as women and men share certain morally relevant capacities—the capacity for rationally directed action, the capacity to form emotional attachments, the capacity to communicate—general norms of human flourishing will still apply equally to both. It is impossible for me to imagine discoverable differences between men and women that could swamp the significance of these commonalities. The properties we manifestly share are sufficient to make clear that there can be no justification for separating men and women—or, indeed, any two groups of human beings—into "rulers or things ruled by Nature's direction."[61]

ACKNOWLEDGMENTS

Thanks to Susan Babbitt, Joe Levine, Sally Haslanger, Geoff Sayre-McCord, Naomi Scheman, and Steve Yablo for discussion of topics in this paper. Thanks also to audiences at the University of Vermont and Tulane University, where earlier versions of this essay were presented.

NOTES

1. With the possible exceptions of Plato and Descartes. But see Genevieve Lloyd, *The Man of Reason: "Male" and "Female" in Western Philosophy* (Minneapolis: University of Minnesota Press, 1984); Susan Bordo, *The Flight to Objectivity* (Albany: State University of New York Press, 1987); and Naomi Scheman, "Though This Be Method, Yet There Is Madness in It: Paranoia and Liberal Epistemology," in

A Mind of One's Own, ed. Louise Antony and Charlotte Witt (Boulder, Colo.: Westview Press, 1993), 145–70.

2. Leslie Stevenson, *Seven Theories of Human Nature*, 2d ed. (New York and Oxford: Oxford University Press, 1987), 3. See also p. viii. I'll discuss Stevenson's discussion of the use of masculine "generics" in detail in the next section.

3. Most of what the major Western philosophers had to say about women can be found in the invaluable collection *Philosophy of Woman*, ed. Mary Mahowald (Indianapolis, Ind.: Hackett, 1978; 2d ed., 1983; 3d ed., 1994). References are to the third edition unless otherwise noted.

4. In all three cases, the concession was made not because women were manifestly capable of rational thought (philosophy has never been seriously constrained by what's obvious) but rather because women would need a modicum of rationality to fulfill their proper roles. See ibid., 30 (Aristotle); 91, 93–95 (Rousseau); 103 (Kant).

5. For further discussion, see Janice Moulton, "The Myth of Neutral 'Man,' " in *Feminism and Philosophy*, ed. M. Vetterling, F. Elliston, and J. English (Totowa, N.J.: Littlefield, Adams, 1977).

6. Aristotle explicitly recognizes and struggles with precisely these difficulties. See Mahowald, *Philosophy of Woman*, 30. For further discussion of Aristotle's views of women see Lynda Lange, "Woman Is Not a Rational Animal," in *Discovering Reality*, ed. Sandra Harding and Merrill Hintikka (Dordrecht: D. Reidel, 1983), 1–15; Elizabeth Spelman, "Aristotle and the Politicization of the Soul," in Harding and Hintikka, *Discovering Reality*, 17–30; and Spelman, *Inessential Woman*, (Boston: Beacon Press, 1988). For discussion of Rousseau and Kant, see Lloyd, *The Man of Reason*.

7. See Mahowald, *Philosophy of Woman*, 31 (Aristotle); 89 (Rousseau); 102 (Kant).

8. Kant, for example, allows that "[t]he fair sex has just as much understanding as the male," but adds the notorious qualification "it is a *beautiful understanding*, whereas ours ['ours'?!—LA] should be a *deep understanding*, an expression that signifies identity with the sublime" (Mahowald, *Philosophy of Woman*, 103). "Her philosophy is not to reason, but to sense" (104). And Rousseau announces baldly: "What would be defects in men are good qualities in women, which are necessary to make things go on well" (90). Evidently the goodness of the feminine virtues lies mainly in their instrumental value to men. Kant concurs: "The content of woman's great science . . . is humankind, and among humanity, men" (104). See Christine Garside-Allen, "Can a Woman Be Good in the Same Way as a Man?" *Dialogue* 10 (1971): 534–44.

9. See Christine Pierce, "Natural Law Language and Women," in Mahowald, *Philosophy of Woman*, 356–68, and Joyce Trebilcot, "Sex Roles: The Argument from Nature," in Mahowald, *Philosophy of Woman*, 349–56.

10. Mahowald, *Philosophy of Woman*, 90. Speaking of women's sensitivity to shame, Kant argues that "since it has the voice of nature on its side, [it] seems always to agree with good moral qualities even if it yields to excess" (106).

11. Ibid., 105. Similarly, Aristotle's slaves *could* not rule because they lacked the deliberative faculty (31).

12. Ibid., 111.

13. Ibid., 103. A personal note: my own experience and that of countless other women my age attest to the durability of Kant's view. Most of us have bitter

memories of someone admonishing us to disguise or downplay our intelligence if we ever wanted to get dates. Judging from my students' reports, a distressing number of girls are *still* being told that boys just don't like smart girls. Yet to my knowledge, not a single one of the studies of sex differences in math and science emerging around puberty takes account of this extremely potent social message. How well would boys do at calculus if you told them—credibly—that they would never get to have sex if they mastered differential equations?

14. John Stuart Mill, *The Subjection of Women*, excerpted in *Philosophy of Woman*, Mahowald (151–70). See especially pp. 153–57.

15. See ibid., and also Mary Wollstonecraft, "Vindication of the Rights of Woman," excerpted in Mahowald, *Philosophy of Woman*, (112–28) and Harriet Taylor Mill, "Enfranchisement of Women," excerpted in Mahowald, *Philosophy of Woman* (170–85), esp. pp. 113–15, 171–73.

16. Steven Goldberg, *The Inevitability of Patriarchy*, excerpted in *Feminist Frameworks*, ed. Alison Jaggar and Paula Rothenberg Struhl (New York: McGraw-Hill, 1978), 81–86.

17. *Time* and *Newsweek* feature cover stories on the "naturalness" of gender differences every few years. See, for example, *Time*'s cover story entitled "Sizing Up the Sexes" (1/20/92) and *Newsweek*'s "The New Science of the Brain: Why Men and Women Think Differently" (3/27/95).

18. ABC News Special Report: "Boys and Girls *Are* Different: Men, Women and the Sex Difference," February 1, 1995.

19. In this I concur with Charlotte Witt, who defends a version of this claim in her essay "Feminist Metaphysics," in Antony and Witt, *A Mind of One's Own*, 273–288.

20. Stevenson, *Seven Theories*.

21. Leslie Stevenson, *The Study of Human Nature* (New York and Oxford: Oxford University Press, 1981).

22. This is to the best of my knowledge. There is no index for the edited collection, and in the monograph's index the only relevant entries are five page citations under "Female, feminism," three of which refer to Stevenson's discussions of his own neglect of the issue of gender differences, added in the second edition.

23. Stevenson, *Seven Theories*, 3.

24. Or, as the characters in *Charlotte's Web* innocently sing, in a Hanna-Barbera video: "We've got lots in common where it . . . really counts! Where it . . . really counts!" (Thanks to my daughter, Rachel Antony-Levine, for bringing this song to my attention.)

25. Stevenson, *Seven Theories*, 3.

26. I would like to acknowledge here my enormous debt to the writings of bell hooks and Elizabeth Spelman, whose works — especially hooks, *Feminist Theory: From Margin to Center* (Boston: South End Press, 1984), and Spelman, *Inessential Woman*)—have informed this entire section. The tacit exclusion of women of color by white feminist theorists is a central critical theme among black feminist and "womanist" writers. See, for example, Audre Lorde, *Sister Outsider* (Trumansburg, N.Y.: Crossing Press, 1984); Barbara Omolade, "Black Women and Feminism," in *The Future of Difference*, ed. Hester Eisenstein and Alice Jardine (Boston: G. K. Hall, 1980), 247–57; and Gloria Joseph, "The Incompatible Menage à Trois: Marxism, Feminism, and Racism," in *Women and Revolution: A Discussion of the Unhappy*

Marriage of Marxism and Feminism, ed. Lydia Sargent (Boston: South End Press, 1981), 91–107.

27. See, for example, bell hooks's discussion of Betty Freidan (hooks, *Feminist Theory*, pp. 1–3, and ch. 4).

28. See Angela Harris, "Race and Essentialism in Feminist Legal Theory," *Stanford Law Review* 42 (1990): 588.

29. Spelman, *Inessential Woman*, 57–79.

30. For an important early statement of the view that the material conditions of femininity constitute an epistemic standpoint in this sense, see Nancy Hartsock, "The Feminist Standpoint: Developing the Ground for a Specifically Feminist Historical Materialism," in Harding and Hintikka, *Discovering Reality*, 283–310. For a more recent development of such a view, see Robin Schott, "Resurrecting Embodiment: Toward a Feminist Materialism," in Antony and Witt, *A Mind of One's Own*, 171–84. For a critique of universal theories of human nature that draws on standpoint theory, see Naomi Scheman, "Feminist Epistemology" and "Reply to Antony," *Metaphilosophy* 26, no. 3 (July 1995): 177–90, 199–200.

31. See Lorde, *Sister Outsider*; hooks, *Feminist Theory*; Harris, "Race and Essentialism"; and Maria Lugones and Elizabeth Spelman, "Have We Got a Theory for You! Feminist Theory, Cultural Imperialism and the Demand for the Woman's Voice," *Hypatia* 6, no. 6 (1983): 578–81.

32. Spelman, *Inessential Woman*.

33. It is difficult to believe that some of them were not. It is a little hard to swallow, for example, that Locke could have seriously believed his own apology for the enslavement of Africans within the colonies: they had been captives in a "just war" who had forfeited their lives "by some Act that deserves death." As Peter Laslett remarks in his notation to section 24 of the *Second Treatise on Government*, Locke's justification of slavery "may seem unnecessary, and inconsistent with his principles, but it must be remembered that he writes as the administrator of slave-owing colonies in America." See John Locke, *Two Treatises of Government*, edited and with introduction and notes by Peter Laslett (Cambridge and New York: Mentor Books of Cambridge University Press, 1963), 325. (Laslett does not comment on Locke's inconsistency in granting husbands a natural right to prevail over their wives.) For further examination of colonial-era discussions of slavery and the natural rights of "man," see Bernard Bailyn, *The Ideological Origins of the American Revolution* (Cambridge, Mass.: Belknap Press of Harvard University Press, 1967). For more on Locke's view of race, see Harry Bracken, "Essence, Accident and Race," *Hermathena* 16 (Winter 1973): 81–96.

34. Carol Gilligan, *In a Different Voice: Psychological Theory and Women's Development* (Cambridge, Mass.: Harvard University Press, 1982).

35. Virginia Held, "Feminist Transformations of Moral Theory," *Philosophy and Phenomenological Research* 50, nos. 3–4, supplement (Fall 1990): 321–44; Nel Noddings, *Caring: A Feminine Approach to Ethics and Moral Education* (Berkeley and Los Angeles: University of California Press, 1984); Sara Ruddick, *Maternal Thinking: Toward a Politics of Peace* (Boston: Beacon Press, 1989).

36. Annette Baier, "Hume, the Women's Moral Theorist?" in *Women and Moral Theory*, ed. Eva Feder Kittay and Diana T. Meyers (Totowa, N.J.: Rowman and Littlefield, 1987). Baier does not condemn all the canonical philosophers: she thinks

that Hume's empiricism provides a promising basis for both a feminist ethics and a feminist epistemology.

37. Susan Okin, *Justice, Gender and the Family* (New York: Basic Books, 1989). See also Okin, "Thinking Like a Woman," in *Theoretical Perspectives on Sexual Difference*, ed. Deborah L. Rhode (New Haven, Conn.: Yale University Press, 1990), 145–59, for a survey and discussion of the range of feminist views on the matter of gender differences in moral thinking.

38. Lloyd, *The Man of Reason*, Marcia Homiak defends Aristotle against the charge that his conception of a life governed by reason is elitist in "Feminism and Aristotle's Rational Ideal," in Antony and Witt, *A Mind of One's Own*, 1–17.

39. Alison Jaggar, *Feminist Politics and Human Nature* (Totowa, N.J.: Rowman and Littlefield, 1983); and Lorraine Code, *What Can She Know? Feminist Theory and the Construction of Knowledge* (Ithaca, N.Y.: Cornell University Press, 1991).

40. See Evelyn Fox Keller, "Cognitive Repression in Physics," *American Journal of Physics* 47 (1979): 718–21; Naomi Scheman, "Othello's Doubts/Desdemona's Death: The Engendering of Skepticism," in *Power, Gender, Values*, ed. Judith Genova (Edmonton, Alberta: Academic Printing and Publishing, 1987); and Scheman, "Though This Be Method," 145–70; Bordo, *The Flight to Objectivity*; and Nancy Chodorow, *The Reproduction of Mothering* (Berkeley and Los Angeles: University of California Press, 1978).

41. Although most of the theorists I have discussed are skeptical that the minimally necessary conditions for successful theorizing are even close to being realized. See, for example, Scheman, "Reply to Antony."

42. See Catherine MacKinnon, *Toward a Feminist Theory of the State* (Cambridge, Mass., and London: Harvard University Press, 1989). For discussion, see Sally Haslanger, "Ontology and Social Construction," *Philosophical Topics* 23, no. 2 (Fall 1995): *Feminist Perspectives on Language, Knowledge, and Reality*, 95–125; and Susan Babbitt, *Impossible Dreams: Rationality, Integrity, and Moral Imagination* (Boulder, Colo.: Westview Press, 1995), 6.

43. Nancy Fraser and Linda Nicholson, "Social Criticism without Philosophy," in *Feminism/Postmodernism*, ed. Linda Nicholson (London and New York: Routledge, 1990), 28. Fraser and Nicholson are not here criticizing the particular theories I referred to, though I think they would agree that the criticism applies. I am simply borrowing their gloss of the term "essentialist."

44. Donna Haraway explains and explores the implications of this absence of fixity through the metaphor of a *cyborg*—a being that defies all distinction between male and female, between animal and machine, and between natural and artificial. See Haraway, "A Manifesto for Cyborgs: Science, Technology, and Socialist Feminism in the 1980's," *Socialist Review* 15, no. 80 (1985): 65–107.

45. Iris Young, *Justice and the Politics of Difference* (Princeton, N.J.: Princeton University Press, 1990), 99.

46. Elizabeth Rapaport, "Generalizing Gender: Reason and Essence in the Legal Thought of Catherine MacKinnon," in Antony and Witt, *A Mind of One's Own*, 127–43.

47. Susan Bordo, "Feminism, Postmodernism, Gender Skepticism," in her *Unbearable Weight: Feminism, Western Culture and the Body* (Berkeley and Los Angeles: University of California Press, 1993), 243.

48. The term "categorical" as a name for nondispositional properties was suggested to me by Stephen Yablo.

49. See Willard V. O. Quine, "Natural Kinds," in *Ontological Relativity and Other Essays* (New York and London: Columbia University Press, 1969), 114–38.

To be more precise, the standard view is that attributions of dispositional properties, *to the extent that they are determinate*, are grounded in some categorical fact about the object.

50. Actually, middle- and upper-class American parents have somewhat incoherent attitudes about intelligence. On the one hand, they have a great deal invested in the idea that their children are inherently smarter (i.e., better) than poorer kids; on the other hand, they are not about to risk leaving their kids' natural intelligence to flourish on its own, so they demand for their own children the most highly enriched educational environment that tax dollars can buy. George Bush used to publicly opine that quality of education had nothing to do with how much was spent per student. His parents then must have been real suckers to shell out the bucks it cost to send him to Andover, which spends eleven thousand dollars per student. See Jonathan Kozol, *Savage Inequalities* (New York: Crown, 1991).

51. I rely here on Richard Lewontin, "The Analysis of Variance and the Analysis of Causes," in Ned Block and Gerald Dworkin, eds., *The IQ Controversy* (New York: Pantheon Books, 1976).

52. Despite this, I'm classified as "white"—a good example of the naming problem (the complex dispositional property of being pale if not exposed to sunlight is conflated with the associated categorical of being pale), aided and abetted by the invisibility of contingencies—"normal" here being partially statistical (I am mostly not in the sun) and normative (what's statistically true for me, an urban professional, is tacitly taken as the standard).

53. See Lewontin, "The Analysis of Variance."

54. See Block and Dworkin, *The IQ Controversy*, and also the discussion of heritability and its abuse in the IQ debate in Richard C. Lewontin, Steven Rose, and Leon J. Kamin, *Not in Our Genes* (New York: Pantheon, 1984), ch. 5.

55. See Harriet Baber, "Choice, Preference and Utility: A Response to Sommers," (paper presented at APA Eastern Division Meetings, December 1994).

56. Nancy Holmstrom makes the same point but argues for a conception of "nature" on which such properties that depend on such stable regularities *are* counted as part of the thing's nature. See "Do Women Have a Distinct Nature?" *Philosophical Forum* 14, no. 1 (Fall 1982): 25–42.

57. See Steven Pinker, *The Language Instinct* (New York: William Morrow, 1994).

58. Although the social contact may be more important than the language. There are cases of spontaneously invented languages: see the discussion of creoles and of invented sign language among congenitally deaf twins in ibid., 32–39.

59. Although see Stephen Jay Gould, "Speaking of Snails and Scales," *Natural History*, May 1995, 14–23, for an intriguing countersuggestion. Gould argues that certain creoles, because they do not carry the syntactic accretions and alterations that appear during the histories of most languages, may provide insight into "default" settings of the parameters specified by Universal Grammar. There is no consensus among linguists as to whether such default settings exist.

60. Cf. Witt, "Feminist Metaphysics."

61. Aristotle, *Politics*, in Mahowald, *Philosophy of Woman*, 31.

Feminist Reconceptualizations in Ethics

VIRGINIA HELD

WHEN FEMINIST perspectives are brought to bear in ethics, they may at first suggest topics overlooked or neglected by the philosophical field of inquiry known as "moral philosophy" or "ethics." Such topics include discrimination against women and justifiable remedies, abortion and reproductive technologies and the moral problems involved, violence against women, and many others.

Soon attention may be turned to the moral theory appealed to in any discussion of ethical problems. And it will be seen that moral theory, like other philosophical theory, has a long history of gender bias.[1] Ethics, like most of philosophy, has been built on assumptions, and constructed with concepts, that are by no means gender-neutral.

In comparison with nonfeminist approaches, feminists characteristically begin with different concerns and give different emphases to the issues we consider. The significance of shifts such as these can be great; as Lorraine Code notes, "Starting points and focal points shape the impact of theoretical discussion."[2] Far from merely providing additional insights that can be incorporated into traditional theory, feminist explorations often require radical transformations of existing fields of inquiry and theory.[3] From a feminist point of view, moral theory, along with almost all theory, will have to be transformed to take adequate account of the experience of women.

I will begin this essay with a brief examination of how various fundamental aspects of the history of ethics have not been gender-neutral. I will discuss three issues where feminist rethinking is transforming moral concepts and theories. And I will suggest some of the profound implications such rethinking has for the transformation of society.

BIAS IN THE HISTORY OF ETHICS

Consider the ideals embodied in the phrase "the man of reason." As Genevieve Lloyd has told the story, what has been taken to characterize the man of reason may have changed from historical period to historical period, but in each, the character ideal of the man of reason has been constructed in conjunction with a rejection of whatever has been taken to be characteristic of the feminine. "Rationality," Lloyd writes, "has been conceived as tran-

scendence of the 'feminine,' and the 'feminine' itself has been partly constituted by its occurrence within this structure."[4]

This has, of course, fundamentally affected the history of philosophy and
of ethics. The split between reason and emotion is one of the most familiar
of philosophical conceptions. The advocacy of reason "controlling" unruly
emotion, of rationality guiding responsible human action against the blind-
ness of passion, has a long and highly influential history, almost as familiar
to nonphilosophers as to philosophers. Lloyd sums it up:

> From the beginnings of philosophical thought, femaleness was symbolically asso-
> ciated with what Reason supposedly left behind—the dark powers of the earth
> goddesses, immersion in unknown forces associated with mysterious female pow-
> ers. The early Greeks saw women's capacity to conceive as connecting them with
> the fertility of Nature. As Plato later expressed the thought, women "imitate the
> earth."[5]

In asserting its claims and winning its status in human history, reason was
thought to have to conquer the female forces of unreason. Reason and clarity of thought were early associated with maleness, and, as Lloyd says,
"What had to be shed in developing culturally prized rationality was, from
the start, symbolically associated with femaleness." In later Greek philosophical thought, the form-matter distinction was articulated, with a similar
hierarchical and gendered association. Maleness was aligned with active,
determinate, and defining form; femaleness with mere passive, indeterminate, and inferior matter. Plato, in the *Timaeus*, compared the defining aspect of form with the father and indefinite matter with the mother; Aristotle
also compared the form-matter distinction with the male-female distinction.
To quote Lloyd again, "This comparison . . . meant that the very nature of
knowledge was implicitly associated with the extrusion of what was symbolically associated with the feminine."[6]

The associations among reason, form, knowledge, and maleness have
persisted in various guises and have permeated what has been thought to be
moral knowledge, as well as what has been thought to be scientific knowledge and the practice of morality. The associations between the philosophical concepts and gender cannot be merely dropped and the concepts retained
regardless of gender, because gender has been built into them in such a way
that, without it, they will have to be different concepts. As feminists repeatedly show, if the concept of "human" were built on what we think about
"woman" rather than on what we think about "man," it would be a very
different concept. Ethics, thus, has not been a search for universal, or truly
human, guidance but a gender-biased enterprise.

Other distinctions and associations have supplemented and reinforced the
identification of reason with maleness, and of the irrational with the female;
on this and other grounds "man" has been associated with the human,
"woman" with the natural. Prominent among distinctions reinforcing the
latter view has been that between the public and the private. Again, these

provide as familiar and entrenched a framework as do reason and emotion, and they have been as influential for nonphilosophers as for philosophers. It has been supposed that in the public realm man transcends his animal nature and creates human history. As citizen, he creates government and law; as warrior, he protects society by his willingness to risk death; and as artist or philosopher, he overcomes his human mortality. Here, in the public realm, morality should guide human decisions. In the household, in contrast, it has been supposed that women merely "reproduce" life as natural, biological matter. Within the household, the "natural" needs of man for food and shelter are served, and new instances of the biological creature that is man are brought into being. But what is distinctively human and what transcends any given level of development to create human progress have been thought to occur elsewhere.

This contrast was made explicit in Aristotle's conceptions of polis and household; it has continued to affect the basic assumptions of a remarkably broad swath of thought ever since. In ancient Athens, women were confined to the household; the public sphere was literally a male domain. The associations of the public, historically male sphere with the distinctively human, and of the household, historically a female sphere, with the merely natural and repetitious, have persisted, even though women have been permitted to venture into public space. These associations have deeply affected moral theory, which has often supposed the transcendent, public domain to be relevant to the foundations of morality in ways that the "natural" behavior of women in the household could not be.

To take some representative examples, David Heyd, in his discussion of supererogation, claims that a mother's sacrifice for her child cannot be an example of the supererogatory because it belongs, in his view, to "the sphere of natural relationships and instinctive feelings (which lie outside morality)."[7] J. O. Urmson had earlier taken a similar position, saying, "Let us be clear that we are not now considering cases of natural affection, such as the sacrifice made by a mother for her child; such cases may be said with some justice *not to fall under the concept of morality*" (emphasis added).[8] And in his article "Distrusting Economics," Alan Ryan argues persuasively about the questionableness of economics and other branches of the social sciences built on the assumption that human beings are rational, self-interested calculators. He discusses various examples of behavior, such as that of men in wartime, which is not self-interested and which shows the assumption to be false; but nowhere in the article is there any mention of the activity of mothering, which would seem to be a fertile locus for doubts about the usual picture of rational man as self-interested.[9] Although Ryan does not provide the kind of explicit reason offered by Heyd and Urmson for omitting mothering from consideration as relevant to his discussion, it is difficult to understand the omission without a comparable assumption being implicit here, as it so often is elsewhere. Without feminist insistence on the relevance for morality of the experience in mothering, this context is largely ignored by moral theorists. And yet from a gender-neutral point of view, how can this vast and fundamental domain of human experience possibly be imagined to lie "outside morality"?

The result of the distinction between public and private, as usually formulated, has been to privilege the points of view of men in the public domains of state and law, and later in the marketplace, and to discount the experience of women. Mothering has been conceptualized as a primarily biological activity, even when performed by human beings, and virtually no moral theory in the history of ethics has taken mothering, as experienced by women, seriously as a source of moral insight, until feminists began to do so in recent years.[10] Women have been seen as emotional rather than rational beings, and thus incapable of full moral personhood. Women's behavior has been interpreted as "natural" and driven by instinct, and thus as irrelevant to morality and to the construction of moral principles, or it has been interpreted, at best, as in need of instruction and supervision by males better able to know what morality requires and better able to live up to its demands.

The Hobbesian conception of reason is very different from the Platonic or Aristotelian conceptions before it and from the later conceptions of Rousseau or Kant or Hegel; all have in common the habit of ignoring and disparaging the experience and reality of women. Consider Hobbes's account of man in the state of nature contracting with other men to establish society. These men hypothetically come into existence fully formed and independent of one another, and decide either to enter civil society or stay outside of it. As Christine Di Stefano writes, "What we find in Hobbes's account is a vital concern with the survival of a gendered subject conceived in modern masculine terms. . . . In the state of nature, Hobbes's masculine egoism carries the day. . . . The specifically gendered dimension of this egoism is underscored by a radical atomism erected on the denial of maternity."[11]

In *The Citizen*, where Hobbes gave his first systematic exposition of the state of nature, he asks us to "consider men as if but even now sprung out of the earth, and suddenly, like mushrooms, come to full maturity, without all kind of engagement with each other."[12] Di Stefano points out that it is an incredible feature of Hobbes's state of nature that the men in it "are not born of, much less nurtured by, women, or anyone else" and that, to abstract from the complex web of human reality an abstract man for rational perusal, Hobbes has "expunged human reproduction and early nurturance from his account of basic human nature and primordial human relations. Such a descriptive strategy ensures that Hobbes can present a thoroughly atomistic subject."[13]

From the point of view of women's experience, such a subject or self is unbelievable and misleading, even as a theoretical construct. The man-made political Leviathan Hobbes erects on these foundations "is effectively composed," Di Stefano writes, "of a body politic of social orphans who have socially acculturated themselves." Hence, Hobbesian man "bears the telltale signs of a modern masculinity in extremis: identity through opposition, denial of reciprocity, repudiation of the (m)other in oneself and in relation to oneself."[14]

Rousseau and Kant and Hegel paid homage, respectively, to the emotional power, the aesthetic sensibility, and the familial concerns of women. But since in their views morality must be based on rational principle and since women were incapable of full rationality, or a degree or kind of rationality comparable to that of men, women were deemed to be inherently wanting in morality. For Rousseau, women must be trained from childhood to submit to the will of men lest their sexual power lead both men and women to disaster. For Kant, women were thought incapable of achieving full moral personhood, and women lose all charm if they try to behave like men by engaging in rational pursuits. For Hegel, women's moral concern for our families could be admirable in its proper place, but it is a threat to the more universal aims to which men, as members of the state, should aspire.[15]

These images of the feminine as what must be overcome if knowledge and morality are to be achieved, of female experience as naturally irrelevant to morality, and of women as inherently deficient moral creatures are all built into the history of ethics. Examining these images, feminists find that they are not the incidental or merely idiosyncratic suppositions of a few philosophers whose views on many topics depart far from the ordinary anyway; they are the nearly uniform reflection in philosophical and ethical theory of patriarchal attitudes pervasive throughout human history. Or they are exaggerations of ordinary male experience, which then reinforce rather than temper other conceptions and institutions reflective of male domination. At any rate, they distort the actual experience of many men as well as women. Annette Baier has speculated why it is that moral philosophy has so seriously overlooked the trust among human beings that in her view is an utterly central aspect of moral life. "The great moral theorists in our tradition," she says, "not only are all men, they are mostly men who had minimal adult dealings with (and so were then minimally influenced by) women." For the most part they were "clerics, misogynists, and puritan bachelors," and thus it is not surprising that they focus their philosophical attention "so single-mindedly on cool, distanced relations between more or less free and equal adult strangers."[16]

As feminists, we deplore the male domination that so much of philosophy and moral theory reflects. But we recognize that the problem requires more than changing patriarchal attitudes, for moral theory as so far developed is incapable of correcting itself without almost total transformation. It cannot simply absorb the gender that has been "left behind," even if both genders want it to. To continue to build morality on rational principles opposed to the emotions and to include women among the rational will leave no one to reflect the promptings of the heart, which promptings can be moral rather than merely instinctive. To simply bring women into the public and male domain of the polis will leave no one to speak for the household. Its values have been hitherto unrecognized, but they are often moral values. Or to

continue to seek contractual restraints on the pursuits of self-interest by atomistic individuals and to have women join men in devotion to these pursuits will leave no one involved in the nurturance of children and the cultivation of social relations, which nurturance and cultivation can be of the
greatest moral import.

There are very good reasons for women not to want simply to be accorded entry as equals into the enterprise of morality as so far developed. In
a recent survey of types of feminist moral theory, Kathryn Morgan laments
that "many women who engage in philosophical reflection are acutely aware
of the masculine nature of the profession and tradition, and feel their own
moral concerns as women silenced or trivialized in virtually all the official
settings that define the practice."[17] Clearly women should not agree, as the
price of admission to the masculine realm of traditional morality, to abandon our own moral concerns as women.

And so we are trying to shape new moral theory. Understandably, we are
not yet ready to offer fully developed feminist moral theories. But we can
suggest some directions our project is taking. As Morgan points out, there is
not likely to be a "star" feminist moral theorist on the order of a Rawls or
a Nozick:

> There will be no individual singled out for two reasons. One reason is that vital
> moral and theoretical conversations are taking place on a large dialectical scale as
> the feminist community struggles to develop a feminist ethic. The second reason is
> that this community of feminist theoreticians is calling into question the very
> model of the individualized autonomous self presupposed by a star-centered male-
> dominated tradition. . . . We experience it as a common labour, a common task.[18]

Promising dialogues are proceeding on feminist approaches to moral theory. As Alison Jaggar makes clear in her useful overview, there is no unitary
view of ethics that can be identified as "feminist ethics." Feminist approaches to ethics share a commitment to "rethinking ethics with a view to
correcting whatever forms of male bias it may contain." While those who
develop these approaches are "united by a shared project, they diverge
widely in their view as to how this project is to be accomplished."[19]

Not all feminists, by any means, agree that there are distinctive feminist
virtues or values. Some are especially skeptical of the attempt to give positive
value to such traditional "feminine virtues" as a willingness to nurture, or
an affinity with caring, or a reluctance to seek independence. They see this
approach as playing into the hands of those who would confine women to
traditional roles.[20] Other feminists are skeptical of all claims about women
as such, emphasizing that women are divided by class and race and sexual
orientation in ways that make any conclusions drawn from "women's experience" dubious.[21]

Still, it is possible, I think, to discern some focal points in current feminist
attempts to transform ethics into an acceptable theoretical and practical activity. In the glimpse I have presented of bias in the history of ethics, I

focused on what, from a feminist point of view, are three of its most questionable aspects: the split between reason and emotion, and the devaluation of emotion; the public-private distinction and the relegation of the private to the natural; and the concept of the self as constructed from a male point of view. In the remainder of this discussion, I will examine further how some feminists are exploring these topics. We are showing that previous treatment of them has been distorted, and we are trying to reenvision the realities and recommendations with which these aspects of moral theorizing should deal.

REASON AND EMOTION

In the area of moral theory in the modern era, the priority accorded to reason has taken two major forms. On the one hand has been the Kantian, or Kantian-inspired, search for very general, abstract, deontological, universal moral principles by which rational beings should be guided. Kant's Categorical Imperative is a prime example. It suggests that all moral problems can be handled by applying an impartial, pure, rational principle to particular cases. It requires that we try to see what the general features of the problem before us are and that we apply to the problem an abstract principle or rules derivable from it. This procedure, it is said, should be adequate for all moral decisions. We should thus be able to act as reason recommends, and resist yielding to emotional inclinations and desires in conflict with our rational wills.

On the other hand, the priority accorded to reason in the modern era has taken a Utilitarian form. The Utilitarian approach, reflected in rational choice theory, recognizes that persons have desires and interests, and it suggests rules of rational choice for maximizing the satisfaction of these desires and interests. While some philosophers in the tradition espouse egoism, especially of an intelligent and long-term kind, many do not. They begin, however, with assumptions that what is morally relevant are the gains and losses of utility to theoretically isolable individuals and that morality should aim to maximize the satisfaction of individuals. Rational calculation about such an outcome will, in this view, provide moral recommendations to guide all our choices. Like the Kantian approach, the Utilitarian approach relies on abstract general principles or rules to be applied to particular cases. And it holds that although emotion is, in fact, the source of our desires for certain objectives, the task of morality should be to instruct us on how to pursue those objectives most rationally. Emotional attitudes toward moral issues themselves interfere with rationality and should be disregarded.

Although the conceptions of what the judgments of morality should be based on and how reason should guide moral decisions are different in Kantian and Utilitarian approaches, they share a reliance on a highly abstract, universal principle as the appropriate source of moral guidance, and they share the view that moral problems are to be solved by the application of such an abstract principle to particular cases. Both admire the rules of reason to be appealed to in moral contexts, and both denigrate emotional responses to moral issues.

Many feminist philosophers have questioned whether the reliance on abstract rules, rather than the adoption of more context-respectful approaches, can possibly be adequate for dealing with moral problems, especially as women experience them. Though Kantians may hold that complex rules can be elaborated for specific contexts, there is nevertheless an assumption in this approach that the more abstract the reasoning applied to a moral problem, the more satisfactory. And Utilitarians suppose that one highly abstract principle, the Principle of Utility, can be applied to every moral problem no matter what the context.

A genuinely universal or gender-neutral moral theory would be one that would take account of the experience and concerns of women as fully as it does the experience and concerns of men. When we focus on women's experience of moral problems, however, we find that they are often especially concerned with actual relationships between embodied persons and with what these relationships seem to require. Women are often inclined to attend to rather than to dismiss the particularities of the context in which a moral problem arises. And many of us pay attention to feelings of empathy and caring to help us decide what to do rather than relying as fully as possible on abstract rules of reason.

Margaret Walker, for instance, contrasts feminist moral "understanding" with traditional moral "knowledge." She sees the components of the former as involving "attention, contextual and narrative appreciation, and communication in the event of moral deliberation." This alternative moral epistemology holds that "the adequacy of moral understanding decreases as its form approaches generality through abstraction."[22]

The work of psychologists such as Carol Gilligan has led to a clarification of what may be thought of as tendencies among women to approach moral issues differently from men. Rather than seeking solutions to moral problems by applying abstract rules of justice to particular cases, many of the women studied by Gilligan were concerned with preserving actual human relationships and with expressing care for those for whom they felt responsible. Their moral reasoning was typically more embedded in a context of particular others than was the reasoning of a comparable group of men.[23] One should not equate tendencies women in fact display with feminist views, since the former may well be the result of the sexist, oppressive conditions in which women's lives have been lived. But many feminists see our own consciously considered experience as lending confirmation to such psychological studies.

Feminist philosophers are in the process of reevaluating the place of emotion in morality in at least two respects. First, many think morality requires the development of the moral emotions, in contrast to moral theories emphasizing the primacy of reason. As Annette Baier observes, the rationalism typical of traditional moral theory will be challenged when we pay attention to the role of parent:

> It might be important for father figures to have rational control over their violent urges to beat to death the children whose screams enrage them, but more than control of such nasty passions seems needed in the mother or primary parent, or parent-substitute, by most psychological theories. They need to love their children, not just to control their irritation.[24]

So the emphasis in traditional theories on rational control over the emotions, rather than on cultivating desirable forms of emotion, is challenged by feminist approaches to ethics.

Second, emotions will be respected rather than dismissed by many feminist moral philosophers in the process of gaining moral understanding. The experience and practice out of which we can expect to develop feminist moral theory will include embodied feeling as well as thought. In an overview of a vast amount of writing, Kathryn Morgan states that "feminist theorists begin ethical theorizing with embodied, gendered subjects who have particular histories, particular communities, particular allegiances, and particular visions of human flourishing. The starting point involves valorizing what has frequently been most mistrusted and despised in the western philosophical tradition."[25] Foremost among the elements being reevaluated are women's emotions. The "care" of the alternative feminist approach to morality appreciates rather than rejects emotion, and such caring relationships cannot be understood in terms of abstract rules or moral reasoning. And the "weighing" so often needed between the conflicting claims of some relationships and others cannot be settled by deduction or rational calculation. A feminist ethic will not just acknowledge emotion, as do Utilitarians, as giving us the objectives toward which moral rationality can direct us; it will embrace emotion as providing at least a partial basis for morality itself and certainly for moral understanding.

Trust is essential for at least some segments of morality.[26] Achieving and maintaining trusting, caring relationships is quite different from acting in accord with rational principles or satisfying the individual desires of either self or other. Caring, empathy, feeling for others, being sensitive to each other's feelings—all may be better guides to what morality requires in actual contexts than may abstract rules of reason or rational calculation.

The fear that a feminist ethic will be a relativistic "situation ethic" is misplaced. Some feelings can be as widely shared as are rational beliefs, and feminists do not see their views as reducible to "just another attitude." In her discussion of the differences between feminist and nonfeminist medical ethics, Susan Sherwin shows why feminists reject the mere case-by-case approach that prevails in nonfeminist medical ethics. The latter also rejects the excessive reliance on abstract rules characteristic of standard ethics, and in this way resembles feminist ethics. But the very focus on cases in isolation makes it difficult to attend to general features in the institutions and practices of medicine that, among other faults, systematically contribute to the oppression of women.[27] The difference of approach can be seen in the treatment of issues in the new reproductive technologies that may further decrease the control of women over reproduction.

This difference is not one of substance alone; Sherwin shows its implications for method as well. With respect to reproductive technologies, one can see clearly the deficiencies of the case-by-case approach: what needs to be considered is not only choice as seen in the purely individualistic terms of the focus on cases but control at a more general level and how such control affects the structure of gender in society. Thus, a feminist perspective does not always counsel attention to specific case versus appeal to general considerations, as some sort of methodological rule. But the general considerations are often not the purely abstract ones of traditional and standard moral theory; they are the general features and judgments to be made about cases in actual (which means, so far, male-dominated) societies. A feminist evaluation of a moral problem should never omit the political elements involved; and it is likely to recognize that political issues cannot be dealt with adequately in purely abstract terms any more than can moral issues.

The liberal tradition in social and moral philosophy argues that in a pluralistic society, and even more clearly in a pluralistic world, we cannot agree on our visions of the good life, on what is the best kind of life for human beings, but we can hope to agree on the minimal conditions for justice, for coexistence within a framework allowing us to pursue our visions of the good life.[28] Many feminists contend that the commitment to justice needed for agreement in actual conditions on even minimal requirements of justice is as likely to demand relational feelings as a rational recognition of abstract principles. Human beings can and do care—and are capable of caring far more than most do at present—about the suffering of children quite distant from them, about the prospects for future generations, and about the well-being of the globe. The mutually disinterested rational individualists of the liberal tradition would seem unlikely to care enough to take the actions needed to achieve moral decency at a global level, or environmental sanity for decades hence, just as they seem unable to represent caring relationships within the family and among friends. Annette Baier puts it thus:

> A moral theory, it can plausibly be claimed, cannot regard concern for new and future persons as an optional charity left for those with a taste for it. If the morality the theory endorses is to sustain itself, it must provide for its own continuers, not just take out a loan on a carefully encouraged maternal instinct or on the enthusiasm of a self-selected group of environmentalists, who make it their business or hobby to be concerned with what we are doing to mother earth.[29]

The possibilities, as well as the problems (and we are well aware of some of them), in a feminist reenvisioning of emotion and reason need to be further developed, but we can already see that the views of nonfeminist moral theory are unsatisfactory.

The Public and the Private

A second questionable aspect of the history of ethics is its conception of the distinction between the public and the private. As with the spilt between reason and emotion, feminists are showing how gender bias has distorted previous conceptions of these spheres, and we are trying to offer more appropriate understandings of "private" morality and "public" life.

Feminists reject the implication that what occurs in the household occurs as if on an island beyond politics. In fact, the personal is highly affected by the political power beyond, from legislation about abortion to the greater earning power of men, to the interconnected division of labor by gender both within and beyond the household, to the lack of adequate social protection for women against domestic violence.[30] Of course we recognize that the family is not identical with the state, and we still need concepts for thinking about the private and the personal, the public and the political; but we do know they will have to be very different from the traditional concepts.

Feminists have also criticized deeper assumptions about what is distinctively human and what is "natural" in the public and private aspects of human life, and what is meant by "natural" in connection with women.[31] Consider the associations that have traditionally been built up: the public realm is seen as the distinctively human realm in which man transcends his animal nature, while the private realm of the household is seen as the natural region in which women merely reproduce the species. These associations are extraordinarily pervasive in standard concepts and theories, in art and thought and cultural ideals, and especially in politics. So entrenched is this way of thinking that it was reflected even in Simone de Beauvoir's pathbreaking feminist text, *The Second Sex*, published in 1949.[32] In thinking about the household and about politics, as about many other topics, feminists need to transcend our own early searches for our own perspectives.

Dominant patterns of thought have seen women as primarily mothers, and mothering as the performance of a primarily biological function. Then it has been supposed that while engaging in political life is a specifically human activity, women are engaged in an activity that is not specifically human. Women accordingly have been thought to be closer to nature than men, to be enmeshed in a biological function involving processes more like those in which other animals are involved than like the rational discussion of the citizen in the polis, or the glorious battles of noble soldiers, or the trading and rational contracting of "economic man."[33] The total or relative exclusion of women from the domain of public life has thus been seen as either fitting or inevitable.

The view that women are more determined by biology than are men is still extraordinarily prevalent. From a feminist perspective it is highly questionable. Human mothering is a different activity from the mothering engaged in by other animals, as different as the work and speech of men is from what might be thought of as the "work" and "speech" of other animals. Of course, all human beings are animal as well as human. But to whatever extent it is appropriate to recognize a difference between "man" and other animals, so is it appropriate to recognize a comparable difference between "woman" and other animals, and between the activities—including mothering—engaged in by women and the behavior of other animals.

Human mothering shapes language and culture, it forms human social personhood, it develops morality. Animal behavior can be highly complex, but it does not have built into it any of the consciously chosen aims of morality. In creating human social persons, human mothering is different in kind from merely propagating a species. And human mothering can be fully as creative an activity as those activities traditionally thought of as distinctively human, because to create new persons and new types of persons can surely be as creative as to make new objects, products, or institutions. Human mothering is no more "natural" or "primarily biological" than is any human activity.

Consider nursing an infant, often thought of as the epitome of a biological process with which mothering is associated and women are identified. There is no more reason to think of human nursing as simply biological than there is to think this way of, say, a businessmen's lunch. Eating is a biological process, but what and how and with whom we eat are thoroughly cultural. Whether and how long and with whom a woman nurses an infant are also human, cultural matters. If men transcend the natural by conquering new territory and trading with their neighbors and making deals over lunch to do so, women can transcend the natural by choosing not to nurse their children when they could, or choosing to nurse them when their culture tells them not to, or singing songs to their infants as they nurse, or nursing in restaurants to overcome the prejudices against doing so, or thinking human thoughts as they nurse, and so forth. Human culture surrounds and characterizes the activity of nursing as it does the activities of eating or governing or writing or thinking.

We are continually being presented with images of the humanly new and creative as occurring in the public realm of the polis or in the realms of the marketplace or of art and science outside the household. The very term "reproduction" suggests mere repetition, the bringing into existence of repeated instances of the same human animal. But human reproduction is not repetition. This is not to suggest that bringing up children in the interstices of patriarchal families, in society structured by institutions supporting male dominance, can achieve the potential of transformation latent in the activity of human mothering. But the activity of creating new social persons and new kinds of persons is potentially the most transformative human activity of all. And it suggests that morality should concern itself first of all with this activity, with what its norms and practices ought to be, and with how the institutions and arrangements throughout society and the world ought to be structured to facilitate the right kinds of development of the best kinds of new persons. The flourishing of children ought to be at the very center of moral, social, political, economic, and legal thought, rather than, as at present, at the periphery, if attended to at all.

Revised conceptions of public and private have significant implications for our conceptions of human beings and relationships between them. Some feminists suggest that instead of interpreting human relationships on the model of the impersonal "public" sphere, as standard political and moral theory has so often done, we might consider interpreting them on the model of the "private," or of what these relationships could be imagined to be like in postpatriarchal society. The traditional approach is illustrated by those who generalize, to regions of human life other than the economic, assumptions about "economic man" in contractual relations with other men. It sees such impersonal, contractual relations as paradigmatic, even, on some views, for moral theory. Many feminists, in contrast, consider the realm of what has been misconstrued as the "private" as offering guidance to what human beings and their relationships should be like in regions beyond those of family and friendship, as well as in more intimate contexts. Sara Ruddick looks at the implications of the practice of mothering for the conduct of peace politics. Marilyn Friedman and Lorraine Code consider friendship, especially as women understand it, as a possible model for human relationships.[34] Others see society as noncontractual rather than contractual.

Clearly, a reconceptualization is needed of the ways in which every human life is entwined with both personal and social components. Feminist theorists are rethinking and reorganizing the private and the public, the personal and the political, and thus morality.

THE CONCEPT OF SELF

Let me turn now to the third aspect of the history of ethics that is being reenvisioned by feminists: the concept of self. A major emphasis in a feminist approach to morality is the recognition that more attention must be paid to the domain between the self as ego, as self-interested individual, and the universal, everyone, others in general. Traditionally, ethics has dealt with these poles of individual self and universal all. Often it has called for impartiality against the partiality of the egoistic self; sometimes it has defended egoism against claims for a universal perspective. But most standard moral theory has hardly noticed as morally significant the intermediate realm of family relations and relations of friendship, of group ties and neighborhood concerns, especially from the point of view of women.

When it has noticed this intermediate realm, it has often seen its attachments as threatening to the aspirations of the man of reason or as subversive of "true" morality. In seeing the problems of ethics as problems of reconciling the interests of the self with what would be right or best for "everyone," standard ethics has neglected the moral aspects of the concern and sympathy that people actually feel for particular others, and what moral experience in this intermediate realm suggests for an adequate morality.

The region of "particular others" is a distinct domain, where what can be seen to be artificial and problematic are the very egoistic "self" and the universal "all others" of standard moral theory. In the domain of particular others, the self is already constituted to an important degree by relations with others, and these relations may be much more salient and significant than the interests of any individual self in isolation.[35] The "others" in the picture, however, are not the "all others," or "everyone," of traditional moral theory; they are not what a universal point of view or a view from nowhere could provide.[36] They are, characteristically, actual flesh-and-blood other human beings for whom we have actual feelings and with whom we have real ties.

From the point of view of much feminist theory, the individualistic assumptions of liberal theory and of most standard moral theory are suspect.[37] Even if we were freed from the debilitating aspects of dominating male power to "be ourselves" and to pursue our own interests, we would, as persons, still have ties to other persons, and we would at least in part be constituted by such ties. Such ties would be part of what we inherently are. We are, for instance, the daughter or son of given parents or the mother or father of given children, and we carry with us at least some ties to the racial or ethnic or national group within which we developed into the persons we are.

If we look at the realities of the relation between mothering person (who can be female or male) and child, we can see that what we value in the relation cannot be broken down into individual gains and losses for the individual members in the relation. Nor can it be understood in universalistic terms. Self-development apart from the relation may be much less important than the satisfactory development of the relation. What matters may often be the health, growth, and development of the relation-and-its-members in ways that cannot be understood in the individualistic terms of standard moral theories designed to maximize the satisfaction of self-interest. Neither can the universalistic terms of moral theories grounded in what would be right for "all rational beings" or "everyone" handle what has moral value in the relations between mothering person and child.

Feminism is, of course, not the only locus of criticism of the individualistic and abstractly universalistic features of liberalism and standard moral theory. Marxists and communitarians also see the self as constituted by its social relations. But in their usual form Marxist and communitarian criticisms pay no more attention than liberalism and standard moral theory to the experience of women, to the context of mothering, or to friendship as women experience it.[38] Some nonfeminist criticisms, such as offered by Bernard Williams, of the impartiality required by standard moral theory, stress how a person's identity may be formed by personal projects in ways that do not satisfy universal norms yet ought to be admired. Such views still interpret morality from the point of view of an individual and his project, not a social relationship such as that between mothering person and child. And nonfeminist criticisms in terms of traditional communities and their moral practices, as seen, for instance, in the work of Alasdair MacIntyre, often take traditional gender roles as given or else provide no basis for a radical critique of them.[39] There is no substitute, then, for feminist exploration of the area between ego and universal, as women experience this area, or for the development of a refocused concept of relational self that could be acceptable from a feminist point of view.

Relationships can be evaluated as trusting or mistrustful, mutually considerate or selfish, harmonious or stressful, and so forth. Where trust and consideration are appropriate, which is not always, we can find ways to foster them. But to understand and evaluate relationships and to encourage them to be what they can be at their best require us to look at relationships between actual persons and to see what both standard moral theories and their nonfeminist critics often miss. To be adequate, moral theories must pay attention to the neglected realm of particular others in the actual relationships and actual contexts of women's experience. In doing so, problems of individual self-interest versus universal rules may recede to a region more like background, out-of-focus insolubility, or relative unimportance. The salient problems may then be seen to be how we ought best to guide or maintain or reshape the relationships, both close and more distant, that we have, or might have, with actual other human beings. Particular others can be actual children in need on distant continents or the anticipated children of generations not yet even close to being born. But they are not "all rational beings" or "the greatest number," and the self that is in relationships with particular others and is shaped to a significant degree by such relations is not a self whose ego must be pitted against abstract, universal claims.

The concept of a relational self is evolving within feminist thought. Among the interesting inquiries it is leading to is the work done at the Stone Center at Wellesley College.[40] Psychologists there have posited a self-in-relation theory and have conducted empirical inquiries to try to establish how the female self develops. In working with a theory that a female relational self develops through a mutually empathetic mother-daughter bond, they have been influenced by Jean Baker Miller's reevaluation of women's psychological qualities as strengths rather than weaknesses. In the mid-1970s, Miller identified women's "great desire for affiliation" as one such strength. Nancy Chodorow's *Reproduction of Mothering* has also influenced the work done at the Stone Center.[41] Chodorow argued that a female sense of self is reproduced by a structure of parenting in which mothers are the primary caretakers and that sons and daughters develop differently in relation to a parent of the same sex, or a parent of different sex, as primary caretaker. Daughters come to define themselves as connected to or in relation with others. Sons, in contrast, come to define themselves as separate from or less connected with others. An implication often drawn from Chodorow's work is that parenting should be shared equally by fathers and mothers so that children of either sex can develop with caretakers of both the same and different sex.

In the early 1980s, Carol Gilligan offered her view of the "different voice" with which girls and women express their understanding of moral problems.[42] Like Miller and Chodorow, Gilligan valued tendencies found especially in women to affiliate with others and to interpret their moral responsibilities in terms of their relationships with others. In all, to value autonomy and individual independence over care and concern for relationships was seen as an expression of male bias. Psychologists at the Stone Center have tried to elaborate on and to study a feminist conception of the relational self. In a series of working papers, researchers and clinicians have explored the implications of the conception of the relational self for various issues in women's psychology (for example, power, anger, work inhibitions, violence, eating patterns) and for therapy.

The self as conceptualized in these studies is seen as having both a need for recognition and a need to understand the other, and these needs are seen as compatible. They are created in the context of mother-child interaction and are satisfied in a mutually empathetic relationship. This requires not a loss of self but a relationship of mutuality in which self and other both express an understanding of each other's subjectivity. Both give and take in a way that not only contributes to the satisfaction of their needs as individuals but also affirms the "larger relational unit" they compose.[43] Maintaining this larger relational unit then becomes a goal, and maturity is seen not in terms of individual autonomy but in terms of competence in creating and sustaining relations of empathy and mutual intersubjectivity.

The Stone Center psychologists contend that the goal of mutuality is rarely achieved in adult male-female relationships because of the traditional gender system, which leads men to seek autonomy and power over others and to undervalue the caring and relational connectedness that is expected of women. Women rarely receive the nurturing and empathetic support they provide. Accordingly, these psychologists look to the interaction that occurs in mother-daughter relationships as the best source of insight into the promotion of the healthy relational self. This research provides an example of exploration into a refocused, feminist conception of the self and into empirical questions about its development.

In a quite different field, that of legal theory, a refocused concept of self is leading to reexamination of such concepts as property and autonomy and the role these have played in political theory and constitutional law. For instance, the legal theorist Jennifer Nedelsky questions the dominant imagery in constitutional law and in our conceptions of property: the imagery of a bounded self, a self contained within boundaries and having rights to property inside a wall—rights to exclude others and to exclude government. The boundary metaphor, she argues, obscures and distorts our thinking about human relationships and what is valuable in them: "The boundedness of selves may seem to be a self-evident truth, but I think it is a wrong-headed and destructive way of conceiving of the human creatures law and government are created for." In the domain of the self's relation to the state, the central problem, she argues, is not "maintaining a sphere into which the state cannot penetrate, but fostering autonomy when people are already within the sphere of state control or responsibility." What we can from a feminist perspective think of as the male "separative self" seems on an endless quest for security behind such walls of protection as those of property. Property focuses the quest for security "in ways that are paradigmatic of the efforts of separative selves to protect themselves through boundaries."[44] But surely property is a social construction, not a thing; it requires the involvement of the state to define what it is and to defend it. Only constructive relationships can provide what we seek to assure through the concept of property.

In a discussion of autonomy, Nedelsky recognizes that, of course, feminists are centrally concerned with the freedom and autonomy to live our own lives. But, she argues, to express these concerns we need a language that will also reflect "the equally important feminist precept that any good theorizing will start with people in their social contexts. And the notion of social context must take seriously its constitutive quality; social context cannot simply mean that individuals will, of course, encounter one another." The problem, then, is how to combine the claim that social relations are a large part of what we are with the value of self-determination. Liberalism has been the source of our language of freedom and self-determination, but it lacks the ability to express comprehension of "the reality we know: the centrality of relationships in constituting the self."[45]

In developing a new conception of autonomy that avoids positing self-sufficient and thus highly artificial individuals, Nedelsky points out, first, that "the capacity to find one's own law can develop only in the context of relations with others (both intimate and more broadly social) that nurture this capacity," and, second, that "the 'content' of one's own law is comprehensible only with reference to shared social norms, values, and concepts."[46] She sees the traditional liberal view of the self as implying that the most perfectly autonomous man is the most perfectly isolated, and this she finds pathological.

Instead of developing autonomy through images of walls around one's property, as do the Western liberal tradition and United States constitutional law, Nedelsky suggests that "the most promising model, symbol, or metaphor for autonomy is not property, but childrearing. There we have encapsulated the emergence of autonomy through relationship with others. . . . Interdependence [is] a constant component of autonomy."[47] And she goes on to examine how law and bureaucracies can foster autonomy within relationships between citizen and government. This does not entail extrapolating from intimate relations to large-scale ones; rather, the insights gained from experience with the context of childrearing allow us to recognize the relational aspects of autonomy. In work such as Nedelsky's we can see how feminist reconceptualizations of the self can lead to the rethinking of fundamental concepts even in terrains such as law, thought by many to be quite distant from such disturbances.

To argue for a view of the self as relational does not mean that women need to remain enmeshed in the ties by which we are constituted. Increasingly, women are breaking free from oppressive relationships with parents, with the communities in which we grew up, and with men—relationships in which we defined our selves through the traditional and often stifling expectations of others.[48] These quests for self have often involved wrenching instability and painful insecurity. But the quest has been for a new and more satisfactory relational self, not for the self-sufficient individual of liberal theory. Many might share the concerns expressed by Alison Jaggar that disconnecting ourselves from particular others, as ideals of individual autonomy seem to presuppose we should, might render us incapable of morality, rather than capable of it if, as so many feminists think, "an ineliminable part of morality consists in responding emotionally to particular others."[49]

I have examined three topics on which feminist philosophers and feminists in other fields are thinking anew about where we should start and how we should focus our attention in ethics. Feminist reconceptualizations and recommendations concerning the relation between reason and emotion, the distinction between public and private, and the concept of the self are providing insights that are deeply challenging to standard moral theory. The implications of this work are that we need an almost total reconstruction of social, political, economic, and legal theory in all their traditional forms, as well as a reconstruction of moral theory and practice at more comprehensive, or fundamental, levels.

TRANSFORMATIONS OF SOCIETY

As we look ahead, we can see some of the directions in which feminist rethinking of the basic assumptions and concepts of standard moral theorizing is leading.

One is toward the view that any moral theory likely to be found satisfactory will have to combine aspects of an ethic of care with aspects of an ethic of justice. An ethic of care is indisputably important for a context in which we feel concern for and engage in the actual care of particular others, and we must insist that this context be recognized as one that is as relevant to moral theory as any of the contexts traditionally attended to. The ethics of care can and should be extended far beyond the household, encouraging more sensitive public policies and greater empathy for those distant from us and unlike ourselves. Still, an ethic of care alone may not be able to ground the criticism that is needed of social inequality and global injustice. Aspects of an ethic of justice continue to be needed, and not only for public or global contexts. Overcoming unjust inequalities in the way work is divided between women and men, in the household and elsewhere, requires clarity concerning what justice demands. And ending unjust violence and coercion against women and children in private as well as public spaces calls for an extension of the ethics of justice. At the same time, justice alone is unable to provide a full and nuanced morality of good lives, trusting relationships, successful families, and healthy communities. An ethic we can accept will need to weave together the moral concerns of care and justice.

Another discernible direction in feminist thought concerns the reshaping of society. We try to envision what society might be like if male dominance were to be overcome. Just because the gender structure is so fundamental, transforming it is likely to transform everything else. We wonder what all the different segments of society would be like, and what the relations between them would be like. How they fit together would almost certainly be transformed, as would each domain.

In a feminist society, some segments might remain relatively intact and distinguishable from other segments—a democratic political system, say, with true equality for women at all levels. But if all such segments are infused with feminist values, and if all are embedded in a society hospitable to feminism, then the relative positions of the segments might change in fundamental ways, as well as many of their internal characteristics.

A feminist society would be fundamentally different from a society composed of individuals each pursuing his own interest, especially his own economic interest, and evaluating public institutions by how well they facilitate or contribute to his own advancement—the traditional model of liberal and pluralistic society. It would be different as well from Marxist conceptions of society, with their neglect of the issues of women and the family, and different as well from conservative communitarian views, with their upholding of patriarchy.

Feminist society might be seen as having various relatively independent and distinct segments, with some not traditionally thought of as especially central and influential now being so, and with all such segments embedded in a wider network of social relations characterized by social caring and trust. Certainly the levels of caring and trust appropriate for the relations of all members of society with all others will be different from the levels appropriate for the members of a family with one another. But social relations in what can be thought of as society as a whole will not be characterized by indifference to the well-being of others, or an absence of trust, as they are in many nonfeminist conceptions. What kinds and amounts of caring and trust might characterize the relations of the most general kind in society should be decided on the basis of experience and practice with institutions that have overcome male dominance.

From the point of view of the self-interested head of household, the individual's interest in his own family may be at odds with the wider political and public interest. And aspects of mothering in patriarchal society have contributed to parochialism and racism. But from a satisfactorily worked-out feminist and moral point of view, the picture of the particularistic family in conflict with the good of society is distorted. The postpatriarchal family can express universal emotions and can be guided by universally shared concerns. A content and healthy child eager to learn and to love can elicit general approval. A child whose distress can be prevented or alleviated should elicit universal efforts to deal with the distress and prevent its recurrence. Any feminist society can be expected to cherish new persons, seeing in the face and body of a child both the specialness of a unique person and the universal features of a child's wonder and curiosity and hope. Feminist society should seek to build institutions and practices and a world worthy of each particular child. But no particular child can flourish in isolation; feminist society should reflect the awareness that for each to do well, children must flourish together in an appropriate global environment.

Although feminist society would have democratic political processes, an independent judicial system to handle the recalcitrant, and probably markets to organize some economic activity, these and other institutions would be evaluated in terms of how well they work to achieve feminist goals. And other segments of society might be recognized as far more central in doing so. Cultural expression would continually evaluate imaginative alternatives for consideration. It would provide entertainment not primarily to serve commercial interests or to relieve for a few hours the distress of persons caught in demeaning and exploitative jobs or with no jobs at all but to enrich the lives of respected members of cultural and social communities.

A society organized along feminist lines would be likely to put the proper care and suitable development of all children at the very center of its concerns. Instead of allowing, as so often at present, family policies and arrangements for child care and for the education and health of children to be marginal concerns, vastly less important than military strength and corporate profits, a feminist society might understand the future of children to be its highest priority. Its practices might then be guided by the fundamental considerations—global and local and in between—needed for all children, as for our own, to begin to lead the lives of their hopes.

ACKNOWLEDGMENTS

This essay is a revised and expanded version of chapter 3 of *Feminist Morality: Transforming Culture, Society, and Politics* (Chicago: University of Chicago Press, 1993).

NOTES

1. See, e.g., Cheshire Calhoun, "Justice, Care, Gender Bias," *Journal of Philosophy* 85 (September 1988): 451–63.
2. Lorraine Code, "Second Persons," in *Science, Morality and Feminist Theory*, ed. Marsha Hanen and Kai Nielsen (Calgary: University of Calgary Press, 1987), 360.
3. See, e.g., Sue Rosenberg Zalk and Janice Gordon-Kelter, eds., *Revolutions in Knowledge: Feminism in the Social Sciences* (Boulder, Colo.: Westview Press, 1992).
4. Genevieve Lloyd, *The Man of Reason: "Male" and "Female" in Western Philosophy* (Minneapolis: University of Minnesota Press, 1984), 104. For detailed argument that the association between reason and maleness is fundamental and lasting rather than incidental and expendable, see Phyllis Rooney, "Gendered Reason: Sex Metaphor and Conceptions of Reason," *Hypatia* 6 (Summer 1991): 77–103.
5. Lloyd, *Man of Reason*, 2.
6. Ibid., 3, 4. For a feminist view of how reason and emotion in the search for knowledge might be reevaluated, see Alison M. Jaggar, "Love and Knowledge: Emotion in Feminist Epistemology," *Inquiry* 32 (June 1989): 151–76.
7. David Heyd, *Supererogation: Its Status in Ethical Theory* (New York: Cambridge University Press, 1982), 134.
8. J. O. Urmson, "Saints and Heroes," in *Essays in Moral Philosophy*, ed. A. I. Melden (Seattle: University of Washington Press, 1958), 202. I am indebted to Marcia Baron for pointing out this example and the preceding one in her "Kantian Ethics and Supererogation," *Journal of Philosophy* 84 (May 1987): 237–62.
9. Alan Ryan, "Distrusting Economics," *New York Review of Books*, May 18, 1989, 25–27. For a different treatment, see Jane Mansbridge, ed., *Beyond Self-Interest* (Chicago: University of Chicago Press, 1990).
10. Pioneering works are Joyce Trebilcot, ed., *Mothering: Essays in Feminist Theory* (Totowa, N.J.: Rowman and Allanheld, 1984); and Sara Ruddick, *Maternal Thinking: Toward a Politics of Peace* (Boston: Beacon Press, 1989).
11. Christine Di Stefano, *Configurations of Masculinity: A Feminist Perspective on Modern Political Theory* (Ithaca, N.Y.: Cornell University Press, 1991), 81–83.
12. Thomas Hobbes, *The Citizen: Philosophical Rudiments Concerning Government and Society*, ed. B. Gert (Garden City, N.Y.: Doubleday, 1972), 205.
13. Di Stefano, *Configurations of Masculinity*, 84.
14. Ibid., 92, 104.
15. For examples of relevant passages, see Mary Mahowald, ed., *Philosophy of Woman: Classical to Current Concepts* (Indianapolis: Hackett, 1978); and Linda Bell, ed., *Visions of Women* (Clifton, N.J.: Humana Press, 1985). For discussion, see Susan Moller Okin, *Women in Western Political Thought* (Princeton, N.J.: Princeton University Press, 1979); and Lorenne Clark and Lynda Lange, eds., *The Sexism of Social and Political Theory: Women and Reproduction from Plato to Nietzsche* (Toronto: University of Toronto Press, 1979).
16. Annette Baier, "Trust and Anti-Trust," *Ethics* 96 (January 1986): 231–60; quotation on pages 247–48.
17. Kathryn Pauly Morgan, "Strangers in a Strange Land: Feminists Visit Relativists," in *Perspectives on Relativism*, ed. D. Odegaard and C. Stewart (Toronto: Agathon Press, 1990).

18. Kathryn Pauly Morgan, "Women and Moral Madness," in *Science, Morality and Feminist Theory*, ed. M. Hanen and K. Nielsen, 223.

19. Alison M. Jaggar, "Feminist Ethics: Some Issues for the Nineties," *Journal of Social Philosophy* 20 (Spring–Fall 1989): 91–107; quotation on page 91. See also Jaggar, "Feminist Ethics: Projects, Problems, Prospects," in *Feminist Ethics*, ed. Claudia Card (Lawrence: University Press of Kansas, 1991).

20. One well-argued statement of this position is Barbara Houston, "Rescuing Womanly Virtues: Some Dangers of Moral Reclamation," in *Science, Morality and Feminist Theory*, ed. M. Hanen and K. Nielsen.

21. See Elizabeth V. Spelman, *Inessential Woman: Problems of Exclusion in Feminist Thought* (Boston: Beacon Press, 1988). See also Sarah Lucia Hoagland, *Lesbian Ethics: Toward New Value* (Palo Alto, Calif.: Institute of Lesbian Studies, 1989); and Katie Geneva Cannon, *Black Womanist Ethics* (Atlanta, Ga.: Scholars Press, 1988).

22. Margaret Urban Walker, "Moral Understandings: Alternative 'Epistemology' for a Feminist Ethics," *Hypatia* 4 (Summer 1989): 15–28; quotations on pages 19, 20. See also Iris Marion Young, "Impartiality and the Civic Public," in *Feminism as Critique*, ed. Seyla Benhabib and Drucilla Cornell (Minneapolis: University of Minnesota Press, 1987).

23. See Carol Gilligan, *In a Different Voice: Psychological Theory and Women's Development* (Cambridge, Mass.: Harvard University Press, 1982); and Eva Feder Kittay and Diana T. Meyers, eds., *Women and Moral Theory* (Totowa, N.J.: Rowman and Littlefield, 1987). See also Joan C. Tronto, "Beyond Gender Difference to a Theory of Care," *Signs* 12 (Summer 1987): 644–63.

24. Annette Baier, "The Need for More Than Justice," in *Science, Morality and Feminist Theory*, ed. M. Hanen and K. Nielsen, 55.

25. Morgan, "Strangers in a Strange Land," 2.

26. See Baier, "Trust and Anti-Trust"; and Laurence Thomas, "Trust, Affirmation, and Moral Character: A Critique of Kantian Morality," in *Identity, Character, and Morality: Essays in Moral Psychology*, ed. Owen Flanagan and Amelie Oksenberg Rorty (Cambridge, Mass.: MIT Press, 1990).

27. Susan Sherwin, "Feminist and Medical Ethics: Two Different Approaches to Contextual Ethics," *Hypatia* 4 (Summer 1989): 57–72.

28. See John Rawls, "Justice as Fairness: Political Not Metaphysical," *Philosophy and Public Affairs* 14 (Summer 1985): 251–75; Rawls, "The Priority of Right and Ideas of the Good," *Philosophy and Public Affairs* 17 (Fall 1988): 251–76; Rawls, "The Idea of Overlapping Consensus," *Oxford Journal of Legal Studies* 7 (Spring 1987): 1–25; and Ronald Dworkin, "Liberalism," in *Public and Private Morality*, ed. Stuart Hampshire (Cambridge: Cambridge University Press, 1978). See also Charles Larmore, *Patterns of Moral Complexity* (Cambridge: Cambridge University Press, 1987).

29. A. Baier, "The Need for More Than Justice," 53–54.

30. See Linda Nicholson, *Gender and History: The Limits of Social Theory in the Age of the Family* (New York: Columbia University Press, 1986); and Jean Bethke Elshtain, *Public Man, Private Woman* (Princeton, N.J.: Princeton University Press, 1981). See also Carole Pateman, *The Sexual Contract* (Stanford, Calif.: Stanford University Press, 1988).

31. See Okin, *Women in Western Political Thought*; and Alison M. Jaggar, *Feminist Politics and Human Nature* (Totowa, N.J.: Rowman and Allanheld, 1983).

32. Simone de Beauvoir, *The Second Sex*, trans. H. Parshley (New York: Bantam, 1953).

33. See Sherry B. Ortner "Is Female to Male as Nature Is to Culture?" in *Woman, Culture, and Society*, ed. Michelle Z. Rosaldo and Louise Lamphere (Stanford, Calif.: Stanford University Press, 1974).

34. See Marilyn Friedman, "Feminism and Modern Friendship: Dislocating the Community," *Ethics* 99 (January 1989): 275–90; and Code, "Second Persons."

35. See Seyla Benhabib, "The Generalized and the Concrete Other: The Kohlberg-Gilligan Controversy and Moral Theory," in *Women and Moral Theory*, ed. E. Kittay and D. Meyers; Caroline Whitbeck, "Feminist Ontology: A Different Reality," in *Beyond Domination: New Perspectives on Women and Philosophy*, ed. Carol C. Gould (Totowa, N.J.: Rowman and Allanheld, 1983); Janice Raymond, *A Passion for Friends: Towards a Philosophy of Female Affection* (Boston: Beacon Press, 1986); and Marilyn Friedman, "Individuality without Individualism: Review of Janice Raymond's *A Passion for Friends*," *Hypatia* 3 (Summer 1988): 13.

36. See Thomas Nagel, *The View from Nowhere* (New York: Oxford University Press, 1986). For a feminist critique, see Susan Bordo, "Feminism, Postmodernism, and Gender-Skepticism," in *Feminism/Postmodernism*, ed. Linda J. Nicholson (New York: Routledge, 1990).

37. See Naomi Scheman, "Individualism and the Objects of Psychology," in *Discovering Reality: Feminist Perspectives on Epistemology, Metaphysics, Methodology and Philosophy of Science*, ed. Sandra Harding and Merrill B. Hintikka (Dordrecht: Reidel, 1983).

38. On Marxist theory, see Lydia Sargent, ed., *Women and Revolution* (Boston: South End Press, 1981).

39. Bernard Williams, *Moral Luck: Philosophical Papers 1973–1980* (Cambridge: Cambridge University Press, 1981); Hampshire, *Public and Private Morality*; and Alasdair MacIntyre, *After Virtue: A Study in Moral Theory* (Notre Dame, Ind.: University of Notre Dame Press, 1981). For discussion, see Susan Moller Okin, *Justice, Gender, and the Family* (New York: Basic Books, 1989).

40. On the Stone Center concept of self, see especially the following working papers from the center, in Wellesley, Massachusetts: Jean Baker Miller, "The Development of Women's Sense of Self," Working Paper no. 12 (1984); Janet Surrey, "The 'Self-in-Relation': A Theory of Women's Development," Working Paper no. 13 (1985); and Judith Jordan, "The Meaning of Mutuality," Working Paper no. 23 (1986). For a feminist but critical view of this work, see Marcia Westkott, "Female Relationality and the Idealized Self," *American Journal of Psychoanalysis* 49 (September 1989): 239–50.

41. Jean Baker Miller, *Toward a New Psychology of Women* (Boston: Beacon Press, 1976); Nancy Chodorow, *The Reproduction of Mothering: Psychoanalysis and the Sociology of Gender* (Berkeley and Los Angeles: University of California Press, 1978).

42. Gilligan, *In a Different Voice*.

43. Jordan, "The Meaning of Mutuality," 2.

44. Jennifer Nedelsky, "Law, Boundaries, and the Bounded Self," *Representations* 30 (Spring 1990): 169, 181. See also Martha Minow, *Making All the Difference: Inclusion, Exclusion, and American Law* (Ithaca, N.Y.: Cornell University Press, 1990).

45. Jennifer Nedelsky, "Reconceiving Autonomy: Sources, Thoughts and Possibilities," *Yale Journal of Law and Feminism* 1 (Spring 1989): 9. See also Diana T. Meyers, *Self, Society, and Personal Choice* (New York: Columbia University Press, 1989). For a discussion of why feminist criticisms of the ideal of autonomy need not weaken arguments for women's reproductive rights, see Sally Markowitz, "Abortion and Feminism," *Social Theory and Practice* 16 (Spring 1990): 1–17.

46. Nedelsky, "Reconceiving Autonomy," 11.

47. Ibid., 12. See also Mari J. Matsuda, "Liberal Jurisprudence and Abstracted Visions of Human Nature," *New Mexico Law Review* 16 (Fall 1986): 613–30.

48. See Mary Field Belenky, Blythe McVicker Clinchy, Nancy Rule Goldberger, and Jill Mattuck Tarule, *Women's Ways of Knowing: The Development of Self, Voice, and Mind* (New York: Basic Books, 1986).

49. Jaggar, "Feminist Ethics," 11.

Feminism and Political Theory

SUSAN MOLLER OKIN

WE ARE SOMETIMES said to be living in a postfeminist era. Whether this is supposed to mean that feminism has been vanquished, or that it has lost its point or its urgency because its aims have been largely fulfilled, the claim is false. Women are still second-class citizens, very far from equality with men in a number of crucial respects. In the United States, 85 percent of elected officeholders (and far more at the highest levels) are still male—a situation more or less replicated in other nations, except for most of the Nordic countries. A similar state of underrepresentation of women exists with regard to influential nonelected offices, such as judgeships, and with regard to other positions that command great power or income. At the other end of the spectrum, women are very well represented among the poor: they make up two-thirds of the adult U.S. population living in poverty and are the sole parents of three-fifths of chronically poor families with children. Thus these women's poverty brings with it the poverty of large numbers of children. Women are now working far more outside of the home, but most are also working almost as hard at home as they were before, and many (because of increased separation and divorce) are working even harder both at home and on the job. Doing more wage work is making women more visible but not necessarily more equal. The labor market is still highly segregated by sex, with most "women's work" paying considerably less than most "men's work"—even in cases where the job title is different but the work identical. After small relative gains, full-time working women are now making about 72 percent as much as men.[1] The media tend to focus their stories about women and work on a small minority of highly visible elite professional women, but this tendency distorts the real picture of women's lives.

Most women can see that many of their rights and their theoretical options in life have increased, in part through the efforts of organized feminism. But, in practice, many women are in some ways worse off now than fifteen years ago. Largely because the structure of wage work, using a male model of the worker, has been built on the assumption of women's unpaid services to men at home, women are often faced with a palette of "choices" that are far from satisfactory, and that are not even available to all women. Either they can remain childless (already in practice a highly constrained choice for poor women, and one that is threatened for all heterosexually active women), or they can take on the double burden of family and wage work, or they can become wholly or partially dependent on a man (an option either not desirable or not available to many, including many African-American and older white women, and lesbians). Once a woman has become dependent on a man, either she must stay with him even if abused or exploited or she must face the considerable chance of taking herself and her children into poverty. Given such "choices," many women must wonder what real difference, if any, feminism has been able to make in their lives.

By interpreting and reinterpreting political theories from the near and the distant past, feminist scholars have aimed at a better understanding of why women are still, in the late twentieth century, far from equal with men. We have thus tried to contribute intellectually to the feminist movement that we hope will change that state of affairs. Though I celebrate the great flourishing of feminist political thought that has occurred during the 1980s, I find it discouraging and ironic that this progress has coincided with the deterioration in various respects of the position of many women, with lack of progress toward—and even retrogression from—desirable public policy goals, and with increased unpopularity of the word "feminism" itself. Of course, these things reflected the generally reactionary political climate of the eighties, which can hardly be attributed to what feminist theorists were or were not saying. However, later in this essay, I shall consider whether there is anything feminist political theorists might do differently, to better help the urgent cause of greater justice for women.

Between 1979 and 1981, three books appeared, catalyzing the vigorous development of feminist scholarship in political theory that has occurred in the subsequent period. They were Lorenne Clark and Lynda Lange's collection of essays, *The Sexism of Social and Political Theory*, my *Women in Western Political Thought*, and Jean Bethke Elshtain's *Public Man, Private Woman: Women in Social and Political Thought*.[2] The critical literature that has emerged is now so vast, rich, and varied that it is very rewarding to teach "Gender and Political Theory" both as a feminist analysis of the tradition and as a course in modes of interpretation.[3] Such is the volume and richness of this literature that I cannot even attempt a thorough survey of it here. But I shall discuss, briefly, some of the directions this work has taken and the challenges it presents to what has often come to be referred to as "malestream thought."[4] I shall point to some of what now seems broadly agreed upon, and discuss some of the current central debates. Finally, I shall broach two subjects that seem to me of considerable significance and that may shed light on the irony pointed out earlier: first, the reluctance of many excellent feminist scholars of political theory to spell out, explicitly, the policy implications that follow from their theoretical conclusions; and second, the issue of why feminist interpretation of political theory is still so marginalized, in comparison with feminist work in many other fields.

FEMINIST CHALLENGES

As the earlier scholars were already aware, it has proved to be no simple matter to integrate women into a tradition of theorizing created by, for, and about men.[5] The three books just mentioned primarily emphasized the distortion of women's "nature," their subordination to men, and their exclusion from what was considered political. Political theorists, it seemed, had largely defined women's nature in relation to men's needs. Instead of asking "What are women like?" and "What is women's potential?" they had asked "What are women for?" and "What should women be like in order to fulfill these functions?" The subordination of women to men was often simply assumed, rather than regarded as something that needed to be questioned or argued about, as inequalities among men have frequently been argued about in political theories. Also, the feminist critics found, it had generally been concluded that, because of the functions within the household that were assumed to be women's, they were regarded as unsuited for or unavailable for participation in political life. In making these discoveries, and in exposing the faulty assumptions and inconsistent reasoning that led to such conclusions, the new feminist analysis challenged the pervasive distinctions in political theory between the political and the personal, the public and the private, and embarked on showing how a feminist perspective affected some of the other central concepts of political theory. They also began to address the crucial question of the fundamental respects in which political theories would have to change in order to include women as men's equals. The counterfactual experiment I set up in the conclusion of *Women in Western Political Thought*—speculating about the effects on the theories of Plato, Aristotle, Rousseau, and Mill if they were required to treat women in all respects as men's equals—was a first attempt at this. Clark and Lange took a more pessimistic view, declaring that the tradition of theory was "utterly bankrupt" from a feminist perspective.[6] Both Elshtain and I argued that politics itself and theories about it would be significantly affected by the inclusion of women, but we were less pessimistic about the possibility of such changes. Elshtain wrote: "Women were silenced in part because that which defines them and to which they are inescapably linked—sexuality, natality, the human body—was omitted from political speech. Why? Because politics is in part an elaborate defense against the tug of the private, against the lure of the familial, against evocations of female power. The question . . . is not just what politics is for but what politics has served to defend against."[7] Where Elshtain and I tended to differ—and still do—is over the questions of the extent to which the public-private dichotomy needs to be challenged, and whether the private domestic sphere needs to be regarded as itself in important ways political. Her tendency, as the preceding passage suggests, is to see the latter trend in feminism as a dangerous threat to the preservation of a private sphere that should be kept free from politics. My tendency, already in 1979 but in a more developed way since, has been—in the company of Carole Pateman, Linda Nicholson, and Anne Phillips, among others—to challenge the dichotomization of public and private and the identification of men with the former and women with the latter, though not to advocate obliterating the distinction entirely. The greater emphasis on political theories' very conceptions of the political than on women's exclusion from them per se has developed much further during the 1980s and 1990s. A number of important books have appeared, primarily concerned to expose and analyze the masculinist construction of such theories. These works have stressed the significance of the fact that almost all of political theory has been written by men, and that this has biased the prevailing view of what is important and what is not. Their authors argue that the division of labor between those who have reproduced and nurtured life, on the one hand, and those who have ruled society and determined its meanings, on the other, has had much impact on political thought—and, indeed, on philosophy in general. Great value has been placed on the things traditionally associated with men—on the allegedly transcendent nonphysical realm, on excessive individualism, on reason as all-important, and on the so-called manly virtues—including competitiveness and aggression. At the same time, the realm of things traditionally associated with women—concern with physical needs and nurturance, emotionality, cooperation (with other people and with nature)—have been much more inclined to be denigrated. Prominent works that have contributed to this argument include Mary O'Brien's *Politics of Reproduction*, Genevieve Lloyd's *Man of Reason*, Hanna Pitkin's *Fortune Is a Woman*, Wendy Brown's *Manhood and Politics*, and Carole Pateman's *Sexual Contract*.[8]

The distinction between concentration on the distortion or exclusion of women and on conceptions of the political should not be overdrawn, however, or seen as more than a difference in emphasis. An anecdote will help to clarify this point. In the mid-1980s I submitted a paper critiquing two contemporary theories of justice to a leading journal of moral philosophy. Rejecting it, the journal sent me a reader's report informing me that, while my argument showed that theory X did not allow for the inclusion of women, I had not shown the effect of this on "the theory itself." It is hard to imagine this being said of a political theory that fails to include men. It should be obvious—though apparently it is not—that to point out that a theory in its present form is incapable of including more than half of humanity is to say something important about the theory itself. As even the first critiques of political thought began to show, it is impossible to reconsider theories from a feminist point of view—that is to say, taking women equally into account with men—without already raising issues central to them. There are a number of conclusions that are now widely (though not necessarily universally) accepted by feminist political theorists, no matter what else they disagree about. First and foremost is the indefensibility of the traditional dichotomy between the public and political and the private and personal, with its identification of men primarily with the former and women almost exclusively with the latter. The exclusion from "politics" of all that is domestic, familial, private, personal, and sexual clearly *depends* on the exclusion of women and cannot be sustained once women are included as full and equal partners in either political theory or political practice. This idea was catalyzed by the early radical feminist slogan "The personal is political."[9] While cautiously raised in relation to the canon in earlier works,[10] it was brilliantly laid out in Carole Pateman's 1983 essay "Feminist Critiques of the Public/Private Dichotomy" and has been further developed in many books and articles.[11]

Most feminist theorists, while by no means claiming that privacy has no value, now recognize that the sharp polarization of "public" and "private" that characterizes virtually all of Western political thought has to give way to the recognition that the two are inextricably interconnected. There are many reasons for this. Power (and therefore politics) exists in both domestic and nondomestic life. Moreover, the distribution of power in the two realms is closely connected: on the one hand, law and public opinion have always regulated and influenced what goes on and who dominates whom in the private sphere; on the other hand, the division of labor between the sexes in the private sphere restricts, both practically and psychologically, women's chances for equality in spheres of life outside the household. Other ramifications of the public-private dichotomy include the devaluation or even nonrecognition of women's work in the private sphere—however crucial to species and social survival—and the failure to acknowledge that our gendered selves are *constructed* primarily by our early experiences in that sphere. Finally, the distinction leads to neglect of the great impact that equality between the sexes at home could have on the achievement of justice and democracy in the world outside of the household. As Pateman wrote in 1983, the "dichotomy between the public and the private is . . . ultimately, what the feminist movement is about." As she has more recently argued: "To develop a theory in which women and femininity have an autonomous place means that the private and the public, the social and the political, also have to be completely reconceptualized; in short, it means an end to the long history of sexually particular theory that masquerades as universalism."[12] As I shall suggest later, however, feminist political theorists' challenge to the public-private dichotomy have not often yielded specific suggestions about *how* it should be reconceptualized or transcended.

The second major challenge to the canon of Western political thought is to its various conceptions of human nature. What was put forward in the tradition as "human nature" turns out to be "male human nature," as female nature is defined very differently. The argument I made in *Women in Western Political Thought* about women's nature being defined functionally, relative to the needs of men, has been virtually ignored. But other theorists have reinforced the notion that, as Ellen Kennedy and Susan Mendus put it, "Woman's (supposed) nature [as emotional, passive, and subservient] is used to justify her social status, and then her actual social status is used as a disqualification for any other status." Many feminist scholars have documented and criticized the extent to which women have been regarded as "naturally" emotional, slaves to their passions, passive, subservient, incapable of rational, universalistic, or principled thinking, and so on. Many feminist scholars agree with, and have greatly refined, the general argument that, if what is defined as "human nature" is actually applicable only to men in a gender-structured society where they dominate women and do not share the responsibilities of domestic life, then clearly "human nature" has to be rethought.[13]

As I shall explain, however, responses to this challenge have been extremely varied, and my own differs from those of many other feminists. Some feminists—variously termed "gynocentric," "cultural," or "maternalist" feminists—are in agreement with the assignment of different natures to women and men. They think women's natures, and women's values, have been largely ignored in Western political philosophy, but they think these natures and values *are* distinctly female and need to be introduced as such into the conversation and into political life itself. Poststructuralists, taking this line of argument further, find no conception of "human nature" viable, since none, in their view, can either encompass or transcend the multiple differences—religious, ethnic, racial, sexual—that characterize humankind. Straussian feminist theorists,[14] on the other hand, are inclined to accept both the tradition's definitions of women's nature and its assignment of women to the domestic sphere, but to stress the importance of these female activities for allowing what they perceive as the separate realm of politics to flourish.

By arguing in *Women in Western Political Thought* that men's nature has been understood to signify potential, whereas women's nature has been defined by the functions they have been expected to serve for men, I was already stating quite clearly that I regarded the vast majority of differences—actual and alleged—between women and men as *constructs* that have been created by, and have in turn reinforced, the patriarchal ordering of society. I believed, and continue to believe, that we must maintain the agnosticism professed by John Stuart Mill about the "natures" of men and women. We still have no idea of what the differences between the sexes might be in a society where they were equal, and where a person's sex was not regarded as a characteristic of major social and political salience. I also believe that the only reliable pathway to equality for women is via the restructuring of society—in particular, through the sharing of responsibilities up to now divided between the sexes—with the likely result that what are now considered masculine and feminine characteristics and values would be spread out among the members of both sexes, so that both would be able to share equally in public as well as private life. However, as I shall discuss, by no means all feminist theorists subscribe to this androgynist approach.

A third major challenge to the traditional canon has been issued by feminist political theorists in the 1980s and 1990s. Scholars have taken on the task of rethinking, one by one, many of the basic *concepts* of the Western political tradition, in light of the feminist requirement that women be included, rather than ignored or assumed subordinate to men. I made a few brief early forays into this enterprise,[15] but my allusions to the rethinking of *self-interest* and *democracy* were bare hints of a whole dimension of feminist theorizing that has since been flourishing.

Feminist theorists have argued that if women's experience is to be taken specifically into account, or if we are to aim for an androgynous polity, concepts such as *autonomy, freedom* and *individualism, contract, consent, power, justice,* and *democracy* must be rethought. For example, theorists such as Mary O'Brien and Wendy Brown have shown how, once women are fully included in a theory and their work in the private sphere is no longer assumed and ignored, freedom can no longer be defined, as it tends to be in the canon, as freedom from the physical, from the demands of everyday life, from the body.[16] Nancy Hirschmann and Christine Di Stefano have given accounts of how freedom and autonomy, respectively, must be rethought, if all that women are and do is not to be taken for granted or ignored.[17] Carole Pateman has radically questioned traditional conceptions of contract and consent, and she and Nancy Hirschmann have both shown how our conception of obligation must change if it is to include women's lives.[18] Kathleen Jones has taken a fresh look at authority and Nancy Hartsock at power, both from a feminist point of view and with illuminating results.[19] Jane Mansbridge has recently discussed some of the effects of feminist theorizing on our concepts of democratic community.[20] Iris Marion Young and I have published books about justice, informed by our feminist perspectives.[21] And Anne Phillips has demonstrated the extent to which even the previously most radical notions of democracy are altered and enhanced by taking account of women and gender.[22] This conceptual approach—now the dominant current in feminist political theory—is continuing to reveal how radical the feminist project really is.[23]

Fourth, and finally, the content of the canon of political theory itself has been challenged by feminist scholars. Shanley and Pateman, for example, ask why Wollstonecraft and de Beauvoir are left out of the canon, while Paine and Sartre are usually included. Why are John Stuart Mill's feminist writings so frequently neglected? These feminist works raised questions that other theorists ignored, and Shanley and Pateman suggest that it is the very focus on these questions that explains their omission from the canon: their subject, the relation between the sexes, is still "treated by contemporary political theorists as outside their subject matter."[24] Another way in which the canon is being challenged is that a professor's assigning *Émile* while conveniently omitting book 5 on the education of Sophie, or ignoring the radical arguments about women in book 5 of Plato's *Republic*, is no longer likely to go unremarked upon, as it would have twenty years ago. It is increasingly difficult to *teach* as if feminist theory does not exist, though, as I shall note later, much of current mainstream scholarship proceeds regardless.

THE POLITICAL SIGNIFICANCE OF DIFFERENCE

Though there is much that most feminist scholars of political theory agree about, there are also issues that divide us quite deeply. Both of the most contentious issues have to do with differences. The first I shall discuss concerns the extent, type, and political significance of differences between women and men, and the second concerns differences among women. Both issues of contention tend to cause divisions among feminists as activists as well as theorists, which may partly explain the disparity between the current health of feminist theory (for theory often thrives on contention) and the relative weakness of feminist politics (which is often impeded by it).

Differences between the Sexes

The claim by some feminist theorists, including myself, that women and men should be treated similarly in social policy and law has been the subject of much discussion. Shanley and Pateman have recently summarized the crucial questions: "What exactly is the significance of sexual difference? Do the different natures and capacities of women and men mean that women cannot be citizens? Or does it mean that, if women are citizens, their citizenship will differ in some ways from that of men?"[25] On these questions, feminist interpreters of political theory tend to divide along the same lines as feminist theorists in general, and legal theorists in particular.[26] A renewed debate has arisen about the extent, type, and significance of differences between the sexes. As I shall discuss, some feminists, as well as antifeminists, have been arguing that those who aim for equality between the sexes are trying to turn women into men.[27]

The "equality-difference" debate is complex; there are actually two fairly distinct ways in which differences between the sexes are claimed to have significance for politics and political theory. In an echo of early twentieth-century "social feminism," one major current in feminist thinking has emphasized and urged the greater valuation of such "feminine" characteristics and ways of thinking as connectedness, contextual thinking, and care and concern for others and for the natural world. These feminists argue that political life would be much improved if such "maternal thinking" influenced it. Jean Bethke Elshtain, inspired by the work of Carol Gilligan and Sara Ruddick, has been the principal proponent of this view among political theorists, and Mary Dietz has been its foremost critic.[28]

Dietz, and some other feminist theorists, including Joan Tronto and myself, are skeptical of the emphasis on the political relevance of women's "different voice," for one or more reasons. We question the strength of evidence for differences between the sexes and doubt that such differences as may exist are anything but the outcome of the deep and pervasive gender structuring of our society (particularly female primary parenting and female lack of power). We suggest that similar differences may occur just as much between other dominant and marginalized or subordinate groups, question the extent of applicability of the ethics of care or contextuality to the political realm, or are concerned that emphasizing difference has more potential for reinforcing than for overthrowing sexism.[29] For these reasons, we think, it is important for feminists who stress differences between the sexes to think hard and critically—as only some do now—not only about the evidentiary basis for their claims but also about what might be the origins of the womanly qualities they celebrate. If, as is usually claimed, "women's values," are superior, and could contribute greatly to the quality of our political life— and if they are *not* innately or necessarily female—should we not try to do our utmost to see that these values are also held by men? So long as the ambiguity about the origins of these values persists, conservative forces that aim to keep women "in their place" could not have better ammunition than to be told (especially by feminists) that women are "naturally" well suited to caring for others, or that politics is a "masculinist" activity.[30] As Wendy Brown writes: "One of the most dangerous things we can do to ourselves is to believe, as have no small number of feminists, that women are what men say we are, e.g., naturally maternal or closer to nature, and proceed to develop an alternative politics out of the uninterrogated stereotype."[31]

If, as some suggest, valuable "feminine" qualities and modes of thought result from female biology, it would seem to be a virtually impossible task to achieve the equal or greater weight of these over "masculine" values. For how are women to continue to assume all of the nurturing activities that allegedly both follow from and reinforce their "naturally" superior virtues, and at the same time challenge men's monopoly of power in the outside world? If, on the other hand, characteristics now associated with femininity have little to do with biology but result from female childrearing or from powerlessness, the implications are entirely different.[32] For it is quite likely that, in a society in which sexual difference were far less salient, the qualities and ways of thinking that may now be differentially found in men and women would be much more evenly shared among members of both sexes. Both sexes would also be far better situated to share equally in political power. Thus the end result aimed at by many cultural feminists—the greater valuation, celebration, and influence of "feminine" qualities—would be achieved not only through the increased influence of women but also in the extension of these desirable qualities in men. Rather than trying to "feminize" politics without strongly challenging the current division of labor between the sexes—which seems a hopeless task—I, as well as others, urge policies that would enable and give incentives to women and men to participate fully in both domestic and nondomestic life, with potential results of great consequence.[33]

The other main strand of theory that stresses the significance of sexual difference is less concerned with differences between women's and men's ways of thinking than with their bodily differences, and with the exclusion of women's bodies from mainstream political thought and practices. As I suggested earlier, there is quite general agreement among feminist scholars that the exclusion of and in some cases repugnance for women's bodies, reproductive powers, and sexuality have very much affected construction of "the political" and of what is worthwhile, creative, and "truly human" in Western political thought. But some theorists, influenced by French post-modernism, place particular emphasis on the political significance of women's bodies, arguing that any attempt to include women as men's equals amounts essentially to ignoring women's bodies and trying to transform women into men.[34]

Elizabeth Gross first concludes that most existing political theories could not include women "without major upheavals and transformations." She continues: "Moreover, even if women were incorporated into patriarchal discourse, at best they could only be regarded as variations of a basic humanity. The project of women's equal inclusion meant that only women's *sameness to men*, only women's *humanity* and not their *womanliness* could be discussed."[35] She concludes that though the aspiration toward equality between men and women was "politically and historically necessary," it is "problematic and ultimately impossible." What we should aspire toward, rather, is female *autonomy*—"women's right to political, social, economic and intellectual self-determination."[36] Obviously, I agree with Gross that major transformations are necessary for women to be included as equals in any formerly patriarchal theory or practice, but her argument against equality as the appropriate aim depends on three weak premises. The first is that equality necessarily implies or requires sameness; the second, that it is objectionable to see oneself or be depicted as a "variation of a basic humanity"; and the third, that the "autonomy" right that she advocates is very different from the equality that many contemporary liberal feminists aspire to. All of these assumptions seem to me to be highly questionable.[37]

In her more recent writings (since about 1986), Pateman has focused increasingly on the imperative for feminist theory to take account of the political significance of women's bodies, to press for the inclusion of "women *as women*" rather than as the equals of men. She writes: "When feminism is taken to be nothing more than equality in the sense of women attaining the same status as individuals, workers or citizens as men, it is difficult to find a convincing defense against the long-standing anti-feminist charge that feminists want to turn women into men."[38] But surely this, too, depends on untenable assumptions, especially that those who advocate equality, or "the same status," for women in these respects think that it can be achieved *without* a transformation of the conception of the individual, the worker, and the citizen. But few feminists these days are thus deluded. If women are to be equal workers and citizens with men, then not only must women attain equal pay for comparable work, and equal political representation, but workers and citizens must also be able to be parents, or caregivers for elderly parents, and to have intimate relations in their lives with others who are also workers and citizens. It also requires that the responsibilities of the previously "nonpolitical" private sphere be shared. These all-too-necessary changes, which require political action as well as changes in the behavior of individual women and men, seem, however, to have far less to do with men's and women's different bodies than with overcoming past and current divisions of labor between the sexes, and the resultant power of men over women.

It is far from clear, as Pateman acknowledges, what making a place for "women *as women*" in the political order, or in political theory, really means. One of the examples that she brings up helps to illustrate her approach, as well as to demonstrate its potential pitfalls. For good reason, she mentions pregnancy as something that is "absurd" to talk about in gender-neutral language, as was clearly demonstrated in some decisions of the U.S. Supreme Court in the 1970s. But sometimes, in the all-too-imperfect world of politics, a gender-neutral approach to reproductive differences can be combined with attention to pregnancy, precisely to promote women's equality with men. In 1987 the Court upheld as nondiscriminatory (against men) a law mandating pregnancy and childbirth leave in a state that did not mandate general disability leave. "By 'taking pregnancy into account,'" the Court reasoned, the statute "allows women, as well as men, to have families without losing their jobs."[39] This "taking pregnancy into account" seems like a very good example of what Pateman may mean by the inclusion of women as women, and of the recognition of the political significance of women's bodies. But, as the Court's subsequent wording makes clear, its purpose in doing this, was to achieve *equality*—meaning the same status as workers and parents—for women and men.

However, as we can see from a brief glance at both past and present policies and legal decisions, taking pregnancy into account has generally worked against the interests of women. It has been used to exclude them from certain jobs, from certain work schedules, from disability and insurance plans, and so on. Thus, unless taking pregnancy into account is done specifically for the purpose of promoting equality between the sexes, it—like other attention to differences between the sexes—should be regarded as suspect.

In my view, the clearest insights on the subject of equality and sexual difference have come from Catharine MacKinnon, radical feminist legal theorist. In a hard-hitting passage that shares some of the concerns of the "women as women" theorists discussed earlier, she does not shrink from demanding equality for women through challenging the many social structures that have been established in the context of male dominance. MacKinnon writes:

> Virtually every quality that distinguishes men from women is already affirmatively compensated in this society. Men's physiology defines most sports, their needs define auto and health insurance coverage, their socially designed biographies define workplace expectations and successful career patterns, their perspectives and concerns define quality in scholarship, their experiences and obsessions define

merit, their objectification of life defines art, their military service defines citizenship, their presence defines family, their inability to get along with each other—their wars and rulerships—defines history, their image defines god, and their genitals define sex. For each of their differences from women, what amounts to an affirmative action plan is in effect, otherwise known as the structure and values of American society.[40]

While a bit hyperbolic in parts, this is a brilliant view of the current significance of sexual difference. Yet bodily differences do not loom large in it, except in the first and last examples; neither does it depend on any notion of "essentially" female values or modes of thinking. MacKinnon does not deny that there are, at present, many differences between men and women, but she interprets them as resulting from male domination: "Can you imagine elevating one half of a population and denigrating the other half," she asks, "and producing a population in which everyone is the same?"[41] Thus nearly all of the respects in which men are now favored could be changed drastically by altering the division of labor between the sexes, eradicating workplace sex discrimination, valuing traditionally female work, and thereby ending women's total or partial economic dependence on men. Men would then no longer have the power to keep any of the other aspects of their "affirmative action plan" in place.

Differences among Women

The second controversy about difference within feminism originated as a dispute within feminist politics as early as 1970 and was only later debated among theorists. Early in second-wave feminism, black, working-class, and lesbian women began to protest that the movement, dominated by white, middle-class, heterosexual women, excluded them and their concerns.[42] Later, theorists—primarily women of color, lesbians, and those strongly influenced by postmodern currents in literary theory and philosophy—entered the debate against what came to be known as "essentialism." It is essentialist, they claimed, to talk about women, the problems of women, and especially the problems of "women as such."[43] Gender is therefore a problematic category, unless always qualified by and seen in the context of race, class, ethnicity, religion, and other such differences. While the work of bell hooks, Audre Lorde, Angela Harris, and others has been influential in this critique, Elizabeth V. Spelman has applied it most specifically to feminist political theory.[44]

Spelman has argued that most feminist interpretations commit, against other women, exclusionary practices similar to those they find committed against themselves in mainstream political thought: "There are startling parallels," she says, "between what feminists find disappointing and insulting in Western philosophical thought and what many women have found troubling in much of Western feminism."[45] It is not enough to simply express the intention of including all women in one's critique of a theory, for "even if we say all women are oppressed by sexism we cannot automatically conclude that the sexism all women experience is the same. We have to understand what one's oppression 'as a woman' means in each case."[46] Forms of sexist oppression are different, and unless the "manyness" of women and the differences among them are taken into account, the critiques authored by feminists are almost as vulnerable to charges of exclusion as are the mainstream theories we critique.

What Spelman has to say is important, and has to be carefully attended to. For example, it is true that feminist interpreters of political theory have focused on the women of the guardian class in reading Plato and on free women in reading Aristotle. In the first case, though, this is partly because much had already been written about Plato's class hierarchy, but very little about his radical proposals about the guardian women, and partly because his tacit assumptions about women in the manual worker class are quite ordinary, whereas his explicit proposals about the guardian women are quite extraordinary. In the case of Aristotle, since he said (to my knowledge) nothing specific about female slaves, we can only speculate whether he would have regarded them as primarily slaves or primarily women. I suspect the former, since he regarded slaves as less rational and therefore less human than women. To some extent, these chapters of Spelman's book come across as critiques of feminist analyses for not being as focused on class, or slave status, or race, as on gender—but this is not what they set out to do.[47] Her main point, however, is important: one should not, in the very act of critiquing a theory for excluding women, render many women invisible because they do not fit some unstated class, race, sexual orientation, or other criterion for inclusion.

Nevertheless, there seem to me to be two related flaws in Spelman's general antiessentialist argument. One is the claim that, unless a feminist theorist perceives gender identity as intrinsically bound up with class, race, or other aspects of identity, she ignores the effects of these other differences altogether. Spelman writes: "If gender were isolatable from other aspects of identity, if sexism were isolatable from other forms of oppression, then what would be true about the relation between any man and woman would be true about the relation between any other man and any other woman."[48] But this simply does not follow. One can argue that sexism is a discrete form of oppression, many of whose effects are felt by women regardless of race or class, without at all subscribing to the view that race or class oppression is insignificant. One can insist, for example, on the significant difference between the relation and the power differential between a wealthy white woman and a wealthy white man, and that between the same woman and a poor black man.

The second flaw is that, in insisting on difference as primary and gender as a category that is meaningful only once differences are taken into account, Spelman misassigns the burden of proof. She asserts: "Precisely insofar as a discussion of gender and gender relations is really, even if obscurely, about a particular group of women and their relation to a particular group of men, it is unlikely to be applicable to any other group of women."[49] But why should this be so? Surely, to be convincing, the antiessentialist critic needs to demonstrate this. She needs to show that, and how, the theory accused of essentialism omits or distorts the experiences of women other than those few the theorist is allegedly focused on (just as feminist theorists have been showing that, and how, mainstream theory, focused on men, has omitted or distorted the experience of women). At one point, Spelman refers to recent research on different women that has been done in many fields, saying that "we have to investigate different women's lives and see what they have in common."[50] Trained as a philosopher, however, she does not engage in this enterprise. When she occasionally gives examples, they are most often about white slave owners' lives and black slave women—examples that seem less relevant to contemporary women than some others she might choose. Like that of many others influenced by postmodernism, Spelman's work, while challenging and deserving of attention, is long on theory and short on evidence.[51] Consistent with her assumption that the burden of proof is on the person who claims that women have anything in common, she tends to substitute the cry "Women are all different" for evidence that or how they are.[52] Partly because of their firmer empirical grounding in evidence about differences between women, I find the antiessentialist arguments of those in some other fields—such as Angela Harris, bell hooks, and Audre Lorde—more convincing.[53]

There are two important things to be learned from those who object that feminists have ignored differences among women. One has to be very careful not to make false generalizations, and to take account of such differences of class, race, sexual orientation, religion, and so on, as are relevant to the argument one is making. It should not be difficult to be aware that black women have hardly been oppressed by being put on pedestals, that lesbian women are oppressed in ways other than by being subordinates in traditional families, and that poor single mothers or single, childless career women experience different forms of inequality from those experienced by middle-class women in traditional marriages. But, unfortunately, most people have a tendency to write partly, even if unconsciously, from their own experiences. This is one of the main reasons it is so important for feminist theory and feminist politics to include a great variety of voices. The other thing we can learn, however, is not from but in reaction to antiessentialist claims: not to jump to the conclusions that gender is simply one among many equally important differences, that differences among women are as or even more important than similarities, and that to generalize about women is always, and necessarily, misleading and/or oppressive to some. This is an important lesson, both for reasons of intellectual integrity and because a certain skepticism about antiessentialism will help to preserve the political potential of feminism from unnecessary fragmentation.

The Tentativeness of Feminist Scholars' Recommendations

In contrast to the power of their critiques of the tradition of political thought, most feminist scholars have been surprisingly tentative or indirect in their conclusions and proposals about "what is to be done." This is not surprising in one sense, since political theorists in general seldom suggest solutions to the problems they analyze and are even less prone to discuss ways of implementing solutions. It is surprising in another sense, though, since the feminist critique of the tradition of political theory grew out of an actual political movement. One might therefore expect its proponents to be concerned with changing the world, as well as criticizing theories about it. I shall offer some examples to show that this is very often not the case.

While Wendy Brown has strongly critiqued the masculine conception of politics that pervades political thought and has expressed her dissent from cultural feminist alternatives, she acknowledges that her own ideas of a "feminist politics of freedom" are "far from complete." We need both to value "the production and reproduction of life," she says, and to strive toward other things, "such that we are not individually divided creatures and are not impelled to divide the species into those who sustain life and those who live 'freely' by transcending life."[54] But how? She offers two explicit suggestions. One—that we try to end our attempts to exploit and dominate external nature—is clear and admirable. The other, however, is much less clear and raises more questions than it answers. She says that we must get away from domination and unfreedom in our intimate relations—certainly also an admirable aim. But seeing the high continuing rate of marriage as a sign of how "terrified of freedom in the 'personal sphere'" we really are, she seems to equate greater freedom in personal relationships with eschewing marriage.[55] What may be meant here, although it is not clear, is an endorsement of lesbian relationships, or at least the ending of heterosexist privilege. Doing away with marriage, however, is more likely to harm than to help heterosexual women, unless along with it comes greater responsibility on the part of men and/or government for raising the children who are likely to result from the vast majority of the theoretically "free" sexual relationships. Brown is clearly as much concerned with equality as she is with freedom, and she looks forward to a time when we "construct both gender and politics in ways far more compatible with justice, with life in the largest sense of the word, and above all, with the rich possibilities contained in being human together."[56] But she refers only vaguely to the social supports that are needed if women are to have either freedom or equality in practice. She seems to miss the point of some feminists' demand that reproductive work be organized and revalued, interpreting it to mean that they overvalue motherhood.[57] Contrary to what she implies, it is precisely because such feminists, while valuing nurturing work, consider that being only a mother is *not* enough for most women that they want it reorganized and shared by men.

Jean Bethke Elshtain's conclusion to *Public Man, Private Woman* is similarly vague when it comes to suggestions for change. She calls for "the redemption of everyday life."[58] She severely and at times unfairly criticizes those whom she takes to be advocating the abolition of the family and the replacement of it by communal child rearing, and she takes other feminist theorists to task for having no political analysis.[59] But such political analysis as is included in her own conclusion is highly elusive. She strongly defends the family as the best, intimate context for child rearing and says that we must "articulate a *particular ideal* of family life that does not repeat the earlier terms of female oppression and exploitation."[60] However, while alluding briefly to the need for a transformation of men so as to make them recognize the imperatives of responsibility to which she sees women as committed, she provides no political vision of what might help us to achieve such a transformation.[61] Specifically, she issues no call for policies that would make nurturing work compatible with economic self-sufficiency and facilitate the sharing of what are now male and female roles.

Pateman's recommendations at the end of *The Sexual Contract* are also hard to pin down, though for very different reasons. Concluding that "the individual" of contract theory is a male figure, whose political standing depends centrally on the subordination of women, she critiques feminism that "argue[s] for the elimination of nature, biology, sex in favor of the 'individual'" for "play[ing] the modern patriarchal game."[62] But rather than asking how we might reconstruct society, particularly its domestic sphere, in such a way that women can also become individuals, Pateman concludes that "as embodied feminine beings we can never be 'individuals' in the same sense as men."[63] While she acknowledges that "what men and women are, and how relations between them are structured, depends on a good deal more than their natural physiology and biology,"[64] her recent focus is clearly on women's bodily differences and their political significance. I think the very elusiveness of her concluding remarks in *The Sexual Contract* results from this focus and from her awareness that to stress women's bodily differences from men is—though this is diametrically opposed to her stated intention—to evoke the possibility of a politics of reaction against feminism. Also, as she says elsewhere, "It is still far from clear exactly what form a feminist theory of the (feminine) body and the body politic will take."[65]

Finally, Kennedy and Mendus state in their introductory discussion that "modern feminists . . . see pregnancy, childrearing and domesticity generally as the barriers to political equality. For them, emancipation can never be anything other than a sham as long as women are identified with their private work of childrearing."[66] As they point out, several of the contributors to their volume remark upon the incompatibility of urging political equality for women and men while recognizing wide differences in their social roles. However, when the editors approach the question "What lesson can feminism learn from [Western] philosophers?" they are much less bold and clear than their initial statements might lead one to expect. After sketching out some of the alternative conclusions that are being drawn from scrutiny of the tradition, they make the very good point that which of these versions of a feminist philosophy and politics is appropriate depends on the situation of women in different political and cultural contexts. Women who lack basic rights, for example, need these before they can afford the luxury of rejecting the realm of the political, which other women might wish to do. Kennedy and Mendus end their discussion by repeating the old point that the "avoidable mistake" throughout Western political philosophy is the reinforcement of a division of labor between those who sustain life and those whose opinions are respected and acted upon. But they have nothing to say about why the "mistake" continues to be made or about what, specifically, we should do to rectify it.

Why do excellent critical theories so often yield such thin or vague suggestions about the practical changes that are needed if the long-standing subordination of women is to end? Perhaps one part of the reason is that the answer is complex, given the diversity of women. But surely there are some policies that would contribute to the greater equality of almost all women. In part, I think the reluctance to follow through is the result of ambivalence on the part of many female theorists, in spite of their deep desires for women's equality, when they contemplate the diminution or even disappearance of gender. Even though "the feminine" has developed in the context of domination, they have an attachment to it, *as* feminine, that is hard to break. Theorists (like Brown) who are sharply aware that "the feminine" has developed in the context of domination are still unwilling to see sexual difference as "a mere or minor biological 'fact,'" or to see "any reason to wish that it could be."[67] Similarly, though Elshtain, in her concluding chapter of *Public Man, Private Woman*, occasionally suggests sharing the special responsibilities and virtues of women with men, she seems not to be so sure of this that she is willing to make concrete suggestions about how it might be achieved. The reason in Pateman's case seems different. Her critique of mainstream theory is such that central concepts, such as "the individual" and "contract" are regarded not just as in need of reformulation or revision but as highly suspect, if not worthless. The vagueness of her concluding suggestions indicates less an attachment to "femininity" than perhaps a sense that one needs to start all over again and that it is not yet clear where or how to start.[68] Pateman may think that women, with the help of feminist theorists, will be able to formulate the answers—to come up with entirely new ways for people to relate to each other—but she has given little hint yet of what such a new set of social relationships might be like.

Among the very few feminist interpreters of political theory who are unambivalent about aiming for the elimination of gender and have ventured some proposals about how we might realize it are Anne Phillips and myself.[69] Phillips, in *Engendering Democracy*, argues strongly that political democracy cannot be complete without democracy and equality in the household. She sees this as crucial both as a means to an end (furthering the larger democracy) and as an end in itself, because of the great effects of the inequalities of sexual power on women's lives. In the relative short term, however, because sexual difference (and therefore, in effect, women) have been excluded from or subordinated within previous democratic theories—even radical ones—she is "in this sense, and to this extent, . . . thoroughly in sympathy with those who highlight sexual difference." Thus, "those who have been previously subordinated, marginalized or silenced need the security of a guaranteed voice and, in the transitional period to a full and equal citizenship, democracies must act to redress the imbalance that centuries of oppression have wrought."[70] She regards this transitional (though not too short-term) measure as a form of affirmative action involving, specifically, various mechanisms to ensure the proportional political representation of women. But eventually, beyond our lifetimes, she looks forward to a future

> when people are no longer defined through their nature as women or men. In this future scenario, the distinction between public and private spheres would have lost its gendered quality. Men and women would move equally between the responsibilities of household and employment, would share equally in bringing up children and caring for parents, would vary as individuals rather than sexes in their priorities or experience, and be equally attracted to (or repulsed by!) a political life. In such a context, the notion of the citizen could begin to assume its full meaning, and people could participate as equals in deciding their common goals.[71]

Unlike almost all other feminist critics of mainstream political theory, moreover, Phillips argues about the specific changes—in the household, the workplace, and the polity—on which a truly nonsexist democracy must be founded.[72] Such is the current emphasis on sexual difference, however, that even Phillips worries that her proposal that we "transcend" difference "slide[s] towards confirming women's difference as the problem, rather than taking it as given and calling on the theories and politics to adjust."[73] I do not understand this concern—which Phillips calls "a major political conundrum"—except as a sign that she is thinking, as she writes, of the postmodernist or gynocentric feminist looking over her shoulder. For wanting the sociopolitical changes that will enable us to transcend the difference between the sexes is no more a sign that one sees women's difference from men as a problem than that one sees men's difference from women as a problem. It is, however, a sign of seeing socially created and reinforced difference as a problem, and of wanting to minimize the differences between the sexes per se, so as to enable persons of both sexes to be as free as possible to develop their own characteristics and ways of thinking. Especially since the differences that constitute gender have developed in the context of domination and oppression, this seems to me to be an eminently reasonable aspiration.

In *Justice, Gender, and the Family*, in the context of critiquing contemporary theories of justice from a feminist point of view, I have expanded the general conclusions I had reached a decade earlier. I reaffirm the position that women cannot be equal citizens until there is a radical rethinking of the public and domestic spheres of life and the relationship between the two, and until public policies both facilitate and encourage the sharing of the work previously assigned on the basis of sex. I argue, as does Phillips, that a just, democratic society needs to have justice and equity in the households that are at its foundation. I also argue that, so long as some people still organize their lives along the lines of gender, those made vulnerable by economic dependence must be protected, both within their gendered relationships and in the event of their dissolution. The attainment of justice within the broader social and political spheres, I argue, is crucially connected with the achievement of justice in families.

The more general tendency I have noted previously—the avoidance by feminist scholars of political thought of explicit programmatic proposals—leads me to think that, perhaps, one of the more urgent matters on the agenda of such theorists should be to reconsider the relationship of political theory to political practice. Perhaps the current feminist rethinking of central concepts of political thought is a step toward a radical rethinking of the whole purpose of the enterprise. Neither the "eternal truths" view of the history of political thought, nor the idea that the great books follow each other in some sort of logical progression, nor the conviction that each theory is intelligible within and of relevance to only its own very specific historical context seems to make much sense from a feminist point of view.[74] It is clearly impossible to regard either the justifications of the exclusion and subordination of women or the distortions of their "nature" as true, much less eternally so. On the other hand, the similarities between many of the rationalizations made about women hundreds and even thousands of years ago and the kinds of arguments that are still made make it impossible to conclude, as Quentin Skinner has, that the study of political thought cannot help us to solve contemporary problems, or even to understand the present—except by showing us how entirely different it is from the past.[75] As Mary Dietz has recently written, "Feminism—at least in its academic guise—needs a calling back to politics."[76] And perhaps the first step is to think again about the political role of political theory.

FEMINIST SCHOLARSHIP: STILL ON THE FRINGES?

Despite the cautiousness of most feminist scholars of political thought in drawing policy conclusions from their findings, feminist work is still quite marginalized within the subfield of political theory. As Anne Phillips says: "Despite a growing weight of feminist critique, political theory has remained largely impervious to . . . [the] contention . . . that gender challenges all our political perspectives, forcing us to examine each position and concept afresh."[77] Carole Pateman has recently concluded that "most current work in political theory repeats the standard readings of the texts, ignores the copious empirical evidence collected by feminist investigators about

women's positions in all areas of social and political life and shows no interest in the broader body of feminist theory."[78] Unfortunately, both statements are all too justified.

During the 1980s, while Reaganism and Thatcherism ruled the Anglo-
American world and the situation of women deteriorated in many respects,
a largely pointless debate between liberalism and communitarianism (in
which almost all participants neglected gender) took center stage in political
theory.[79] While varieties of feminist theory (especially postmodernist varieties) were becoming extremely influential in some disciplines, such as literary
criticism, and at least accepted and noticed in others, like history, feminist
political theory has, by comparison, remained on the fringes. One of the
most obvious indicators of this marginalization is that many interpretations
of political theories still take no account of the feminist objections that have
been raised about the theories. Two obvious recent examples are Leslie
Green's and Don Herzog's books on social contract theory, which fail to pay
attention to the fact that all the contract theorists leave women out of their
respective contracts.[80] Neither mentions the feminist arguments of Carole
Pateman's *Problem of Political Obligation* (though Green refers to the book
in other contexts) or any of the other feminist literature on the contract
theorists.[81] Those works of political theory, whether of interpretation or of
original argument, that constitute exceptions to this rule are so rare that they
are frequently cited as such by appreciative feminists—in democratic theory,
for example, Philip Green's *Retrieving Democracy: In Search of Civic
Equality* and David Held's *Models of Democracy*. Will Kymlicka's *Contemporary Political Philosophy: An Introduction* is another welcome exception,
treating feminism as a major current in recent political thought.[82]

Why is this? Why is feminist political theory still so marginalized? Pateman has suggested persuasively that it is at least partly because feminist
arguments call for the redefinition of the fundamental terms of the debate—
in particular, what is to be regarded as political: "to engage with feminist
criticisms political theorists have to be willing to think again about fundamental premises of their arguments."[83] I agree. I think there is a strong belief
within male-dominated academia that if something—a paper, a book, a
course—is about gender, it is "only" about women, and not about politics,
and can therefore be readily ignored. A male colleague asked me, shortly
before the publication of *Women in Western Political Thought*, how, "given
that it's about women, it could be of any *real, intellectual* interest." Students, too, sometimes complain when feminist scholar-teachers spend time
in general political theory courses addressing the issue of whether the theory
being discussed includes women, or could include women, and if not, why
not. "This isn't a women's studies course, it's a political science course,"
some have said, "so why do you talk about women?"

I think there is more to the problem than this rather drastic misunderstanding, however. Clearly, so does Pateman. She writes elsewhere that the
radicalness of feminist questions touches "on some emotions, interests, and

privileges very different from those disturbed by arguments about class."[84] The most important reason for the marginalizing of feminist theory, in this view, is less a matter of labels than that those in power do not like its messages at all. Most feminist political theory is, at least by implication, *so political*, so radical, that it is not at all to the liking of most of the men (or the occasional strongly male-identified woman) who have largely dominated the field.[85]

It has been very convenient, to put it mildly, for men in general (and not just political theorists!) to dominate women—to be in a position to exploit our labor, to devalue what we do, and to exclude us from positions of power from which we might change all this. Mainstream political theories have served an important ideological function by justifying or obscuring male domination. Feminist political theory—far more directly than the versions of feminist theory prevalent in some other disciplines—challenges those who accept the theories that have helped to sustain patriarchal practices to confront the high probability that they will find them, in important respects, devoid of intellectual or ethical legitimacy. Given that most men have benefited and many continue to benefit from such practices, this is a tough, and often a deeply personal, challenge. Only rarely do we see it taken up explicitly, as by Allan Bloom, who defends the Rousseauian sexual order as a "natural" and necessary injustice, and blames contemporary feminists for destroying the family by claiming a degree of equality that men, in his opinion, can only find intolerable.[86] More often, the challenge is dealt with by ignoring or marginalizing feminists' arguments. The message of most feminist political theory—especially its most androgynist and its most radical versions—is unwelcome; thus its messengers have often not been welcomed.

Recently, this has begun to change in several significant respects, at least in the United States. Partly because of pressure from feminist studies or women's studies programs, but sometimes on their own initiative, departments of political science and philosophy in many universities and colleges have come to perceive feminist political theory as a subfield that should be taught and should have scholarly representation within their walls. Even this, though, despite being a substantial improvement, can constitute marginalization, if it is understood to relieve the pressure on other members of the relevant department to take up the challenges of feminist theory in their own teaching and research. Another indication that feminist political theory is becoming less marginalized is that, as well as appearing on specifically feminist panels at professional meetings, feminist scholars are increasingly present—whether giving papers or serving as commentators—on a wide variety of panels.[87] Also, books of essays on general issues in political theory are increasingly including at least one feminist essay.[88]

If these trends continue, it will become more and more difficult for scholars to ignore feminist perspectives and findings. Feminist political theory is here to stay, and its impact on the rest of political theory is very likely to grow. To the extent that we can drop our caution and refuse to let internal disagreements paralyze us, we should be able to spell out the policy implications of our theoretical conclusions, loudly and clearly. If we can succeed in doing this, we may well not only help to revitalize political theory but, in addition, provide part of the theoretical basis for the next wave of feminism.

ACKNOWLEDGMENTS

This chapter is adapted from the afterword to the second edition of my *Women in Western Political Thought* (Princeton, N.J.: Princeton University Press, 1992). I am grateful to Robert O. Keohane, Janet Kourany, Jane Mansbridge, Mary L. Shanley, and Joan Tronto, who offered very helpful suggestions on earlier versions.

NOTES

1. For an excellent account of the present status of women and an analysis of why sex inequality is so widely not perceived as a problem, see Deborah L. Rhode, *Speaking of Sex: The Denial of Gender Inequality* (Cambridge, Mass.: Harvard University Press, 1997). On women's increased work and poverty, see Barbara R. Bergmann, *The Economic Emergence of Women* (New York: Basic Books, 1986), and Victor Fuchs, *Women's Quest for Economic Equality* (Cambridge, Mass.: Harvard University Press, 1988).

2. Lorenne Clark and Lynda Lange, *The Sexism of Social and Political Theory* (Toronto: University of Toronto Press, 1979); Susan Moller Okin, *Women in Western Political Thought* (Princeton, N.J.: Princeton University Press, 1979); Jean Bethke Elshtain, *Public Man, Private Woman* (Princeton, N.J.: Princeton University Press, 1981).

3. For some clear examples of the variance in interpretations, compare: on Aristotle, chapter 4 of *Women in Western Political Thought* with chapter 4 of Arlene W. Saxonhouse, *Women in the History of Political Thought: Ancient Greece to Machiavelli* (New York: Praeger, 1985); on Locke, Melissa Butler, "Early Liberal Roots of Feminism: John Locke and the Attack on Patriarchy," *American Political Science Review* 72 (1978): 135–50, with Lorenne Clark, "Women and Locke: Who Owns the Apples in the Garden of Eden?" in Clark and Lange, eds., *The Sexism of Social and Political Theory*. Saxonhouse's chapter and Butler's article both appear, somewhat abridged, in Mary L. Shanley and Carole Pateman, *Feminist Interpretations and Political Theory* (University Park, Pa.: Pennsylvania State University Press, 1991). Since this essay was written, a series entitled *Re-Reading the Canon* has begun to be published by Pennsylvania State University Press, under the general editorship of Nancy Tuana. Volumes published so far include: Nancy Tuana, ed., *Feminist Interpretations of Plato* (1994); Margaret A. Simons, ed., *Feminist Interpretations of Simone de Beauvoir* (1995); and Bonnie Honig, ed., *Feminist Interpretations of Hannah Arendt* (1995).

4. This phrase was coined by Mary O'Brien in *The Politics of Reproduction* (London: Routledge and Kegan Paul, 1981).

5. For example, see Okin, *Women in Western Political Thought*, pp. 10, 12, 286. See also Carole Pateman's introduction to Carole Pateman and Elizabeth Gross, eds.,

Feminist Challenges: Social and Political Theory (Boston: Northeastern University Press, 1987), pp. 3–4; Pateman, *The Sexual Contract* (Stanford, Calif.: Stanford University Press, 1988), esp. pp. 1–2, 13–14; Pateman, *The Disorder of Women: Democracy, Feminism and Political Theory* (Stanford, Calif.: Stanford University Press, 1989); see also Pateman and Shanley's introduction to *Feminist Interpretations*, pp. 1–2. I think Elizabeth Gross is wrong in saying that, at first, feminist interpreters "rejected . . . [some] patriarchal discourses . . . outright" and thought others acceptable with minor adjustments" ("Conclusion: What Is Feminist Theory?" in *Feminist Challenges*, p. 191). It is not clear who is supposed to have accepted this dichotomization.

6. *The Sexism of Social and Political Theory*, p. xvii. However, Lange at least has revised this view. See her "Rousseau and Modern Feminism," in Shanley and Pateman, *Feminist Interpretations*, pp. 95–111.

7. *Public Man, Private Woman*, pp. 15–16.

8. Genevieve Lloyd, *The man of Reason* (Minneapolis: University of Minnesota Press, 1984); Hanna Fenichel Pitkin, *Fortune Is a Woman* (Berkeley: University of California Press, 1984); Wendy Brown, *Manhood and Politics* (Totowa, N.J.: Rowman and Littlefield, 1988).

9. For a brief summary of the origins of this idea see Ellen Willis, "Introduction," in Alice Echols, *Daring to Be Bad: Radical Feminism in America (1967–1975)* (Minneapolis: University of Minnesota Press, 1989), pp. 16–18.

10. For example, Okin, *Women in Western Political Thought*, and "Women and the Making of the Sentimental Family," *Philosophy and Public Affairs* 11 (1982): 65–88; see also Lange, *The Sexism of Social and Political Theory*; and Elshtain, *Public Man, Private Woman*.

11. Carole Pateman, "Feminist Critiques of the Public/Private Dichotomy," in Stanley Benn and Gerald Gaus, eds., *Private and Public in Social Life* (London: Croom Helm, 1983), and reprinted in *The Disorder of Women*; Olsen, "The Family and the Market: A Study of Ideology and Legal Reform," *Harvard Law Review* 96 (1983): 1497–1578; Olsen, "The Politics of Family Law," *Journal of Law and Inequality* 2 (1984): 1–19; Olsen, "The Myth of State Intervention in the Family," *University of Michigan Journal of Law Reform* 18 (1985): 835–64. See also Pateman's introductions to *Feminist Challenges* and *The Disorder of Women*; Linda Nicholson, *Gender and History* (New York: Columbia University Press, 1986); Anita Allen, *Uneasy Access: Privacy for Women in a Free Society* (Totowa, N.J.: Rowman and Allanheld, 1988); Ellen Kennedy and Susan Mendus, *Introduction to Women in Western Political Philosophy: Kant to Nietzsche* (Brighton: Wheatsheaf, 1987); Okin, "Gender, the Public and the Private," in David Held, ed., *Political Theory Today* (Cambridge: Polity Press, 1991); Okin, "Humanist Liberalism," in Nancy Rosenblum, ed., *Liberalism and the Moral Life* (Cambridge, Mass.: Harvard University Press, 1989); Okin, *Justice, Gender and the Family* (New York: Basic Books, 1989), chap. 6; Anne Phillips, *Engendering Democracy* (University Park: Pennsylvania State University Press, 1991), esp. chap. 4; and Mary L. Shanley, *Feminism, Marriage, and the Law in Victorian England* (Princeton, N.J.: Princeton University Press, 1990).

12. Pateman, "Feminist Critiques," in *The Disorder of Women*, p. 118; introduction to *Feminist Challenges*, pp. 9–10.

13. This is a major theme of the essays in Kennedy and Mendus's collection, and is well introduced in their introduction, pp. 10–13. The quotation above is from page

11. See also Lloyd, *The Man of Reason*; Pateman, "'The Disorder of Women': Women, Love and Sense of Justice," *Ethics* 91 (1980): 20–34, reprinted in *The Disorder of Women*. I also have pursued the question further, in "Thinking Like a Woman," in Deborah L. Rhode, ed., *Theoretical Perspectives on Sexual Difference* (New Haven, Conn.: Yale University Press, 1990).

14. I use this phrase, though it seems to me oxymoronic. When Straussians are Straussians, they cannot be feminists, and when their feminism prevails, they are no longer Straussians. Mary Nichols, for example, is a Straussian in her reliance on traditional views of women's "nature," as is Delba Winthrop in her argument that in Tocqueville's discussion of the situation of American women, he is primarily concerned not with women but with making an attack on excessive democracy. Arlene Saxonhouse is quite distinctly Straussian—and not feminist—in some chapters of *Women in the History of Political Thought* (such as the one on Aristotle), and distinctly more feminist—but less Straussian—in others (such as the one on early Christianity). Nichols, "Women in Western Political Thought," *American Political Science Review* 13 (1983): 241–60; Winthrop, "Tocqueville's American Woman and 'The True Conception of Democratic Progress,'" *Political Theory* 14 (1986): 239–61.

15. See Okin, *Women in Western Political Thought*, pp. 285–89.

16. O'Brien, *The Politics of Reproduction*; Brown, *Manhood and Politics*, esp. pp. 193–99.

17. Nancy Hirschmann, "Revisioning Freedom: Relationship, Context, and the Politics of Empowerment," and Christine Di Stefano, "Autonomy in the Light of Difference," chs. 3 and 5 of Hirschmann and Di Stefano, eds., *Revisioning the Political: Feminist Reconstructions of Traditional Concepts in Western Political Theory* (Boulder, Colo.: Westview Press, 1996).

18. Carole Pateman, "The Fraternal Social Contact," in J. Keane, ed., *Civil Society and the State: New European Perspectives* (London and New York: Verso, 1988); Pateman, "Women and Consent," *Political Theory* 8 (1980): 149–68, both reprinted in *The Disorder of Women*; Pateman, *The Sexual Contract*; Nancy J. Hirschmann, *Rethinking Obligation: A Feminist Method for Political Theory* (Ithaca, N.Y.: Cornell University Press, 1992).

19. Kathleen Jones, "On Authority: Or, Why Women Are Not Entitled to Speak," in J. Roland Pennock and John W. Chapman, eds., *Authority Revisited* (New York: New York University Press, 1987); Nancy Hartsock, *Money, Sex and Power: Toward a Feminist Historical Materialism* (New York: Longman, 1983).

20. Jane Mansbridge, "Feminism and Democratic Community," in Ian Shapiro and John Chapman, eds., *Democratic Community* (New York: New York University Press, 1993).

21. Iris Marion Young, *Justice and the Politics of Difference* (Princeton, N.J.: Princeton University Press, 1990); Okin, *Justice, Gender, and the Family*.

22. Anne Phillips, *Engendering Democracy*; also *Democracy and Difference* (University Park: Pennsylvania State University Press, 1993).

23. Two excellent new anthologies of feminist reconstructions of political concepts are Hirschmann and Di Stefano, eds., *Revisioning the Political*, and Mary L. Shanley and Uma Narayan, eds., *Reconstructing Political Theory* (Oxford: Polity Press, 1997). For a fruitful use of this approach in another subfield of political science, see J. Ann Tickner's recent challenge to conventional concepts and assumptions of international relations theory, in *Gender in International Relations* (New York: Columbia University Press, 1992).

24. Shanley and Pateman, *Feminist Interpretations*, pp. 2–3.

25. Ibid., p. 5.

26. For some indication of the dimensions of the "difference" debate in feminist legal theory, see my review essay, "Sexual Difference, Feminism, and the Law," *Law and Social Inquiry* 16 (1991): 553–73, and the sample of legal literature cited there in notes 1–3.

27. See, for example, Moira Gatens, "A Critique of the Sex/Gender Distinction," in J. Allen and P. Patton, eds., *Beyond Marxism? Interventions after Marx* (Sydney: Intervention Publications, 1983), pp. 143–63; Merle Thornton, "Sex Equality Is Not Enough for Feminism," in *Feminist Challenges*, pp. 77–98. Pateman and Gross have both put forward the view that aiming at equality was a necessary step, but is no longer (if it ever was) sufficient. See Pateman, *The Sexual Contract*, esp. pp. 231–33; and Gross, "Conclusion: What Is Feminist Theory?" in *Feminist Challenges*.

28. Carol Gilligan, *In a Different Voice* (Cambridge, Mass.: Harvard University Press, 1982). Joan Tronto has recently noted that there were over 1,100 citations to Gilligan's book, according to the Social Science and Science Citation Indices, between 1986 and 1991. See Tronto, "Reflections on Gender, Morality and Power: Caring and the Moral Problem of Otherness" (forthcoming). Sara Ruddick, "Maternal Thinking," *Feminist Studies* 6 (1980): 342–67; Elshtain, *Public Man, Private Woman*, esp. chap. 6; Elshtain, "Feminism, Family and Community," *Dissent* 29 (1982): 442–49; Elshtain, "Antigone's Daughters," *Democracy* 2 (1982): 46–59; Dietz, "Citizenship with a Feminist Face: The Problem with Maternal Thinking," *Political Theory* 12 (1985): 19–35; "Context Is All: Feminism and Theories of Citizenship," *Daedalus* 116 (1987): 1–24.

29. Dietz, "Citizenship with a Feminist Face," and "Context is All"; Okin, "Thinking Like a Woman" and esp. critical sources cited there from other disciplines in note 43; Tronto, " 'Women's Morality': Beyond Gender Difference to a Theory of Care," *Signs* 12 (1987): 644–63; "Political Science and Caring," in Maria J. Falco, ed., *Feminism and Epistemology: Approaches to Research in Women and Politics* (Binghamton, N.Y.: Haworth Press, 1987); Dietz articles cited in note 26; Brown, *Manhood and Politics*, chap. 10. For critiques of the more general literature on differences between the sexes, see Anne Fausto-Sterling, *Myths of Gender: Biological Theories about Women and Men* (New York: Basic Books, 1985); and Cynthia Fuchs Epstein, *Deceptive Distinctions: Sex, Gender, and the Social Order* (New Haven, Conn.: Yale University Press, 1988). One revealing finding is that research that yields no or slight differences between the sexes attracts far less attention than studies showing differences.

30. Pope John Paul II's 1988 Apostolic Letter, "On the Dignity of Women," clearly capitalizes on the "different moralities" strain in feminism, appealing to women's special capacity to care for others in order to justify their special callings to motherhood or celibacy. On the dangers of categorizing politics as "masculinist," see, for example Kennedy and Mendus, *Women in Western Philosophy*, p. 18.

31. Brown, *Manhood and Politics*, p. 191.

32. See Nancy Chodorow, *The Reproduction of Mothering: Psychoanalysis and the Sociology of Gender* (Berkeley, and Los Angeles: University of California Press, 1978); Dorothy Dinnerstein, *The Mermaid and the Minotaur: Sexual Arrangements and Human Malaise* (New York: Harper, 1977); Jean Baker Miller, *Toward a New Psychology of Women* (Boston: Beacon Press, 1977).

33. For example, Okin, *Justice, Gender, and the Family*, esp. chaps. 1, 5, and 8; Phillips, *Engendering Democracy*.

34. The most obvious influences behind this way of thinking are the works of French postmodernist or poststructural feminists—including but not restricted to Hélène Cixous, Claudine Herrmann, Luce Irigaray, Julia Kristeva, and Annie Leclerk. For a sampling of their writings in translation, see Elaine Marks and Isabelle de Courtivron, eds., *New French Feminisms* (New York: Shocken, 1981). For critical commentary on some of these theorists, see Nancy Fraser and Sandra Lee Bartky, eds., *Revaluing French Feminism: Critical Essays on Difference, Agency, and Culture* (Bloomington: Indiana University Press, 1992).

35. "Conclusion," *Feminist Challenges*, p. 191.

36. Ibid., pp. 192–93.

37. Extreme androcentrism of the "turning women into men" sort is, of course, found in the work of some feminists, such as Simone de Beauvoir and Shulamith Firestone. But it is certainly not characteristic of the thinking of all feminists who aim at equality between the sexes, or of all those who aim at an androgynous or gender-free future.

38. Pateman, "Introduction," *Feminist Challenges*, pp. 7–8.

39. *California Federal v. Guerra*, 107 S. Ct. 683 (1987). This case was highly controversial among U.S. feminists, who testified on both sides. Some feared, reasonably enough considering the lessons of history, that what seemed to them to be "special treatment" for pregnancy would re-evoke precedents that have been very harmful to women. Despite the stance I take on these issues in chap. 11 of *Women in Western Political Thought*, I do not see this case (given its careful wording, and given that it involved pregnancy and childbirth, but not leave for child care) as forming a harmful precedent for women. See Sylvia A. Law, "Rethinking Sex and the Constitution," *University of Pennsylvania Law Review* 132 (1984): 955; Christine A. Littleton, "Equality and Feminist Legal Theory," *University of Pittsburgh Law Review* 48 (1987): 1043; Littleton, "Reconsidering Sexual Equality," *California Law Review* 75 (1987): 1279.

40. Catharine MacKinnon, "Difference and Dominance," in *Feminism Unmodified* (Cambridge, Mass.: Harvard University Press, 1987), p. 36. As MacKinnon is aware, societies other than the United States have as thorough, often more thorough, "affirmative action plans" for men.

41. Ibid., p. 37.

42. For a good account of this, see "The Eruption of Difference," chap. 5 of Echols, *Daring to Be Bad*.

43. In the context of feminist theory, "essentialism" seems to have two principal meanings. The other refers to the tendency to regard certain characteristics or capacities as "essentially" female, in the sense that they are unalterably associated with being female. Used in this other sense, essentialism is very close to, if not identical with, biological determinism.

44. Angela P. Harris, "Race and Essentialism in Feminist Legal Theory," *Stanford Law Review* 42 (1990): 581–616; bell hooks, *Feminist Theory: From Margin to Center* (Boston: South End Press, 1984); Audre Lorde, "Age, Race, Class, and *Sex: Women Redefining Difference*," *Sister Outsider* 114 (1984): 114–23; Elizabeth V. Spelman, *Inessential Woman: Problems of Exclusion in Feminist Thought* (Boston: Beacon Press, 1988).

45. Spelman, *Inessential Woman*, p. 6.
46. Ibid., p. 14.
47. See, for example, Okin, *Women in Western Political Thought*, pp. 11–12.
48. *Inessential Woman*, p. 81.
49. Ibid., p. 114.
50. Ibid., p. 137.
51. There is a similar tendency to simply assume difference, rather than present evidence of it, in Nancy Fraser and Linda Nicholson's "Social Criticism without Philosophy: An Encounter between Feminism and Post-Modernism," in Nicholson, ed., *Feminism/Postmodernism* (New York: Routledge, 1990). However, Nicholson's *Gender and History* is much more of an exception to the rough generalization I have asserted.
52. For an attempt to investigate some cross-cultural evidence about gender inequalities, see Okin, "Gender Inequality and Cultural Differences," in Martha Nussbaum and Janathan Glover, eds., *Human Capabilities: Women, Men, and Equality* (Oxford: Clarendon Press, forthcoming).
53. For example, in Harris, "Race and Essentialism in Feminist Legal Theory," *Stanford Law Review* 42, 581–616; hooks, *Feminist Theory: From Margin to Center* (Boston: South End Press, 1984); Lorde, "An Open Letter to Mary Daly," in *Sister Outsider* (Trumansburg, N.Y.: Crossing Press, 1984).
54. Brown, *Manhood and Politics*, pp. 210, 196.
55. Ibid., pp. 200–201.
56. Ibid., p. 211.
57. Ibid., pp. 204–5.
58. Elshtain, *Public Man, Private Woman*, p. 335 (emphasis omitted).
59. The critiques of Firestone and de Beauvoir are quite fair, but those of Chodorow and Dinnerstein are not. Elshtain writes: "Chodorow presents one of the strongest cases for where, and how, [the stresses and shortcomings of one of our present arrangements] get reproduced" (*Public Man, Private Woman*, p. 292). But then she concentrates her energies on criticizing Chodorow's brief suggestions about communal child-rearing arrangements—unfairly calling them "Chodorow's route"—and neglects Chodorow's much more emphasized and important proposal: parenting equally shared by women and men.
60. Elshtain, *Public Man, Private Woman*, p. 323.
61. Ibid., p. 349.
62. Pateman, *The Sexual Contract*, p. 226.
63. Ibid., p. 224.
64. Ibid., p. 225.
65. Pateman, "Introduction," *Feminist Challenges*, p. 9.
66. Kennedy and Mendus, *Women in Western Political Philosophy*, p. 13.
67. Brown, *Manhood and Politics*, p. 211. I have taken the liberty of using the phrase "sexual difference" where Brown uses "gender," because I have been using the word "gender" to refer to the social construction and/or institutionalization of sexual difference. In the context of my usage of the term, her passage would be rendered incomprehensible without this substitution.
68. Perhaps a clue to this is to be found in Pateman's acknowledgment that her argument has been to some extent influenced by the anarchist wing of the socialist movement. See *The Social Contract*, p. 14.

69. I do not mean to imply by this statement that few feminists take this position. There are many feminists on both sides of the question. Among political theorists, Mary Dietz is another who has endorsed androgyny but said little about how we may achieve it. She has argued in a recent essay that Hannah Arendt's analysis of the human condition, though astonishingly lacking in consciousness about gender, can contribute much to feminist theory. Once we realize that Arendt is by no means as entirely negative about the production and reproduction of life as she is sometimes presented, and once we argue that her realms of labor, work, and action can all be conceived of as "genderless realms," the androcentrism of Arendt's own worldwide view gives way to an androgynous feminist one, which Dietz clearly endorses. But she gives little hint as to how feminism might transform conceptions of citizenship, and she is surprisingly silent about the enormous obstacles that lie in the path of women's equal citizenship and how they might be overcome. See "Hannah Arendt and Feminist Politics," in *Feminist Interpretations*, pp. 232–52, and "Context Is All: Feminism and Theories of Citizenship," *Daedalus* 116 (1987: 1–24).

70. Phillips, *Engendering Democracy*, pp. 6–7.

71. Ibid., p. 7.

72. This occurs in various passages of *Engendering Democracy*, but see esp. pp. 99–101, 110–11, 156–58.

73. Ibid., p. 8.

74. For a clear statement and analysis of some of these—the most diametrically opposed—viewpoints, see Quentin Skinner, "Meaning and Understanding in the History of Ideas," in James Tully, ed., *Meaning and Context: Ouentin Skinner and His Critics* (Cambridge: Polity Press, 1988).

75. Ibid., pp. 65–67.

76. Dietz, "Hannah Arendt and Feminist Politics," in Shanley and Pateman, *Feminist Interpretations*, p. 250. See also the editors' "Introduction," pp. 9–10.

77. Phillips, *Engendering Democracy*, p. 2.

78. Pateman, "Introduction," *The Disorder of Women*, p. 2. See also Pateman and Shanley's introduction to *Feminist Interpretations*, p. 1.

79. Notable exceptions to both the pointlessness and the neglect are Seyla Benhabib's "The Generalized and the Concrete Other," in Benhabib and Druscilla Cornell, eds., *Feminism as Critique* (Minneapolis: University of Minnesota Press, 1987) and Marilyn Friedman's "Feminism and Modern Friendship: Dislocating the Community," in Cass R. Sunstein, ed., *Feminism and Political Theory* (Chicago: University of Chicago Press, 1990). I have discussed the neglect of gender by those on both sides of the debate in "Humanist Liberalism," esp. pp. 46–53. The reasons I regard the debate as largely pointless are, first, that no one has produced a good positive argument for communitarianism—only critiques of liberalism, and not very compelling ones either. See Will Kymlicka, *Liberalism, Community and Culture* (Oxford: Clarendon Press, 1989), pt. 1, for a convincing response to several of the more prominent communitarian objections to liberalism. Second, few communitarians indicate clearly what they mean by "a community."

80. Leslie Green, *The Authority of the State* (Oxford: Clarendon Press, 1988); Don Herzog, *Happy Slaves: A Critique of Consent Theory* (Chicago: University of Chicago Press, 1989).

81. Feminist arguments were present even in the first (1979) edition of Pateman's book and were much expanded in the second (1985) edition, especially in the after-

word. Although Pateman's *Sexual Contract* was not published in time for Green or Herzog to have read it before their books went to press, there were numerous other feminist critiques of contract theory available, such as Clark, " 'Who Owns the Apples?'; Okin, "Women and the Making of the Sentimental Family"; Teresa Brennan and Carole Pateman, " 'Mere Auxiliaries to the Commonwealth,' Women and the Origins of Liberalism," *Political Studies* 27 (1979): 183–200; Pateman, "Women and Consent," *Political Theory* 8 (1980): 149–68; and Shanley, "Marriage Contract and Social Contract in Seventeenth-Century English Political Thought," *Western Political Quarterly* 32 (1979): 79–91. All of these argue that including women poses major problems for traditional contract theories of political obligation.

82. Publishers and dates of these works are Green (Totowa, N.J.: Rowman and Allanheld, 1985); Held, (Cambridge: Polity Press, 1987); and Kymlicka (Oxford: Clarendon Press, 1990). Green's and Held's works are cited as exceptions among recent democratic theories by Pateman in her introduction to *The Disorder of Women*, p. 5, and by Phillips in *Engendering Democracy*, p. 98. In the context of theories of justice, I have recently (in *Justice, Gender, and the Family*, p. 9) cited Green and, as a partial exception to the general rule of ignoring feminism, Michael Walzer's *Spheres of Justice* (New York: Basic Books, 1983).

83. Pateman, "Introduction," *The Disorder of Women*, p. 14. She also writes: "In the texts of the famous theorists there are . . . discussions of the power of men over women, but contemporary political theory does not acknowledge this form of jurisdiction as political power and pays no heed to feminist theorists who attack the legitimacy of patriarchal government," p. 3.

84. Pateman, "Introduction," in Pateman and Gross, eds., *Feminist Challenges*, p. 12.

85. The recent election of Carole Pateman to the presidency of the International Political Science Association is a welcome breach in this wall.

86. Allan Bloom, *The Closing of the American Mind* (New York: Simon and Schuster, 1987). See also my critique in *Justice, Gender, and the Family*, chap. 2.

87. Compare, for example, the listing of panels and participants at the 1991 or 1992 APSA meetings with those of even five or six years earlier!

88. For example, Benn and Gaus, *Public and Private*; Amy Gutmann, ed., *Democracy and the Welfare State* (Princeton, N.J.: Princeton University Press, 1988); Held, *Political Theory Today*; Pennock and Chapman, eds., *Authority Revisited*; Rosenblum, *Liberalism and the Moral Life*; and Shapiro and Chapman, *Democratic Community*.

Perceptions, Pleasures, Arts: Considering Aesthetics

CAROLYN KORSMEYER

FEMINIST ANALYSES have been especially productive in the critical scrutiny of basic, formative concepts of a field. So many of the fundamental concepts of philosophy have been discovered to carry a gendered significance, that the old assumptions about the universal scope of philosophical claims regarding human nature, values, knowledge, ontology, perception, and the mind can no longer be taken for granted. All of these categories have a place in aesthetics, and in this essay I shall outline feminist critiques as they have developed within aesthetics and related areas in philosophy and art theory.[1]

The field of aesthetics is unusually diverse, for it participates not only in the discourses of philosophy but also in some of the problems and debates of related fields, such as literary criticism and theory, film studies, art history, and musicology. Feminist perspectives in aesthetics have developed from all of these sites, as well as from ideas generated from the activist women's movements and the work of politically engaged artists. In order to organize these developments and to emphasize their philosophical dimensions, I shall open with an analysis of the concept of the aesthetic itself. This will introduce several arenas where feminist perspectives have developed in studies of perception and the arts and will illuminate the connections of aesthetics with other branches of philosophy.

In the discussion to come I begin each section with an account of the history of a concept and feminist critiques of the genesis of the terms of philosophical debate, for the history of a discipline shapes its present in ways that can be difficult to erase. This is not to say that philosophy has to be mired in its roots or that a concept forever retains the elements of its birth. But the framing of basic concepts significantly influences the choice of what counts as a philosophical problem to be investigated, as well as the terms by which the investigation is conducted. Thus when we find some gender asymmetry at the historical root of an idea, we are well advised to look for what philosophy has neglected to consider.

While theories of art have as long a history as philosophy itself, so many views relevant to contemporary aesthetics were formulated in the context of early modern European philosophy that the discipline is often conceived as having taken form in the eighteenth century. The very term "aesthetic" was introduced into modern discourse by a German philosopher, Alexander

Baumgarten, who borrowed it from the Greek as a term of reference for a type of knowledge gained from sense experience. (Kant employs this meaning in the *Critique of Pure Reason* [1781].) In the course of his work *Aesthetica*, Baumgarten shifted the term to mean a kind of sensory cognition attained through the perception of beautiful objects and art. (Poetry was his special focus for analysis.) This meaning quickly supplanted the earlier, and "aesthetic" came to refer to immediate experience of a special kind: the apprehension of *beauty*. (Kant uses the term in this way in the *Critique of Judgment* [1790].)[2]

In English, the term does not appear until the early nineteenth century,[3] and before that some influential British aesthetic theory was written using the terminology of beauty and taste. "Beauty" was employed in that early theory to develop general theories of value and of perceptual pleasure, whether taken in nature or in art. But the term "beauty" increasingly came to be seen as too tame a word with which to formulate theories that included not only that which is pleasant to behold, hear, or imagine but also stronger experiences such as the sublime, the picturesque, the grotesque, the comic and tragic, even the ugly and the terrible. So "aesthetic" became the serviceable concept of greatest generality for theories of the apprehension of perceptual values in art and nature.

Thus this crucial term does not have an idiomatic provenance in vernacular usage, and it has been beset with shifting connotations. Eighteenth-century philosophers devoted considerable care to specifying the scope of aesthetic pleasure and aesthetic judgments, also known as judgments of taste; such clarifying specifications continue into the twentieth century. Kant (so often in this role) sums up the general usage and ensures its perpetuation when he notes that the pure judgment of taste is one that takes pleasure in the perceptual presentation of an object without any interest in that object. Aesthetic pleasure has nothing to do with the instrumental or practical use of an object, with its religious or moral meaning, or with any desire to possess or employ the object. Kant and his predecessors believed that such qualifications were also the prerequisites for a subjective judgment of pleasure that could still be considered universal and necessary, because the restrictions on aesthetic pleasure eliminate all that is idiosyncratic or personal about the act of evaluation, leaving the common disposition of human nature at the core of the apprehension of aesthetic value. Thus as aesthetics developed, grounds for standards of taste were also formed. And as philosophical concepts of taste were refined, so were notions of the objects of taste, whether natural objects or art. A good portion of later nineteenth- and twentieth-century work was devoted to articulating a concept of art that summarizes the special values that art possesses. This effected an expansion of the concept of aesthetic value, since according to many theories the principal value of a work of art is aesthetic.

So far, this account of the idea of the aesthetic may sound neutral, untainted by gender. But gender is only hidden. In fact it operates in all of the aforementioned ideas that make up notions of the aesthetic and of art, both in their historical origins and in their continued use in contemporary theory. To support this claim, I shall organize the following discussion into four sections. First, I shall discuss the foundational views of perception and the aesthetic senses that emerge from the oldest epistemic traditions of Western philosophy. Second, I shall consider analyses of value and the nature of aesthetic qualities, linking these with theories of taste and critical judgment. The concept of art is the subject of the third section, which also discusses notions of the creative artist and of artistic canons. The fourth section considers issues of philosophy of mind, including aesthetic pleasure, perception, emotion, and interpretation. Finally, I shall conclude with some thoughts about the importance of aesthetics for the concerns of feminism to acknowledge differences among persons and to accommodate a plurality of experiences and values.

AESTHETIC SENSES

I begin by discussing the relationship of the concept of the aesthetic with sense experience. Not only is this historically a generative place to start, but it also permits early introduction of the feminist critique that subtends all areas of philosophy—an analysis of reason and rationality. Rationality so dominates Western theories of knowledge, of morals, of politics, of human nature, of culture, that there is no area of philosophy not under its long influence. It is also one of the most complexly gendered of theoretical concepts. Though critiques of rationality were developed early by feminist scholars and are by now familiar, let me summarize several points that are especially germane to the aspects of aesthetics I shall discuss.

Reason is traditionally designated the faculty of the mind that both distinguishes human from nonhuman activity generally and elevates male over female within our species. This has resulted in a tangled set of conceptual counterparts that pair up reason and "masculine" activities and traits, and nonreason and "feminine" correlates. Insofar as women are human, they are rational. Insofar as they are feminine, they are drawn into a system of symbols that represent the nonrational regions of mind and uncontrolled and inchoate nature. This has presented women with an unstable and often peripheral place within the various areas philosophers study. In epistemology the paradigmatic knower is modeled on a concept of male nature, while to female nature is ascribed an emotional and intuitive temperament. Because emotions are standardly regarded as unreliable and idiosyncratic, this description has had both theoretical and practical consequences for the idea of female moral responsibility. In moral theory, the model of responsibility, just principles, and free choice is a male agent, while the image of femininity is merciful and vacillating, swayed by particular circumstances and practical exigencies and apt therefore to be inconsistent and irresponsible. In politics the sphere of the male is public and abstract, associated with the "mind," that of the female, domestic and associated with the "body." It has seemed to follow in philosophies from Aristotle onward that cognitive abilities and natural proclivities have been unequally distributed in males and females. In the infamous binary oppositions that line up within conceptual hierarchies, reason and the mind, justice, activity, and public responsibility are all associated with a masculine domain, while emotion and the body, whim, passivity, and domesticity are assigned to the feminine realm.

Because women are ascribed roles associated with the body and its senses as contrasted to the mind and its reason, it may seem at first that the early ties to sense perception that characterize the aesthetic might make it a more "feminine" concept than others that operate in philosophical discourse. But no. The senses themselves have gendered meanings that influence the notions of beauty, aesthetic perception, and art.

The senses by which we both perceive art and learn about the world are distinguished from the bodily senses of smell, taste, and touch. The eyes and the ears have a long-established status as the primary senses of cognition, the senses most allied with reason that human beings use in abstracting propositional knowledge from experience and discovering truths about the world. By the time that Plato wrote, the senses were already recognized as having "higher" and "lower" ranks. Hearing and sight are elevated above touch, taste, and smell because they appear less intimate with the body and are more "distant" from our physical being. As the terminology of aesthetics develops in modern philosophy, the cognitive senses are also deemed the "aesthetic senses."[4] While the bodily senses can offer sensuous pleasure, it is only the more distanced objects of hearing and sight that provide genuine aesthetic pleasure and furnish the foundation upon which the fine arts build.

The conventional ranking of two of the five senses as superior on both epistemic and aesthetic grounds accords with the elevation of mind over body; of reason over sense; of man over beast and culture over nature—and of masculine over feminine. Not surprisingly, the cognitive abilities associated with certain senses are ascribed differently to male and female as well. If the greater abilities of abstract reason drift to the "masculine" side of things, the cognitive capacities of the eyes and the ears are carried in their wake. The eyes and the ears are also the principal aesthetic senses, and the bodily senses of touch, taste, and smell remain grounded in the feminine.

In spite of the sometimes complicating dominance of distance and disinterestedness in modern theories of aesthetic perception—a subject to be discussed in the next section—theories of art have rarely strayed very far from theories of knowledge. The prevalence of the idea of imitation in the history of Western art reflects the attachment of the arts to intellectual activity, since enjoyment of imitation is founded upon love of learning, as Aristotle observed. The rejection of the bodily senses in favor of cognitive/aesthetic senses also appears in the classicist idea that art nourishes the soul through the eye, informing while pleasing. Until rather recently, in fact, truth was held to be a central value for both painting and poetry. Insofar as aesthetic perception is conceived as a mode of understanding, a grasping of truths manifest in art, this mode of achieving insight has traditionally referred to the sensory conduits of sight or hearing. Taste, smell, touch may please or not, but their cognitive dimensions are held to be dull. In short, the identification of the fine arts as objects of the cognitive and aesthetic senses of seeing and hearing is parallel to the identification of knowledge with the faculty of reason, and is deeply connected with the exclusion of the bodily senses that traditionally have been associated with concepts of femaleness.[5]

This division has had very basic importance for philosophy because it has influenced what is considered to be a legitimate philosophical issue. The "problem of taste" that powers virtually all eighteenth-century aesthetic theory is seen to arise only with the objects of the cognitive and aesthetic senses. Whether or not we all enjoy the same food, on the other hand, has never been considered of philosophical interest, and *de gustibus non est disputandum* is the commonplace that reigns over objects of the bodily senses.[6] Therefore, at the outset the division of the senses automatically removes from philosophical attention such stereotypically "feminine" activities as those that take place in the kitchen.[7] This has had consequences for the idea of fine art and the fate of domestic creative activities most practiced by women, a point to be elaborated in the third section of this essay. In sum, fundamental philosophical assumptions about sense experience carry gendered meanings regarding modes of perception, aesthetic value, the nature of aesthetic objects and art objects, and paradigms of artistic creativity.

AESTHETIC VALUE

We see in the development of the notion of aesthetic senses something of a conundrum. While one may enjoy and appreciate pleasurable experiences from any of the senses, only the distance senses of vision and hearing count philosophically; only these senses mingle insight and beauty with sense experience. Thus the kinship between the aesthetic and the sensible is both stressed and denied. Similar tensions pervade other dimensions of the aesthetic, including the central concept of aesthetic value.

Aesthetic Pleasure as Disinterested Enjoyment

Pleasures from the aesthetic senses are of philosophical interest because, although subjective experiences, they seem to be more than signals of individual preferences. Therefore, they demand theories to explain how pleasures can transcend relativity. The language developed to negotiate this delicate combination of subjectivity and objectivity is that of disinterestedness or distance. The eighteenth-century idea of aesthetic pleasure supplanted a long tradition in which beauty was analyzed along platonic lines as an objective quality. Hobbes was a major catalyst in the development of theories of disinterestedness, for he argued that value qualities of any sort refer ultimately to pleasure, an analysis further developed by later empiricists. But Hobbes also argued (along then-standard lines) that pleasure is occasioned by the real or imaginary satisfaction of a desire; and desires are selfish or self-interested. The idea that not only beauty but also goodness would be reduced to egocentric satisfaction galvanized other philosophers to make some theoretical repairs to the notion of pleasure. The result was the articulation of the concept of *disinterested* pleasure, enjoyment taken in a thing for its own sake regardless of the interest or advantage of the perceiver.

The notion of disinterested pleasure made possible arguments that judgments of taste could be both subjective (as pleasures obviously are) and exemplary guides for other perceivers. For if interests are self-directed, *disinterested* pleasures might be occasioned only by elements of human nature that are shared by all. By such accounts, the similarity of constitution of all human perceivers is sufficient grounds to expect that among those whose experience is not muddled by desire, interest, bad cultural education, or emotional overload, there will be a general commonality of opinion about matters of beauty in nature and art. The sheer number of such theories in the eighteenth century is evidence of the weight given this issue, those of Kant and Hume being but the most famous.

Thus modern theories of aesthetic judgment are also theories that defend a notion of value that is "universal," that posit a common human nature present in all, and that confirm the grounds for agreement of judgments of "good taste." Such assertions of universality, of course, are deeply challenged by some recent philosophies, including feminism. They are suspected of reifying a historically specific social philosophy in their descriptions of basic human traits, a social philosophy that includes both androcentric attitudes and views blinkered by presumptions of class, race, and nationality concerning who represents our "common nature."[8] Terry Eagleton has argued that the rise of the concept of aesthetic value that posits individuals conforming with one another in their very sensed reactions represents the development of political ideology according to which the middle classes regulate their own order by natural sense and temperament and without the need of old feudal authority and regulations.[9] Janet Wolff's sociological analysis of the history of aesthetics similarly confirms the cultural specificity and the class bases for concepts of universal aesthetic value.[10] Certainly descriptions of the aesthetic and how it supposedly operates are highly colored with social detail. Paradoxically, the notion of pure aesthetic value transcending cultural and historical divisions is formulated in language that alludes repeatedly to differences of society and of gender. This can be discovered both in views of the perceiving *subject* and in characterizations of the *objects* of aesthetic attention.

In the course of formulating their ideas about aesthetic pleasure, theorists came to assign different appreciative roles to males and females. With the rise of interest in the notion of the sublime at the end of the eighteenth century, a new binary was added to the old list mentioned earlier. The meaning of beauty shrunk to the tamer connotations of pretty, charming, lovely, while the sublime was conceived to encompass power, boundlessness, and the exhilaration experienced in the face of dangerous reaches of nature, or in such extremes expressed in art. By means of this contrast beauty became characterized as a feminine companion to the masculine domain of the sublime.[11]

A complicating element in the claim that the domain of critical judgment is governed by a masculine model of the ideal perceiver ensues from the common characterization of feminine temperament as naturally tasteful. Indeed, women were (are?) stereotyped as refining, softening, acculturating forces, just as they were idealized as the protectors of domestic goodness and personal morals. But the ambit of feminine taste was believed to reach only to tame beauties such as decoration and domestic entertainment, rarely to great, difficult, or sublime art. Moreover, the apparent compliment frequently paid women, that they have an intuitive sense of taste absent in men, was also a way to deny them both the intellectual rigor needed for analysis of the abstract foundations of taste and the control over interest that permits reliable aesthetic judgments.[12]

Gender skew is even more evident when one considers treatments of the objects of judgments of taste. For alongside nature and lovely designs, women also standardly figure as objects of beauty in theoretical discussions of the nature of taste. This is peculiar, since the experience of beauty is supposedly disinterested, yet women are regarded (in these theories) as beautiful partly because of their sexual desirability, and sexual desire is an obvious "interest." The recommended disinterested attitude thus must serve as a brake not just on desire but specifically on heterosexual male desire, in order to keep women proper objects of aesthetic judgment along with paintings, sculptures, and scenery. This assigns women as well as other aesthetic objects the passive role of being-looked-at (rather than active looking), objects presented for the delectation of a perceiver. Even when women are not explicitly referred to as examples of aesthetic objects, there is arguably a parallel between the characteristics that make something an appropriate aesthetic object and characteristics that connote femininity. Both are passive, available for admiration, awaiting response from a more active appreciator. The presumption that it is appropriate to take an aesthetic attitude toward art and toward women actually helps to constitute a functioning notion of their natures.[13]

The Male Gaze

The idea that the object for appreciation is constituted as feminine and the appreciative subject as masculine can be summed up with the concept of the "male gaze." Especially associated with feminist film theory, theories of the

gaze draw upon psychoanalytic and deconstructionist methodologies, discussion of which I shall save for the fourth section of this essay. I mention
them now because they have contributed so much to the feminist critiques of
the concept of the aesthetic and the notion of distanced, disinterested visual
perceptual enjoyment.

Study of framing techniques and camera angles reveals that the vantage
points of spectator, filmmaker, and actor virtually always reinforce a masculine position in relation to the action of a film and toward the bodies of the
female characters. The types of bodies to be savored, moreover, are restricted by additional factors such as social class, race, and age. The prevalence of the adoption of masculine visual points of view in movies, and by
extension in other visual arts, has prompted the idea of the male gaze to
account for the reinforcement of authoritative social and cultural positions
to which the meaning of cultural artifacts is geared. (As with film, it is noteworthy how much of European painting depicts nudes, often females posed
for the visual pleasure of the spectator, whose imaginative position is thus
both masculine and heterosexual.)[14] In order to adopt an appropriate stance
from which to appreciate art, female spectators also are led to assume a
masculine position when they engage with imaginative products of culture.[15] (Appreciative spectators from outside the cultural group immediately
addressed might also find themselves switching back and forth from the prescribed viewing position to that of an "outsider.")[16]

Analyses of the male gaze support the suspicion that the canon of art most
valued for its aesthetic excellence is that which is produced for male pleasures and shapes taste that perpetuates masculinist values. This claim has
been made about both the content and the style of certain genres of art.
Literary narrative, for example, is commonly crafted around heroes who
surmount obstacles to their autonomy, or around the struggles of heroines
that are resolved by marriage. Certain feminists have developed even more
radical textual critiques arguing that narrative itself is masculinist, with its
linear plotlines and its employment of a language of discrete meanings and
grammatical rigidities.[17] In short, the actual, recorded judgments of the pleasures afforded by art are evidently infected by values more patriarchal than
"aesthetic."

In sum, the notion of the aesthetic, so long conceived as the neutral,
universalist mode of perception par excellence, has been revealed through
feminist analyses to be far from neutral in practice, and to achieve its universality at the expense of suppressing all but a limited range of critical perspectives. Where to go with this recognition? If feminist perspectives reveal a
dominant masculinist tenor to art and concepts related to the aesthetic, can
they also discover a feminine counterpart in a subculture or subgenre of art,
perhaps those produced by women artists? Is there a "feminine aesthetic"
that both combats the dominance of the male gaze and serves as an alternative stylistic tradition?

Is There a Feminine Aesthetic?

The form of this frequently posed question is misleadingly simple, for the subject of inquiry has multiple possibilities. Does the question urge an empirical study to seek some common trait in the work of female artists? If so, how many artists need to be studied to compile a reliable pool from which one can make a generalization about female style or creativity? Is this a more theoretical question regarding the sources of creative voice and sexual difference? How does one identify feminine aesthetic qualities, and, particularly, how would a search for characteristically feminine styles avoid simply perpetuating the infamous binaries that feminism has subjected to so much analysis and criticism? Are we to look for values in art that can be identified not as *feminine* but as *feminist*, a more politically self-conscious position? In seeking artistic styles that are either feminine or feminist, need the artists or authors actually be women?

For the philosopher, all of these issues are further complicated by the slippery notion of the aesthetic. The task of searching for a female/feminine/feminist philosophical aesthetic *theory* is different from discovering distinctive aesthetic values at play in the creative work of (male or female) artists. But this confusion cannot be resolved simply by demarcating theory from practice; rather, it presents the further query: What relationships obtain between philosophical aesthetic theories and periods, styles, or trends in art? I shall not even attempt to provide answers to all of these questions here but shall settle for a brief review of some work that attempts different approaches to sorting through the issues.

Many early feminist efforts in the critical disciplines directed attention to the work of female artists and writers. Some literary and art theorists have identified certain texts, styles, and themes as more present in works by female artists than in works by males.[18] Such qualities may be the outcome of common differences in social experience: women assigned domestic roles will naturally write about different possibilities for life than men who frequent public places. Their values might be less confrontational and dramatic, more compromising and routine. However, attempts to generalize about the work of women has been sharply debated among feminist scholars, for many are skeptical of the evidence for such claims and of the presumptions that must be made in order to defend them. Not only does the diversity of art produced by women defy stylistic generalization, but so does the diversity of women themselves. Since women, like men, are not a uniform class of people but live within communities described by class, nationality, race, and the histories that complicate those categories, the art they produce is unlikely to yield any discernible tradition of its own.[19]

The possible role of the body in the development of subjectivity has suggested other approaches to the question of female creativity. A group of theories with roots in psychoanalysis and poststructuralism radically extends critiques of the patriarchal traditions of philosophy to language itself, arguing that the feminine is unrepresentable in traditional discourse. Writers such as Luce Irigaray and Hélène Cixous (the two figures most well known in North America) understand language and writing as modes of self-creation along lines developed by Derrida. Language helps to create subjectivity, according to this view; the self should not be pictured as an independent entity who "chooses her words" to match her particularly female experience. Irigaray not only examines language for patriarchal values (she has subjected the history of Western philosophy to a sweeping critique) but also advances the idea of writing as a woman, with the body of a woman. Irigaray insists that "sexuate" being pervades one's identity, and that the pretense of shedding one's sex when writing or speaking requires the feminine to disappear into the masculine/neutral discourse that dominates the patriarchal order.[20] Writing from the body potentially overturns this order. It is radically disruptive writing that would elude the structures of patriarchal discourse and order that have defined the feminine as nonmasculine, lacking subjectivity of its own.[21]

Provocative ideas about writing and the feminine have also been advanced by Julia Kristeva, whose psychoanalytic account posits that some poetic writing proceeds from pre-Oedipal experience of the mother-child dyad—before language develops and patriarchal discourse predominates—that breaks through into language. This writing is discoverable in the poetry of men as well as women and thus is "feminine" in a somewhat different sense, in that it is not governed by the laws of the symbolic, patriarchal order.

There are obviously many ways to locate a feminine "voice" in theory and in art, and equally obviously each of these methods is contested within feminism, for the issues are immensely complex and require affinity with vastly different philosophical methods. I shall not attempt to resolve their differences here but end with a comment about what they have in common. Whether the method is empirical, psychoanalytic, or deconstructive, the positing of a feminine voice brings to the fore what has recently been dubbed "positionality." One perceives, appreciates, and creates *from* some place, and that place is a vortex of history and other social descriptors as well as individual identity. Moreover, one's identity emphatically includes bodily and gender identity. (Since "the body" is traditionally dismissed by philosophers as one of those inconvenient accidents that hampers mind, it can be a temptation to take the body as something "natural" and untheorized. But this view itself represents a theoretical construal of the body, which has not escaped the conceptual shaping of philosophy.) Locating the effects of position and embodiment both in the formation of theories and in artistic texts is an important contribution of feminist aesthetics. Not only does it prompt critical scrutiny of traditional philosophies, but it also contributes to understanding women's consciousness and lives as they are distilled in cultural artifacts.

Aesthetic Properties and Critical Assessment

The feminist critique of the neutrality and universality of aesthetic values has reopened a related analytical issue crucial to the interpretation of art: the nature of the distinction of aesthetic and nonaesthetic qualities. This has always been a contested area, it must be emphasized, and few aesthetic theories have employed a pure notion of the aesthetic in their treatment of art (only the strictest of formalists can do this). Nevertheless, there is a solid tradition within aesthetic theory, perhaps particularly the Anglo-American school, that has drawn a distinction between what can be termed "internal" and "external" properties of works of art and held that only the internal properties are relevant to assessing the meaning or quality of the work.

This distinction is tied to presumptions about the autonomy of art and the idea that distinctive artistic value is that which the work has by itself without consideration of factors that an observer could not grasp in the experience of reading or listening or looking. Upon looking at a painting, listening to a concerto, or reading a poem, one is unlikely to be able to discern the gender of the artist.[22] Therefore, it is customarily argued, the mere fact that the artist is male or female constitutes an external property of art. Marxism, psychoanalysis, and more recently feminism are the chief examples of theoretical schemes that have been faulted because they intrude consideration of external characteristics into the process of evaluating a work of art.

The distinction between internal and external properties is a basic point of contention, for feminist perspectives proceed from the claim that art is a culturally embedded activity that cannot be understood in isolation from the social factors that went into its production. Once such factors are entered into the calculus of what art "means," it is not so easy to distinguish "internal" from "external." Thus feminist theories of criticism have dramatized and complicated the perennial problem of distinguishing the boundaries of aesthetically relevant qualities. Feminist scholars from the critical disciplines have provided much valuable evidence for this debate. The issue remains unresolved within philosophy and has begun to generate discussion about the compatibility of feminist perspectives with recent philosophical treatments of art.[23]

Variations of this issue are present not only in scholarly discourse but also in public debates about pornography and the thin, contested line between pornographic and erotic art. Feminist spokespersons have participated on all sides of this tangled argument, the contribution of philosophers often focusing on the role that the traditional notions of creative freedom and artistic autonomy should play in understanding the aesthetic and social value of works of art.[24] Pornography and erotic art remind us that the relatively academic distinction between internal and external qualities and debates over artistic freedom and autonomy also breach the standard division between aesthetics and ethics, for it is an arena where the practical consequences of art practice are impossible to ignore.

ART AND ARTISTS

Ideas about art have a long and shifting history, and we can find in these notions several more variations of the ways a concept may possess gendered elements. Correspondingly, feminists have taken a number of routes to analyze and deconstruct the concept of art.

Who Creates? What Counts as Art?

In spite of the fact that apparently women have participated in making art throughout its history, the term "artist" usually conjures up the image of a male creator—visionary, bold, acquainted with the inspiring (feminine) muses. Prevalent notions such as "natural talent" and "born genius" provide feminists with yet another focus for disputing what is "natural" and what culturally constructed.

Women's absence in large numbers from much of the history of art may be traced in part to their relative lack of education, which proceeded both from their domestic roles and from presumptions about their lesser abilities to learn. In 1971 Linda Nochlin published an essay that was to launch feminist art history and prompt studies of the effects of those presumptions on the notion of the artist. "Why Are There No Great Women Artists?" outlines the limited instruction available to female painters from the Renaissance through the early twentieth century, including the exclusion of women from studios where male artists practiced drawing nude models.[25] Nochlin stresses the social conditions that permit the development of virtuosity, undermining the romantic idea that artists are born rather than made. Moreover, she also suggests that there are conceptual prejudices that surround the notion of art and further masculinize the concept.

One such prejudice that is vividly gendered is that of artistic genius. Throughout its protean history, genius has been the proper possession of men, and reverence for creative artistic imagination burgeoned in the romantic period. Christine Battersby argues that during this time the notion of genius takes its most perniciously gendered form, for the idea of creativity as artistic parturition caused what are traditionally deemed feminine characteristics to leech into the masculine preserve of genius.[26] Rather than resulting in an androgynous or egalitarian concept, however, the artist was assigned "feminine" life-giving qualities but retained the explicit gender of masculinity. The insistent praise of creative powers in masculinist language has long put the female artist in the awkward position of either disavowing her femininity insofar as she is an artist, and/or having her work downgraded from "original" to "derivative" on the suspected grounds that, since she produced it, it *could not be* a work of true genius.[27] We can see in the notion of the creative artistic genius an instance of a theoretical concept both tailored for a particular type of individual and more or less guaranteed to describe that type alone, for the concept of genius—the maker of the highest, most original, and most important art forms—virtually excludes female members. Probably the better term for this phenomenon is "preclusionary" rather than "exclusionary," for the narrow beam of theory that illuminates the objects called "art" is rarely even aware of the scope of activities left in shadow. We can discover similar exclusions at work in many definitions and concepts surrounding art.

For much of the modern period, art has been tied to concepts of expression, in which the romantic notions of genius and imagination play continuing roles. A particularly clear example of how expression itself takes on a gendered significance is provided by the influential work of R. G. Collingwood, whose writings are still widely reprinted in textbook anthologies of aesthetics. Because Collingwood holds art to be essentially expressive, he must formulate a concept of expression that distinguishes it from nonartistic activities that might be confused with expression proper, such as the betrayal or arousal of emotion. A true expression, he argues, is the coming-to-clarity of an idea or feeling that was hitherto vague and inchoate. When the artist creates, he brings the expression into being; when the observer appreciates, something of that clarity of consciousness is re-created.[28]

This definition is articulated with the purpose of setting real art apart from, among other things, craft.[29] The craft product is not expressive, according to Collingwood, since the goal or end product (e.g., a basket for fruit or a pillowcase) is known in advance. The craftsperson simply follows prescribed means to reach the desired end. But it is the expressive artist who has the truly creative mind and who produces Art.

The distinction between art and craft does not prima facie discriminate by gender. But theories of art are never far from practice, and despite the considerable numbers of females who practice in the world of fine art, for centuries by far the greater number of women's creative products have been domestic decorations or artifacts for use. Earlier I observed that the distinction between aesthetic and nonaesthetic senses removes from the domain of philosophical attention many of the traditional activities of women (such as cooking). Similarly, the limits placed on what counts as genuine expression divert theoretical attention from craft products, many of which are produced not only by women but also by men outside the recognized territory of "high" art.[30] Since their exclusion is buttressed by the very concepts of art and aesthetic value we standardly employ, it is not easy simply to expand the application of the term "art" to include what has been omitted. "Art," while a flexible concept, is still a highly selective label disposed to attach to only certain sorts of artifacts.

The notions of expression and of fine art tie into other preclusionary concepts related to art. Whatever "art" is (and competing definitions abound), all but maverick theories assume that a work of art is essentially a public object. (The paradigm cases invoked usually are visual works hanging in galleries or museums, or works in readily available print or film or sound media.) "Public" not only means "available to scrutiny by anyone"; it also conveys the conditions that make the autonomy of art possible: artworks are objects that stand by themselves, broadcasting their value to any sensitive observer who happens to be there. Now, as feminists have been observing for some time, the public-private dichotomy is also one that conventionally corresponds to masculine-feminine space. What has this implied for the idea of the artist and artworks?

Griselda Pollock has presented a powerful argument about the public-private distinction in a study of the development of modernism that examines nineteenth-century French Impressionist painting. The concept of modernism, she argues, develops alongside the notion of the artist as urban, public man. The subjects of the influential painting of this period are frequently public squares, bars, streets. Moroever, these venues often feature sexually charged subjects such as prostitutes and barmaids. The modern artist is the consummate observer of this public scene, the *flaneur* or stroller in the city, taking in all before him and distilling it in art. While Impressionism included among its participants respected women artists such as Berthe Morisot and Mary Cassatt, the work of these artists is markedly limited by subject matter to domestic scenes. Indeed, the very rendering of space in the formal composition of their paintings evokes the more confined circuit of the woman artist herself. Pollock concludes that "modernism" is not a period term that one may amend with the simple inclusion of women because it is tied to a notion of public space that is linked with its converse: domestic, private, feminine space.[31] As Janet Wolff confirms, "There is no question of inventing the *flaneuse*: the essential point is that such a character was rendered impossible by the sexual divisions of the nineteenth century."[32]

"Feminine Arts": Alternative Models and Traditions?

The idea that fine art is public art entails that it be comprehensible in the comparatively blank context of a gallery. This is a space that, until recently, few women entered as practitioners. Indeed, some would argue that even the world of modern art galleries is still "masculine" space.[33] If the notion of art as public is a male-oriented concept, what does it leave out? Might consideration of the things produced in private contexts and therefore hitherto overlooked reveal artistic traditions where women are the principal practitioners?

The search for feminine art traditions is often conflated with the search for a feminine aesthetic, which was discussed in the previous section. However, there are important differences between the two inquiries. Looking for a feminine aesthetic is apt to fall into essentialist presumptions insofar as one is led to scrutinize the paintings, music, and literature of women to discover some common stylistic flavor. The discovery is not only unlikely; the very search presumes that there exists some set of characteristic feminine aesthetic qualities. By contrast, inquiring after distinctive artistic traditions that women have created makes no presumptions that their products are going to share any similar aesthetic qualities. Rather, it acknowledges that the opportunity for making things that are valued as art has been influenced by circumstance. So rather than look only at canonical genres to find their few female practitioners, one searches out the places where the majority of women of certain social groups spent their time to see if the conventional notion of art might be supplemented.

Anne Higgonet observes that in the eighteenth and nineteenth centuries, arguably a heightened time of domesticity for middle- and upper-class women, it was customary for women to keep picture albums that circulated among family and friends. Higgonet believes these constitute an alternative tradition of art that disappeared with the increasing acceptance of the idea that *real* art is that which hangs in galleries and does not require a domestic context to be understood.[34] There are numerous additional ways to branch away from the idea of art as public object; the attention paid by literary scholars to private letters and diaries was inspired partly by the search for women's writings.

While historians of the arts search the past for the neglected work of women, other feminists use critical discoveries about the traditional notions of art to envision the forms that feminist art might take. Venerating creative genius and setting art objects apart from the activities of daily life have seemed to some feminists to be deeply masculinist notions thoroughly imbedded in patriarchal traditions. Indeed, the very idea of an art *object* presented for the delectation of the *observer* participates in the subject-object dichotomies aligned with familiar masculine-feminine binary opposites. Artists and theorists alike have explored art forms that do not employ conventional distinctions between art and audience. Dance and music are forms where active participation may supplant passive appreciation.[35] Because participation makes connoisseurship difficult, these art forms subvert the standard positions of art object and critic, and undermine attention to formalist values and the elevation of aesthetic quality as the most important characteristic of art. The relationship of subject and object, and the blurring of clear distinctions between the two; an emphasis on aesthetic dimensions of daily life; art as an activity rather than a product—all these ideas have found their way into feminist aesthetic theory and the practice of feminist artists.[36]

SUBJECTIVITY: PERCEPTION, EMOTIONS, AND PLEASURE

As we have seen, feminist critical scrutiny has both challenged traditional treatments of art and aesthetic value and suggested alternate concepts to pursue. This section returns to theories of aesthetic response and explores more deeply feminist reflections on subjectivity.

Questions of subjectivity and point of view are at the center of postmodernist debates and have left hardly an area of philosophy untouched. The relationship of feminism to postmodernism is complex and contested, but without doubt feminist discoveries about the dubiousness of basic philosophical claims to refer universally to all human subjects have powerfully fueled postmodernism's declaration to fragment "the subject."

The previous analyses of concepts involving the aesthetic referred largely to the tradition of Kant and his British predecessors. To discuss feminist theories of perception and interpretation we must shift to more recent European traditions, those that have also strongly influenced literary theory. Upon the basis of hermeneutics and theories of the interaction of reader and text, European thinkers have built a complex set of philosophies that draw variously on psychoanalysis and deconstruction to understand the phenomena of subjectivity, culture, and meaning. While philosophy (particularly Anglo-American philosophy) has generally been skeptical about psychoanalytic theory, that approach to understanding gender has provided inspiration to many feminists, and partly via feminist philosophy has entered philosophical discourse. Because it has become so much a part of interpretive theories of literature and the arts, it is now a contender for attention within aesthetics. The widespread use of the concept of a male gaze has further disseminated psychoanalytic assumptions. It is possible to use this term chiefly to describe the socially constituted ideal viewer of art, but most theorists develop a deeper analysis about the formation of visual pleasure that relies upon psychoanalytic categories. In what follows I sketch a brief account of the uses of this tradition in aesthetics. I follow this with a supplementary suggestion, for this is an area where I believe some trends in recent Anglo-American philosophy potentially have much to offer feminism and its goals of diversifying the "voices" of theory.

Feminism and Philosophy of Mind

As we saw earlier, theories of aesthetic pleasure originally developed alongside eighteenth-century philosophies of mind. Such theories typically posit a model of aesthetic pleasure in which the perceiver employs a generic consciousness that takes in the physical world through the senses, reflects on that world with intellect and imagination, and evaluates its own "mental contents" by introspection. This approach stresses the universal elements of perception and appreciation, and as such it deliberately omits analysis of the aspects of individuals that make them different from one another (unless difference is invoked to account for a failure of taste).

In none of its forms has the philosophical tradition within which aesthetics arose inspired widespread feminist adaptation, and this is because with the emphasis on universality, none of these forms accommodates more than a superficial understanding of the development of *gendered* consciousness. Many feminist theorists have turned instead to psychoanalysis for a dynamic model of consciousness that links gender to the psychological and physical development of the subject. This move has seemed particularly compelling for those feminists who have concluded that gender asymmetry is a far more intransigent fact of culture than sociological description can explain, and that the sources of gender difference lie far deeper than the reaches of legislation or social reorganization.[37] Therefore, some feminist theorists, seeking a way to account for the formation of gender divisions at their earliest stages, have cast another look at Freud, whose philosophy of mind, though originally focused on the developing psyche of male children, employs a model of the subject as split into conscious and unconscious processes that account for the development of gender identity.

There are too many varieties of feminist perceptual-interpretive theory to do justice to any of them in one summary. I shall outline here a skeleton account of perception of art that takes gender analysis as central to the understanding of aesthetic pleasure, for this is an aspect of feminist theory that directly challenges traditional philosophical accounts of the aesthetic.

The roots of feminist theories of pleasure are eclectic. From Foucault comes an understanding of pleasures as occupying a site where power relations take their initial form.[38] From deconstruction comes the suspicion that the meanings of cultural products reside as much in what is absent from a text or artifact as in what is apparent. From Freud and Lacan comes an understanding of pleasure as issuing out of the same regions of the unconscious where erotic charge and gender identity come into being.

Many feminist critics make use of the concept of "scopophilia," which is Freud's term for pleasure in looking, to account for aesthetic pleasure. It is a salient notion to compare to standard accounts of aesthetic pleasure, for the latter are also frequently developed using vision as the model for aesthetic perception. Scopophilia is traceable to a prearticulate level of consciousness and the experience of the infant looking at the mother while suckling. As the child develops a sense of its own separate identity, scopophilia takes the form of pleasure in looking at another. There is also counterpart pleasure in identifying with what is seen, in being the object of the look. The former, more active position is labeled "masculine," and the latter "feminine." But since these are positions of viewing and not simply designations of the sex of the perceiver, gender identity is potentially fluid, another useful flexibility for feminist adaptation.[39]

The developing subjectivity that experiences scopophilia is also forming gender identity; thus visual pleasure is also eroticized. So as well is another aspect of pleasure that is offered by artistic representation. Scopophilic pleasure covers over a traumatic moment of identity formation: the realization that one is not a part of the maternal body and is forever separate from that experience of primal unity. The discomfort at this realization of loss and incompleteness is an instance of what is referred to generally as castration anxiety, an anxiety about loss, separation, and absence, which functions deeply in the unconscious and colors the experience of pleasure. The image of woman, representing lost maternal plenitude and the absent phallus, prompts castration anxiety. At the same time, as an unconscious reminder of the maternal body, it serves to allay that anxiety. Thus women become the objects of fetishistic pleasure, the fetish being the object that substitutes or stands in for absence.

By implication, therefore, pleasure in the experience of visual perception is formed from erotic, unconscious desire. Even if beauty appears to consciousness as pleasurable in and of itself, it is really a displaced construct ultimately traceable to fetishistic scopophilia. By this analysis, the terms that stand for the pinnacle of intrinsic value, such as beauty and other positive aesthetic qualities, actually denote substitute pleasures that either cover an anxiety or signal a pleasurable satisfaction formed from infantile, now unconscious drives.

The contrast between the traditional understanding of beauty as a pleasure recognizing a pure, intrinsic value and psychoanalytic deconstructions is evident in Laura Mulvey's assertion that "fetishistic scopophilia builds up the physical beauty of the object, transforming it into something satisfying in itself." Similarly, Griselda Pollock's rhetorical questions imply an affirmative answer: "What role has beauty to play in securing visual pleasure? Is the beauty of the physical object, the painting, a defense against anxieties excited by the represented object, woman?" Even "pure" or formal beauty is rendered opaque and thoroughly suspect by this account. As Eagleton wryly remarks, for "conventional aesthetic theory, Freud is exceedingly bad news."[40]

Theories of scopophilic pleasure also position males and females differently with regard to the pleasure derived from art, because the formation of gendered consciousness differs male to female. The identification of female children with the body of the mother, that is, a recognition that her body is the same as their own, creates an identity that is less prone to draw lines of demarcation than is the case with male gender identity, which forms with the recognition of the difference between its body and the mother's.[41] Thus not only the differing reactions to the content of art but also the very sources of immediate pleasure are prone to vary with gender.

There are many compelling elements to this approach to perception and pleasure, not the least of which is the fact that what appears as an immediate aesthetic reaction to a complex work of art is understood as immediate only because certain elements of culture and power, especially those concerning gender, have been so deeply absorbed that they leap into consciousness with the immediacy of sensory reaction. Moreover, this approach effectively counters the formalism that has dominated both philosophical aesthetics and art history, insofar as these disciplines have tended to concentrate on style and composition as the locus of aesthetic value and artistic innovation. Feminists have been effective in directing attention to the content of artistic representation and how it is rendered for the pleasures of the male gaze.[42]

But there are some disadvantages to the account as well. For one thing, the components of aesthetic pleasure are so buried in the unconscious that they can only be speculated about, and aesthetics' traditional recourse to introspection to check the reasonableness of a conclusion is stymied. Perhaps more important, the terms of analysis make the "discovery" of gender difference virtually a foregone conclusion. While the term "male gaze" brilliantly distills the general truth that cultural productions construct an appreciative audience as masculine and heterosexual, the disjunction between masculine and feminine viewpoints is not exhaustive, and it tends to shadow the multitude of critical perspectives that may issue from viewers with different sexual desires and groups outside the socially dominant culture.

This is no news to feminism, and psychoanalytic theorists have been mindful of the need neither to essentialize gender nor to ignore cultural diversity. Just how one manages this difficult task is one of the deepest challenges facing feminism at present, and for many it is also the stumbling block that cautions against promiscuous postmodernism. I have no solution to the general problems facing feminist theory. But in the arena of aesthetics I believe—following a suggestion of Noël Carroll's—we can profit from the advances made by feminist appropriations of psychoanalysis by putting them to use with another body of work that is ready-to-hand in recent philosophy: theories of emotion.[43]

Emotions and Aesthetic Responses

Because of the important role that concepts of expression have in philosophies of art, one might expect that the role of emotion in aesthetic responses is already firmly established. However, the great bulk of philosophical expression theory, especially in the analytic tradition, takes pains to distance the feeling of the audience from whatever might be expressed in art. The standard distinction is between "expression" and (mere) "arousal" of emotion.[44] Neglect of actual *felt* emotions has probably been almost as prevalent in aesthetics as in other branches of philosophy.

Available analyses of emotion are fertile ground for understanding aesthetic responses for a variety of reasons. First of all, a major impetus behind the philosophical study of emotions has been to reveal their cognitive dimensions. Far from the irrational and uncontrollable forces caricatured by many philosophers since Plato, emotions are educable and intelligent affective responses that can deliver information about the world, as well as about the experiencing self.[45] Responses to art must have a cognitive dimension, at least insofar as subject matter and its treatment is a source of aesthetic attention; so emotive theories of aesthetic response are equipped to capture this dimension of artistic comprehension. Second, emotions are deeper experiences of affect than the language of pleasure captures, and yet they include aversion or attraction and thus a dimension of pleasure and pain, which again both accords with and deepens traditional analyses of aesthetic appreciation.[46] Furthermore, emotions also tally with the experience of immediacy so long taken to describe aesthetic appreciation. Thus emotions satisfy some basic intuitions about aesthetic pleasure without sacrificing the complexity of the art object.[47]

Even more useful for employment in feminist analyses is the diversity of emotions and their openness to both cultural and individual development. If psychoanalysis illuminates gender constants in aesthetic reactions, theories of emotion shed light on individual differences that complicate those constants. While it might seem that emotions take place at a basic level of the psyche where variation is minimal (as with the operation of the senses), this is probably the case only with some emotions considered in general terms. Love of children, for example, seems likely to be a constant in virtually all human communities, but the shades and varieties of this emotion are demonstrably variable, from the familiar image of the overprotective parent of our own time to the famous Spartan mother who ordered her son to return from battle with his shield or on it. Because emotions are enormously diverse, there is less temptation to speak of a single phenomenon (as with reason or pleasure). Therefore, they foster one of the oft-stated goals of feminism: understanding that seeks to do justice to the diversities of the arts and the plural identities of audiences.

Finally, emotion does not line up on the "masculine" side of the binary oppositions that so often govern thought. One's ideas are perhaps less likely to run into familiar and habitual channels. They are thus conducive to disrupting the power of binary thinking altogether, so long a stated goal of feminists.

Much of the philosophical literature on emotions has centered on the definitional question, Just what is an emotion? There is widespread doubt that the noun actually describes a single category of mental phenomena, a position that reaches an extreme of sorts in Ronald de Sousa's claim that there are no generic emotions, just emotion-types that are themselves constructed out of the experiences ("paradigm scenarios") of individuals. By his formulation, emotions are products of polyadic relations that may have as many as seven terms.[48] Perhaps he overdoes this, but his emphasis on polyadicity usefully prevents a slide into the philosophers' habit of constructing a universal norm for how "we" all behave, think, and feel.

In her analysis of emotion, Amélie Rorty makes note of four elements of the emotive experience: a target object (the object of an emotion extensionally defined), an intentional object (the target described as present to consciousness), the intentional state of the perceiver (the emotive state), and the general character of the perceiver (or magnetized disposition).[49] The latter permits unconscious factors to participate in the genesis of an emotion, for a magnetized disposition is the result of a personal history that has become embedded in the psyche and is no longer as such present to consciousness.

If we keep the notion of magnetized disposition in mind when thinking about the subject experiencing an emotion, then there is ample room for noticing variation by gender in affective responses and for employing theories of the unconscious. Terms describing dispositions with gender variants are supplied not only by theories of the unconscious but also by familiar sociological factors more accessible to introspection. And if we remember that emotions are also charged negatively and positively, then we will also retain the idea of pleasure built into the affective response and importantly welded with the cognition that is also a component of emotion.

But there is more, for here we are interested in a particular genre of affect, that referring to art; thus the facility or cultural fluency of the subject will play a critical role in the formation of emotive responses to art, for artworks are not objects of uniform comprehension in a heterogeneous society. Cultural fluency includes not only at-homeness with works of art and the art world but the perspective from which one achieves fluency: as a practitioner, an outsider, a lay appreciator, a critic, a member of the society that produced the object, a member of the group represented as artistic subject matter, a member of a group slighted or ignored by the work. Of course, one's actual social position does not determine one's aesthetic reaction, for imaginative experiences are often far more flexible and generous than those summoned up in practical reality.

The goal of spinning out the many possible components of affective cognition is twofold: to indicate how gendered subjectivity may be systematically accounted for without wholesale reliance on the unconscious formation of gender identity, and to do so in a way that defies reassemblage along the traditional dichotomies of "masculine" and "feminine" that so easily reassert themselves in our habitual paths of thought. Moreover, emotions satisfy other elements of aesthetic perception classically understood: its immediacy, its ability to combine feeling and insight, the complexities of its pleasures. This view of the mind and of aesthetic comprehension is not simple or even particularly neat. But feminists have learned to distrust overly comprehensive systems with all their loose ends tucked away. Complex models guard against oversimplification, which is another way to label the problem of generalization that feminist perspectives combat in philosophy.

This essay has attempted to present something of the flavor and diversity of issues in aesthetics that feminist scholarship has fostered, and to organize the insights of various disciplines according to traditional philosophical concerns. Feminist scholarship in philosophy—indeed, in all disciplines—began with challenges to reigning theory and methodologies. It has revealed the partiality of many concepts basic to philosophy that previously were regarded as a neutral bedrock upon which an understanding of universal truths could be founded. Once one absorbs the power of these critiques, it becomes evident that philosophy, despite its long history of subjecting everything under the sun to scrutiny, has missed some interesting areas of inquiry. They have been neglected because they have not been considered important for understanding either truths about the external world or "the human condition." Often such subjects are the very ones that cluster around less important "feminine" concepts such as the body, feeling, and emotion. Feminism has redirected philosophical interest to many of these areas.

Not only do feminist perspectives bring fresh insights and challenging issues to aesthetics, but aesthetics and its own established concerns can contribute usefully to feminist theory. In this assertion, I am seconding Hilde Hein's observations regarding the methodological compatibility between traditional aesthetics and the concerns of contemporary feminism to acknowledge and respect plural values and differences among women. For despite the foregoing critiques of the field, aesthetics—often conceived as the misfit stepchild of philosophy—has always had to keep the particularity of experience at the forefront of theory. Aesthetic apprehension was conceived as a glimpse of a particular, sensed truth resistant to general rules that operate with intellectual reasoning. Similarly, attention to the individuality of works of art requires that philosophies of art be grounded in the actual experience of art and acquaintance with its histories. Consequently, the methods traditionally observed within aesthetic theory are tailored for observance of plurality, of individuality, of difference. Because of its need "to preserve the diverse and disorderly," Hein argues, aesthetics offers a model for feminist theorizing that is attentive to difference.[50]

Therefore, as feminism continues its search for friendly philosophical methods and possibilities for adjustments to traditional paradigms that have excluded gender from analyses, it will find congenial company within the realm of aesthetics. It is frequently remarked that feminist scholarship has spurred interdisciplinary scholarship to the mutual benefit of researchers in other disciplines. Similarly, feminist philosophy itself would profit from greater incorporation of issues of aesthetics into its endeavors. I have ended with mention of one such area: studies of emotion. Many assumptions that philosophy has perpetuated about the relations among reason, emotion, the senses, pleasures, and knowledge, are now being revised. This area of study is one where moral theory, philosophy of mind, epistemology, feminist theory, and aesthetics converge in enacting the many changes that philosophy is undergoing at present.

ACKNOWLEDGMENTS

For their helpful discussions of this essay I would like to thank Peg Brand, Hilde Hein, Betsy Cromley, Claire Kahane, Liz Kennedy, Isabel Marcus, and Carol Zemel.

NOTES

1. Portions of this essay were first developed in "Gender Bias in Aesthetics," *APA Newsletter on Feminism in Philosophy* 89, no. 2 (Winter 1990): 45–48; and in "Pleasure," *Journal of Aesthetics and Art Criticism* 51, no. 2 (Spring 1993): 199–206.

2. For a thorough account of the history of theories of aesthetic judgment, see David Summers, *The Judgment of Sense: Renaissance Naturalism and the Rise of Aesthetics* (Cambridge: Cambridge University Press, 1987).

3. *Oxford English Dictionary*, vol. 1 (1971), p. 37. See also Raymond Williams, *Keywords: A Vocabulary of Culture and Society* (New York: Oxford University Press, 1976), pp. 27–28.

4. For just one of many opinions of this sort, see George Santayana, *The Sense of Beauty* (New York: Scribner's, 1896).

5. Terry Eagleton argues that attention to the aesthetic in the eighteenth and nineteenth centuries puts the body at the center of cognition of particulars. Thus aesthetic experience grounds abstract knowledge in concrete experience, making the body an indispensable component of a full account of knowledge. I believe his account neglects the importance of the distinction between aesthetic and bodily senses and induces him to overemphasize the prominence of the body in philosophy of this time. See *The Ideology of the Aesthetic* (Oxford: Basil Blackwell, 1990), introduction and chap. 1.

6. Immanuel Kant, *Critique of Judgment*, trans. Werner Pluhar (Indianapolis: Hackett, 1987), p. 55; Eva Shaper, "The Pleasures of Taste," in Eva Shaper (ed.), *Pleasure, Preference and Value* (Cambridge: Cambridge University Press, 1983).

7. A recent collection that establishes food as a philosophical topic is Deane W. Curtin and Lisa M. Heldke (eds.), *Cooking, Eating, Thinking* (Bloomington: Indiana University Press, 1992). See also Elizabeth Telfer, *Food for Thought: Philosophy and Food* (London: Routledge, 1996).

8. Critiques of "universalist" directions in theory often target Enlightenment European philosophy and the elitist and imperialist presumption that a man of social privilege is in an optimal position to stand for all "mankind." While a strong case can be made for this challenge to universalist concepts, many philosophies across the globe have also presumed that differences among people are superficial variations on a single uniform model.

9. Eagleton, *The Ideology of the Aesthetic*, esp. chapters 1 and 2.

10. Janet Wolff, *Aesthetics and the Sociology of Art*, 2d ed. (Ann Arbor: University of Michigan Press, 1993); Wolff, *The Social Production of Art* (London and Basingstoke: Macmillan, 1981). An earlier critique of aesthetic value as perpetuating class hierarchies is made by Pierre Bourdieu, *Distinction: A Social Critique of the Judgment of Taste*, trans. Richard Nice (Cambridge, Mass.: Harvard University Press, 1984).

11. Gender analyses of eighteenth-century aesthetics include Paul Mattick, "Beautiful and Sublime: Gender Totemism in the Constitution of Art," Timothy Gould, "Intensity and Its Audiences," and Christine Battersby, "Stages on Kant's Way," all in Peggy Zeglin Brand and Carolyn Korsmeyer (eds.), *Feminism and Tradition in Aesthetics* (University Park: Pennsylvania State University Press, 1995); Mary Wiseman, "Beautiful Exiles," and Jane Kneller, "Discipline and Silence: Women and Imagination in Kant's Theory of Taste," both in Hilde Hein and Carolyn Korsmeyer (eds.), *Aesthetics in Feminist Perspective* (Bloomington: Indiana University Press, 1993); Naomi Schor, *Reading in Detail: Aesthetics and the Feminine* (New York: Methuen, 1987), esp. part I.

12. Carolyn Korsmeyer, "Gendered Concepts and Hume's Standard of Taste," in *Feminism and Tradition in Aesthetics*.

13. Hilde Hein, "Refining Feminist Theory: Lessons from Aesthetics," in *Aesthetics in Feminist Perspective*, op. cit.; Sally Markowitz, "Feminism and the Aesthetic

Point of View" (paper presented to the American Society for Aesthetics, Philadelphia, 1992).

14. Norma Broude and Mary D. Garrard (eds.), *The Expanding Discourse: Feminism and Art History* (New York: HarperCollins, 1993), contains a selection of art historical essays that examine the depiction of female bodies and the eroticization of political and cultural power.

15. For two influential discussions of the male gaze see Laura Mulvey, "Visual Pleasure and Narrative Cinema," in Gerald Mast and Marshall Cohen (eds.), *Film Theory and Criticism* (New York: Oxford University Press, 1985); and E. Ann Kaplan, "Is the Gaze Male?" in Marilyn Pearsall (ed.), *Women and Values: Readings in Recent Feminist Philosophy* (Belmont, Calif.: Wadsworth, 1993). The male gaze and aesthetic theory is discussed in Mary Devereaux, "Oppressive Texts, Resisting Readers and the Gendered Spectator: The New Aesthetics," in *Feminism and Tradition in Aesthetics*.

16. bell hooks, "The Oppositional Gaze," in her *Black Looks* (Boston: South End Press, 1992); Griselda Pollock, *Avant-Garde Gambits 1888–1893: Gender and the Color of Art History* (London: Thames and Hudson, 1993).

17. Teresa de Lauretis, *Alice Doesn't: Feminism, Semiotics, Cinema* (Bloomington: Indiana University Press, 1984).

18. Some examples include Elaine Showalter, *A Literature of Their Own* (Princeton, N.J.: Princeton University Press, 1977) and *Sister's Choice: Tradition and Change in American Women's Writing* (New York: Oxford University Press, 1991); and Elizabeth Abel (ed.), *Writing and Sexual Difference* (Brighton, U.K.: Harvester Press, 1982). See also Josephine Donovan, "Towards a Nondominative Aesthetic," Estella Lauter, "The Reenfranchisement of Art," and Renée Cox, "A Gynecentric Aesthetic." The latter three essays, on literature, visual art, and music, respectively, can be found in *Aesthetics in Feminist Perspective*. See also Silvia Bovenschen, "Is There a Feminine Aesthetic," and Heide Göttner-Abendroth, "Nine Principles of a Matriarchal Aesthetic," both in Gisela Ecker (ed.), *Feminist Aesthetics*, trans. Harriet Anderson (Boston: Beacon Press, 1985).

19. Rita Felski, *Beyond Feminist Aesthetics* (Cambridge, Mass.: Harvard University Press, 1989); Felski, "Why Feminism Doesn't Need an Aesthetic (And Why It Can't Ignore Aesthetics)," in *Feminism and Tradition in Aesthetics*; Janet Wolff, *Feminine Sentences: Essays on Women and Culture* (Cambridge: Polity Press, 1990); and Toril Moi, *Sexual/Textual Politics* (London: Routledge, 1985).

20. See especially Luce Irigaray, "The Power of Discourse and the Subordination of the Feminine," in her *This Sex Which Is Not One*, trans. Catherine Porter (Ithaca, N.Y.: Cornell University Press, 1985); and Irigaray, *Je tu, nous: Toward a Culture of Difference*, trans. Alison Martin (New York: Routledge, 1993). See also Hélène Cixous and Catherine Clément, *The Newly Born Women*, trans. Betsy Wing (Minneapolis: University of Minnesota Press, 1986); and Margaret Whitford, *Luce Irigaray: Philosophy in the Feminine* (London: Routledge, 1991). Jeffner Allen and Iris Young (eds.), *The Thinking Muse* (Bloomington: Indiana University Press, 1989), is a collection of feminist essays on the adaptation of French feminism to American feminist philosophy.

Though her philosophy is different (she argues against the abandonment of Enlightenment ideals), the literary work of Monique Wittig is a good example of antipatriarchal writing along similar principles. See her novels *Les Guerillères* and *The Lesbian Body*.

21. Speculations about feminine expression are not confined to literature, for painter Nancy Spero has adopted the idea of *la peinture feminine* in her own work, celebrating the female body and commenting ironically on artistic traditions of rendering images of women. See Elizabeth Ann Dobie, "Interweaving Feminist Frameworks," in *Feminism and Tradition in Aesthetics*.

22. However, as Ismay Barwell argues, this does not rule out the relevance of gender positions in what artworks mean or "say." See her "Who's Telling This Story, Anyway? Or, How to Tell the Gender of a Storyteller," *Australasian Journal of Philosophy* 73, no. 2 (June 1995): 227–38.

23. See Anita Silvers, "Has Her(oine's) Time Now Come?" in *Feminism and Tradition in Aesthetics*; Silvers, "Pure Historicism and the Heritage of Hero(ine)s: Who Grows in Phyllis Wheatley's Garden?" *Journal of Aesthetics and Art Criticism* 51, no. 3 (1993): 473–82; Peggy Brand, "Feminism in Context: A Role for Feminist Theory in Aesthetic Evaluation," in H. Gene Blocker and John W. Bender (eds.), *Contemporary Philosophy of Art: Continuity and Change, the State of the Art in Analytic Aesthetics* (New York: Prentice Hall, 1993); Susan L. Feagin, "Feminist Art History and De Facto Significance," in *Feminism and Tradition in Aesthetics*.

24. Mary Devereaux discusses autonomy in "The Philosophical and Political Implications of the Feminist Critique of Aesthetic Autonomy," in Glynis Carr (ed.), *Turning the Century: Feminist Theory in the 1990s* (Lewisburg, Pa.: Bucknell University Press, 1992); and "Protected Space: Politics, Censorship, and the Arts," *Journal of Aesthetics and Art Criticism* 51, no. 2 (1993): 207–15. A powerful critique of pornography as violence against women can be found in Catharine MacKinnon, *Only Words* (Cambridge, Mass.: Harvard University Press, 1993).

25. Nochlin's essay is reprinted in her *Women, Art, and Power and Other Essays* (New York: Harper and Row, 1988). Whitney Chadwick, *Women, Art, and Society* (London: Thames and Hudson, 1990), notes that women were not taught mathematics during the important time when linear perspective was being developed.

26. Christine Battersby, *Gender and Genius: Towards a Feminist Aesthetics* (Bloomington: Indiana University Press, 1989). I have based these remarks about genius on Battersby's study. Genius is also discussed in Rozsika Parker and Griselda Pollock, *Old Mistresses* (London: Routledge and Kegan Paul, 1981).

27. Studies of such cases may be found in Germaine Greer, *The Obstacle Race* (New York: Farrar, Straus and Giroux, 1979), and in Chadwick, *Women, Art, and Society*.

28. R. G. Collingwood, *Principles of Art* (London: Oxford University Press, 1938). Collingwood's theory is idealist in that, for him, the work of art proper is the mental expression of the artist.

29. Many scholars trace the roots of the idea of "fine art" to the eighteenth century, the same time when aesthetic theory takes its modern form. See Paul Osker Kristeller, "The Modern System of the Arts," in his *Renaissance Thought II* (New York: Harper Torchbook, 1965); Lawrence Lipking, *The Ordering of the Arts in Eighteenth-Century England* (Princeton, N.J.: Princeton University Press, 1970); Paul Mattick, Jr. (ed.), *Eighteenth-Century Aesthetics and the Reconstruction of Art* (Cambridge: Cambridge University Press, 1993).

30. See Larry Shiner, *The Invention of Art*, forthcoming.

31. Griselda Pollock, "Modernity and the Spaces of Femininity," in her *Vision and Difference* (London: Routledge, 1988); and Pollock, "Feminism and Modernism," in Rozsika Parker and Griselda Pollock (eds.), *Framing Feminism: Art and the*

Woman's Movement 1970–1985 (London: Pandora, 1987).The freight borne by the private-public distinction is a problem that Richard Rorty imports into his recommendation about ironism and solidarity in *Contingency, Irony, and Solidarity* (Cambridge: Cambridge University Press, 1989).

See also Frieda High W. Tesfagiorgis, "In Search of a Discourse and Critique/s That Center the Art of Black Women Artists," in Stanlie M. James and Abena P. A. Busia (eds.), *Theorizing Black Feminisms* (New York: Routledge, 1993); James M. Saslow, "Disagreeably Hidden," in *The Expanding Discourse*. Saslow argues that Rosa Bonheur's paintings contain self-portraits that offer a lesbian alternative to conventional female portraiture.

32. Janet Wolff, "The Invisible *Flaneuse*," in her *Feminine Sentences*, p. 47.

33. Carol Duncan, "The MoMA's Hot Mamas," is a witty and persuasive argument to this effect. It is reprinted in *The Expanding Discourse*. See also her *Aesthetics of Power: Essays in the Critical History of Art* (Cambridge; Cambridge University Press, 1993).

34. Anne Higgonet, "Secluded Vision," in *The Expanding Discourse*. In *Berthe Morisot's Images of Women* (Cambridge, Mass.: Harvard University Press, 1992), Higgonet demonstrates the continuity between domestic picture making and the recognized art of Morisot.

35. For example, Renée Lorraine believes that some non-Western dance and music traditions, such as those of tribal Africa and native America, provide models that are suitable for feminist projects in their nonhierarchic structures and goals of communal unity. See Renée Lorraine [Cox], "A Gynecentric Aesthetic," in *Aesthetics in Feminist Perspective*; see also Lorraine, "A History of Music," in *Feminism and Tradition in Aesthetics*.

See also Claire Detels, "Autonomous/Formalist Aesthetics, Music Theory, and the Feminist Paradigm of Soft Boundaries," *Journal of Aesthetics and Art Criticism* 52, no. 1 (Winter 1994): 113–26; Naomi Scheman, *Engenderings: Constructions of Knowledge, Authority, and Privilege* (New York: Routledge, 1993), chaps. 9 and 10.

36. They are also components of a venerable American philosophical tradition, pragmatism, in which some feminist philosophers find congenial company. See "Feminism and Pragmatism," special issue of *Hypatia*, Charlene Haddock Seigfried (ed.), 8, no. 2 (Spring 1993). A revival of Dewey's aesthetic ideas is Richard Shusterman's *Pragmatist Aesthetics* (Oxford: Basil Blackwell, 1992).

37. The most radical philosophical account to date of the construction of both gender and sexuality is probably Judith Butler's *Gender Trouble* (New York: Routledge, 1990). This is usefully paired with Thomas Laqueur's historical analysis of concepts of sex differences in *Making Sex* (Cambridge, Mass.: Harvard University Press, 1990). See also Butler, *Bodies That Matter* (New York: Routledge, 1993).

38. See Jana Sawicki, *Disciplining Foucault* (New York: Routledge, 1991); Lois McNay, *Foucault and Feminism* (Boston: Northeastern University Press, 1992); and Irene Diamond and Lee Quinby (eds.), *Feminism and Foucault* (Boston: Northeastern University Press, 1988).

39. Like empiricist aesthetics, psychoanalytic aesthetics is weighted to vision and the visual arts. Some of its most influential spokespeople have been film theorists. See, for example, Mary Ann Doane, *The Desire to Desire* (Bloomington: Indiana University Press, 1987); Doane, *Femmes Fatales: Feminism, Film Theory, Psychoanalysis* (New York: Routledge, 1991); Anne Friedberg, *Window Shopping: Cinema and the Postmodern* (Berkeley and Los Angeles: University of California Press,

1993); E. Ann Kaplan (ed.), *Psychoanalysis and Cinema* (New York: Routledge, 1990); Laura Mulvey, *Visual and Other Pleasures* (Basingstoke: Macmillan, 1988); and Constance Penley (ed.), *Feminism and Film Theory* (New York: Routledge, 1988). A selection of philosophical discussions of film is presented in Cynthia A. Freeland and Thomas E. Wartenberg (eds.), *Philosophy and Film* (New York: Routledge, 1995).

Psychoanalysis and literary studies have been pursued heavily as well; see, for example, Jane Gallop, *The Daughter's Seduction* (Ithaca, N.Y.: Cornell University Press, 1982); Gallop, *Reading Lacan* (Ithaca, N.Y.: Cornell University Press, 1985); and Claire Kahane, *Passions of the Voice: Hysteria, Narrative, and the Figure of the Speaking Woman 1850–1915* (Baltimore, Md.: Johns Hopkins University Press, 1995).

40. Laura Mulvey, "Visual Pleasure and Narrative Cinema," in Penley (ed.), *Feminism and Film Theory*, p. 64; Griselda Pollock, *Vision and Difference* (New York: Routledge, 1988), p. 126; Eagleton, *The Ideology of the Aesthetic*, p. 265. See also Naomi Scheman, "Missing Mothers/Desiring Daughters: Framing the Sight of Women," in her *Engenderings*.

It should be noted that many eighteenth-century philosophers speculated that the origin of feelings of beauty might be sexual attraction; however, they left those primitive beginnings behind in the articulation of the conscious experience of beauty.

41. The consequences for these differences are developed in Nancy Chodorow's influential feminist object relations theory. See *The Reproduction of Mothering* (Berkeley and Los Angeles: University of California Press, 1978) and *Feminism and Psychoanalytic Theory* (New Haven, Conn.: Yale University Press, 1989).

42. While most psychoanalytic accounts are particularly suited for analyzing representation, some also focus on formal aspects of art. Consider, for example, Julia Kristeva's speculations about sounds from the "semiotic chora" that irrupt into poetic language.

43. In this line of thought I am following a suggestion made by Noël Carroll in "The Image of Women in Film: A Defense of a Paradigm," in *Feminism and Tradition in Aesthetics*. Carroll offers his view as a criticism and alternative to psychoanalytic-minded film theory. I prefer to retain a place for theories of the unconscious.

The usefulness of analytic philosophical methods to feminism is discussed in Peg Brand and Carolyn Korsmeyer, "Aesthetics and Its Traditions," in *Feminism and Tradition in Aesthetics*; Brand, "Feminism in Context."

44. There are numerous accounts of expression in art that follow this distinction. Perhaps one of the most widely read is John Hospers' entry "Aesthetics, Problems of," in the *Encyclopedia of Philosophy*, Paul Edwards, ed., vol. 1 (New York and London: Macmillan, 1967).

45. Ronald de Sousa defends what he calls the "rationality" of emotions in *The Rationality of Emotions* (Cambridge, Mass.: MIT Press, 1987). In addition to the fact that they can be evaluated as rational or irrational, emotions perform a crucial cognitive function by determining the salience of information (see pp. 195, 202–3). Caution about "cognitivist" accounts of emotion is spelled out in Cheshire Calhoun's "Cognitive Emotions?" in Cheshire Calhoun and Robert C. Solomon (eds.), *What Is an Emotion?* (New York: Oxford University Press, 1984).

Some suggestions about emotions and gender variability are made by Alison Jaggar, "Love and Emotion in Feminist Epistemology," in Alison Jaggar and Susan Bordo (eds.), *Gender, Body, Knowledge* (New Brunswick, N.J.: Rutgers University

Press, 1989); Elizabeth V. Spelman, *Inessential Woman* (Boston: Beacon Press, 1988); and Naomi Scheman, "Anger and the Politics of Naming" and "Individualism and the Objects of Psychology," in her *Engenderings*.

46. Patricia Greenspan sees attraction and aversion or approval and disapproval as a kernel at the heart of all emotions. See her *Emotion and Reason* (New York: Routledge, 1988).

47. Susan L. Feagin explores emotions as aesthetic responses to fiction in *Reading with Feeling: The Aesthetics of Appreciation* (Ithaca, N.Y.: Cornell University Press, 1996). See also Jenefer Robinson, "*L'Éducation Sentimentale,*" *Australasian Journal of Philosophy* 73, no. 2 (June 1995): 212–26.

48. $R(Stfacmp)$: where R = emotion-type, S = subject, t = target object, f = focal property of t, a = the motivating aspect of the emotion, c = the cause of having the emotion, m = the aim of the emotion, and p = the propositional object of the emotion. There is much subtlety in de Sousa's robust account of emotions, though I believe he insists needlessly that there are no generic emotions. He argues that, unlike beliefs and desires, which all have the same formal objects (truth and goodness, respectively), emotions do not; their formal objects vary according to what the emotion is. Moreover, the formal object both defines the emotion and serves as the salient axiological property of the intentional object. I believe de Sousa's account runs into difficulty by assigning too many roles to the formal object.

49. Amélie O. Rorty, "Explaining Emotions," in Amélie Rorty (ed.), *Explaining Emotions* (Berkeley and Los Angeles: University of California Press, 1980).

50. Hilde Hein, "Refining Feminist Theory: Lessons from Aesthetics," in *Aesthetics in Feminist Perspective*, p. 4. See also Hein, "The Role of Feminist Aesthetics in Feminist Theory," in *Feminism and Tradition in Aesthetics*.

Philosophy of Religion in Different Voices

NANCY FRANKENBERRY

> History shows that the moral degradation of woman is due more to
> theological superstitions than to all other influences together.
>
> —*Elizabeth Cady Stanton*[1]

> God alone can save us, keep us safe. The feeling or experience of a positive,
> objective, glorious existence, the feeling of subjectivity, is essential for us.
> Just like a God who helps us and leads us in the path of becoming, who keeps
> track of our limits and infinite possibilities—as women—
> who inspires our projects.
>
> —*Luce Irigaray*[2]

RANGING FROM the scalding critique of Stanton to the reconstructive reflections of Irigaray, feminist philosophy of religion has been marked by a complex set of relations to the subject matter of religion, as well as to the discipline of philosophy. For those who find that the backlash against feminism and the revival of the religious right threaten to contribute as much to "women's degradation" as old "theological superstitions" do, Stanton's reasoning is still persuasive: the Word of God is the word of man, used to keep women in subjection and to hinder their emancipation. For others, who tend to identify with communities of faith and resistance, gynocentric efforts to create a possible space for the divine hold considerable appeal. Whether offering critique or reconstruction, women are (re)writing philosophy of religion today according to a variety of strategies whose overall rationale was articulated more than a hundred years ago by Anna Julia Cooper, an African-American feminist who appealed to the creation of a wholeness of vision: "It is not the intelligent woman vs. the ignorant woman, nor the white woman vs. the black, the brown, and the red,—it is not even the cause of woman vs. man. Nay, it is woman's strongest vindication for speaking that *the world needs to hear her voice*. It would be subversive of every human interest that the cry of one half of the human family be stifled. Woman . . . daring to think and move and speak,—to undertake to help shape, mold and direct the thought of her age, is merely completing the circle of the world's vision."[3]

My purpose in this essay is to consider the ways in which philosophy of religion is currently being written in different voices and to offer a critique of the dominant direction of the discipline. By critique I mean the practice, as described by Jeffner Allen and Iris Marion Young, of showing the limits of a mode of thinking by forging an awareness of alternative, more liberating, ideas, symbols, and discourses.[4] Although I will suggest ways in which gender as an analytic category and gender studies as a body of knowledge can not only challenge but also enrich and inform the methodological and substantive assumptions of philosophers of religion, I do not mean to suggest that gender hierarchy comprises a simple or exclusive category of analysis.[5] Given the interflowing streams of class, race, ethnicity, age, sexual orientation, and nationality that shape the complex modalities of social experience, it is unlikely that any one factor could ever suffice as a single or unitary focal point. And of course women cannot be presumed to speak in a single voice or to share a uniform "experience." Nevertheless, gender constitutes perhaps the most fundamental factor creating human difference, and it remains among the most ignored philosophically.

In the history of the philosophy of religion, gender bias has long operated to shape the ways in which the traditional problems and orientations of the field have been constructed. Like the cultural phenomenon of religion itself, philosophy of religion not only originated in a male tradition of production and transmission, with a history of excluding and devaluing women, but it has also been defined by many concepts and symbols marked as "masculine," which stand in oppositional relation to those marked as "feminine." Unlike the cultural phenomenon of religion, however, which is embedded in multiple cultural contexts, philosophy of religion has been largely Eurocentric and Anglo-American in its orientation. In addition to gender bias, its ethnocentrism constitutes the second major weakness of the field. For a long time, philosophy of religion has been written from a standpoint not unlike that of the Reverend Thwackum, the character in Henry Fielding's novel *Tom Jones*, who announced: "When I say religion, I mean the Christian religion, and when I say the Christian religion, I mean the Protestant religion, and when I say the Protestant religion, I mean the Church of England!" If not always the Church of England, it is for the most part Protestant Christianity that has been conflated with "religion" in the modern period of philosophy of religion. Most philosophers when they consider the field no doubt think of the standard topics and problems treated in the more familiar anthologies and textbooks: arguments for and against the existence of God; the nature and attributes of deity; the validity of religious knowledge claims; the question of theodicy; the justifiability of religious belief and language; the hope of immortality; the relation of faith and reason; evaluation of the nature of religious or mystical experiences, and so forth. Called upon to teach a course in philosophy of religion, many philosophers are likely to turn to the classic texts in the field, updated by contemporary readings, most of which conform in one way or another to Parson Thwackum's definition.

Undaunted by two such severe deficiencies—gender bias and ethnocentrism—the dominant Anglo-American analytic school of philosophy of religion has proved surprisingly healthy. Whereas at the midpoint of the twentieth century philosophy of religion was virtually defined by the assumptions and methods of logical positivism and empiricism, in the last few decades new and technically rigorous contributions by religiously committed philosophers have enlivened old theistic arguments. After long decades of dormancy when logical positivism seemed to yield only negative conclusions in the philosophy of religion, a resurgence of interest in traditional theism is occurring in mainstream philosophy of religion.[6] Thanks to the work of a variety of analytic philosophers, we now know, for example, that modal logic can be used to formulate a more perspicacious version of the ontological argument, that Bayesian models of probability can breathe new life into inductive justifications of religious belief, that rational choice theory can propel Pascal's wager once again to center stage, and that language-game analysis can offer a prima facie justification of religious language. Such developments, imported from other areas of philosophy, have prompted Richard Gale to suggest that "philosophy of religion is to the core areas of philosophy—logic, scientific methodology, the philosophy of language, metaphysics, and epistemology—as Israel is to the Pentagon. The former are a proving ground for the weapons forged in the latter."[7] Far from the days of wondering what Athens has to do with Jerusalem, philosophy and religion now appear to have entered a period of détente as comrades-in-arms. None of the new and sophisticated military hardware, however, engages the questions posed by feminist inquiry or aims at disarmament of the sexist elements of the traditional theistic model. Instead, in the work of philosophers such as Richard Swinburne, Alvin Plantinga, William Alston, and D. Z. Phillips, philosophy of religion has been deployed in defense of the cogency of a standard form of Western monotheism, in the service of a conception of "God" that is patriarchal, and in the vested interests of staunchly traditional forms of Christianity.[8]

Philosophy of religion in the last days of the twentieth century needs to shed both its gender bias and its ethnocentrism if it is to open out in new directions adequate to the twenty-first century. Not only is much of its content sexist and patriarchal, but its understanding of religion is parochially defined and monoculturally impaired. By contrast, the constructive contours of several new research programs that I will trace in this chapter offer an exciting potential for reshaping the field.

THE PROBLEM OF GOD AND THE CRITIQUE OF
PHILOSOPHY OF RELIGION

With its very subject matter—religion—so notoriously riddled with misogyny and androcentrism, the philosophy of religion can hardly ignore questions of gender ideology. Indeed, gender bias in religion has not been accidental or superficial. Elizabeth Johnson likens it to a buried continent whose subaqueous pull shapes all the visible landmass; androcentric bias has massively distorted every aspect of the terrain and rendered invisible, inconsequential, or nonexistent the experience and significance of half the human race.[9] Of all the manifold forms sexism takes, none has been more pernicious than the religious and theological restrictions on women's lives. For philosophers studying the intellectual effects and belief systems of religions, the opportunity to critique and correct sexist and patriarchal constructions in this field is as ample as it is urgent, given the ubiquitous presence of gender ideology in all known religions. Not one of the religions of the world has been totally affirming of women's personhood. Every one of them conforms to Heidi Hartmann's definition of patriarchy as "relations between men, which have a material base, and which, though hierarchical, establish or create interdependence and solidarity among men that enable them to dominate women."[10] All sacred literatures of the world display an unvarying ambivalence on the subject of women. For every text that places well-domesticated womanhood on a religious pedestal, another one announces that, if uncontrolled, women are the root of all evil. Religion thus comprises a primary space in which and by means of which gender hierarchy is culturally articulated, reinforced, and consolidated in institutionalized form. Religion is hardly the only such space, of course, but it appears to have been a particularly persistent and recurrent way of undergirding and sanctifying gender hierarchy in the West.

Not only does gender bias saturate the subject matter of philosophy of religion but it also permeates its practice, in ways that range from the sublime to the recidivist. On the recidivist side, a series of familiar lapses appears: the dearth of female authors in the leading journals or standard textbooks; the almost complete absence of attention to feminist philosophy on the part of mainstream authors, male and female; the exclusively male-authored and monochromatic complexion of the standard anthologies of readings and editorial boards. Even the use of inclusive language has been remarkably slow in finding its way into the scholarly publications and conceptual patterns of the field.[11] It is not unusual to find authors who discuss concepts of justice and fairness at length, using throughout the male pronoun. The "simple matter of pronouns," as Elizabeth Kamarck Minnich has remarked, "contains the whole of our problem, and there is no shortcut to fixing it. Every time we stumble over a pronoun, we stumble over the root problem that entangles the dominant tradition in its own old errors."[12] The dominant tradition, however, has barely begun to register the seriousness of the feminist criticism of patriarchal religious language.

This lapse is most apparent at the sublime end of the scale, where discussion of the problem of God, a topic that has been standard fare for all schools of philosophy of religion, epitomizes the pervasive gender bias infecting the field. Long a linchpin holding up other structures of patriarchal rule, the concept of a male God has been judged by every major feminist thinker, including Mary Daly, Rosemary Radford Ruether, Naomi Goldenberg, Judith Plaskow, Julia Kristeva, and Luce Irigaray, to be both humanly oppressive and, on the part of believers, religiously idolatrous. Why should a single set of male metaphors be absolutized as though supremely fitting about the subject? Contrary to the literary gesture of writers hoping to avoid sexist language with ritual disclaimers, it has not been persuasive simply to declare that the concept of God transcends gender and, therefore, "he" is not literally male, and then to presume that all can go on as before. The problem remains that once the masculine has been raised to the univeral human, beyond gender, the feminine alone must bear the burden of sexual difference.

Despite the de-anthropomorphizing efforts of many generations of theologians and philosophers, the sign God remains stubbornly gendered male in Western thought. Philosophers of religion have sometimes marked a distinction between the crudely anthropomorphic language of myth and popular piety, on the one hand, and the loftily conceptual and gender-neutral language of philosophy, on the other hand, while failing to account for the fact that the *Vorstellung*, or image, of a male personage is firmly inscribed in every major philosophical *Begriff*, or concept, of deity in the West, and the referent in the long history of philosophical arguments both for and against the existence of God is for the most part subliminally envisioned as male. Whether taken as real or unreal, inferred validly or invalidly, experienced directly or projected illusorily, the divine identity in classical theism has been unmistakably male. More problematically, the supreme, ruling, judging, as well as loving, male God envisioned as a single, absolute subject and named Father has been conceived as standing in a relation of hierarchical domination to the world. In ways both implicit and explicit, this has tended in turn to justify various social and political structures of patriarchy that exalt solitary human patriarchs at the head of pyramids of power. Drawn almost exclusively from the world of ruling-class men, traditional theistic concepts and images have functioned effectively to legitimate social and intellectual structures that grant a theomorphic character to men who rule but that relegate women, children, and other men to marginalized and subordinated areas. The discursive practices that construct the divine as male have been so intimately connected to the production of ideologies which devalue all that is not male that they have formed a constitutive element in the oppression of women and other "Others." Mary Daly pronounces the perfect apothegm on this form of sexism when she writes, "If God is male, then the male is God."[13]

At the same time, the problem of gender bias is more subtle than the dominance of male signifiers for deity alone indicates. It encompasses other topics and gender-inflected categories of traditional philosophy of religion, as well as the basic conceptual tools assumed in this field. Like a prism that refracts all the surrounding light, the gendering of God has skewed the way in which other problems in philosophy of religion have traditionally been constructed. The problem of *religious language*, for example, is frequently cast in terms of the meaning and use of metaphors and models, and questions of reference and truth. But the metaphors and models employed by mainstream philosophers of religion often trade uncritically on intrinsically hierarchical patterns of relations. Metaphors such as Father, King, Lord, Bridegroom, Husband, and God-He go unmarked. Let an occasional female model or metaphor intrude into this homosocial circle and it will immediately be remarked upon, usually producing nervous laughter in the classroom. In considerations of the so-called *divine attributes*, none receives more discussion in the literature than that of "omnipotence," by which some version of "perfect power" is meant. In the eleventh century, Peter Damian could quote approvingly the biblical passage "O Lord, King Omnipotent, all things are placed in your power, and there is no one who is able to resist your will" as he argued that divine omnipotence is even able to "restore a virgin to purity after her fall."[14] In twentieth-century studies, "perfect power" has not improved any.[15] On standard definitions of the concept of omnipotence, ranging from "unilateral power to effect any conceivable state of affairs" to more moderate "self-limiting power," the kind of power in question is in principle one of domination, or power-over, and has been persistently associated with the characteristics of ideal masculinity. Like the two favorite heroes of modern philosophy, the Cartesian cognitive subject and the Kantian autonomous will, an omnipotent deity reflects the mirror image of idealized masculinist qualities. At the same time, philosophical arguments on behalf of the concept of divine aseity or self-sufficiency reinforce the disparagement of reciprocal power relations that is characteristic of patriarchy in its social and intellectual expressions. Among contemporary schools, only process philosophers of religion have explicitly argued against the attribute of omnipotence on the grounds that it is conceptually incoherent, scientifically superfluous, and morally offensive in its association of the divine with Male Controlling Power.[16]

In a related way, the topic of *theodicy* has also been deeply shaped by male-defined constructions of power and interest. The very form of the question, How can an all-powerful deity permit evil? implies a meaning of "allpowerful" that is embedded in a discourse of domination. Also exemplary are the types of evil overlooked in the many hypotheticals, counterexamples, and possible worlds that are generated in discussions of theodicy by male philosophers. Misogyny and rape rarely make the list of evils. The whole drift of theodicy as an intellectual exercise points back to the question of God, and rarely to the world of cruelty and suffering.[17]

Philosophical debates on the topic of *immortality*, it could be argued, have also been deeply shaped by androcentric interests—centering on self-perpetuation and individual, rather than collective, survival. Charlotte Perkins Gilman, rightfully regarded as a foremother in feminist philosophy of religion, located the gender difference in *His Religion and Hers* (1923) this way: "To the death-based religion, the main question is, 'What is going to happen to me, after I am dead?'—a posthumous egoism. To the birth-based religion, the main question is, 'What is to be done for the child who is born?'—an immediate altruism."[18] Forgiving Gilman for the simplicity of her anthropology, we see her point. In philosophically emphasizing the absolute transcendence of God over the world, the dominating and all-encompassing nature of the divine power, and the splendid self-sufficiency and independence of the divine will, classical philosophical theism produced a perfect reflection of patriarchal consciousness in which it is possible today to see only "man." Religiously, as well, classical theism's entire repertoire of beliefs concerning God, creation, redemption, and future hope have been interwoven with characteristics that are oppressive to half of the human race.

A still deeper critique involves the differentiation of embedded levels of bias and androcentrism in the crucial assumptions, methods, and norms of traditional philosophy of religion. Rooted in an ancient dualistic worldview whose philosophical inadequacy has been harder to detect, until recently, than its social and legalistic inequities, Western religious categories have been inextricably bound up with "a certain metaphysical exigency," as Derrida calls it. The metaphysical worldview that once supported the sacred canopy may have lost all cogency for the modern mind, along with the arguments of medieval Scholastics that sailors cannot kiss their wives good-bye on Sundays, or hangmen go to heaven, but the dualisms associated with that worldview have continued to haunt the philosophical imagination, betraying an androcentric bias. Beginning with Greek philosophy's equation of the male principle with mind and reason and act, the female principle was left with only a contrasting identification in terms of matter, body and passion and potency. The subsequent history of Western philosophy, despite major conceptual shifts, displayed a characteristic logic and form. Taking the form of hierarchical opposition, the logic of binary structuring mutually opposed such elements as mind and body, reason and passion, object and subject, transcendental and empirical. As argued by any number of feminist philosophers, these hierarchical oppositions are typically gender-coded. Body, matter, emotions, instincts, and subjectivity are coded as feminine, while mind, reason, science, and objectivity are coded as masculine.[19] Western monotheism has constructed the meaning of "God" in relation to "world" around these binary oppositions of mind/body, reason/passion, male/female. In this way, not only religion in the West but also traditional philosophy of religion remain complicitous with the very system of gender constructs and symbolic structures that underlie women's oppression.[20] In the binary opposition between "God" and "world," "God" occupies the privileged space and acts as the central principle, the One who confers identity to creatures to whom "He" stands in hierarchical relation. Oppositional pairing of God/world has served in turn to organize others, such as heaven and earth, sacred and profane. The widespread dichotomy of sacred/profane, employed by many authors, thus comes already encoded with the hierarchical oppositions of male/female and masculine/feminine onto which it is mapped, along with the structurally related pairs, white/black and heterosexual/homosexual.[21] The first term in each pair is sacralized, while the second is rendered profane.

Along with the broad dissemination of the foregoing critique has come an increasing awareness that the relation between symbolic structures, on the one hand, and gender constructions, on the other, cannot be specified in terms of a single explanatory model. The power of symbolic orders to invoke and reinscribe implicit gender understandings works in varied and complex ways, as shown in recent studies. Emphasizing the polysemic and multivalent quality of religious symbols, Caroline Bynum's work, for example, stresses the ability of a symbol to hold different meanings for different people. Never a simple matter of sheer reflection of the social order, the relation between society and symbol, or between psyche and symbol, is open-ended. Relations of reversal or inversion of actual social structures may also obtain, making it risky for the interpreter to posit a single unidirectional cause-and-effect relation between symbol and social setting. As Bynum points out, meaning is not so much imparted as it is appropriated "in a dialectical process whereby it becomes subjective reality for the one who uses the symbol," allowing for the possibility that "those with different gender experiences will appropriate symbols in different ways."[22] An important implication of this is that no necessary correlation can be assumed between goddess-worshiping cultures and actual egalitarian social structures in the lives of females and males of that culture. Similarly, the male Father God may open up a range of different interpretative possibilities for both women and men. In culturally specific and historically unstable ways, religious symbols, even of the male Father God, have been useful in resisting and subverting the social order, not only in reflecting or reinforcing it. In light of these considerations, it is risky to generalize across cultures, religious traditions, or historical periods with respect to the different ways in which males and females appropriate or construct religious symbolism. More detailed historical and philosophical analyses are needed of the relations between symbolic structures and gender constructions.[23]

Although mainstream philosophers have so far failed to take explicit account of the gendered dynamics of religious thought, for over two decades a variety of other scholars, including biblical exegetes, theologians, ethicists, and feminist philosophers of religion, have produced an extraordinary explosion of research resulting in feminist thealogies, critical hermeneutics of suspicion, and woman-affirming writings on spirituality. In these, "the problem of God" reappears as a crucial site of reconstruction, to which I selectively attend in the next section.

RECONSTRUCTING THE MEANING OF THE DIVINE

The medieval theologian Hildegard of Bingen, struggling to capture her vision of the Spirit of God, wrote with a cascade of vivid images, a mélange of metaphors. As rendered by Elizabeth Johnson in the following passage, Hildegard's vision encompasses many of the themes that appear in the writing of twentieth-century feminist writers. The divine spirit, according to Hildegaard, is the very life of the life of all creatures; the way in which everything is penetrated with connectedness and relatedness; a burning fire who sparks, ignites, inflames, kindles hearts; a guide in the fog; a balm for wounds; a shining serenity; an overflowing fountain that spreads to all sides. "She is life, movement, color, radiance, restorative stillness in the din. Her power makes all withered sticks and souls green again with the juice of life. She purifies, absolves, strengthens, heals, gathers the perplexed, seeks the lost. She pours the juice of contrition into hardened hearts. She plays music in the soul, being herself the melody of praise and joy. She awakens mighty hope, blowing everywhere the winds of renewal in creation."[24] This, for Hildegard in the eleventh century, is the mystery of the God in whom humans live and move and have our being.

Eight centuries later, Paula Gunn Allen has written in similarly provocative language of the spirit that is pervasive of her Laguna Pueblo/Sioux peoples: "There is a spirit that pervades everything, that is capable of powerful song and radiant movement, and that moves in and out of the mind. The colors of this spirit are multitudinous, a glowing, pulsing rainbow. Old Spider Woman is one name for this quintessential spirit, and Serpent Woman is another . . . and what they together have made is called Creation, Earth, creatures, plants and light."[25]

In Ntozake Shange's well-known play, a tall black woman rises from despair and cries out, "i found god in myself and i loved her, i loved her fiercely."[26] Alice Walker, in a frequently cited passage in *The Color Purple*, voices a similar note as Shug recounts to Celie the epiphany that came over her when she learned to get the old white man off her eyeball:

> It? I ast.
> Yeah, It. God ain't a he or a she, but a It.
> But what do it look like? I ast.
> Don't look like nothing, she say. It ain't a picture show. It ain't something you can look at apart from anything else, including yourself. I believe God is everything, say Shug. Everything that is or ever will be. And when you can feel that, and be happy to feel that, you've found It.[27]

In recent theological constructions, Rosemary Ruether has worked with the unpronounceable written symbol "God/ess," used to connote the "encompassing matrix of our being" that transcends patriarchal limitations and signals redemptive experience for women as well as for men. Modeling God for a nuclear age, Sallie McFague has experimented with metaphors of God as Mother, Lover, and Friend of the world which is conceived of as God's own body. Correlating the Tillichean notion of the power of being with the empowerment women know in freeing themselves from patriarchy, the early Mary Daly posited God as "Verb," a dynamic becoming process that energizes all things. Using process philosophy's categories, Marjorie Suchocki has given new resonance to the meaning of Whitehead's metaphors of God as "the lure for feeling" whose "power of persuasion" aims to effect justice and peace. Blurring the lines between psychological, somatic, and religious experiences, Luce Irigaray projects a concept of "the feminine divine" grounded in the morphology of women's bodies in all their multiplicity and fluidity.[28] Significantly in all the cases cited here, contemporary women's articulation of a relation between God and the world depicts the divine as continuous with the world rather than as radically transcendent ontologically or metaphysically. Divine transcendence is seen to consist in total immanence. But images and metaphors are not philosophical concepts, and the reference range of "the divine" as it appears in these and other feminist writings is not always clear. While theologians are frequently satisfied to work imaginatively with symbols, images, and metaphors, without regard to the question *what* the symbols are symbolic *of*, philosophers of religion normally seek more precision and conceptual clarification.

On the difficult question of the meaning and reference of God-talk, two contemporary schools of philosophy of religion offer potentially promising reconstructive and revisionist avenues. Both the tradition that employs the classical ontology of being, extending from Thomas Aquinas to Paul Tillich and the early Mary Daly, and the tradition that employs an ontology of becoming, extending from Alfred North Whitehead to Charles Hartshorne, John Cobb Jr., Marjorie Suchocki, and Catherine Keller, afford systematic conceptual schemes for explicating the metaphors that appear in various contemporary writings concerning "the sacred" and any of its variants, such as "the divine," "spirit," "God," "transcendence," or "higher power." Both traditions can be modified, moreover, according to qualifications I will suggest, and thereby seen to converge in a single conceptual model, rendered as "creativity" in Whitehead's system and as being (*esse*) in Aquinas's.

The school of thought known as process philosophy has been re-writing philosophy of religion in a radically different voice for several decades, providing the basis for a revisionist theism that is better termed "panentheism," or all-in-god. Preeminently among those who have labored in this century to construct a coherent philosophy of God that is also consistent with scientific cosmology and evolutionary theory, process philosophers of religion have produced, in addition, a model relatively free of sexism and androcentrism. The underlying values of the process worldview are organic, relational, dynamic, and embodied. Whitehead's 1929 elaboration of the idea that "it is as true to say that God creates the World as that the World creates God"[29] anticipated the themes of interrelatedness and mutual conditioning that feminist philosophy has developed in multiple ways in recent decades.[30]

In the process paradigm everything comes into being by grasping or "prehending" antecedently actualized things to integrate them into a new actualized thing, its own self. Supplanting substance philosophy's idea that it takes an agent to act, process philosophy proposes a model whereby agents are the results of acts and subjects are constituted out of relations. Quantum units of becoming achieve momentary unity out of a given multiplicity in a never-ending rhythm of creative process whereby "the many become one and are increased by one."[31] Creativity within each occasion is spontaneous, the mark of actuality, and free, within the limits determined by its antecedent causes. Creativity unifies every many and is creative of a new unifying perspective that then becomes one among the many. In a process ontology, creativity is ultimate reality not in the sense of something more ultimate behind, above, or beyond reality but in the sense of something ultimately descriptive of all reality, or of what the biologist Charles Birch and the theologian John B. Cobb Jr. call "the Life Process."[32] As a category, creativity is the "ultimate of ultimates" in Whitehead's words, but as such it is only an abstraction, the formal character of any actual occasion. Creativity as concrete, however, signifies the dynamism that is the very actuality of things, their act of being there at all. Everything exists in virtue of creativity, but creativity is not any *thing*.

The proposal to view the divine as equivalent to creativity marks a crucial departure from Whitehead's own notion of God as an actual entity in the process of becoming, but it acquires support from its correlation with the tradition that employs the language of being, rather than becoming, to explicate the meaning of the divine. In its classical medieval synthesis in Aquinas, this tradition conceptualizes the divine as *esse ipsum* and holds that in God essence and existence are one; that is, God's very nature is *esse*, to be. Everything that exists does so through participation in divine being, or being itself. Although for Aquinas and classical thinkers, being was thought to be already concretized in a single source that was supremely actual, precisely this assumption undergoes modification in the shift from a substance metaphysics to one in which processive-relational categories are taken as ultimate. Desubstantialized and freed from static fixity in neo-Scholastic metaphysics, being signifies the source and power of all that exists. Dynamized and pluralized according to the process paradigm, being does not repose in an originary source antecedent to every event; rather, it constitutes the very act of be-ing, of liv-ing, of exist-ing in the present moment as a new one emergent from an antecedent many. As such, being or creativity is inherently relational and processive. It is immanent within each momentary event as its spontaneous power; and it is also transcendent to that event of becoming in the sense that it is never exhausted by the forms in which it is found but is always potentially a "more" that is "not yet" actualized. As long as being, like creativity, is not construed as something a being *has* but rather as what it means *to be* at all, the identification of God with being in the West can be understood to point to sheer livingness or that which energizes all things to exist. Although no-thing particular in its own right, being is the very actuality of things, their act of being there at all. Being-itself is therefore not construed as a particular being, thus ruling out pictorial theism's anthropomorphisms; it is not the sum of beings, thus ruling out a simple aggregation; it is not a property of things nor an accidental quality, not a substance, and not a class of things.

Articulating this tradition in light of recent feminist writings about God, Elizabeth Johnson explicates the concept of *esse* to signify "pure aliveness in relation, the unoriginate welling up of fullness of life in which the whole universe participates."[33] Like the theologian–philosopher of religion Paul Tillich, Johnson understands the symbol God to refer to the creative ground of all that is and the re-creative ground of the energy to resist nonbeing toward the good that may yet be, the future promised but unknown. For Johnson the religious "naming toward God" as "Holy Mystery" is not an utterly agnostic gesture but analogical in that the dynamic and immanental idea of God is the idea of that which energizes all things. The concept of God as *esse* within this ontological framework refers to the sheer actuality of things, an act common to all things. Dynamic and living, being is yet elusive. Signifying the moment-to-moment reality in virtue of which everything exists, the philosophical concepts of creativity (as explicated by Whitehead) and of *esse* (as explicated dynamically) are useful for interpreting what philosophy of religion in a new and different voice could mean by "divine reality," "holy mystery," "empowering spirit," and a variety of other metaphors and symbols.

By providing a unifying concept that articulates a common feature of various experiences of the presence and absence of empowerment, reconstruction of the concept of God along the lines adumbrated here can illuminate and give coherence to the varieties of women's and men's experiences at three levels: the personal and interpersonal; social systems and institutional structures; and the all-encompassing natural world. Any person, for example, who survives horrible crime, assault, war, or famine, and who wants to praise the power or powers that permit her being in the face of nonbeing, experiences the meaning of creativity, of being, even if she can no longer give credence to the faith of the fathers. Anyone who experiences life's fresh starts of vitality and freedom, of courage renewed, or of love restored in unlikely circumstances, encounters the mystery of the divine. All those women and men who in their sheer grit to keep on keeping on find the strength to march, organize, protest, sue, walk out, tear down, make peace, or rebuild, are animated by the spirit. And anyone who has ever felt awe before the power of ocean and sky, the majesty of mountain, the peace of prairie, or the wildness of any part of nature's terrible beauty, has been stirred by the same living God.[34]

While revisionist and depatriarchalized philosophies of God will clearly continue to engage some philosophers of religion, others are willing to see even that topic cease to hold center stage in future philosophies of religion. As new waves of historicism and antiessentialism begin to register among a new generation of postanalytic philosophers of religion, dissatisfaction is developing with the way in which the traditional table of contents has been constructed. Michael McGhee, for example, criticizes the tendency of philosophers silently to assimilate questions about religion to questions about "belief in the existence of God." Complaining of the slippery slope whereby philosophers slide from "religion" to religious "belief" and from that to "belief in God," McGhee laments the way that "philosophical reflection about religion is transformed without a pause into reflection on the existence of God, and questions about the rationality of belief, the validity of the proofs, and the coherence of the divine attributes cannot be far behind." The established methodology that causes this slide may be historically understandable in terms of the influence of natural theology on philosophy of religion, but the real issue, McGhee notes, "is whether such preoccupations should remain central to the philosophy of religion, and, if not, what should replace them."[35] Strong examples of alternative preoccupations are appearing in recent work considered in the next section.

ENGENDERING NEW PHILOSOPHIES OF RELIGION

Two major thematic concerns serve to distinguish the new generation of texts from mainstream analytic philosophy of religion. First, the body, a recurrent theme in a variety of recent interdisciplinary studies, figures as the material or symbolic basis for much new writing, in contrast to the fiction of disembodied subjectivity that marks most mainstream epistemology.[36] Second, analysis of the complex relations between power and knowledge recurs in the new philosophies of religion, in contrast to the dominant paradigm's failure to take seriously enough the social processes that construct subjectivity, the discursive practices that construct the discipline of philosophy itself, and the relations of power that inform both.

Reinclusion of the embodied character of subjectivity produces, for example, such subtle and provocative investigations as Paula Cooey's *Religious Imagination and the Body*. Giving the body a major epistemological role as medium, Cooey explores its ambiguous double role as site and as sign, and demonstrates how wide a range of new inquiries can be opened up for philosophy of religion by this focus. Among the new questions that emerge from the conjunction of the body, sexuality, and religious experience are those that Cooey formulates for further study; they are worth quoting at length to highlight the difference between a religious epistemology oriented

to embodied subjectivity and mainstream ones in which such questions never get posed in connection with the topic of mystical or religious
experience:

> What role does eroticism play in mystical experience? Given contemporary claims
> that sexual exploration liberates and empowers, are there material and historical
> relations between mystical self-transcendence and disciplined transgression of sex-
> ual taboos, and, if so, what are they? What kinds of meaning and value do such
> experiences produce? How does acknowledging the involvement of sexuality in
> mystical experiences, whether sexuality is suppressed or exercised, materially af-
> fect the central symbols or concepts themselves? Does acknowledging the involve-
> ment of the body in mystical experiences tell us anything new about the role of
> central symbols as place-setters, or the prescription of limits on language itself?
> Given that transgression may include violence perpetrated by a self upon the self
> or others, how does disciplined transgression of sexual taboos (for example, sado-
> masochistic practices) relate to other contexts of violence (for example, torture,
> war, domestic violence, and rape)? Does the occurrence of sexual transgression in
> the context of a religious symbol system substantively differ from any other con-
> text? What does it mean that believers attribute wrath, carnage, sexual transgres-
> sion, erotic behavior, and sexual acts to their deities? Does the absence of such
> attributions simply mask and deny the reality of the violence of human
> existence?[37]

In another kind of body-based study, Howard Eilberg-Schwartz's provocative work *God's Phallus and Other Problems for Men and Monotheism* is
indicative of a new alliance of philosophy of religion with gender studies and
social theory, rather than with natural theology and speculative metaphysics.[38] Dozens of feminist studies over the past twenty-five years have explored the way in which male deities authorize male domination in the social
order. Written mostly by women, these studies typically have attended to the
way in which a male divinity undermines female experience by both legiti-
mating male authority and deifying masculinity. Left unconsidered until
very recently has been the question whether a male divinity generates certain
dilemmas and tensions for the conception of masculinity, rendering its
meaning unstable. Overturning the conventional assumption that Jewish
monotheism centered on an invisible, disembodied deity, Eilberg-Schwartz
shows through careful analysis of numerous myths that ancient Israel did
image God in human form, while at the same time veiling the divine phallus.

Two consequences in particular arise for masculinity in a religious system
that imagines a male deity with a phallus. First, the dilemma of homoerotic
desire is posed when men worship a male God in a culture based on heterosexual complementarity. Although the expression of divine-human intimacy
is couched in the language of male-female complementarity, it is males, not
females, who enter into the covenantal marriage with the deity. Collectively,
Israelite men were constituted discursively as "she" and were said to be
"whoring" when they strayed from monotheism (monogamy) into idolatry

(adultery). Suppression of the homoerotic impulse in the divine-human relationship, however, could take several forms: hiding and veiling the body of God through prohibitions against depicting God; feminizing Israelite males so that they could assume the role of God's wife; and exaggerating the way in which women are "other" so as to minimize the ways in which men are made into others of God.

The solution of imagining Israel as a metaphoric woman, in an exclusive relation to the divine maleness, may have solved the first dilemma of homoerotic desire only by generating another. The second major dilemma for masculinity is posed by being made in the image of a sexless Father God in a culture defined by patrilineal descent. The sexlessness of a Creator Father God sets up major tensions for men who must procreate. In contrast to the Christian religion, whose different logic of a God fathering a Son could render a human father irrelevant, Hebrew logic placed great importance on the human father, generating tension around a Father God who was thought to be sexless and therefore without a son. When the dilemma of homoerotic desire is again posed for Christian men in relation to a male Christ's body, it, too, is avoided by speaking collectively of the Christian community as a woman.

Just as feminist theorists have yet to explore fully the question of how a male God is problematic for men's conceptions of self, feminist critique has left unthought the difference between God as male and God as Father, according to Eilberg-Schwartz. Strict focus on the ways in which a masculine image of God undermines female experience tends "to conflate human and divine masculinities into one undifferentiated symbol."[39] Differentiating between images of male deities and images of father deities, Eilberg-Schwartz contends that the maleness of God may have different implications than the fatherliness of God. Fatherly images of God can and should be used, he argues, "but only if equally powerful female images are also celebrated." Repudiating the incorporeal, distant God that helped to generate the hierarchical associations of masculinity and femininity, he favors an image of "a tender loving Father who faces and embraces the child," in the apparent expectation that a loving and embodied God may support a different kind of masculinity, one more capable of intimacy and tenderness.[40]

An indication of another new direction available to philosophers of religion appears in the growing influence of poststructuralist criticism, which accords great significance to the webbed relations of language, experience, power, and discourse. The links frequently assumed among these terms, however, leave a lot of open, untheorized space. Mary McClintock Fulkerson brilliantly exposes and attempts to fill these gaps in *Changing the Subject*, a study of women's discourses, feminist theology, and the import of the poststructuralist revolution. One of the most powerful insights of the poststructuralist discourse analysis that Fulkerson deploys is its challenge to three inadequate notions of language, gender, and power: (1) the idea that linguistic signs re-present the thing; (2) the Cartesian assumption of the subjective consciousness as the origin of meaning; and (3) the understanding of power only in terms of external, unidirectional, and negative oppression. Poststructuralist method also critiques the related liberal logic of inclusion that appeals to "women's experience" as though it is an unproblematic or uncoded content of some kind. All such strategies and methods, Fulkerson shows, fail to recognize and account for the multiplicity of differences among myriad subject positions. In contrast to the liberal humanist goal of accommodating as many "different voices" as possible, discourse analysis seeks a more radical reading of the ways "voice" itself is produced and knowledge is power. In order to flesh out the multiple orderings that create differences in women's positions, a major epistemic shift is needed, one that has already been more fully accomplished by theologians and literary critics than by philosophers of religion. According to Fulkerson, taking into account the inextricable and multiplicative character of the link between knowledge and the social relations out of which knowledge emerges changes the question, as well as the subject. The question is not, for example, whether a given religious belief system is oppressive or liberating to women. Such generic and wholesale frames need to be replaced by more complex appreciation of the construction of multiple identities according to different locations in the social formation of patriarchal capitalism.

Calling explicit attention to the priority of interpretive interest on the part of scholars, Fulkerson examines the way that social relations and political elements in the form of postindustrial capitalism and modern disciplinary technologies are implicated in the construction of both readers and texts. In this account, signifying processes constitute the very objects that philosophers of religion consider and often reify as natural. At the same time, philosophers of religion occupy social positions of power, which further construct their own complex identities, discourses, and desires. Therefore, philosophies that regard language or ideas as straightforward reflections of, or homologous with, the social relations of their proponents turn out to be quite inadequate. Equally, the pretense to be interest-free belies the situated, interested nature of all knowing and disguises the way the philosopher of religion's own theoretical discourse is impacted by power.

Fleshing out the multiple orderings that create differences in women's positions should result in a clarification of what is at stake in appeals to "women's experience," often taken as a "source" and/or "norm" for feminist thought in an earlier generation of texts. Rather than as a "content" that is representative of a natural realm of women's consciousness, religious or otherwise, "women's experience" can be understood as constructed from "converging discourses, their constitution by differential networks, and their production of certain pleasures and subjugations."[41] There is, therefore, no essential woman, or inner consciousness, or natural body that transcends all particularities to which one can appeal in order to join women together in a shared dilemma/oppression and a shared vision of emancipation. Experience is not the origin of (feminist) philosophy of religion in the sense of offering evidence for its claims, but the very reality that needs to be explained. Similarly, in theorizing the link, for example, between the maleness of divine imagery and the legitimation of male dominance, what needs to be *explained* is how the maleness of divine imagery gets distributed and interrelated with material realities, and *how* the discourse itself carries out the oppression of women.

Once the false universal of "women's experience" or "human experience" is replaced with Fulkerson's "analytic of women's discourses," philosophers of religion can begin to consider the specific productions of positions for women, asking such questions as: What discourses construct the middle-class white churchwoman's positions? The poor Pentecostal woman preacher's? The liberal academic liberation feminist's? In extended accounts of Appalachian Pentecostal women preachers' discourse and of the discourse of Presbyterian women's groups, Fulkerson illuminates how these two very diverse women's subject positions have wrestled with a religious tradition in ways both liberating and constraining. By approaching the world of faith as a system of discourses, rather than as representational interpretations or cognitive belief claims, she displays how women's faith positions can be constitutive of their emancipatory practices. The call stories and worship performances of poor Pentecostal women ministers, accompanied by ecstatic and bodily displays of joy, produce particular forms of resistance to patriarchal constraints, just as the faith practices of middle-class Presbyterian housewives produce other possibilities for transgression, pleasure, and desire.

The merit of this methodological shift for philosophy of religion is a greatly enhanced display of the complexity of gender discourse, of the constraints and resistances found in faith practices, and of the social conditions of signification. Above all, poststructuralist criticism has the merit of fully displaying a feminist commitment to the situated character of knowledge. Unlike mainstream analytic philosophy, it creates space in which it is possible to ask what philosophy of religion has occluded from its angle of vision by virtue of the abstract and distanced discourse that characterizes it. The problem is not that philosophy of religion employs abstractions; all theoretical discourse must employ critical and abstract reasoning. The problem occurs when philosophy's abstractions are presented as disembodied and independent of the philosopher's social position, as though innocent of the philosopher's own complicity in the power/knowledge relation. Failing to pursue the implications of the central insight that discourse (including the very discourse of mainstream analytic philosophy of religion) produces meaning effects, philosophers of religion are unlikely to be able to problematize their own writing.

Even as she invokes a feminist theological principle that "only that which supports the full humanity of women is revelatory," Fulkerson points out that "the standard for 'full humanity' is precisely what we do not have or know."[42] Her use of a poststructuralist account of discourse rules out the possibility of claims that can be validated outside of particular communities and their languages. Appealing to nonfoundationalism, the position that eschews the search for justifying beliefs or experiences that can in turn support other beliefs derived from them, Fulkerson apparently does not find it necessary to offer reasoned arguments for the faith claims and theological commitments she both makes and invokes.[43] This aspect of the method of discourse analysis may be more or less disturbing to philosophers of religion insofar as they find the project of proving or defending the existence or nonexistence of God to be an interesting one. Fulkerson clearly does not. The pertinent discursive practices she analyzes are those of resistance, survival, agape, and hope—practices, she freely admits, that *assume* the existence of God rather than problematize it.

How far discourse analysis such as Fulkerson's can go toward ever *subverting* the belief structures of Pentecostal women ministers or Presbyterian housewives remains an open question. Are certain structures of belief more emancipatory or enslaving than others? When the object of belief is assumed to be unreal, can the language of transcendence still be retained as poetic probes? Might women-centered beliefs and gynocentric practices deconstruct and show the partiality of masculinist models of deity? This constellation of questions is at the heart of another new direction available to philosophy of religion, appearing at the intersection of philosophy, psychoanalytic theory, and French feminist thought. An increasingly influential source for those who would fashion a more inclusive philosophy of religion is the work of Luce Irigaray, whose explicit insistence on the importance of the religious dimension to the creation of women's subjectivity and self-transcendence stands in some contrast to other analyses, such as Simone de Beauvoir's. Indeed, Irigaray goes so far as to claim: "Divinity is what we need to become free, autonomous, sovereign. No human subjectivity, no human society has ever been established without the help of the divine. There comes a time for destruction. But, before destruction is possible, God or the gods must exist."[44] The gynocentric models of "God or the gods" that Irigaray favors go hand in hand with the project of a new ethics of sexual difference that would recognize the subjectivity of each sex instead of symbolically splitting the maternal to the feminine and the spiritual to the masculine.

But how are Irigaray's recent calls for "a feminine divine" to be understood? Although a number of critical analyses of Irigaray's texts and their implications for Anglo-American philosophy of religion are beginning to appear,[45] the work of Amy Hollywood is perhaps the most lucid and philosophically important of these. Hollywood's analysis discloses that Irigaray's acceptance of a Feuerbachian projection theory of religion, in which God is the projection of human wishes, attributes, and desires, complicates her efforts to construct a new "feminine divine." "What Irigaray appears to forget," Hollywood notes, "is Feuerbach's central claim (and the grounds for his hope that the hold of religion might be *broken*): for religious projection to function, its mechanism must be hidden so that its object might inspire belief."[46] Irigaray recognizes that the "exposure" of this mechanism has not destroyed religion for many, and hence asserts the importance of adequate projections. But how is such projection possible or meaningful for those, like Irigaray herself, who assume that the object of belief is unreal? If Irigaray maintains a Feuerbachian human referent for her own projection of religious discourse in terms of female representations of the divine, the feminine divine, too, would seem to facilitate its own destruction. What possibilities does this leave for female transcendence? Can belief be simultaneously posited *and* deconstructed? Can the strong female subjectivity created in and by a mystic such as Teresa of Avila become available to women *without* Teresa's acceptance of a transcendent Other who is the divine? Because transcendence for Irigaray is associated with the "male" and a sacrificial economy, it is not clear how women are expected to claim the new subjectivity that she thinks religion, reconstituted, can offer. According to Hollywood, "Her ambivalence with regard to belief and transcendence leads her immediately to deconstruct the very deities she invokes." For all of its intriguing promise, this gynocentric project in philosophy of religion creates distinctive tensions, leading Hollywood to inquire "how far the immanent can be reinscribed as the site of transcendence without returning to the logic of sacrifice and bodily suffering seemingly endemic to the incarnational theologies of Christianity." There is also the related question of "whether belief can be mimed without re-inscribing women into a logic of the same such as that which Irigaray sees underlying Christianity."[47]

Insofar as preoccupation with the very concept of belief itself stands at the center of much modern philosophy of religion, Irigaray's 1981 essay entitled "Belief Itself" is of special interest.[48] In Amy Hollywood's reading of this allusive text, "Irigaray argues that the constitution of the normative subject of religion and philosophy depends on the mastery and silencing of the mother('s) body, and hence the denial of real differences between the sexes and between subjects."[49] Irigaray's argument is not only the familiar feminist one that the *object* of belief is male-defined but also the more radical claim that the *structure* and discourse of belief itself are masculinist and in need of deconstruction. Irigaray's development of this argument relies upon critical appropriations of psychoanalysis and Derridean reading practices to show how the related issues of embodiment and presence and absence are implicated in the formation of the subject, belief, and sexual difference. The constitution of normative (Western, bourgeois) subjectivity depends on the association of the body with the mother and femininity and an always incomplete and ambivalent mastering, concealment, or denial of the mother's body. Freud's own account of the *fort-da* game ("gone"-"there") played by his grandson, Ernst, exposes the relationship between belief and the little boy's mastery of the mother's presence and absence, concealedness and unconcealedness. Despite her apparent absence, she is there, the boy comes to believe, and in so believing he experiences his own power. For Irigaray, God, as the Father and the source of meaning, is the object of a belief first articulated in the (male child's) attempt to master the mother's absence; according to Hollywood's gloss, the dismantling of the subject as master, then, implies a concomitant deconstruction of the object of belief.

In the final analysis, it may be that Irigaray refuses simply to reduce the divine to Feuerbachian new "ego ideals" projected for women, for on her own terms this could only mean a reversion to the logic of the same and negation of the possibility of radical alterity. Not wanting to negate the divine entirely, as she also wants to hold out the hope to women of transcendence, Irigaray can be interpreted as reinscribing a religious language that leads neither to theism nor to atheism but, rather, to a dialectic of immanence and transcendence that is strongly reminiscent of certain medieval Christian mystics. The medieval mystics Mechthild, Hadewijch, and Marguerite Porete are important as well to Amy Hollywood because, among other things, they afford philosophy of religion new ways of talking about the divine or the sacred that do not in any way assume an "object of belief" along hierarchical lines of verticality.[50]

As is evident from even this limited discussion, the effort of engendering philosophy of religion anew in the different voices noted here raises new questions, identifies alternative kinds of issues as relevant, and focuses attention on the value judgments, the political effects, and the power dimensions of philosophical work in this field. One important way in which women, in conjunction with other elided groups and perspectives, hope to change the contours and texture of mainstream philosophy of religion consists in making epistemological questions an explicit point of focus. What has the status of knowledge? What gets valorized as worth knowing? What are the criteria evoked? Who has the authority to establish meaning? Who is the presumed subject of belief? How does the social position of the subject affect the content of religious belief? What is the impact upon religious life of the subject's sexed body? What do we learn by examining the relations between power, on the one hand, and what counts as evidence, foundations, modes of discourse, and forms of apprehension and transmission, on the other hand? In view of the intimate connection of power/knowledge, how do we handle the inevitable occlusion that attends all knowledge production? What particular processes constitute the normative cultural subject as masculine in its philosophical and religious dimensions? Questions such as these have not previously been asked in philosophy of religion; their answers will depend upon the intellectual capaciousness and undisciplined, because interdisciplinary, freedom of a new generation of philosophers.

Multiculturalism and Philosophy of Religion

Not only the gender bias but also the ethnocentrism of contemporary Anglo-American philosophy of religion can be understood historically in the context of colonization processes occurring from the seventeenth through the eighteenth century in Europe and coinciding with the very origins of the modern period of the philosophy of religion. The same politics of exclusion that work against those in the category of "woman" also work against all those in the category of "Others," and those who inhabit the intersection of both spaces are doubly marginalized. In marked contrast to the interdisciplinary and cross-cultural space in which religious studies has operated for the last several decades in the academy, philosophy of religion, like the discipline of philosophy as a whole, has been largely Eurocentric and Anglo-American in its orientation rather than conceiving of itself as a philosophy of *world* religions. This has produced a philosophical study not so much of *religious* ideas as of *Christian* religious ideas, and usually of relentlessly traditional ideas rather than of modernist or postmodernist reconstructions of those ideas. Mainstream philosophy of religion has shown no interest in Chinese philosophies or religions, nor in those of Indian origin, and not even in Islam, where strict monotheism might be thought to constitute some common ground.[51] Judaism is usually considered in philosophy of religion only insofar as it contributes ideas of interest within Christian thought. Not only have whole traditions of Asian, Amerindian, and African religions been excluded from the dominant tradition of philosophy of religion, but even the many contexts and consequences of its own narrowly constructed shape have been ignored. Although the Christian religion remains the dominant tradition studied, no attention is given to understanding class or racial or regional differences in the meaning of the Christian belief structure as it is variously found, for example, among Irish working-class Protestants in Belfast, or African-American southern Baptists, or Croatian Catholics in Bosnia, or Womenchurch gatherings. Once the cultural and political contexts are removed from the study of even the one (Christian) tradition invariably examined, only the most homogenized and orthodox version of Christianity remains visible as the touchstone for what is studied in philosophy of religion.[52]

To the extent that gender, race, and multicultural perspectives are increasingly important categories of analysis and understanding, philosophy of religion stands to gain a great deal by stretching its usual parameters in order to think *in* and *with* these categories. In a postcolonial era of cultural studies, when multicultural interests are inspiring scholars in all fields to take account of the philosophy, religion, art, and literature of diverse cultures, one of the most important developments that could take place in philosophy of religion would be its multicontextualization across ethnic, cultural, and religious lines. By problematizing the taken-for-granted background of Christian categories that now frame most work in philosophy of religion, philosophers of religion might come to see religion less as a vestige of metaphysics than as a primary motor of cultural production. As Gayatri Spivak has remarked, "Given the connection between imperialism and secularism, there is almost no way of getting to alternative general voices except through religion." Spivak's concern, like Foucault's, to make sense of how the subject becomes ethical, leads her to regard religions as mechanisms of such production, without which "one gets various kinds of 'fundamentalism.'" Workers in cultural politics and its connections to a new ethical philosophy, according to Spivak, have to be interested in religion in the production of ethical subjects. "There is much room for feminist work here," she points out, "because western feminists have not so far been aware of religion as a cultural instrument rather than a mark of cultural difference."[53]

John Hick, one of the few mainstream philosophers of religion to rise to the challenge of religious pluralism, has urged the following view: "A philosopher of religion must today take account not only of the thought and experience of the tradition within which he or she happens to work, but in principle of the religious experience and thought of the whole human race."[54] It is exceedingly difficult, however, for any one philosopher to acquire the kind of expertise that Hick calls for. Knowledge of religion in Asia, South and Central America, or Africa is specialized, and dependent upon crucial linguistic tools and long periods of study. Faced with the vast variety of symbolic expressions, cultic forms, and creedal formulations of the religions of the world, philosophers confront a challenging set of demands. Many will object that it is unfair and unrealistic to expect philosophers to become scholars of religion as well. But in a way perhaps analogous to philosophy of science, a good working knowledge of the first-order subject matter must be presumed if the second-order philosophical theories are to be *about* it. Indeed, the same could be said of most branches of philosophy, including aesthetics, philosophy of language, and philosophy of mathematics. These parallel second-order inquiries demand knowledge of the subject matter in order even to establish the necessary assumptions, questions, and methods suitable to it. In these as well as other areas of philosophy, it is commonly recognized that it would be impossible as well as presumptuous to give a normative account of science, art, language, or mathematics without also mastering the descriptive side. And yet, in philosophy of religion, it has been customary for philosophers to know the descriptive side of only one religion, at best, and even then to abstract from all the most concrete aspects of religious life and to focus on the problematic category of "belief."

The next crucial stage of philosophy of religion will require engagement with and inquiry into a plurality of religious traditions for the sake of creating a truly cross-cultural philosophy of religions. Methodologically, this will mean taking as much account of history of religions and cultural anthropology as previous practitioners have of speculative metaphysics and natural theology. Practically speaking, several ways of working with multicultural religious materials are open to philosophers. At the most basic level of curricular innovation, it is easy enough to pair, splice, or otherwise inject a good dose of cross-cultural or comparative readings even when working with the standard (Western) list of topics considered "problems in philosophy of religion." Lao-tzu's reflections on the nature of the Tao that cannot be spoken compare cogently with certain of Wittgenstein's injunctions, if not with Kant's critique of pure reason. The sixth-century C.E. philosophy of the Buddhist logician Dignāga would compare interestingly with the deconstructive strategies of Derrida. The autobiography of the Islamic philosopher al-Ghazālī would make a vivid contribution to any consideration of theodicy.[55]

Turning also to the multicultural expressions of the Christian religion, philosophers of religion should look to the burgeoning new literature being created under the rubric of "feminist theology." African-American women are developing a wealth of writings around Womanist theology and ethics, as evident, for example, in Jacquelyn Grant's *White Woman's Christ, Black Woman's Jesus* and in Dolores Williams's *Sisters in the Wilderness: The Challenge of Womanist God-Talk.*[56] A new generation of Hispanic women is creating the critical perspective known as Mujerista theology, as seen in Ada Maria Isasi-Diaz's *En La Lucha: Elaborating a Mujerista Theology.*[57] Third World women in Asia, Africa, and Latin America are now actively contributing to the global phenomenon of women's religious discourse.[58]

Philosophy of religion in different voices can also draw upon the distinctive voices of lesbian women and gay men for a critique of the normative heterosexist framework in which religious symbols have been constructed.[59] Further investigation of and reflection upon the new theologies emerging across cultures, religions, and sexual orientations should be very productive in stimulating different voices in philosophy of religion, just as detailed philosophical analysis and criticism of the reasoning and faith assumptions in these emerging works should be beneficial to theologians.

Moving beyond Christianity, one finds decisive work being done by Jewish women such as Judith Plaskow in *Standing Again at Sinai* and by Buddhist women such as Rita Gross in *Buddhism after Patriarchy: A Feminist History, Analysis and Reconstruction.*[60] Both texts provide illuminating reinterpretations of the male-defined categories of these religions. Among Muslim women, serious rethinking of the interpretation of the Koran and the Sharia has begun, and among Hindu women, new discussions are aimed at understanding how Indian myths and laws might be ruptured as much as respected, and criticized as well as re-created.[61]

One advantage of broadening the banks of the mainstream to embrace religious traditions other than Western ones is that rather than regarding the world's religions as exotic sites on which to erect the latest philosophical theories, philosophers might also find in them novel grounds for testing their own (Western-generated) claims in order to discover possible limitations. Buddhist religious philosophy, for example, provides an excellent testing ground for appraising certain ontological claims generated by poststructuralism's emphasis on fragmented selfhood. As Anne C. Klein has shown, the practice of "mindfulness" in Indian, Tibetan, and other Buddhist traditions facilitates a concentrated centering of the self, leading to a different style of subjectivity altogether. Postmodernists, Klein argues, overlook an important distinction long held crucial by Buddhists between experiencing one's qualitative state of mind, on the one hand, and experiencing its contents, on the other hand. By focusing only on the latter, Western theorists operate with a disembodied notion of mind, according to Klein. Although both Buddhists and postmodernists share a common rejection of any unitary or essentialist subjectivity, they part company over their views of the role of language in knowledge and experience. Only knowledge that is conceptually based and linguistically mediated matters to Western conceptions of subjectivity, but Klein calls to mind the visceral knowledge of the body valued in Buddhist religion wherein selves can achieve both centeredness without essentializing and constructedness without fracturing.[62]

Maria Lugones has called upon philosophers to become genuine "world-travellers," thinkers who explore reality wearing the other's shoes, all the while recognizing that the other's perspective is fully realized, not just an add-on to one's own sight-seeing.[63] "World-traveling" philosophers of religion do not necessarily need to visit "foreign" shores; the point is to take responsibility for studying, mediating, interpreting, and including a variety of cultural voices in our research and teaching. Great tensions and not a few risks lurk here, including the risk, ironically, of occluding the Other. The problem is not only that our (Western) philosophical texts are partial and incomplete accounts of the Other but that our very texts *produce* the Other as a result of where *we* are.[64] The chief challenge to those writing philosophy in a different voice is posed by the risk of eliding the *many* different voices and generating only a new set of exclusions and unconscious privilegings. In the present historical moment, we know that the "dream of a common language" (Adrienne Rich) is elusive, but we do not yet know how to make the vision of a "powerful infidel heteroglossia" (Donna Haraway) any more coherent.

Other Issues

The perennial problem of justification of religious beliefs has yet to receive due attention from either a feminist or a multicultural perspective. Among mainstream philosophers, it is commonly agreed that contemporary philosophy of religion encompasses two distinct but related tasks, the first dealing with issues of justification and the rationality of religious belief; the second having to do with hermeneutical attempts to elucidate the distinctive character and meaning of religious practices, beliefs, and experiences. Those philosophers of religion whose basic interest is in questions of justifiability have typically concentrated on the belief aspect of religion, with the apparent assumption that the elucidation of other elements of a religious system, such as ritual, moral choice, cosmology, and so on, is ultimately related to the justifiability of some belief or set of beliefs. Recently, some have interpreted the task of justification narrowly to consist in showing the rational defensibility of various religious beliefs, as though a minimal not-yet-proved-false defense could serve as a positive recommendation. Others have maintained that sheer defensibility should not be confused with plausibility and that a stricter account of plausibility conditions also needs to be provided. Hermeneutical efforts in contemporary philosophy of religion, on the other hand, have usually attempted to disclose some common core or essence of religion, or else to exhibit the distinctive grammar and rules of religious "forms of life." Purely descriptive accounts that aim only to elucidate the meaning and structure of religious life often circumvent the difficult justifiability and rationality debates, but at the risk of incurring the criticism that they harbor apologetic purposes. Both tasks, explanation as well as understanding, would seem essential to any fully adequate philosophy of religion. However, one of the chronic dilemmas of philosophy of religion is that sheer elucidation alone proves insufficient, and neither justification nor refutation ever assumes a conclusive form. This irresolution is felt by some with a sense of gnawing futility and accepted by others as a sign of infinite undecidability.

In light of the implications of religious pluralism, mainstream philosophy of religion needs to revise what have been thought of as philosophical issues. Insofar as the field faces the challenge of encounter with traditions expressing practices and beliefs that are not predominantly associated with European, white, or male modes of understanding, it will be required to elaborate new models of interpretation, a broader theory of evidence, a cross-culturally adequate conception of human rationality, and a more complex appraisal of the norms applicable to cases of divergent, rival religious claims and disagreements. Insofar as philosophy of religion studies the strictly intellectual interpretations of any religious tradition, it encounters beliefs, symbols, and ideas that are embedded in specific sociocultural power relations. New work is now needed that reflects on the dynamics of power relations, analyzes inherited oppressions, searches for alternative wisdom and suppressed symbolism, and risks new interpretations of the tricky truth and justification questions in light of religious pluralism.

The irreducible fact of human convictional diversity has yet to be properly theorized by philosophers of religion without leading either to the absolutizing of some one convictional set above all others or to the relativizing of the notion of truth altogether. Lacking in this field any well-established theory of the necessary and sufficient conditions or the transcultural evidential basis for assessing rival truth claims, many scholars have been primarily concerned to understand and expound a descriptive and historical account of various religious claims, bypassing the tough questions of philosophical assessment of competing conceptual systems. In order to do more than simply accept the diversity of religious interpretations, paradigms, frameworks, and language games, however, it will be necessary to face up philosophically to the presence of genuine conflicts among the truth claims of the world's religions.

In this essay I have tried to suggest a number of critical questions and interests that I believe any future philosophy of religion must accommodate if it is to be adequate. Whether philosophy of religion can rise to the new occasion ushered in by these questions in our time remains an open question that can only be answered in terms of a new awareness of the challenge of feminists, of people of color, of Third World cultures, of all those different voices who find the mainstream preoccupations of the field irrelevant—not simply because those preoccupations are implicated in a religious worldview that for an intellectual elite has become *untrue* but because they are implicated in an economic and political worldview that for most women, and many men, remains *unjust*.

ACKNOWLEDGMENTS

I am indebted to Janet Kourany, Amy Hollywood, Terence Tilley, and John Konkle for criticisms of an earlier version of this essay, and to Marilyn Thie, Sarah Coakley, and Sandra Bartky for stimulating conversations on the topic of feminist philosophy of religion.

NOTES

1. Elizabeth Cady Stanton, "Has Christianity Benefitted Women?" *North American Review* 140 (1885): 389–90.

2. Luce Irigaray, "Divine Women," in *Sexes and Genealogies*, trans. Gillian C. Gill (New York: Columbia University Press, 1993), p. 67. I am indebted to Amy Hollywood for calling this quotation to my attention.

3. Anna Julia Cooper, "A Voice From the South," in *Schomburg Library of Nineteenth-Century Black Women Writers* (New York: Oxford University Press, 1988 [1892]), pp. 121–23.

4. Jeffner Allen and Iris Marion Young, eds., *The Thinking Muse: Feminism and Modern French Philosophy* (Bloomington: Indiana University Press, 1989).

5. Neither do I intend to invoke a distinction between gender and sex that allows naturalized assumptions about the sexed body to go unquestioned.

6. Indicative of this resurgence is the volume *Contemporary Perspectives on Religious Epistemology*, edited by R. Douglas Geivett and Brendan Sweetman (New York: Oxford University Press, 1992). Significantly, this volume consists entirely of contributions from twenty-four male authors and includes not a single female author. The epistemological perspectives represented in this volume are uniformly concerned with traditional modes of Christian belief. For an argument that Anglo-American philosophers are now addressing an expanded range of topics, see Eleonore Stump's claim that new work in philosophy of religion is currently characterized, first, by "a broad extension of subjects seen as appropriate for philosophical scrutiny" and, second, by "a willingness to bridge boundaries with related disciplines." But what Stump means by "new work" is that "philosophers have gotten up their courage and ventured into such areas as providence, creation, conservation, and God's responsibility for sin," and by "related disciplines" she refers only to theology

and biblical studies. Cf. Eleonore Stump, ed., *Reasoned Faith: Essays in Philosophical Theology in Honor of Norman Kretzmann* (Ithaca, N.Y.: Cornell University Press, 1993), p. 1.

7. Richard Gale, *On the Nature and Existence of God* (Cambridge: Cambridge University Press, 1991), p. 2.

8. See, for example, Richard Swinburne, *The Coherence of Theism* (Oxford: Clarendon, 1977); Swinburne, *The Existence of God* (Oxford: Clarendon Press, 1979); Swinburne, *Faith and Reason* (Oxford: Clarendon Press, 1981); Alvin Plantinga, "Is Belief in God Properly Basic?" *Nous* 15, no. 1 (1981): 41–52; Plantinga, "Reason and Belief in God," in Alvin Plantinga and Nicholas Wolterstorff, eds., *Faith and Rationality* (Notre Dame: University of Notre Dame Press, 1983); Plantinga, *Warrant: The Current Debate* (New York: Oxford University Press, 1993); Plantinga, *Warrant and Proper Function* (New York: Oxford University Press, 1993); William P. Alston, *Perceiving God: The Epistemology of Religious Experience* (Ithaca, N.Y.: Cornell University Press, 1991); and D. Z. Phillips, *Faith after Foundationalism* (London: Routledge, 1988). See also Phillips's uncritical assumption that the Christian God exhibits the three characteristics of "independence of the way things go, unchangeability, and immunity from defeat," in "Faith, Skepticism, and Religious Understanding," in Ann Loades and Loyal D. Rue, eds., *Contemporary Classics in Philosophy of Religion*. (La Salle, Ill.: Open Court, 1991), pp. 123–38.

9. See Elizabeth A. Johnson, *She Who Is: The Mystery of God in Feminist Theological Discourse* (New York, Crossroad, 1993).

10. Heidi Hartmann, "The Unhappy Marriage of Marxism and Feminism: Toward a More Progressive Union," in Lydia Sargent, ed., *Women and Revolution: The Unhappy Marriage of Marxism and Feminism* (Boston: South End Press, 1981), p. 14.

11. For example, John Hick's widely used text, *Philosophy of Religion* (Englewood Cliffs, N.J.: Prentice-Hall, 1989), now in its fourth edition, went through three editions before the author amended it with more inclusive language. Despite Hick's explanation in the 1983 preface that he has "desexized" (*sic*) his language, it is apparent that conceptually his notion of God is still what Lacan calls the "good old God," the Father, the omnipotent One of classical theism.

12. Elizabeth Kamarck Minnich, *Transforming Knowledge* (Philadelphia: Temple University Press, 1990), p. 175.

13. Mary Daly, "Feminist Post-Christian Introduction," in her *The Church and the Second Sex*, 2d ed. (New York: Harper and Row, 1975), p. 38.

14. Peter Damian, "On Divine Omnipotence," in John F. Wippel and Allan B. Wolter, eds. *Medieval Philosophy* (New York: Free Press, 1969), p. 143–45.

15. John Mackie's definition may stand as representative: "We might suggest that 'God is omnipotent' means that God can do anything that is logically possible. . . . So omnipotence includes the power to make X to be only where there is no contradiction either in X itself or in making X to be. . . . if God is omnipotent every coherently describable activity or production is within his power." See his "Omnipotence" in Linwood Urban and Douglas N. Walton, eds., *The Power of God: Readings on Omnipotence and Evil* (New York: Oxford University Press, 1978), pp. 76, 77.

16. See in particular John B. Cobb Jr. and David R. Griffin, *Process Theology: An Introductory Exposition* (Philadelphia: Westminster Press, 1976); Charles Hart-

shorne, *Omnipotence and Other Theological Mistakes* (Albany: State University of New York Press, 1984); and Marjorie Suchocki, *The End of Evil: Process Eschatology in Historical Context* (Albany: State University of New York Press, 1988).

17. This is the point of Marilyn Thie's critique in "Epilogue: Prologomenon to Future Feminist* Philosophies of Religions," in *Hypatia: A Journal of Feminist Philosophy* 9, no. 4 (Special Issue on Philosophy of Religion, edited by Nancy Frankenberry and Marilyn Thie; Fall 1994): 234. For two important exceptions, see Wendy Farley, *Tragic Vision and Divine Compassion: A Contemporary Theodicy* (Louisville, Ky.: Westminster/John Knox Press, 1990), and Kathleen M. Sands, *Escape from Paradise: Evil and Tragedy in Feminist Theology* (Minneapolis, Minn.: Fortress Press, 1994).

18. Charlotte Perkins Gilman, *His Religion and Hers* (New York: Century, 1923), p. 46.

19. See Susan Bordo, *The Flight to Objectivity: Essays on Cartesianism and Culture* (Albany: State University of New York Press, 1987); Sandra Harding and M. B. Hintikka, eds., *Discovering Reality: Feminist Perspectives on Epistemology, Metaphysics, Methodology, and Philosophy of Science* (Dordrecht: Reidel, 1983); Luce Irigaray, *This Sex Which Is Not One* (Ithaca, N.Y.: Cornell University Press, 1985); and Genevieve Lloyd, *The Man of Reason* (London: Methuen, 1985).

20. Inevitably, I am conflating my critique of mainstream philosophy of religion with a critique of its subject matter, Western monotheistic religious beliefs. When religion is construed this narrowly, philosophy of religion acquires an impaired view of what is appropriate for its philosophical scrutiny.

21. For a development of this theme in connection with the work of Durkheim and Weber, see Victoria Lee Erickson, *Where Silence Speaks: Feminism, Social Theory, and Religion* (Minnneapolis, Minn.: Fortress Press, 1993).

22. Caroline Walker Bynum, Stevan Harrell, and Paula Richman, *Gender and Religion: On the Complexity of Symbols* (Boston: Beacon Press, 1986), p. 9.

23. For a preliminary analysis in connection with three models of divinity, see Nancy Frankenberry, "Classical Theism, Panentheism, and Pantheism: The Relation between God Construction and Gender Construction," *Zygon Journal of Science and Religion* 28, no. 1 (March 1993): 29–46. For a brief discussion of why such analysis is not more common in philosophy of religion, see my "Introduction: Prolegomenon to Future Philosophies of Religion," *Hypatia: A Journal of Feminist Philosophy* 9, no. 4 (Special Issue on Philosophy of Religion, edited by Nancy Frankenberry and Marilyn Thie; Fall 1994): 1–14.

24. Johnson, *She Who Is*, pp. 127–28. Cf. Hildegaard of Bingen, *Scivias*, trans. Mother Colubia Hart and Jane Bishop (New York, Paulist Press, 1990).

25. Paula Gunn Allen, *The Sacred Hoop: Recovering the Feminine in American Indian Traditions* (Boston: Beacon Press, 1986), p. 22.

26. Ntozake Shange, *for colored girls who have considered suicide/when the rainbow is enuf* (New York: Macmillan, 1976), p. 63.

27. Alice Walker, *The Color Purple* (New York: Harcourt Brace Jovanovich, 1982), pp. 177–78.

28. See Rosemary Radford Ruether, *Sexism and God-Talk* (Boston: Beacon Press, 1983); Sallie McFague, *Models of God: Theology for an Ecological, Nuclear Age* (Philadelphia: Fortress Press, 1987); Mary Daly, *Beyond God the Father* (Boston: Beacon Press, 1973); Marjorie Suchocki, *The End of Evil: Process Eschatology*

in Historical Concept (Albany: State University of New York Press, 1988); and Irigaray, *Sexes and Genealogies.*

29. Alfred North Whitehead, *Process and Reality,* corrected edition, ed. David R. Griffin and Donald Sherburne (New York: Free Press, 1978), p. 348.

30. An excellent account of these themes in process philosophy from a feminist perspective is found in Catherine Keller, *From a Broken Web: Separation, Sexism, and Self* (Boston: Beacon Press, 1986). See also Nancy Howell, "The Promise of a Process Feminist Theory of Relations," *Process Studies* 17 (Summer 1988): 78–87.

31. Whitehead, *Process and Reality,* pp. 31–34, 342–51.

32. Charles Birch and John B. Cobb Jr., *The Liberation of Life: From the Cell to the Community* (Cambridge: Cambridge University Press, 1981).

33. Johnson, *She Who Is,* p. 240. Given other aspects of Johnson's ontology, however, it is unlikely that she would favor the radically pluralized and temporalized interpretation of creativity/*esse* that I recommend here.

34. A more developed treatment of the concept of the divine as creativity would consider the ways in which divine power is not always and everywhere "good" in any unambiguous sense. While the power of being may always be good, what is is not always good. While creativity is an ontological good, it may also turn out to be a practical or social evil in context.

35. Michael McGhee, "Introduction," in Michael McGhee, ed., *Philosophy, Religion and the Spiritual Life* (Cambridge: Cambridge University Press, 1992), p. 1.

36. For important critiques of the dominant tradition's neglect of what constitutes a real, socially located epistemic subject, see Lorraine Code, *What Can She Know? Feminist Theory and the Construction of Knowledge* (Ithaca, N.Y.: Cornell University Press, 1991); Jane Duran, *Toward a Feminist Epistemology* (Savage, Md.: Rowman and Littlefield, 1991); and Terence W. Tilley, *The Wisdom of Religious Commitment* (Washington, D.C.: Georgetown University Press, 1995).

37. Paula M. Cooey, *Religious Imagination and the Body: A Feminist Analysis* (New York: Oxford University Press, 1994), p. 127.

38. It is also indicative of the fact that the "different voice" in which philosophy of religion is being written is not limited to the female register.

39. Howard Eilberg-Schwartz, *God's Phallus and Other Problems for Men and Monotheism* (Boston: Beacon Press, 1994), pp. 5–6.

40. Ibid., pp. 239, 240.

41. Mary McClintock Fulkerson, *Changing the Subject: Women's Discourses and Feminist Theology* (Minneapolis, Minn.: Fortress Press, 1994), p. 115.

42. Ibid., p. 103.

43. See, for example, ibid., pp. ix, 7, 24 n. 10, 29, 372–77. This assimilation of "theology" to "testimony" is mistaken, in my judgment; the crisis of legitimation of theology's cognitive claims cannot be so easily circumvented.

44. Irigaray, *Sexes and Genealogies,* p. 62.

45. In particular, see C. W. Maggie Kim, Susan M. St. Ville, and Susan M. Simonaitis, *Transfigurations: Theology and the French Feminists* (Minneapolis, Minn.: Fortress Press, 1993); Philippa Berry and Andrew Werncik, eds., *Shadow of Spirit: Postmodernism and Religion* (New York: Routledge, 1992); and Elizabeth Grosz, *Sexual Subversions: Three French Feminists* (Sydney: Allen and Unwin, 1989).

46. Amy M. Hollywood, "Beauvoir, Irigaray, and the Mystical," *Hypatia: A Journal of Feminist Philosophy* 9, no. 4 (Special Issue on Philosophy of Religion,

edited by Nancy Frankenberry and Marilyn Thie; Fall 1994): 175. Cf. Ludwig Feuerbach, *The Essence of Christianity*, trans. George Eliot. (New York: Harper Torchbooks, 1957).

47. Hollywood, "Beauvoir, Irigaray, and the Mystical," pp. 176–77.

48. Luce Irigaray, "Belief Itself," in *Sexes and Genealogies*, pp. 25–53.

49. Amy M. Hollywood, "Deconstructing Belief: Irigaray and the Philosophy of Religion" (paper presented at the annual meeting of the American Academy of Religion, Chicago, November 1994).

50. For an extended analysis, see Amy M. Hollywood, *Soul as Virgin Wife: Mechthild of Magdeburg, Marguerite Porete, and Meister Eckhart* (South Bend, Ind.: Notre Dame University Press, 1995).

51. Important exceptions include the comparative work of Robert C. Neville and Paul Griffiths in Chinese and Indian Buddhist studies, and of William Lane Craig, Eric Ormsby, and David Burrell in Christianity and Islam.

52. The parochialism of much philosophy of religion in college and university courses may be tested by asking such questions as: How often do philosophers include in their syllabi any readings from non-Western religious texts or philosophies? Within the Western context, how many philosophers are receptive to the variety of perspectives outside the dominant analytic tradition, including such revisionist modes of thought as process philosophy? How many philosophers are cognizant of the field of history of religions as providing a wealth of data that has made the very meaning of "religion" a contested and constructed site? My own impression is that very little is occurring that is either new or interesting from the standpoint of gender, race, or multiculturalism in mainstream philosophy of religion as it is taught and written by the predominantly white, male, English-speaking philosophers who currently dominate the field.

53. Gayatri Spivak, "The Politics of Translation," in Michelle Barrett and Anne Phillips, eds., *Destabilizing Theory: Contemporary Feminist Debates* (Stanford, Calif.: Stanford University Press, 1992), p. 192. I am indebted to Amy Newman for calling my attention to this source.

54. John Hick, *An Interpretation of Religion: Human Responses to the Transcendent* (New Haven, Conn.: Yale University Press, 1989), p. xiii.

55. Needless to say, I do not mean to advocate only the Great Men approach in which, now, the recipe is to take one "other" great man (Mencius, Lao-tzu, Ghandi) and stir. Furthermore, I would urge something more politically powerful than simple appreciation of the multiple varieties of women's subject positions and the humanism of hearing them all into speech, but that is the subject for another paper.

56. See Jacquelyn Grant, *White Woman's Christ, Black Woman's Jesus: Feminist Christology and Womanist Response* (Atlanta: Scholars Press, 1989); and Dolores Williams, *Sisters in the Wilderness: The Challenge of Womanist God-Talk* (Maryknoll, N.Y.: Orbis Books, 1993).

57. Ada Maria Isasi-Diaz, *En La Lucha: Elaborating a Mujerista Theology* (Minneapolis: Fortress Press, 1993). See also Ada Maria Isasi-Diaz and Yolanda Tarango, *Hispanic Women, Prophetic Voice in the Church: Hispanic Women's Liberation Theology* (San Francisco: Harper and Row, 1988).

58. See Virginia Fabella and Sun Ai Lee Parks, eds., *We Dare to Dream: Doing Theology as Asian Women* (Maryknoll, N.Y.: Orbis Books, 1990); C. H. Kyung, *Struggle to Be the Sun Again: Introducing Asian Women's Theology* (Maryknoll, N.Y.: Orbis Books, 1990); Mercy Amba Oduyoye, *Hearing and Knowing*

(Maryknoll, N.Y.: Orbis Books, 1986); and Elsa Tamez, *Through Her Eyes: Women's Theology from Latin America* (Maryknoll, N.Y.: Orbis Books, 1989). For a collection of feminist and Third World perspectives, see Susan Brooks Thistlethwaite and Mary Potter Engel, eds., *Lift Every Voice: Constructing Theologies from the Underside* (San Francisco: Harper and Row, 1990).

59. See, for example, Carter Heyward et al., "Lesbianism and Feminist Theology," *Journal of Feminist Studies in Religion* 2 (1986): 95–106; and Mary Hunt, *Fierce Tenderness: A Feminist Theology of Friendship* (New York: Crossroad Press, 1990).

60. See Judith Plaskow, *Standing Again at Sinai: Judaism from a Feminist Perspective* (San Francisco: Harper and Row, 1990); and Rita Gross, *Buddhism after Patriarchy: A Feminist History, Analysis and Reconstruction* (Albany: State University of New York Press, 1992).

61. Riffat Hassan, Leonard Grob, and Haim Gordon, eds., *Women's and Men's Liberation: Testimonies of Spirit* (New York: Greenwood Press, 1991).

62. See Anne C. Klein, "Presence with a Difference: Buddhists and Feminists on Subjectivity," *Hypatia: A Journal of Feminist Philosophy* 9, no. 4 (Special Issue on Philosophy of Religion, edited by Nancy Frankenberry and Marilyn Thie; Fall 1994): 112–30. Cf. also Anne C. Klein, *Meeting the Great Bliss Queen: Buddhists, Feminists and the Art of the Self* (Boston: Beacon Press, 1995).

63. Maria Lugones, "Playfulness, 'World'-Travelling, and Loving Perception," *Hypatia* 2, no. 2 (1987): 3–20.

64. Cf. Fulkerson, *Changing the Subject*, p. 381.

Voice and Voicelessness: A Modest Proposal?

LORRAINE CODE

IN A 1986 ESSAY, I contend that stories "convey something about cognitive and moral experiences . . . that slips through the formalist nets of moral principles and duties, or standards of evidence and justification." I continue: "The modest proposal urged here is that perhaps, by taking stories into account, theorists will be able to repair some of the rifts in continuity . . . between moral theory and moral experiences, and theory of knowledge and cognitive experiences."[1] A student in my 1992 Philosophy and Feminism course has prompted me to take this passage as my point of departure here. Why, he asked, do I cast as a modest proposal this challenge to the founding assumptions of twentieth-century epistemology and moral theory? In this essay, I grant his point: the proposal asks radical questions of epistemologists and moral theorists alike. Its appeals to experience are contestable in ways that I did not address in 1986; yet it can be opened out to engage many of the issues central to feminist critical and revisionary epistemological projects. Here I explain how such an amplification could work.

VOICES

In feminist epistemological projects, the issue is less of doing philosophy "in a feminist voice," or even "in a different voice"—as some feminists propose[2]—than of discerning whose voices have been audible, and whose muffled, in the articulations of prevailing theories; of showing whose experiences count, and how epistemic authority is established and withheld. These issues are more basic than that of developing *a* different voice: they require finding the voices of the epistemology makers, uncovering the processes of theory and knowledge production, relocating epistemic activity from the "no-one's-land" that it has seemed to occupy into human speaking and listening spaces where dominant conceptions of experience, knowledge, and subjectivity have systematically suppressed other contenders. I am framing my discussion with questions about voice and voicelessness to emphasize and "make strange" the disembodied, disconnected—hence unstoried, nondiscursive—character of the dominant versions of Anglo-American epistemology: theories that are spoken from nowhere and as if by no one in particular. No one voices the assumptions and problems of these theories; no one's voice is heard in the exemplary knowledge claims around which they are built; and no one is answerable for their effects in people's lives.

The stories that are implicated variously in the making of knowledge and epistemologies are neither homogeneous nor independent of one another. I am thinking of stories about the provenance and hegemony of theories of knowledge; about interconnections between theory and practice; and about how it is to experience the world in certain ways. Telling such stories locates epistemology within the lives and projects of specifically situated, embodied, gendered knowers. It establishes continuities between the experiences and circumstances that people seek to explain, and the theories that purport to explain them.

Consider first, stories—genealogies—that map the processes out of which certain kinds of knowledge come to hold sway as exemplary and theory shaping; stories that expose the complex interconnections between examples and theories. The point is not just that examples illustrate theories, which remain intact through exemplification processes. Rather theories, and the background assumptions that they generate and are generated by, predispose privileging certain examples; and the apparent self-evidence of the examples strengthens the presumption that theories can be shaped around them. Thus, for example, an assumption that knowledge caused by immediate experience—whether of "sense-data" or, derivatively, of medium-sized material objects—is foundational, exemplary, and reliable both produces and is produced by early-twentieth-century positivist-empiricist theories of knowledge. These theories develop out of and sustain faith in the powers of instrumental reason in capitalist, highly (materially) productive societies, and they generate faith in the power of science to trump all other contenders for first place in the ranks of truth producers. These are just some of the factors that a story of the triumph of empiricism would reveal.

This brief example is merely a plot summary of a story that locates a philosophical theory historically and geographically, as a human product.[3] Such stories affirm the local contingency of human intellectual projects. They show that although a particular "style of reasoning" may prevail here and now,[4] in another spatiotemporal configuration, out of another intersection of subjectivities, circumstances, and social structures, something quite different might have prevailed.

Stories tell of the provenance of governing theories. Hence for philosophers who believe that epistemic progress is enhanced by "the breakdown of narrative knowledge in the wake of the advance of scientific knowledge,"[5] they belong to the history of philosophy, metaphilosophically conceived, rather than to philosophy "proper." Distinguishing between scientific and narrative (=folk?) knowledge enables such thinkers to discount the epistemological significance of narratives of scientific knowledge itself, whereas the narrative voice locates theory, knowledge, and experience production within social-historical situations and epistemic struggles. Yet a storied epistemology assumes neither that there is a single, "true" story nor that the implications of a story can be read off its surface. Telling and listening to stories exposes the artificiality of separating philosophy and metaphilosophy, and breaks with the practice of representing the history of modern-day epistemology as a voiceless history—an inevitable, impersonal march toward an ideal epistemic convergence.

Philosophers have not always discounted the narrative voice. Jonathan Rée, for example, suggests that the history of rationalist (especially Cartesian and Hegelian) philosophy can be reread as a series of interconnected and well-crafted tales of epistemic practice. He argues persuasively that although a "high-minded disdain for stories and verses went back to Plato" and "echoed through the philosophical canon, . . . it was only [with] Jeremy Bentham that anti-narrativism achieved a full and literal embodiment."[6] Even after Bentham, antinarrativism did not prevail absolutely. A notable exception is the work of R. G. Collingwood, which enlists some of the interpretive storytelling strategies that I advocate here. Collingwood's "question and answer logic" aims to attend to the voices of past history makers and philosophy makers, to engage, empathetically, with the problems that engaged them.[7] Only by reenacting their preoccupations and puzzlements as they would have experienced them, Collingwood believes, can a historian (or a historian of philosophy) hope to know what is at stake for past thinkers and actors. And despite an epistemological individualism that he retains unexamined,[8] Collingwood's writings open a resourceful critical space for articulations of a storied epistemology. Yet they have not achieved the influential status they deserve in a discourse dominated by the antistoried epistemologies of Anglo-American philosophy. Out of their veneration of a rarefied conception of scientific validity, these epistemologies have perpetuated the illusion that all knowledge worthy of the label is—like science as they conceive it—ahistorical, and exempt from self-reflexive accountability. Evidence presents itself unequivocally to a mind prepared to assent. The belief that science "has no history," the fact that the "stories science tells are usually about 'nature,' rarely about its own past,"[9] preserves a division between science (and hence knowledge "in general") and stories.

Stories about how knowledge and belief are made maintain a connection between practice and theory for which the practical, situated processes of knowledge/belief production are as significant as the products of cognitive activity. Practice and theory are mutually implicated, linked in a reciprocity that precludes granting primacy to either. Practices can attest to the strengths and inadequacies in theories just as readily as theories can generate or legitimate certain practices and forestall others; and neither practices nor theories are singly self-explanatory. Yet their cross-fertilization cannot be understood from the "one-liners" of which philosophical examples often are made. Stories shift epistemic inquiry from the lofty, extraterrestrial places that many theorists have claimed to occupy into the localities, situations, and specific academic "disciplines" where people seek to produce knowledge that will make it possible for them to act well, in their circumstances, with the resources at their disposal. Joseph Rouse, for example, proposes a laboratory model of localized scientific research, to displace an older spectator model. He argues that science—and, analogously, most secular knowledge—is produced within "locally, materially, and socially situated skills and practices," and within "self-adjudicating" communities, whose critical-interpretive activities are essential to the very possibility of "truth" emerging.[10] And Elizabeth Potter shifts the site of knowledge production into communal, interactive, epistemic negotiations, maintaining that isolated individuals "cannot produce language—much less the knowledge it embodies."[11] It is impossible to decide before the fact which specificities and practices will be salient in any epistemic tale, but it is clear that in their tellings questions about logical possibility will often yield to the demands of practical possibilities.

Interwoven with genealogical tales, and with stories of how practice and theory are mutually informative, are experiential stories of how it is for cognitive or moral agents to be located as they are, and to experience the world from there. Such stories are often told in a first-person voice; they are as often dismissed as anecdotal evidence, and contrasted pejoratively with data, "hard facts"; such stories are often cast as the stuff of which folklore, gossip, as opposed to knowledge "proper," is made.[12]

It is odd to exclude such stories from the epistemic terrain staked out even by the Anglo-American epistemologies that maintain allegiance to an older empiricism that privileges first-person, observational reports. Excluding them suggests that the starker versions of empiricism come apart around a paradox: for all their alleged grounding in experience, the experience to which orthodox empiricisms appeal is itself an abstraction. Classical empiricists and their successors have neither the conceptual nor the theoretical apparatus to account for real, specifically located experiences. Historical, gendered, and other locational differences reduce to individual bias, aberration; to errors that have to be eradicated and thence discounted in verification or justification procedures. In anti-narrative thinking, an alleged fact-narrative distinction often seems to parallel the old positivistic justification-discovery distinction, both evaluatively and descriptively.[13] Just as the chaos of discovery was to be left behind in the purification processes of justification, so the anecdotal character of narrative is to be left behind in the abstraction processes through which factuality is established.[14] In both processes, voice and specificity are suppressed in the name of a higher neutrality and generality.

The stories I have sketched out—like those that Collingwood tells—are primarily historical-genealogical rather than fictional. In calling them stories, I am drawing on Rée's minimal definition: "by 'story' I mean a sequence of the actions and experiences of one or more characters."[15] Yet my reading emphasizes the *poiesis* (=making) function of stories, where the "character(s)" are at once artificers and artifacts of "their" actions and experiences. And I am amplifying the definition with the assumption that stories manifest

a certain coherence—both internal and external, both spatial and temporal—that holds them together as stories rather than as mere assemblages of
statements. Coherence is at once produced by narrative structure, and can
have the effect of disrupting, interrogating, reconfiguring other alleged co-
herences, even including its own. This reading leaves open questions about
whether the stories at issue are factual or fictional; and about how their
"factuality" is discursively, narratively realized. My purpose is to destabilize
the self-certainty of the unstoried projects of which these stories tell; to show
that these stories are about human agency, even though they often contest
received conceptions of agency. More specifically, these are stories about a
situated, socially produced and exercised human agency whose newly audible voice requires "changing the subject" of the individualist tradition in
epistemology.[16]

Stories of this third, experiential variety most closely approximate the
narratives that philosophers contrast with arguments, proofs, demonstrations, to sustain a separation between fact and fiction. I appeal to them not
to collapse the distinction but to show that it is not as neat as the purists
wish. Because experiences, knowing, and theories of knowledge are embedded in community and social structures, and because epistemic activities are
interconnected across and among communities, whether consensually or
critically, there is no single Archimedean point from which analysis can
begin. Hence elaborated stories (=personal, local histories) are some of the
most productive sites for epistemological investigation.[17] Yet I am not
presenting first-person testimonials as clear and uncontested sites of fact-
finding.

Stories make audible the multiplicity of voices of which knowledge and
epistemologies are made, challenging assumptions of linear progress toward
establishing self-evident necessary and sufficient conditions, and contesting
the hegemonic claims of the dominant, yet not self-identifying, epistemic
voices. They offer fuller descriptions than propositional analyses commonly
have at their disposal. Yet a storied epistemology does not eschew normativ-
ity in favor of purely descriptive accounts of knowledge making. Rather, it
makes normative decisions qualitatively dependent upon descriptive evidence, and locates that evidence in practices and subjectivities where its effects and implications can be assessed. The multifaceted evidence on which
such normative judgments depend makes it unlikely that a single, universal
criterion of assessment will emerge; yet the normative judgments it informs
will be more adequate to the circumstances in which people need to be able
to know well than formal analyses have tended to be.

I have told a story of the epistemic potential of stories somewhat untidily,
to capture a sense that the old paradigm in epistemology is being displaced,
both horizontally and vertically. I am referring to the paradigm that derives
from upholding science (=theoretical physics) as the supreme human intellectual achievement and establishes positivist empiricism as the reigning
epistemology. In its purest form, this paradigm's ascendancy was quite

short, but its residues are still tenacious in shaping problems and epistemological puzzles. And its popular and intellectual appeal is indisputable for the promises of clarity and certainty that it advances.

Yet vertically the paradigm no longer stands, monolithically, as the regulative ideal of what epistemology aspires to achieve. And horizontally epistemology can no longer claim to be an umbrella inquiry that subsumes and speaks (evaluatively) for all inquiry, setting out the principles and methods to which all disciplines—and all everyday knowledge seeking—must adhere. Nonetheless, by contrast with periods of true paradigm shift in the natural sciences, where a clear case, historically, could be made that a single paradigm rules, epistemology has been less univocal. And by contrast with other periods of paradigm strain, it is unlikely that this period will produce a single new paradigm, a single different, or a single feminist, voice. Several of the strain-producing forces coalesce around the postcolonial, postimperialist contention that there could not be a single paradigm, a single conception of knowledge and epistemology that would not achieve its status by dominance and subordination; by colonizing other contenders. And although paradigms may, traditionally, have done just this to make normal science possible, many feminist and other critical epistemologists of the late twentieth century resist such homogenizing moves, of which the very idea of "normal" science, or "normal" epistemology, counts as one.

THE VOICELESS TRADITION

I shall characterize the paradigm-governed stage of twentieth-century epistemology with a cameo sketch of the purest, most influential of epistemic visions—the one that has shaped popular conceptions, in western capitalist societies, of what knowledge is and what an ideal knower is like. I focus here on the residual, but once strong, foundational empiricism that runs through modern Anglo-American epistemology and often combines with a conception of "pure reason," drawn more from the rationalist tradition, to inform commonsense beliefs about what knowledge is. The epistemologists I refer to do not constitute a homogeneous group; hence my aggregating them is somewhat artificial. Nor are they the only philosophers to have addressed matters of knowledge: rationalists, phenomenologists, Marxists, existentialists, hermeneuticists, and pragmatists, to mention only a few, deal with knowledge quite differently. Yet the features of the "epistemology project" that I highlight form a loosely constructed grid of assumptions, methods, and purposes that extend beyond the boundaries of this starkly conceived empiricism.[18]

Underwriting the assumptions I outline is a tacit consensus to the effect that epistemologists need not ask "Who knows?" Nor need they pose the question "What is knowledge?" in any but a formulaic sense, to which a response such as the claim that "knowledge is justified true belief" could suffice. Inquiry proceeds as if the answers to such questions were so obvious that no bona fide epistemologist need worry about them. My "modest" proposal moves these questions to the top of the epistemic agenda and shows that stories have to be told if they are adequately to be answered.

Twentieth-century epistemology in the English-speaking world still bears the marks of this empiricist legacy. It traces its principal (more recent) origins to the disaffection of such British philosophers as Bertrand Russell and G. E. Moore, in the early years of this century, with the idealism in which many of them were trained; and to the logical positivism endorsed by members of the Vienna Circle at about the same time. Its central ideas are most familiarly—if starkly—articulated in Bertrand Russell's *Problems of Philosophy* and A. J. Ayer's *Language, Truth and Logic*.[19] I am reading these versions of empiricism as emblematic for the expectations that ordinary people have about what knowledge amounts to, and about what critical examinations of their own and other people's knowledge should enable them to do. These everyday expectations persist through philosophers' critical reassessments of empiricist theory.

In these projects, a veneration of logic, mathematics, and physics as the highest human intellectual achievements translates into a regulative ideal that knowledge "in general" should aim to approximate. The ideal in some (historically mutable) form is by no means new: it figures in Plato's writings on knowledge and is a powerful shaping force in classical rationalist metaphysics and theories of knowledge, where its realization is quite differently envisaged. Its twentieth-century empiricist reinstatement and its secularization in everyday observational moments have had far-reaching effects, both horizontal and vertical, in the twentieth century. Many of the effects I discuss persist even through refinements and neorationalist variations that have sought to soften the stringency of this ideal in its postpositivist versions.

Horizontally, across the epistemic terrain, the ideal has worked to demarcate the "scope and limits" of human knowledge, hence to establish lateral barriers to separate what can "properly" be known from what can merely be opined, believed, or felt. The logical positivists' verifiability principle, according to which the meaning of a statement is the method of its verification, illustrates this point. Any proposition that was not immediately verifiable, commonly in direct observation, was rendered meaningless by this principle. Hence—famously—because religious, aesthetic, and ethical claims ("God is good"; "Kathe Kollwitz is a fine painter"; "Safe abortion is every woman's right") could not be verified, they reduced to expressions of emotion, to mere expletives with no more epistemic status than "boo" or "hurrah." Epistemologies that bear the traces of this ideal still commonly map out their terrain so that aesthetics, religion, ethics, and, analogously, other forms of qualitative inquiry are relegated to places beyond the boundaries of epistemological evaluation, places where "it's all a matter of opinion." The assumption prevails that knowledge properly so called consists of facts, information, neutrally (=objectively) found and observationally testable: facts whose "factuality" depends on the extent to which they are free of the taint of subjectivity, and hence are value-neutral. Values become noncognitive by this same lateral mapping process: in consequence of their affective character they count only as subjectively whimsical. They fall outside the domain of ideal objectivity, where facts are established. What counts as a fact for the more austere adherents of this position, then, is determined by a standard according to which quantifiable or empirically verifiable claims are the most plausible contenders for assessment as true or false. Ideally, a fact is a piece of information about a discrete state of affairs in the material world, expressible in such simple propositions as "dogs have four legs," "I know that this is a rock," "S knows that p," whose necessary and sufficient truth conditions, apparently, can be determined.[20] Exemplary knowledge is "of" things that have no particular significance for the knower, because mattering, too, is evaluative, and obscures the possibility of objective clarity.

On a Russellian, classical reading, knowledge about aspects of the world other than medium-sized, observable, material objects could approach incontestable certainty only if those aspects could be reduced, manipulated, or broken down into comparable, observable units so that they could, likewise, be verified. Hence for Russell "knowledge by acquaintance" is always more secure, more reliable than "knowledge by description"; and knowledge by description increases in epistemic worth to the extent that it can be analyzed into moments of direct observational acquaintance.[21] In more modern versions of empiricism, concentration upon simple perceptual examples often gives way to a search for conditions of "warranted assertability," or to assessing epistemological coherence or the fit of a knowledge claim with a subject's "acceptance system."[22] Yet throughout these changes, the presumed ubiquity of observational and conceptual access to objects in the world, together with a formalization process derived from what scientists (especially theoretical physicists) apparently do, insulates an entrenched, yet once-stipulated, definition of knowledge-as-information from any need to tell the story of its own stipulation. The continued hegemony of this definition—as evidenced, for example, in social-scientific resistance to "qualitative research"—yields the consequence that people, too, can be known only to the extent that their behavior can be observed. Any other reactions or responses to them remain just that: reactions, hence of no epistemological significance, because of their affective (value-laden) character. Even in late-twentieth-century academic social science departments, theorists are relatively rare, and a belief persists that social sciences can claim the status of knowledge only for their observational and/or quantifiable results. History and archaeology become contentious disciplines owing to the inaccessibility of their "data" to direct observation; and women's traditional arts and skills are judged "unscientific," hence unworthy of the label "knowledge."[23] Thus an assumed, unarticulated conception of what knowledge *is* still moves like a regulative cursor across the epistemic terrain, giving its stamp of approval here, withholding it there.

Positivist-empiricist epistemologists, both classical and modern, assume that most of what goes into making valid knowledge claims is available on the surface, so to speak, of experience: that the conditions of its provenance and possibility, broadly construed, have no epistemic bearing—indeed, that invoking them commits the "genetic fallacy." Implicated in this (horizontal) assumption is the belief that seeing—even "seeing as"—is a direct and unmediated route to knowing: that in the right conditions it amounts to perception without bias or distortion; and that those conditions can readily be brought about.

Yet for such conditions to hold, it has also to be assumed that would-be knowers are distributed evenly across a surface that is equally traversable by all, furnished with objects, animals, plants, and other people that are equally accessible to everyone. Standard propositional paradigms *("S* knows that *p")* can be accorded epistemic salience only if it can be taken for granted that experiences and experiencers are all alike and perfectly transparent—hence, again, that no stories need to be told about the circumstances in which every cognitive act is embedded. That assumption is achieved in the character of the knower who is taken for the principal actor in these epistemic events. He—and I use the masculine pronoun advisedly here[24]—is the abstract individual of post-Enlightenment epistemology and moral theory, whose intellectual activities and capacities vary according to whether he appears in an idealist, a rationalist, or an empiricist setting. Throughout these variations, certain commonalities are discernible. Most striking, for my analysis here, is the fact that this "individual" is not individuated: he is an infinitely replicable knower whose personal and situational peculiarities are preanalytically eradicated to enable him to stand as *the* epistemic (or moral) agent, *the* knower. Whether in rationalist appeals to introspective examinations of the contents of the mind, or in empiricist appeals to experiential givens, the assumption is that the route to certain knowledge is a solitary one; yet that every "individual" can go that journey on his own and, by following proper procedures, can achieve valid, reliable knowledge. The individualist presumption is reinforced by the low esteem in which "testimony" is held in many of these theories of knowledge: by the tendency to align testimony with opinion or hearsay (and to denigrate it accordingly). Assumptions such as these condone relegating stories to the category of "anecdotal evidence," contrasting them sharply and unfavorably with "empirical facts." Knowledge claims become stylized responses to passively received stimuli, and particular circumstances or experiences reduce to variables. In short, in the starkest moments of postpositivist empiricism, and residually, in disciplines informed by its latter-day variants, epistemologists have tended to work with a stimulus-response model of knowing that does not address its conative and affective aspects—that ignores the desires and interests that motivate most people's cognitive projects, in situations where their very survival may depend on what they can know.

And what, in these terms, is knowledge? For early-twentieth-century empiricists, it is the propositional product of a perceptual confrontation between a sentient creature (a subject) and an insentient item (an object) that is accessible to the creature's sensory apparatus. Standing in that vertical (onlooker) relation to the object, the subject is able to utter statements about it that name or quantify some of its properties or indicate how they are spatially interrelated. Those statements become the elements of knowledge when/if there is "sufficient" evidence to support the conclusion that the object is just as the propositions state: evidence that may be available to one observer as a result of repeated observations, or/and evidence that is available, separately and singly, to other observers in identical observational conditions. Verifiability is closely linked to repeatability of observations about the same object(s): to the assumption that any observer, independently, will make the same observations as every other; and that his monologic reports count as representative knowledge claims. The voice in which he utters his claims is the voice of "everyman"—and no man. Hence its (impersonal) objectivity is assured. Relations between subject and object do not figure in such knowledge claims, nor does the social-political positioning of the subject. Nor do these inquiries consider the relations between and among subjects, and their cooperative, argumentative, or otherwise interactive, knowledge-making activities. Rather, these projects tend to count as no more than the sum of their parts, with every participant separately accountable to the evidence. Results (=knowledge) become his individual achievement, neutrally presented to an objective and disinterested public. Nor does it matter what these knowers might do with their knowledge, how it might bear upon their being in the world.

Now this reading of the positivist-empiricist legacy is stark, and overstated in glossing over more recent refinements and nuances. Yet such a conception of knowledge still trickles down to inform everyday, commonsensical conceptions of what knowing is all about: it produces the folk wisdom that enjoins people to go and see for themselves, it upholds the assumption that "seeing is believing," and grants overriding credence to "eye-witness evidence."[25]

What difference, then, would it make to take stories seriously, and how would it open up spaces where feminist voices would be clearly audible? Stories challenge the anonymous and universalist pretensions of dominant theories and afford rich opportunities for self-reflexive theory making. Because they presuppose tellers and listeners, they are good candidates for shaping revisionary projects and transformational agendas. In such projects it is vital to understand where we are now and how we got here, and to recognize that "we" is also a contestable signifier, shaped and delineated, perhaps only strategically, in the tellings. Storytelling engages its listeners not so much by rhetorical spellbinding as responsively, interrogatively, interpretively, and confrontationally. It presents loci for identification and differentiation, agreement and dispute, and presents them over a textured range of possibilities that are linked, yet contingent and available for assent or refusal. The story I am telling is a story of this sort: a reading I put forward for discussion, not a final telling.

My plea for stories focuses as much on locating philosophical developments within larger social and historical narratives as it does on seeking narrative starting points for critical inquiry. Taking as one of its catalysts Ruth Hubbard's claim that "every fact has a factor, a maker,"[26] my proposal says that the same is true of theories and experiences, whose "makers" are enabled and constrained by the situations in which they find themselves, and which they need to understand. It exhorts these "makers" to announce themselves and to examine the implications of their historical-geographical-cultural locations. Contra the charge that such a move commits the "genetic fallacy," telling stories does not explain away the artifacts, the products, of these makings. Rather, it situates them, diachronically and synchronically. Taking stories into account eschews individualism and dispels any illusion that "experiences" come parceled in discrete propositional units; it shows that such a parceling, as a prelude to formal analysis, leaves "experiences" behind in the very explanations that purport to elucidate them.

I am suggesting that the examples that have counted as "typical" have shaped the results that epistemology can yield, in form, in content, and in their (limited) implications for people's epistemic lives. Hence in their very neutrality, their presumed innocence, they exercise an exclusionary power, homogenizing circumstantial differences and situational variability. My point is neither that stories become necessary conditions for the possibility of knowledge nor that they could ever be sufficient. Experiential stories do, nonetheless, approach the status of sine qua non conditions for achieving the imaginative understanding that is often a prerequisite for acting well both epistemically and morally (i.e., for knowing circumstances—both one's own and someone else's—well enough to act appropriately). Developing a well-constructed story is different from occupying a perspective: it requires situating the self reflexively and self-critically. Nor can it be done incontrovertibly, for it is a matter of putting plots together, of achieving a factual and artifactual coherence and plausibility, and of constant revisions even in the process of establishing nodal points that make action possible.

In stories, experience is read in greater "semantic depth" than in merely observational reports; yet taking experience seriously also affirms its contestability.[27] No longer are first-person, experiential reports simply accepted as read, as "pure," innocent tellings of how reality has imprinted itself upon a receptive consciousness. Experiences are mediated by their locations within particular spatial-temporal points, produced out of intricate complexes of identities, circumstances, and events, to become starting points for ongoing analysis, interpretation, and critique. My proposal contests the presumed privilege of traditional, privileged-access knowledge claims and challenges their exemplary and uncontrovertible status. In the always-contestable readings that stories generate, discussion and debate displace univocal utterance, exclusions are as significant as inclusions, and the monologic voice yields to a plurality of sometimes consonant, sometimes dissonant voices.[28]

MULTIPLE VOICES

There is no linear story to tell of feminist interrogations of "the epistemological project," no single, unbroken narrative line with a beginning, middle, and end. Yet epistemology was late among the traditional branches of philosophy to come under feminist scrutiny: knowledge, and particularly scientific knowledge, seemed, to early second-wave feminists, to be secure and outside the fray of critical debate. Only logic and mathematics seemed to be more stable. True, philosophers throughout history had contended that women were deficient in reason, that their approaches to the world were ineluctably subjective because of their reliance on intuition, and that they were incapable of abstract thought.[29] Yet the very idea that reason, knowledge, methodology, objectivity, abstraction—even thought itself—could be indelibly masculine because they were based in male experience and fostered highly valued male character traits seemed at best preposterous, at worst a manifestation of ideological excess. The "problem" was with "woman," not with these constant, and largely extramundane ideals. Against the background of such entrenched assumptions, the rallying call sounded in the 1983 introduction to Sandra Harding and Merrill Hintikka's *Discovering Reality* was nothing short of revolutionary. The editors write: "We must root out sexist distortions and perversions in epistemology, metaphysics, methodology and the philosophy of science—in the 'hard core' of abstract reasoning thought most immune to infiltration by social values. [C]ontributors to this volume . . . identify how distinctively masculine perspectives on masculine experience have shaped the most fundamental and most formal aspects of systematic thought in philosophy and in the social and natural sciences—the aspects of thought supposedly most gender-neutral."[30] Residues of positivism were especially perceptible in the intellectual climate into which this text was inserted. There the immunity of science and formal systems to social-political interests still amounted to what Collingwood would call an "absolute presupposition": a presupposition about which questions of truth and falsehood do not arise for it constitutes the basis, the framework, that makes inquiry possible and stands outside all interrogatory projects, to provide their very terms of reference.[31]

Equally strong contenders for "absolute presupposition" status in western philosophy, both rationalist and empiricist, are the mutually sustaining beliefs that "the mind has no sex" and that "reason is alike in all men."[32] They attest to a pervasive conviction that accidents of gendered embodiment are just that: accidents. They have no more bearing upon the operations of reason than accidents of eye color or food preferences might have. Yet two landmark stories—Genevieve Lloyd's *The Man of Reason* and Evelyn Fox Keller's *A Feeling for the Organism: The Life and Work of Barbara McClintock*[33]—contested even these seemingly unshakable beliefs, and in so doing prepared the way for the analyses in which feminist epistemologists have subsequently been engaged.

The story of Barbara McClintock's practice as a geneticist enables Keller to examine how scientific knowledge "grows out of the interaction—sometimes complex, always subtle—between individual creativity and communal validation."[34] What is interesting about the story is the fact that its outcome, with respect to the gendered associations it seeks to establish, is equivocal. Notable discrepancies emerge between McClintock's scientific methods and orientation and those of the overwhelmingly male establishment in which she worked and sought recognition. Yet McClintock professed a commitment to an ideal of gender-free science and resisted any suggestion that her "feeling for the organism" might derive from her femaleness. Hence Keller presents McClintock as a supremely individual thinker and researcher, whose maverick vision of the "oneness of things"[35] led her to depart radically from received practice in genetics. Nonetheless, the analysis in the biography is of a piece with Keller's work on gender and science, in which she uncovered notable coincidences between the traits attributed to ideal knowers and the norms of affluent, male psychosexual development in science-oriented, western societies.[36] The character traits that appear to inform McClintock's approach to her work—and hence to shape her results—are more closely aligned with traits that have been fostered in female psychosexual development in the same segments of those societies. Hence the McClintock story challenges the very idea of a gender-free science: a project in which many feminists have been involved in recent years.[37] In so doing, it contests the sanctity of privileged-access claims even to cherished aspects of "one's own" experiences, suggesting that McClintock's responses may not count as the last words on the matter. Opening them to critical reinterpretation can maintain respect for the sincerity of her testimony, while approaching it within an ongoing reinterpretive process that keeps the tensions in feminist inquiry alive and productive. Keller has told a good story. Her historical essays that expose the sexual imagery of mastery and domination that shapes Baconian science, and those that examine the imagery of love and sex in Platonic epistemology, open up an ongoing contestation of the presumed neutrality and sexlessness of reason, objectivity, and knowledge.[38]

Genevieve Lloyd's genealogical story of the "maleness" of reason reveals the coincidences Keller uncovered, between idealized (western) maleness and scientific rationality, as twentieth-century manifestations of an entrenched practice of defining reason, rationality, and objectivity through the exclusion of traits commonly associated with femininity. Lloyd's is not the facile contention that what is true and rational for men is untrue and irrational for women: that reality, knowledge, reason, and rationality divide neatly into "his" and "hers." Her point is that even despite explicit avowals to the contrary (by such philosophers as Augustine and Descartes), reason persists as an ideal articulated through the symbols and metaphors that also articulate ideal maleness. The symbolic content of ideal reason is established by a suppression of traits devalued by their associations with "the feminine." Although no unified, constant, "male" principle has prevailed since ancient times, between the definitions, symbolisms, and associations that define masculinity and those that define reason there is a coincidence too remarkable to be merely coincidental.

These engrained metaphors are not *merely* symbolic accretions to an otherwise literal linguistic mapping of a neutral or sexless reason. Reason is not just something one comes across, there in the world: it becomes available only conceptually. Hence, Lloyd notes: "The metaphor of maleness is deeply embedded in philosophical articulations of ideas and ideals of reason. It has been constitutive of ways of thinking of reason which have deep repercussions in ways of thinking of ourselves as male or female. Metaphorical though it may be, maleness has been no mere embellishment of reason."[39] Lloyd shows that ideals of reason, throughout their shifting and evolving history, designate what it is to be a good knower, determine what counts as knowledge and as a proper object of knowledge—and prescribe the "proper relations between our status as knowers and the rest of our lives."[40] These ideals have had a constitutive effect in western metaphysics, epistemology, and ethics: an effect that has shaped popular conceptions of knowledge and of whose knowledge can claim epistemic authority.

Lloyd's and Keller's stories set in motion two lines of investigation that have become central to feminist and other postessentialist analyses of knowledge and subjectivity: one line (Lloyd's) traces how historical-social-cultural patterns and discourses position thinkers within circumscribed yet never closed sets of conceptual possibilities; one (Keller's) focuses on historically specific psychosocial forces that shape "individual" epistemic practice.[41] These stories leave little doubt that the invisible, voiceless, knowing subject in mainstream epistemology and philosophy of science has a voice after all: it is presumptively male. It is no wonder that the knowledge he produces is androcentric, for it derives from typically male experiences.

Acknowledging the maleness of reason and the androcentricity of epistemic practice generates a set of tensions that are not easily resolved. Kirstie McClure summarizes the situation thus: "Feminist political theory . . . is necessarily normative in its prescriptions for solving the problem of women's oppression. It is empirical and scientific in its comprehensive causal analysis of that oppression; practical in its intent to explain, justify, and guide feminist action in ending that oppression; and philosophical in the systematic character of its ideals. . . . By virtue of its practical purpose . . . the requisite foundations of feminism include reliable knowledge of the world."[42]

Feminists need reliable knowledge to ground their emancipatory political projects and to claim the epistemic authority from which women have been systematically excluded. Yet when the most effective knowledge-producing tools and strategies are demonstrably masculine, and when the knowledge that is produced and validated tends to confirm male privilege, the options are by no means straightforward.

Nor are these tools simplistically masculine in the sense that they are produced by and for all men. The regulative ideals that have shaped western epistemic practice are created by and address the situations of only a small group of men: affluent, educated, culturally Eurocentered, usually Christian, white men. It is they who have produced the master narratives in which "the man of reason" has been the principal actor: they who, in the nineteenth and early twentieth centuries, colonized vast sections of the world, not just materially but intellectually. Their standards of rationality have provided the foundations for judging other cultures primitive, irrational, prescientific—and not just other cultures in other countries but nondominant cultures within their own countries.

Feminists have found resonances with other participants in critical and revisionary epistemology projects in their insistence that the privilege of anonymity and feigned ubiquity of voicelessness can no longer be maintained. These critics contest the assumed invisibility that cloaks standard knowers, requiring accountability only to "the evidence," represented as neutrally there, as found, not made. In these critical-revisionary projects, questions about knowledge become questions about subjectivities, where subjectivity means something different from the "personhood" or "selfhood" of the Anglo-American (liberal) tradition. It recalls the subjectivity evanescently realized in choices and the exercise of agency in the existentialist writings of Simone de Beauvoir and Jean-Paul Sartre; yet its freedom is not nearly so radical as the early de Beauvoir and Sartre maintained. It is materially, situationally constrained, and multiply realized, articulated, and positioned. As in the writings of de Beauvoir and Sartre, this is a subjectivity whose projects and problems are often best articulated in stories.

The epistemological narratives in which such subjectivities are implicated are about power and empowering, and about accountability not just *to* the evidence but *for* the positions from which knowers speak, and *to* the society or social group where knowledge is circulated or withheld and differentially distributed. Because stories about the production of theories, knowledge, and experience are about human agency, they are at once and inextricably epistemological, moral, and political.

Feminist epistemologists have found allies and resources in other successor epistemologies and philosophies of science. Many see in Thomas Kuhn's *The Structure of Scientific Revolutions*[43] a crucial interruption of an otherwise unbroken story of linear scientific epistemological progress. Kuhn reinserts scientists into stories of the generation of scientific paradigms to prepare the way for such socioanthropological studies of science making as Bruno Latour and Steve Woolgar's *Laboratory Life* and Latour's later *Science in Action*. In the latter book, Latour tells stories of the "disorderly mixture revealed by science in action" as a way of demystifying and contextualizing "the orderly patterns of scientific method and rationality."[44] Feminists have drawn, albeit critically, upon Richard Rorty's challenge to Enlightenment epistemology in *Philosophy and the Mirror of Nature*,[45] and upon the consequent revival of pragmatism in North American philosophy;[46] and some feminists have seen in Quinean "naturalized epistemology" a subtler empiricism that opens possibilities for answering the "whose knowledge" question.[47] This list must expand to include cross-fertilizations between Continental and Anglo-American philosophy, whose epistemological effects would have astonished professional English-speaking philosophers of the 1960s and early 1970s. Most notable has been the work of Michel Foucault, whose histories of reason and analyses of the interconnections between power and knowledge dispel any illusion that dislocated, disembodied critique is possible; and of Jacques Derrida, whose deconstructions of western "logocentrism" and its hierarchical dichotomies (reason/emotion, mind/body, nature/culture) expose instabilities in language and metaphysics that demand revisionary reconstructions of speaking positions.

Feminists have found analytic resources in many of these critical endeavors, despite their frequent misogyny and androcentricity, and their failure to engage adequately with issues of gendered specificity. Many feminist epistemologists thus tell histories/stories about how sex-gender systems continue, in late capitalist societies, to sustain theories of knowledge and rationality that are fundamentally androcentric. Although this project is "storied" in many of the senses I invoke, it is by no means "single-storied," for sex-gender systems are not unified, homogeneous loci of power and marginality. They do not produce uniform speaking positions, separable from the other "identities" and "attributes" that position people differentially across social orders. These positionings are always shaped and constrained by some of the others so that a concentration on sex-gender issues is always an explicit choice to examine how subjectivities are thus positioned, to highlight sex-gender systems out of a cluster of conspiring and opposing factors that, in their turn, shape sex-gender positionings. Class, race, ethnicity, sexual orientation, economics, religion, age, sexuality, bodily size, ability, and other privilegings and marginalizings too numerous to mention produce subjectivities variously, throughout their biographical life-lines. Hence there can be no single "different" feminist voice.[48]

A FEMINIST EPISTEMOLOGY?

Born of 1960s consciousness-raising practices, with their commitment to taking stories seriously, feminist critiques of the master narratives of epistemology have exposed gaps and cognitive dissonances between women's diverse experiences and the theories that purport to explain—to *know*—them. Feminists, consequently, are suspicious of efforts to determine necessary and sufficient conditions for knowledge and for cognitive practice. The silencing effects of those projects are well documented, as are their implications for perpetuating women's oppression.[49] Hence feminists examine *practices* of knowledge construction to produce critical retellings of what historically and materially "situated" knowers actually do. Denying that epistemology should aim to derive a regulative theory of "knowledge in general," they are looking at how knowledge is produced in specific disciplines and areas of inquiry; how hypotheses are circulated and evidence selected; how conclusions are drawn and enacted; how disciplinary power structures work. Their purposes are as much to reveal the permeability of disciplinary boundaries as to work within them.

Joan Hartman and Ellen Messer-Davidow's edited collection, *(En)gendering Knowledge: Feminists in Academe* (1991), exemplifies this process. Its structure is as interesting as its content. The editors want to develop a "social epistemology" that views "the production or transformation of academic knowledge as a practice that constitutes both knowers and the institutions that enable and constrain them."[50] They distinguish their project from sociology of knowledge by insisting that normative imperatives are integral to the descriptive inquiries: that studies of how knowledge is constructed show how it *should* be constructed and circulated by exposing the exclusions that are effected by the inclusions of received theories and the distributions of power they legitimate. Practitioners discuss knowledge production in sociology, art history, literature, physics, classics, biology, to name but a few; each section concludes with an analytic reading of the contributions by an epistemologist/philosopher of science. The book exemplifies the practice of moving in and out of epistemology, telling diverse stories of how knowledge—scientific, social scientific, and humanistic—is made, and reflecting critically on those makings.

The Hartman and Messer-Davidow book is not without its problems: many of the analyses are less radical than feminists of the late 1990s might wish, and the authoritative status that the book preserves structurally for philosophy appears to beg the very questions that critics of philosophical master narratives find most pressing. But it is provocative in representing epistemology as a storied project of (descriptively) understanding how people can know and (prescriptively) showing how they should negotiate their local circumstances and the global situations in which their localities are embedded. With other critical-revisionist theorists, these feminists face the challenge of showing how avowedly engaged and political inquiries yield knowledge that can guide feminist action.

Endeavoring to meet this challenge, some feminists of the "second wave" have drawn on the radical potential of older-style epistemologies, sometimes separately and sometimes more eclectically. In these projects, where again they move in and out of epistemology, feminists at once contest and use the tools that it has produced. Many of them engage in these projects by appealing to, or developing, storied analyses.

Feminists who see empiricism as the most promising resource for successor epistemological projects tend to take issue with postpositivist versions of empiricism for many of the reasons I have discussed. They argue that the knower who occupies the S position in the standard *"S-knows-that-p"* rubric is male in the autonomy that produces his detachment from the object of knowledge, in the ideal objectivity he claims to attain, and in the instrumental rationality that informs his cognitive projects. His location is a generic one, within the options and privileges of white maleness. Yet these same feminists are well aware of the impressive successes of empirical knowledge seeking and of scientific inquiry that is empirically, even positivistically, based. Hence they argue that an unabashedly value-laden yet rigorous empiricism, informed by feminist commitments, can produce more adequate knowledge than standard empiricist epistemologies: that politically informed, gender-sensitive inquiry can yield a better empiricism. The goal of inquiry is to produce knowledge cleansed of androcentric and sexist biases, and (latterly) of racist, classist, and other "distortions."

Feminist empiricism is a curious hybrid, for a feminist knower cannot be the abstract, ahistorical, disembodied individual that classical empiricist theories of knowledge take for granted. Her political commitments seem so flagrantly to violate a basic empiricist principle that the point of retaining the label is often unclear. Yet for Sandra Harding, the multifaceted objectivity that feminist inquiry demands is stronger than the older, ideal objectivity of the empiricist tradition.[51] It is objective both in its approach to the objects of knowledge and in knowing its own social situation and background beliefs. Hence it amounts to a storied objectivity: one that produces stories about its own claims to objective status—and that recognizes the need for such stories, resisting any temptation to assume that its "successes" are self-justifying.

In Helen Longino's contextual empiricism, evidential reasoning is context-dependent, data count as evidence only in relation to background assumptions and hypotheses, and science is social knowledge. She writes: "The development of knowledge is a necessarily social rather than individual activity, and it is the social character of scientific knowledge that both protects it from and renders it vulnerable to social and political interests and values."[52] Knowledge production is rigorously accountable to empirical evidence, yet there are choices about what to count as evidence and how to determine its significance: choices shaped by the background assumptions that inquirers bring to research. Because knowledge-producing activities are thoroughly social, acknowledging the effects of values, ideology, and background assumptions leads not to an indiscriminate tolerance of subjective preferences but to ongoing social criticism. Longino's elaborated stories of sex difference research, in which she explains the implications of competing explanatory models of causality and human action, exemplify the complex interactions of theory and practice in reading and interpreting evidence.

For Lynn Nelson, post-Quinean "naturalized" epistemologies offer a promising resource for developing a specifically feminist, empirically rigorous theory of knowledge.[53] Quinean empiricism demands neither the stark individualism nor the theory neutrality of the classical theories. Indeed, as Nelson presents it, Quine's could count as a "storied" epistemology, for it develops "firmly *within* science" (even though it seems not to be explicitly "voiced").[54] It includes "as its primary task an effort to provide an account of how we go about constructing theories and positing objects":[55] studying what "we" do "naturalizes" Quinean epistemology. Naturalized epistemologies assume that people can and do have knowledge, arguing that their survival behaviors alone attest to it. Drawing upon the findings of cognitive psychology, naturalists abandon any claims to dislocation, transcendence, to examine how people actually know, individually and socially.

In a story about the politics of knowledge in sociobiology, Nelson examines the accountability requirements its metaphysical commitments engender. Like Longino, she maintains that it is communities, not "individuals," who know: that although, "based on our experiences, we can each contribute uniquely to what we know, . . . none of us knows what no one else could."[56] Their adherence to principles of empirical objectivity persuades nonfeminist naturalists that they can offer effective tools for producing and adjudicating knowledge of the physical and social world. They eschew methodological individualism and theory neutrality, to address many of the same charges feminists have leveled at the older empiricisms. The promise of the project is apparent. Yet its radical, prefeminist potential is thwarted by the fact that the scientific psychology to which the orthodox Quineans appeal presupposes a constancy in a "human nature" exemplified in "representative selves" who have commonly been white, male, and middle-class. It has fallen to feminists such as Nelson to show that the power-saturated processes that confirm or withhold membership in the company of "natural" knowers cannot escape critical scrutiny. Hence feminist naturalists have to maintain a wariness about the scope of the "we" whom the post-Quineans study, and to remember that appeals to "nature" have been notoriously complicit in the exclusion of women and other marginal groups.[57]

These neoempiricist stories do not sit well with feminist standpoint theorists, who object that no version of empiricism can tell the whole story. Contending that neither orthodox nor feminist empiricists can account for the historical and material conditions out of which people produce knowledge and are themselves produced as knowers, standpoint theorists[58] turn to Marxist historical materialism as their principal theoretical resource. They remind feminists that exemplary, authoritative knowledge in western societies has been derived from and tested against the social experiences of white, propertied, educated men, to be presented as the universal truth. It is based on, and perpetuates, stories about the proper places for women and men to occupy m capitalist societies, and about the relative worth of their labor, both cognitive and material. Women (like the proletariat) are oppressed in underclass epistemic positions that are represented as their "natural" places in the social hierarchy, and the naturalness of these assumptions is upheld by a scientific practice to whose esoteric discourse few women gain ready access.

Standpoint theorists claim that women's oppression can be turned into an epistemic advantage. Just as, in Marxist theory, consciousness-raising enables the oppressed to understand the structures that subordinate them better than those who benefit from those same structures, so a feminist-achieved understanding of their marginal position often enables women to know their oppressors and the systems that legitimate them more clearly than the oppressors know themselves. Experiential knowledge—narratives—can "denaturalize" and make strange women's presumed inferior cognitive and political capabilities.

Some critics object that because there is no single, unified female/feminist situation, standpoint theory obliterates differences and hence fails by its own standards. Others challenge its claims to epistemic privilege, arguing that its "locatedness" produces a perspective on social reality that is as limited as any other. Its defenders respond that its specific rootedness in material exigencies gives standpoint theory an emancipatory edge and a ready-formulated political agenda that even the most sensitive empiricism cannot hope to achieve. They insist on the importance of faithful, yet critical and necessarily partial, stories of women's experiences and material circumstances for producing critical understandings of how patriarchal oppression is legitimated by hegemonic epistemic values.

For all of these theorists, knowledge production is a social practice of embodied, gendered, historically, racially, and culturally located knowers whose products bear the marks of their makers and whose stories need, therefore, to be told. The "constructivism" implicit in the suggestion that knowledge is *made*, not found, is constrained by the intransigence of things and practices that will neither go away nor lend themselves to just any construction; and by the stubborn conservatism of traditions, institutions, and social structures that resist wishful negation or reconstruction. Yet that intransigence is not absolute: within its gaps feminists have shown that interventionist, transformative strategies can be remarkably effective.

Once epistemologists acknowledge the limitations of knowers and the partiality of every "perspective," the demands of *epistemic responsibility* assert themselves insistently.[59] Their reliance on a purified physical-science model of knowledge exempted positivist-empiricists from facing such questions. They worked with a conception of doxastic involuntarism for which seeing indeed was believing; faced with "the evidence" spread out neutrally before him, a knower could not rationally withhold assent. Moving the "whose knowledge" question to the top of the agenda challenges these taken-for-granted assumptions so radically that even so seemingly universal an ideal as objectivity is reconstructed as a socially produced and mediated value.[60] Nor is it any wonder that objectivity—with subjectivity, rationality, and experience—should count among the candidates for deconstruction and transformation. These concepts cannot simply be translated into "a feminist voice" for—like reason in Lloyd's analysis—their operative meanings are so saturated with the androcentered specificities of their histories that they have to be respecified, retold whenever they are employed in revisionary projects.

In many feminist stories of knowledge production, objectivity is as much a consequence of negotiation and communal criticism—the secular counterparts of peer review in the academy—as of scrupulous attention to "the evidence." Evidence counts as evidence within contexts determined as much by social as by purely observational criteria. Burdens of proof are redistributed *laterally*, across communities of inquirers; they no longer pertain merely vertically, from a transcendent observer *to* the data. It is as important to know about the credibility of knowledge claimants, their critics and interlocutors as it is to know how, empirically, to verify a claim "on its own merits"; and knowledge claimants are as accountable to their communities of inquiry as to the facts. Thus the ideal of pure inquiry fragments into locational specificity. Indeed, according to some persuasive feminist stories, only people with the resources and power to believe that they can transcend and control their circumstances would see the detachment that the ideal demands as even a theoretical option. Inquiry comes out of, and is interwoven with, human purposes, whether at commonsensical or at esoteric, scientific levels. Those purposes have to be evaluated if knowledge is to achieve its emancipatory potential, locally and globally.

Informed by postmodern critiques, many feminists contend that the detached, disinterested knower, the neutral spectator of the world, can no longer count as the hero of the story. Subjectivity is produced in social-political-racial-class-ethnic-cultural-religious circumstances so diverse that attempts to tell one true story, to develop a single master narrative, amount only to grossly reductive exercises.[61] Yet in an essay patently wary of postmodern attempts to undo the achievements of the Enlightenment, Seyla Benhabib argues for "an epistemology and politics which recognizes the lack of metanarratives and foundational guarantees but which nonetheless insists on formulating minimal criteria of validity for our discursive and political practices."[62] Her plea engages directly with some of the tensions that feminists of the 1990s are working within as they recognize the postmodern implications of feminist projects while retaining a commitment to producing valid accounts of "reality."

Feminists have to determine criteria for adjudicating knowledge claims when foundational appeals are no longer viable, and to devise methods for analyzing knowledge that both is socially constructed and bears the marks of its makers, *and* is constrained by a reality that is not wholly compliant with their wishes. They have to be attentive to the specificities of their subject matters (their intractability to reductive analysis) yet open to critical debate across a plurality of locations and methods. These tensions cannot be resolved merely by introducing a "different voice," or a single "feminist voice" into the rhetorical spaces where epistemology is made. Yet out of these same tensions, feminists have to effect temporary closures at nodal points that can permit strategic, informed knowledge and action.

This project of taking stories into account proposes a way of engaging with these issues. It picks up a thread from my *Epistemic Responsibility*, where I argue that people are epistemically interdependent and that narratives (i.e., stories), historical, political, personal, social, fictional, are among the principal vehicles of self-understanding and self-critique. I draw upon an extended story of Philip Gosse's struggles to reconcile Darwinian evolutionary theory with his Christian fundamentalism, to illustrate the demands of epistemically responsible inquiry. I pick up this thread in *What Can She Know?* where I argue that persons are essentially "second persons" who realize their "personhood" in addressing one another as "you" (both singular and plural), affirming the delineation of "I" and "we" in so doing. People need interpretive communities if they are to make sense of and interrogate their experiences, and the social structures that make these experiences possible. In (storied) analyses of how androcentered epistemologies engender a double standard of credibility, and how knowledge itself is a commodity of privilege, I have shown that subjectivities (in this case, people) have tended, in the knowledge that these epistemologies legitimate, to be *known*, represented, categorized in empowering and disempowering ways, according to whether they come in male or female bodies; and that femaleness is consistently disempowering, even across its historically and culturally varied manifestations. This thread connects with the projects of feminists who are telling the stories of science making and knowledge making as communal, social stories and producing specifically located interrogations of epistemic agency in the process.[63]

But what, at the end of this story, is knowledge? Any search for a univocal answer must yield, now, to a Wittgensteinian appeal to a "family of meanings," of which propositional information is one—perhaps junior—member. Knowing becomes a way of engaging with the world, where "world" is conceived as much circumstantially and socially as physically, materially. It is about how people find their way about, understand, and intervene in events; how they make commitments and engage in cooperative projects; how they confer epistemic authority and expertise. Its effectiveness is pragmatic (where pragmatic does not reduce to instrumentality) in the living situations and personal relations it fosters and prevents. Yet that effectiveness has also to be assessed in collaborative, critical stories that expose the impact of apparent "successes" on the lives that are directly and indirectly affected. Being knowledgeable requires an ecological sensitivity to the interconnections of which the world is made, and hence to the accountability issues that are implicated in practices and the knowledge that informs them. It can include skills, as in knowing how to take a child's temperature. Often it is about depth of acquaintance, as in knowing de Beauvoir's philosophy, knowing the implications of pay equity legislation, know who is a good teacher, and why. Some kinds of knowledge are manifested in an attunement, say to the need to give or withhold empathy. The list goes on, and it usually matters who is giving the answers, telling the stories.

ACKNOWLEDGMENTS

Thanks to Brock Winsor for the question that prompted these thoughts. I am grateful to Kathy Davis, Janet Kourany, Richard Schmitt, and Nancy Tuana for comments on an earlier version of this essay.

NOTES

1. Lorraine Code, "Experience, Knowledge, and Responsibility," in Morwenna Griffiths and Margaret Whitford, eds., *Feminist Perspectives in Philosophy* (London: Macmillan, 1988), p. 201; reprinted in Ann Garry and Marilyn Pearsall, eds., *Women, Knowledge and Reality.* (Boston: Unwin Hyman, 1989), p.169.

2. I am thinking both of the title of this book—*Philosophy in a Feminist Voice*—and of Carol Gilligan's landmark work, *In a Different Voice: Psychological Theory and Women's Development* (Cambridge, Mass.: Harvard University Press, 1982).

3. Michel Foucault's stories of the historical contingency of "knowledges," and of breaks and discontinuities in epistemic history, in his archaeological works, such as *The Order of Things* (New York: Vintage, 1973), and his geneaological works, such as *Discipline and Punish*, trans. Alan Sheridan (New York: Vintage, 1977), illustrate the scope of such an inquiry. For discussions of Foucault's significance for feminists, see Irene Diamond and Lee Quinby, eds., *Feminism and Foucault: Reflections on Resistance* (Boston: Northeastern University Press, 1988), especially the editors' introduction; Lois McNay, *Foucault and Feminism* (Boston: Northeastern University Press, 1992); and Jana Sawicki, *Disciplining Foucault* (New York: Routledge, 1992).

4. I owe the phrase "style of reasoning" to Ian Hacking, in "Language, Truth and Reason," in Martin Hollis and Steven Lukes, eds., *Rationality and Relativism* (Cambridge, Mass.: MIT Press, 1982). Hacking observes: "I have no doubt that our discoveries are 'objective,' simply because the styles of reasoning that we employ determine what counts as objectivity," (p. 49).

5. The phrase is used by the editors in the introduction to their selection from the writings of Jean-François Lyotard, in Kenneth Baynes, James Bohman, and Thomas McCartney, eds., *After Philosophy: End or Transformation?* (Cambridge, Mass.: MIT Press, 1987), p. 68.

6. Jonathan Rée, *Philosophical Tales* (London: Methuen, 1987), p. 97.

7. See R. G. Collingwood, *An Autobiography* (Oxford: Oxford University Press, 1939), especially chap. 5, for an outline of his question and answer logic.

8. For a further discussion of the significance of this claim for my discussion here, see my "Collingwood's Epistemological Individualism," *The Monist* 72 (October 1989) 542–67.

9. The phrases are from George Levine, "Why Science Isn't Literature," in Alan Megill, ed., *Rethinking Objectivity I: Annals of Scholarship* Vol. 8, no. 3/4, p. 376;

reprinted in Alan Megill, ed., *Rethinking Objectivity* (Durham, N.C.: Duke University Press, 1994).

10. Joseph Rouse, *Knowledge and Power: Toward a Political Philosophy of Science* (Ithaca, N.Y.: Cornell University Press, 1986), pp. 72–73.

11. Elizabeth Potter, "Gender and Epistemic Negotiation," in Linda Alcoff and Elizabeth Potter, eds., *Feminist Epistemologies* (New York: Routledge, 1993), pp. 164–65.

12. Hence researchers in the Chilly Climate project at the University of Western Ontario in 1990 were criticized for basing their analysis on first-person testimonial evidence of women who had experienced its "chilliness." See the Chilly Collective, eds., *Breaking Anonymity: the Chilly Climate for Women Faculty* (Waterloo, Ontario: Wilfrid Laurier University Press, 1995). Hence, also, a colleague suggested that if I do not need access to the university's computer mainframe for statistical data, then it must follow that my work relies only on "anecdotal evidence."

13. Writing of positivistic orthodoxy, Donald Polkinghorne notes that "Hempel refused to accord any epistemological value to those procedures of understanding or interpretation used by historians. . . . He took it for granted that narrative was simply too elementary a form of discourse even to pretend to satisfy the requirements for scientific deductive-nomological explanation." Donald E. Polkinghorne, *Narrative Knowing and the Human Sciences* (Albany: State University of New York Press, 1988), p. 45.

14. See also, in this connection, my "Gossip, or in Praise of Chaos," in Lorraine Code, *Rhetorical Spaces: Essays on (Gendered) Locations*. (New York: Routledge, 1995).

15. Rée, *Philosophical Tales*, p. 8.

16. Here I quote the title, and appeal to the spirit, of Julian Henriques, Wendy Hollway, Cathy Urwin, Couze Venn, and Valerie Walkerdine, eds., *Changing the Subject: Psychology, Social Regulation and Subjectivity* (London: Methuen, 1984).

17. Here I include, as a minimal sampling, such disparate endeavors as Edward Said, *Orientalism* (New York: Random House, 1978); Said, *Culture and Imperialism* (New York: Knopf, 1993); V. Y. Mudimbe, *The Invention of Africa: Gnosis, Philosophy, and the Order of Knowledge* (Bloomington: Indiana University Press, 1988); Thomas Lacquer, *Making Sex: Body and Gender from the Greeks to Freud* (Cambridge, Mass.: Harvard University Press, 1990); Minnie Bruce Pratt, "Identity: Skin Blood Heart," in Elly Bulking, Minnie Bruce Pratt, and Barbara Smith, *Yours in Struggle: Three Feminist Perspectives on Anti-Semitism and Racism* (Ithaca, N.Y.: Firebrand Books, 1984); and especially Patricia Williams, *The Alchemy of Race and Rights: Diary of a Law Professor* (Cambridge, Mass.: Harvard University Press, 1991). I list them as examples of works that analyze the integrated makings of experiences, knowledge, and subjectivities in specified locations.

18. For a representative collection of the range of positions I refer to here, see the articles in Peter A. French, Theodore E. Uehling Jr., and Howard K. Wettstein, eds., *Midwest Studies in Philosophy V 1980: Studies in Epistemology* (Minneapolis: University of Minnesota Press, 1980).

19. Bertrand Russell, *The Problem of Philosophy* (1912; Oxford: Oxford University Press, 1970); Alfred Jules Ayer, *Language, Truth and Logic* (1936; New York: Dover, n.d.).

20. Examples of this sort are still presented as typical, for instance, in Keith Lehrer's *Theory of Knowledge* (Boulder: Colo.: Westview Press, 1990); and in

Richard Foley's *Theory of Epistemic Rationaltiy* (Cambridge, Mass.: Harvard University Press, 1987). I raise some feminist concerns about Foley's position in my "Taking Subjectivity Into Account," in Linda Alcoff and Elizabeth Potter, eds., *Feminist Epistemologies*; reprinted in my *Rhetorical Spaces*.

21. See Russell, *The Problems of Philosophy*, chap. 5 ("Knowledge by Acquaintance and Knowledge by Description").

22. See, for example, Gilbert Harman, *Thought* (Princeton, N.J.: Princeton University Press, 1973); Laurence Bonjour, "The Coherence Theory of Truth," *Philosophical Studies* 30 (1976) 281–312; and Keith Lehrer, "Knowledge, Truth and Ontology," in *Language and Ontology: Proceedings of the Sixth International Wittgenstein Symposium* (Vienna: Verlag Holder-Pichler-Tempsky, 1982).

23. See in this connection Ruth Ginzberg, "Uncovering Gynocentric Science," in Nancy Tuana, ed., *Feminism and Science* (Bloomington: Indiana University Press, 1989); and Linda Alcoff and Vrinda Dalmiya, "Are 'Old Wives' Tales' Justified?" in Alcoff and Potter, eds., *Feminist Epistemologies*.

24. I discuss the maleness of reason and the individualist tradition in the next section of this essay.

25. George Levine notes that a "standard" notion of science "is still held . . . by the culture at large and by most practicing scientists [according to which] science is distinguished (1) by the 'objectivity' and 'rationality' of its procedures, and the disinterest of its practitioners; (2) by its rigorous requirements of verification, by replication of results; (3) by the universal validity of its conclusions . . . " (Levine, "Why Science Isn't Literature," p. 368).

26. Ruth Hubbard, "Science, Facts, and Feminism," in Nancy Tuana, ed., *Feminism and Science*, p. 119.

27. I am indebted in my comments about experience, here and elsewhere in this essay, to Joan W. Scott's "Experience," in Judith Butler and Joan W. Scott, eds., *Feminists Theorize the Political* (New York: Routledge, 1992).

28. See in this regard Mieke Bal's provocative reading, in her "First Person, Second Person, Same Person: Narrative as Epistemology," *New Literary History: A Journal of Theory in Interpretation* 24, no. 2 (Spring 1993): 293–320, of the position I develop in my *What Can She Know? Feminist Theory and the Construction of Knowledge* (Ithaca, N.Y.: Cornell University Press, 1991).

29. See chap. 1, "Is the Sex of the Knower Epistemologically Significant?" of my *What Can She Know?* for a brief survey of these views and a discussion of some early feminist endorsements of "different" female ways of knowing.

30. Sandra Harding and Merrill Hintikka, eds., *Discovering Reality: Feminist Perspectives on Epistemology, Metaphysics, Methodology, and Philosophy of Science* (Dordrecht: Reidel, 1983), pp. ix, x.

31. See R. G. Collingwood, *An Essay on Metaphysics* (1940; Chicago: Gateway Edition, 1972), chaps. 4 and 5.

32. Londa Schiebinger attributes "The mind has no sex" (*L'esprit n'a point de sexe*) to François Poullain de la Barre (1673) in the epigraph to the introduction of her book *The Mind Has No Sex? Women in the Origins of Modern Science* (Cambridge, Mass.: Harvard University Press, 1989), p. 1. The idea that "reason is alike in all men" is a focal point in Genevieve Lloyd's demonstration of the maleness of reason in her *The Man of Reason: "Male" and "Female" in Western Philosophy*, 2d ed. (London: Methuen, 1993).

33. Evelyn Fox Keller, *A Feeling for the Organism: The Life and Work of Barbara McClintock* (New York: W. H. Freeman, 1983).

34. Ibid., p. xii.

35. Ibid., p. 205.

36. I am referring to the essays collected in Evelyn Fox Keller, *Reflections on Gender and Science* (New Haven, Conn.: Yale University Press, 1985).

37. See, for example, Ruth Bleier, *Science and Gender: A Critique of Biology and Its Themes on Women* (New York: Pergamon Press, 1984); Bleier, ed., *Feminist Approaches to Science* (New York: Pergamon Press, 1986); Donna Haraway, *Primate Visions: Gender, Race, and Nature in the World of Modern Science* (New York: Routledge, 1989); Sandra Harding, *The Science Question in Feminism* (Ithaca, N.Y.: Cornell University Press, 1986); Cynthia Eagle Russett, *Sexual Science: The Victorian Construction of Womanhood* (Cambridge, Mass.: Harvard University Press, 1989); and Tuana, *Feminism and Science.*

38. Evelyn Fox Keller, "Love and Sex in Plato's Epistemology," "Baconian Science: The Arts of Mastery and Obedience," and "Spirit and Reason at the Birth of Modern Science," all in her *Reflections on Gender and Science.* Keller's 1992 collection, *Secrets of Life, Secrets of Death: Essays on Language, Gender and Science* (New York: Routledge, 1992), reclaims her respect for the achievements of physical science, while offering subtle analyses of (often gender-specific) power dynamics in the "insider/outsider" communities that scientific practice creates.

39. See Lloyd, preface, *The Man of Reason*, p. viii. And see also her "Maleness, Metaphor, and the 'Crisis' of Reason," in Louise Antony and Charlotte Witt, eds., *A Mind of One's Own* (Boulder, Colo.: Westview Press, 1993).

40. Lloyd, *The Man of Reason*, p. xviii.

41. For further psychosocial analyses, see Susan Bordo, *The Flight to Objectivity* (Albany: State University of New York Press, 1987); and Naomi Scheman, "Othello's Doubt/Desdemona's Death: On the Engendering of Scepticism," in Judith Genova, ed., *Power, Gender, Value* (Edmonton, Alberta: Academic Printing and Publishing, 1987); and her "Though This Be Method, Yet There Is Madness in It: Paranoia and Liberal Epistemology," in Antony and Witt, eds., *A Mind of One's Own.* Scheman's essays are reprinted in *Engenderings: Constructions of Knowledge, Authority, and Privilege* (New York: Routledge, 1993).

42. Kirstie McClure, "The Issue of Foundations: Scientized Politics, Politicized Science, and Feminist Critical Practice," in Butler and Scott, eds., *Feminists Theorize the Political*, p. 349.

43. Thomas S. Kuhn, *The Structure of Scientific Revolutions* (Chicago: University of Chicago Press, 1962).

44. Bruno Latour and Steve Woolgar, *Laboratory Life* (London: Sage, 1979); and Bruno Latour, *Science in Action* (Cambridge, Mass.: Harvard University Press, 1987), p. 15.

45. Richard Rorty, *Philosophy and the Mirror of Nature* (Princeton, N.J.: Princeton University Press, 1979). And see Nancy Fraser "Solidarity of Singularity: Richard Rorty between Romanticism and Technocracy," in her *Unruly Practices: Power, Discourse and Gender in Contemporary Social Theory* (Minneapolis: University of Minnesota Press, 1989).

46. See the special issue, "Feminism and Pragmatism," of *Hypatia: A Journal of Feminist Philosophy* 8, no. 2 (Spring 1993), guest editor, Charlene Haddock Seigfried; and Seigfried's *Pragmatism and Feminism: Reweaving the Social Fabric* (Chicago: University of Chicago Press, 1996).

47. See Jane Duran, *Toward a Feminist Epistemology* (Savage, Md.: Rowman and Littlefield, 1991); Lynn Hankinson Nelson, *Who Knows: From Quine to a*

Feminist Empiricism (Philadelphia: Temple University Press, 1990); Louise Antony, "Quine as Feminist: The Radical Import of Naturalized Epistemology," in Antony and Witt, eds., *A Mind of One's Own*; and Lorraine Code, "What is Natural about Epistemology Naturalized?" *American Philosophical Quarterly* 33, no. 1 (January 1996): 1–22.

48. For a representative sampling of some of this work, see Kathleen Lennon and Margaret Whitford, eds., *Knowing the Difference: Feminist Perspectives in Epistemology* (London: Routledge, 1994).

49. Many of these effects are detailed in the feminist works I cite in the notes to this essay, many of which include comprehensive bibliographies.

50. Joan E. Hartman and Ellen Messer-Davidow, eds., *(En)gendering Knowledge: Feminists in Academe* (Knoxville: University of Tennessee Press, 1991), p. 2.

51. See Sandra Harding, *Whose Science? Whose Knowledge? Thinking from Women's Lives* (Ithaca, N.Y.: Cornell University Press, 1991), especially chap. 5, "'Strong Objectivity' and Socially Situated Knowledge."

52. Helen Longino, *Science as Social Knowledge: Values and Objectivity in Scientific Inquiry* (Princeton, N.J.: Princeton University Press, 1990), p. 12.

53. Nelson, *Who Knows.*

54. Nelson, *Who Knows*, p. 83.

55. Ibid., p. 85.

56. Lynn Hankinson Nelson, "Epistemological Communities," in Alcoff and Potter, eds. *Feminist Epistemologies*, p. 142.

57. I discuss these issues briefly in "Critiques of Pure Reason" in my *Rhetorical Spaces* and again in my "What Is Natural about Epistemology Naturalized?"

58. See Nancy Hartsock, "The Feminist Standpoint: Developing the Ground for a Specifically Feminist Historical Materialism," in Harding and Hintikka, eds., *Discovering Reality*; Hartsock, *Money, Sex, and Power: Toward a Feminist Historical Materialism* (Boston: Northeastern University Press, 1983); Harding, *Whose Science? Whose Knowledge?* pp. 119–34; Harding, "Rethinking Standpoint Epistemology: 'What Is Strong Objectivity?'" in Alcoff and Potter, eds., *Feminist Epistemologies*; Hilary Rose, "Hand, Brain and Heart: A Feminist Epistemology for the Natural Sciences," *Signs: Journal of Women in Culture and Society* 9, no. 1 (1983); and Rose, *Love, Power and Knowledge: Towards a Feminist Transformation of the Sciences* (Cambridge: Polity Press, 1994).

59. See my *Epistemic Responsibility* (Hanover, N.H.: University Press of New England, 1987).

60. For an instructive project of this sort, see Megill, *Rethinking Objectivity.*

61. See, also, in this connection, Susan J. Hekman, *Gender and Knowledge: Elements of a Postmodern Feminism* (Boston: Northeastern University Press, 1983), and McClure, "The Issue of Foundations."

62. Seyla Benhabib, "Epistemologies of Postmodernism," in Linda Nicholson, ed., *Feminism/Postmodernism* (New York: Routledge, 1990), p. 125.

63. In addition to the works I have cited in this essay, see the section on "Personal Narratives: A Selection of Recent Works," in *Signs: Journal of Women in Culture and Society* 18, no. 2 (Winter 1993), and especially Camilla Stivers's article "Reflections on the Role of Personal Narrative in Social Science."

A New Program for Philosophy of Science, in Many Voices

JANET A. KOURANY

> Science, it would seem, is not sexless; she is a man, a father, and infected too.
>
> —*Virginia Woolf*, Three Guineas

SCIENCE, A MAN? Science, infected? Isn't this all nonsense? A category mistake? An oxymoron? And what does this have to do with philosophy of science?

MANLY SCIENCE

Certainly some of the most distinguished founders of modern Western science—the "fathers," as it were, present at, and participating in, its (motherless) "birth"—did not think it nonsense to speak of their new charge in masculine terms. With the birth of modern Western science the proper objects of knowledge had shifted from forms—whether Platonic transcendent forms or Aristotelian abstract intelligible principles informing material things—to matter, nature construed as mere mechanism, a machine devoid of mind. And correspondingly, the mind's task in knowing had shifted from the contemplation of forms to the careful, sustained observation and manipulation of matter.[1] Some of the most distinguished fathers of modern science represented this shift in gendered terms. For example, Bacon suggested in *The Masculine Birth of Time* that older science represented only a female offspring, passive and weak, whereas now a son was born, active, virile, and generative.[2] And Henry Oldenburg, secretary of the Royal Society, announced from its inception that the explicit goal of that body was "to raise a Masculine Philosophy . . . whereby the Mind of Man may be ennobled with the knowledge of Solid Truths."[3] What made the new science masculine in these men's eyes was their vision of its aims and methods: "to follow and as it were hound nature in her wanderings," "to lay hold of her and capture her," "to bind her to [man's] service and make her [man's] slave" (Bacon), to "render ourselves the masters and possessors of nature"

(Descartes), "to know nature" and "to command her," "to bring nature to be serviceable to [men's] particular ends, whether of health, or riches, or sensual delight" (Boyle).[4] And, in contrast to the barrenness of the older, merely contemplative and impractical, feminine science, what was to come from this new masculine science, this "chaste and lawful marriage between [masculine] Mind and [feminine] Nature" (in Bacon's words), was "an increase beyond all the hopes and prayers of ordinary marriages, to wit, a blessed race of Heroes or Supermen who will overcome the immeasurable helplessness and poverty of the human race, which cause it more destruction than all giants, monsters or tyrants, and will make [the human race] peaceful, happy, prosperous and secure."[5] These gendered representations of the new science on the part of its fathers helped to define it, and define it in a way that left no plausible role for women within it. And given the strong associations—positive for masculine, negative for feminine—that already existed, these gendered representations of the new science helped to garner support for it as well. But they also helped to define a new conception of masculinity and femininity.[6] Science and masculinity, in short, were being made for each other.

If Western science and masculinity were bound together in the seventeenth century, the strength of the bonds continues undiminished. Indeed, Western science and scientists still aim for prediction and control—dominance—over nature: they seek to "master" the genetic code, "control" reproduction, "smash" the atom and "harness" its energy, "fight" cancer, and "win" the "war" against AIDS. And nature—"mother nature"—and the feminine are still firmly associated. Similarly, masculinity still involves superiority to, and dominance over, the feminine.[7] What's more, Western scientists are trained to be objective, impartial, logical, unemotional, disinterested, and independent—these are norms of scientific behavior, part of scientific method. But they are also norms of masculine behavior, in sharp contrast to the very opposite norms of feminine behavior. And Western scientists are expected to be aggressive and competitive, and they jeopardize their careers when they do not exhibit these traits.[8] Indeed, some have argued that these, also, are important aspects of scientific method.[9] But aggressiveness and competitiveness also are defining traits of masculinity. In short, Western science, its aims and methods, are as tied to masculinity as they ever were.

Bolstered by the masculinity of the enterprise, men have controlled modern Western science right from its beginning, and this is a second way in which such science is masculine. In the past the control took such obvious forms as denying women with scientific talents access to universities and other centers of scientific learning, denying them all but menial research roles, and denying them membership in prestigious scientific academies and professional organizations.[10] More recently men's control of Western science has taken subtler forms: restrictive admissions quotas for undergraduate and graduate women students, or deliberate recruitment and selection by (masculine) gender; less financial assistance for women students; research positions for women with inferior work space and equipment and pay, and with little authority or possibility of advancement; exclusion of women from the most important scientific meetings and collaborations and information networks, and restricted access to prestigious scientific academies; a system of expectations and rewards structured for the lives that men traditionally have led, free of family responsibilities; and, of course, such newly recognized phenomena as sexual harassment.[11] As a result, "women have been swelling the lower and middle ranks of science for years, yet still have not managed to pierce the upper scientific strata in anything beyond token numbers."[12]

Men's control of Western science, in turn, has affected its content. Indeed, Western science has tended to leave women largely invisible in its knowledge and research, and this is a third way in which Western science is masculine. For example, medical researchers have often failed to include females in animal studies in basic research, as well as in clinical research, unless the research centered on controlling the production of children. This has led, among other things, to drugs not adequately tested for women patients before being marketed and lack of information about the etiology of some diseases in women. Indeed, research on conditions specific to women (e.g., dysmenorrhea, incontinence in older women, and nutrition in postmenopausal women) has received low priority, and research on diseases (like heart disease) that affect both sexes has been primarily concerned with the predisposing factors for the disease in men (in this case, white, middle-aged, middle-class men), while very little research has been concerned with high-risk groups of women (e.g., older women and poor black women who have had several children).[13]

In the social sciences abstract models based on male experience and male perception have been presupposed in the formulation of ongoing research projects. For example, the model of the rational actor in sociology has been "the abstracted model of organizational or bureaucratic man, whose motives, methods, and ego structure are organized by the formal rationality structuring his work role."[14] The model of human nature presupposed by a dominant strand of contemporary political science has been that of a narrowly calculating masculine being "who adapts, conforms, and engages in self-interested behavior, rather than in action with a social as well as a private meaning."[15] And more generally, "political science [in the words of Borque and Grossholtz] 'insists upon a narrow and exclusive definition of politics which limits political activity to a set of roles which are in this society, and many others, stereotyped as male. . . .' Thus, what women do is conceptually excluded from the purview of political science."[16] Again, the model of the healthy, mature, socially competent adult in psychology has been that of a male adult rather than a female adult.[17]

The problem is that social science "often assumes a 'single society' with respect to men and women, in which generalizations can be made about all participants, yet men and women may actually inhabit different social worlds."[18] It is only the men's world that social science takes to be the single social world, however. Thus, for example, in the conceptual schemes of sociology and economics all human activity is either work or leisure, a dichotomy that more accurately describes men's lives than women's. As a consequence, housework and volunteer work, which are not quite work (wage labor, part of the gross national product) and not quite leisure, cannot easily be conceptualized even though they form significant parts of women's experience. Nor can women's more concrete and caring modes of moral evaluation be easily captured within the Piaget-Kohlberg model of moral development in psychology that was originally abstracted from male experience.

When Western science *has* considered women, on the other hand, it has often portrayed us in negative terms, and this is a fourth way in which Western science is masculine. A favorite theme has been women's intellectual capacity. In the seventeenth century, for example, women's brains were said to be too "cold" and "soft" to sustain rigorous thought. In the late eighteenth century, the female cranial cavity was considered too small to hold a powerful brain. In the late nineteenth century, the exercise of women's brains was thought to shrivel our ovaries. In our own century, the way women process visuospatial information (supposedly by using the left hemisphere of the brain in addition to the right) supposedly makes women inferior in visuospatial skills (including mathematical skills).[19] But comparably negative stands have been taken with regard to many of women's other traits. Indeed, this situation is related to the problem of women's general invisibility, noted previously. That is to say, if men's bodily processes or social world or mode of psychological development, or whatnot, is the described state of affairs in science, the norm or standard, then to the extent that women's situation is different, it is no large step to conceiving of women as deviant, defective, or inferior. In this way women's moral and sexual and social development has been thought to be inferior because it does not fit the model of development applied to men.

"... A FATHER, AND INFECTED TOO":
A ROLE FOR PHILOSOPHY OF SCIENCE?

Modern Western science, then, has been masculine right from the start, in at least four ways. First, it has sought from the start to dominate a nature conceived of as feminine, with a method characterized by disinterestedness and emotional detachment, and (at least in recent times) aggression and competitiveness; second, men have controlled it right from the start; third, that enterprise has tended to leave women largely invisible in its knowledge and research; and fourth, that enterprise has often portrayed women, and things feminine, in negative terms when it *has* considered us. Turn, now, to the achievements of this masculine science—the progeny of Bacon's "chaste and lawful marriage between Mind and Nature." Has this progeny been "a blessed race of Heroes or Supermen who ... overcome the immeasurable helplessness and poverty of the human race . . . and . . . make [the human race] peaceful, happy, prosperous and secure," as Bacon predicted? The quest for dominance over nature and the methods of disinterestedness and emotional detachment from nature, along with aggressiveness and competitiveness for quick and dramatic results, have yielded or helped to yield such things as food in greater variety and abundance, produced more quickly and efficiently; the near annihilation of such dreaded diseases as scarlet fever, tuberculosis, polio, cholera, and malaria; better-insulated, more comfortable homes, with more conveniences, produced more quickly and efficiently; more sophisticated communications systems; and quicker, more convenient modes of transportation. But the quest for dominance over nature and the methods of disinterestedness and emotional detachment from nature, along with aggressiveness and competitiveness for quick and dramatic results, have also yielded, or helped to yield, such things as a food supply tainted with every manner of pesticides, herbicides, antibiotics, growth hormones, and other harmful chemicals; polluted air and water and a depleted ozone layer; ever-rising mountains of garbage and toxic wastes; ever more prevalent heart disease and strokes, cancer, diabetes, gallbladder disease, and other dreaded diseases related to overadequate (over-fatty, over-protein-filled, over-calorie-filled) diets and polluted environments; ever more depleted supplies of the world's resources and widespread extinction of plant and animal life; and, of course, enormous stockpiles of nuclear and other weapons. Moreover, men's control of science and exclusion of women from the most important activities in science have inflicted much injustice on women scientists and would-be scientists, and robbed science of much of its pool of available talent, and thus of much of its progress. Finally, the invisibility and negative portrayals of women, and things feminine, in scientific knowledge and research has yielded, or helped to yield, such things as inferior educational and athletic opportunities for women, inferior medical treatment for women, and inferior positions for women in the workplace, the family, and every institution of human life. In short, Bacon's "marriage between [masculine] Mind and Nature" has failed to make the human race "peaceful, happy, prosperous and secure," and certainly has failed to make the female half of the human race so. Nor does it augur anything different in the future. Indeed, to say nothing of the billions of dollars of taxpayers' money spent in the United States alone on projects (like the now-defunct superconducting supercollider and "star wars" projects) that promise no real help for United States and world problems, and the lack of funding for projects (like research on solar energy and long-term sustainable agriculture) that *would* be of help, expensive research programs like the human genome project (and reductionism in general) are already threatening major new ills for the future, especially for women.[20] What's more, if women are among those most likely to make women visible and fairly portrayed in scientific knowledge and research, then men's continuing control of science and exclusion of women from the most important activities in science promise to perpetuate the invisibility and negative portrayals of women in science. And, in turn, the invisibility and negative portrayals of women in science also promise to perpetuate—to "justify"—men's control of science. And just as men's control of science and women's invisibility and negative treatment within science promise to perpetuate—since science so profoundly shapes our attitudes and our world—the inequality women confront in society at large, so too, the inequality women confront in society promises to perpetuate these conditions in science.

Modern Western science, in short, is afflicted with serious ills related to its masculinity. And this being the case, it deserves careful diagnosis and treatment. The question I would like to raise is, What role ought philosophy of science to play in this venture? Certainly, the history of science, whose task is to reconstruct science's past, has tended systematically to ignore significant parts of that past, including the masculinity of Western science's aims and methods, women's scientific contributions both within and outside organized science, the obstacles women scientists faced, and the treatment of women within the content and methods of science. And the sociology of scientific knowledge, whose task is to show that and to show how scientific knowledge is constitutively social right through to its technical core, has systematically ignored the *gender* component of the social. The history of science and the sociology of scientific knowledge have thus far, therefore, played significant roles in keeping invisible and intact the masculinity of modern Western science and its associated ills. And by the same token, these fields can play significant roles in treating the situation, not only by informing us of the problems, but also by providing us with some of the conceptual resources we will need to solve them. Our understanding of science, however, is shaped at least as much by inquiries in the philosophy of science as by those in the history of science and the sociology of scientific knowledge. Has philosophy of science also helped to keep the masculinity of modern Western science and its associated ills invisible and intact, and can philosophy of science also offer anything useful in its treatment?

THE PRESCRIPTIVE PROGRAM OF LOGICAL EMPIRICISM

It is often said that the task of the philosophy of science, unlike that of the history of science and the sociology of scientific knowledge, is to provide a systematic and comprehensive picture of science, its aims and methods, its foundations and results. Thus, the basic issues it deals with include the nature of scientific observation and experiment and their roles in scientific research; the nature of the claims scientists make (factual statements, empirical laws, theories, and so forth), their explanatory and other functions in science, and the ways they are validated; the way science, its aims and methods and subject matter, develops over time; the nature of the results of scientific inquiry, whether science provides truth about the world, or only useful information; and the like. In the heyday of logical empiricism this task was interpreted in a very narrow way: providing a systematic and comprehensive picture of science, its aims and methods, its foundations and results, meant characterizing it within the conceptualizations provided by formal logic and empiricist epistemology. Thus, a scientific theory was an axiom system together with a set of rules that partially defined selected nonlogical terms of the system ("theoretical terms") by terms defined on the basis of observation ("observational terms"). A scientific explanation was the (deductive or inductive) logical derivation of a statement to be explained (the "explanandum") from a set of general laws and statements of initial conditions (the "explanans"). The process of evaluating a hypothesis consisted in logically deriving observation statements ("predictions") from the hypothesis in conjunction with statements of initial conditions, and comparing these with statements describing the results of observation or experiment. Scientific development consisted in the extension of scientific knowledge (e.g., the addition of new empirical laws or theories to existing ones) and, especially, in the greater (deductive) systematization of that knowledge—the (deductive) explanation of scientific laws and theories by more general theories, and the (deductive) reduction of scientific theories, and even whole disciplines, to other theories and disciplines. And so on. This characterization of the various aspects of science provided by logical empiricism portrayed science in a very abstract, idealized way. Indeed, it portrayed only the "logic of science": disembodied "observations" and "observation statements," "experiments" detached from the individuals and groups who design them, fund them, and carry them out, "scientific explanations" detached from their proponents, their purposes, their audiences, their effects. All social details—who is doing what, who has been excluded from doing what, whose questions are being settled by what mechanisms, and with what effects—were antiseptically removed. And with them, all details of gender were removed. But this characterization of science was, nevertheless, held to be a comprehensive picture of science, its aims and methods, its foundations and results, or, at least, everything that was important to science as a knowledge-producing activity. In short, science as a knowledge-producing activity was "pure"—purely logical and empirical, detached from the social, and, of course, gender-free. Or so philosophy of science under the aegis of logical empiricism unmistakably suggested.

The way in which logical empiricism kept the masculinity of science invisible and intact went deeper than this, however. The characterization of science it provided functioned more as a prescription to science than as a description of it: it told us what scientific explanations, theories, empirical laws, processes of hypothesis evaluation, instances of scientific development, and the rest, were, *in the sense of* the logical and empirical conditions statements or inferences had to fulfill to *be* scientific explanations, theories, empirical laws, processes of hypothesis evaluation, instances of scientific development, and the rest. The program of logical empiricism was, thus, a very normative program: it served to describe what ideal science was, and what actual science was aspiring to be—and sometimes was, if it was truly science at its best. And, of course, the foundation of this normative program was formal logic and empiricist epistemology. What's more, this foundation made any other prescriptive role toward science problematic. In particular, its empiricist criterion of meaning analyzed moral and political prescriptions as devoid of cognitive significance—useful for expressing (venting) attitudes and emotions, perhaps, but not for critiquing and improving science. In consequence, logical empiricism not only kept the masculinity of science invisible, and hence intact, but provided conceptual structures (in the form of the empiricist criterion of meaning) that ultimately safeguarded science and its masculinity from criticism—that *kept* the masculinity of science intact.

What led to the downfall of logical empiricism was none of this, however. What led to its downfall—aside from the difficult logical and epistemological problems it confronted in carrying out its program—were the historical researches of Thomas Kuhn, Paul Feyerabend, and others[21] showing that some of our greatest examples of science failed to satisfy the logical and empirical conditions of adequacy prescribed by logical empiricism, and, in some cases, *were* some of our greatest examples of science *just because* they failed to satisfy logical empiricism's conditions of adequacy. Not only that, these historical researches of Kuhn, Feyerabend, and others seemed to suggest that science had no (one enduring) nature to be defined, at least no very specific nature like the one logical empiricism was seeking. Indeed, the nature of science's aims and methods, science's theories, explanations, evidence, and the like seemed to be different for different sciences, and for any one science at different times. What the history of science suggested, in short, was that logical empiricism had lost contact with actual science. In seeking to define science for all time, it was not describing *actual* science, even a truly great actual science, *at all*—which was, after all, the only science there was to describe. And, of course, in not describing actual science at all, logical empiricism neither informed us of the problems of actual science, including the problems related to the masculinity of science, nor provided us with resources for solving them, for bringing us closer to the ideal science it described.

THE DESCRIPTIVE PROGRAM OF THE "NEW" PHILOSOPHY OF SCIENCE

The prescriptive program of logical empiricism having failed in its task of providing a systematic and comprehensive picture of science, its aims and methods, its foundations and results, many philosophers of science, influenced by Kuhn and others, shifted in the early 1960s to a more straightforwardly descriptive program for philosophy of science. The program was now to examine the actual processes and products of scientific research, past and present, and to characterize science accordingly. Indeed, it was argued, how could philosophers of science presume to *prescribe* what science should be like when they had no clear idea what science *was* like, when their "characterizations" did not in any way match the sophistication and diversity of actual science. Surely scientists are the appropriate authorities in matters of empirical knowledge, and philosophers should respectfully study what they do. The aim was, then, and still is, to *describe* general patterns of scientific change, clarify *actual* concepts, depict the structure and functions of *actual* theories, make epistemological sense of *actual* episodes in the history of science, all to understand science as an *actual* knowledge-producing enterprise.

At least this is what is *said* to be the aim of the descriptive program in the philosophy of science. When we consider the typical *method of approach* used in this program, however, the situation is not so clear. Consider Kuhn, who did more than anyone else to define the new program, both by the work he produced and by the influence he exerted on others. Kuhn sought to provide a general descriptive account of science—its fundamental components and the process by which they develop, as well as the process by which they undergo fundamental change. When Kuhn proceeded to support/illustrate his general descriptive account of science, however, he referred exclusively to the work of scientists like Copernicus and Lavoisier, Newton and Einstein, those scientists generally regarded as the greatest of all time—all physical scientists, of course, and all men, and white, and Western, and of upper- or middle-class origins. ("We shall deal repeatedly with the major turning points in scientific development associated with the names of Copernicus, Newton, Lavoisier, and Einstein. More clearly than most other episodes in the history of at least the physical sciences, these display what all scientific revolutions are about."[22]) And Kuhn treated his descriptive account of science as having normative impact as well, insinuating, for example, that the social sciences were still in their immature, pre-paradigm stages.[23] Other philosophers of science seemed to follow suit.

There was, of course, a barrage of critical discussion of Kuhn's general descriptive account of science on the part of philosophers of science.[24] Much of it concerned the nature and viability of Kuhn's fundamental concepts (like "paradigm" and "incommensurability") and of Kuhn's fundamental distinctions (between normal science and revolutionary science, for example). Much of it, again, concerned the nature and acceptability of the implications of Kuhn's general descriptive account of science (Was scientific change *irrational*, according to Kuhn? Is scientific knowledge really all *relative*?). But none of it seemed to question the strategy of first constructing a descriptive account of science to fit the work of the greatest (Western white male) physical scientists and then normatively applying it to other cases of science. When philosophers raised the question of application at all, they tended to inquire whether Kuhn's account could helpfully be applied to cases of the greatest physical science (e.g., What was the relation between Cartesian physics and Newtonian physics?). But they tended simply to *ignore* other cases of science.[25] Philosophers never seemed to *challenge* Kuhn's account by its failure to apply to these other cases of science. Imre Lakatos appeared both to capture and to clarify what was going on when he explicitly set out to analyze the work of the greatest (Western white male physical) scientists with the aim of constructing a normative-descriptive account of science, an account that would at once *describe* this greatest science and *prescribe* to other science.[26]

The descriptive program in the philosophy of science, pursued in just this way, could not have had any coherent justification, however—in fact, had to be in part a residue of logical empiricism's intense fascination with physical science and reductionism and the unity of science, and in part a manifestation of our continuing intense fascination with things Western and white and male. After all, the aim of the descriptive program was to learn empirically about science—science in general, any and all of it. So no one could have been expected to know, before the research was done, that selected cases of the greatest science were representative of science in general, or could be used as a normative model for science in general, that white, Western, men's science was just like (or could be used as a normative model for) Western women's science, or Eastern science, or African science, that the aims and methods and standards of some of the greatest physical science could be fruitfully applied to the social sciences, and the like.

Justified or not, however, what have been the consequences of this program? What kind of intellectual climate has it promoted? Since, most frequently, only the greatest physical science of white, Western, men scientists is given in support of our conceptions of science, our conceptions of science are shaped accordingly. When we think of science, we think of the greatest physical science of white, Western, men scientists. And this may make men's control of Western science appear more justifiable. Furthermore, with so much attention focused in this way on great physical science, women's invisibility and negative treatment within other areas of Western science become matters of small concern, if noticed at all. After all, women are not misrepresented within *physical* science, and if there are no gender-related problems within the content and methods of physical science, there are no gender-related problems within "real science," the only area of science that counts. And finally, with so much reverence bestowed on physical science, practitioners of the social sciences cannot but be encouraged to model their research goals and methods and concepts on those of the physical sciences. But this kind of research has yielded negative portrayals of women and other "minorities" as results.

For example, research design in the past in psychology, modeled as it was on that of the physical sciences, tended to emphasize physiological or biochemical variables, and variables defined by performance on psychological tests or manipulation of circumstances in the research situation, and it tended to de-emphasize the background, personal history, and gender of subjects and experimenters, as well as research situations outside the laboratory or in naturalistic settings. And this had the effect (among others) of producing gender bias in the results of that research. In the past it was frequently reported in social psychology texts, for instance, that women are more susceptible to persuasive influences or suggestions than men. More recently, however, this has been corrected by research demonstrating that influenceabilty or suggestibility is affected by a variety of factors, including whether a topic is of concern to a subject, and the gender of the researcher in relation to the topic. It was demonstrated, for example, that women are more suggestible with a male researcher when the topic is socially defined as one of male interest, but that men respond in parallel fashion when a woman researcher tries to influence them on a topic socially defined as interesting to women. The result of this more recent research, research that takes into account such factors as the gender of the researcher, the experimental context, and the interests and self-definition of subjects, is that there is now no basis whatsoever for saying that women are more suggestible or influenceable than men.[27]

But modeling the research methods, concepts, and goals of a discipline like psychology on those of the physical sciences can have other effects than gender bias, as psychologist Mary Brown Parlee has pointed out. For when psychological phenomena are stripped of their sociocultural, political, and personal dimensions to fit patterns appropriate to the physical sciences, the individual is represented "not as an agent who acts for reasons in a social and moral order but as a being subjected in natural-law-like ways to various causal influences conceptualized as variables or factors." And

> To the extent that this representation of persons in mechanistic, agentless, nonmoral language becomes part of public discourse (or part of the discourse of the educated elites), it deprives the general public of the richer linguistic resources for self-interpretation and self-understanding inherent in the everyday language of persons, actions, reasons, motives, and values. These resources enable or even encourage people to experience and think of themselves as agents who can act politically and in other ways in a world of meaning toward ends they value. The mechanistic, pseudoscientific language of psychology thus plays its role in the reproduction of the existing social order by pervading public discourse and the interpretations of ourselves that are shaped by it, displacing a discourse more compatible with the self-interpretations necessary for people to act together for social change.[28]

The *method of approach* of the "new" philosophy of science, then, does its part to promote the status quo. But so does the *content* of the "new" philosophy of science. Consider, again, Kuhn as an example, and the pathbreaking, provocative account of science he enunciated. According to this account, paradigms—scientific theories and the concrete applications ("exemplars") that accompany them—are the mainstay of science, rather than the observation statements and logic of the logical empiricists. Indeed, it is paradigms that determine the research agenda of science, in the form of problems the paradigms' first appearance leaves unsolved or incompletely solved; it is paradigms that provide the methods to be used in solving these problems, and the standards to be used in assessing the solutions; and hence, it is paradigms that determine what counts as "scientific success" and "scientific progress." It is even paradigms that shape what is observed and determine how what is observed is to be described. So once again science is portrayed as independent of the social and its economic/political/cultural— including gender—and other modes of influence, not because it is claimed that observation and logic are powerful enough to construct science all by themselves, as logical empiricism suggested, but because it is claimed that *paradigms* are[29]—or "research programmes," or "research traditions," or "scientific domains," or any of the other central players of the "new" philosophy of science.[30] And once again we are discouraged from engaging in a social (moral, political) critique of science, not because the empiricist criterion of meaning renders such a critique devoid of cognitive significance, as logical empiricism suggested, but because the actions that such a critique enjoins are likely to impede "scientific progress"—as the intervention of social needs impedes the internally directed development of the social sciences for Kuhn[31]—or worse, are likely to be "irrational."[32] As a consequence, the social character of science as a knowledge-producing enterprise, including its masculinity, is once again kept invisible and intact, now by the "new" philosophy of science as well as the old.[33]

Of course, the "new" philosophy of science is exceedingly diverse.[34] It explores the whole gamut of traditional issues in philosophy of science and some new ones as well, and in order to develop and support its views of science it makes use—in addition to case studies in the history of science and contemporary science—of a wide spectrum of resources, from mathematics (for the semantic approaches to scientific theories, for example) to the cognitive sciences (for the cognitive theory of science). But the limitations regarding method and content I have discussed and illustrated in the work of Kuhn are entirely general, and they are matched by comparable limitations in other current work in the philosophy of science that continues to show the influence of logical empiricism.

THE NEW "NEW" PHILOSOPHY OF SCIENCE:
PHILOSOPHY OF BIOLOGY TO THE RESCUE?

So what is the upshot? At the outset we considered four ways in which modern Western science has been masculine right from its beginning: first, Western science has sought from the start to dominate a nature conceived of as feminine, with a method characterized by disinterestedness and emotional detachment, aggression and competitiveness; second, men have controlled it right from the start; third, that enterprise has tended to leave women largely invisible in its knowledge and research; and fourth, that enterprise has often portrayed women, and things feminine, in negative terms when it *has* considered us. Noting the seriousness of the effects of this masculinity on women, and, in fact, on all of us, I asked what role philosophy of science should play in responding to it. More specifically, I asked whether philosophy of science has helped to keep the masculinity of Western science and its harmful effects invisible and intact, and whether philosophy of science can offer anything helpful to deal with this situation. The assumption, of course, was that the philosophy of science, at least as much as science itself, the history of science, and the sociology of scientific knowledge, shapes the conception of science of many persons—scientists and teachers and students of science, social scientists of science and historians of science, science policy makers and science funders—including many persons who will find themselves in a position to directly or indirectly deal with problems related to the masculinity of science. We have found that two of the most important programs in philosophy of science in our century—the older prescriptive program of logical empiricism and the newer, more descriptive program ushered in by Thomas Kuhn and others in the 1960s—have portrayed science as detached from the social, including gender, and have provided conceptual structures to safeguard science from social critique, including gender critique; and the newer program has focused attention solely on great (white, Western) men scientists and physical sciences as paradigmatic of science, and insofar, has made either less visible or more acceptable the masculinity of Western science in each of its several forms. We have found, in short, that two of the most important programs in philosophy of science in our century have helped in various ways to keep the masculinity of Western science and its harmful effects invisible and intact. Does philosophy of science, then, offer nothing helpful for dealing with the masculinity of science?

Recently a small number of philosophers of science, mostly from philosophy of biology, have striven to integrate the social dimensions of science in a serious way[35] into their general accounts of science, mostly in response to work in the sociology of scientific knowledge.[36] And a few of these philosophers of science—among them David Hull—have recognized gender as a component of the social. In his book *Science as a Process*, Hull has fully combined interests and expertise in the history, philosophy, and sociology of science to provide "an evolutionary account of the interrelationships between social and conceptual development in science."[37] What's more, Hull has made use of extended historical narratives to support his evolutionary account of science, narratives that cover the work of ordinary scientists as well as those generally regarded as among the greatest, and women scientists as well as men, and he has focused on biology rather than the physical sciences. According to the account of science Hull has provided, the evolution of science is to be conceptualized in the same terms as biological evolution. Thus, just as genes are passed on to future generations in biological evolution, so concepts (memes) are transmitted to other scientists in scientific evolution. And just as organisms attempt to maximize their genetic inclusive fitness in biological evolution, so scientists attempt to maximize their conceptual inclusive fitness in scientific evolution—that is, they attempt to gain recognition for their work (especially via the *use* of that work) from those working in their area whom they respect—and this attempt largely accounts for the social organization and behavior of scientists and, ultimately, the process of conceptual change. For example, scientists behave in ways calculated to encourage other scientists to use their work, they use the work of others for the support it provides their own work, they form research groups to provide themselves with receptive audiences, and the like. As a result, science and scientists have been "elitist and competitive"[38] right from the beginning. And aggressive: "If we are genuinely interested in educating students who are most likely to contribute to the growth of science, we might well give applicants to graduate school aggressiveness tests as well as achievement tests."[39] And cooperative, too. But the cooperation, as pervasive as the competition, has been of a kind, claims Hull, as accurately characterized as "mutual exploitation" as cooperation: "Scientists cooperate to the extent that they do because it is in their own self-interest to do so. The degree of cooperation among scientists varies directly with the degree of benefit that the scientist receives."[40]

In short, Hull has made visible in his account of science one of the ways in which Western science is masculine, and not only that, he has made it a central feature of his account. In a remark buried in a footnote he says:

> In this book, I have ignored the claims made by some feminists that science is itself sexist. By this they do not mean simply that scientists have been and continue to be sexists, i.e., that their views about sexual dimorphism in the human species are frequently biased, but that scientific methods are themselves in some significant sense male-biased. . . . However, if I am right about the central role of competition and aggression in science and if these characteristics are more common among males than females (regardless of why), then there may be a sense in which the social organization of science is male-biased.[41]

Hull has studied modern Western biological science, then, he has found that competition and aggression play a central role in it, and he has declared, as a result, that the social organization of science (all science, everywhere?) may favor males over females. What changes does Hull suggest to deal with this situation? "The functional perspective does lead one to be somewhat cautious in attempting to change a system. . . . To the extent that a system is functionally organized, changes are sure to ramify, and these ramifications may well be extensive, not to say unpredictable. Unless one is willing to risk the destruction of the system that one wants to change, caution is called for."[42] And in another place: "Perhaps scientists could be raised so that they were not so strongly motivated by curiosity and the desire for individual credit, but I am not sure that the results would be worth the effort. In fact, such efforts, if successful, might bring science to a halt. At the very least, in the absence of the mechanism which I have sketched, science could be likely to proceed at a very leisurely pace."[43] And while Hull cautions, he also reassures: "Thus far, even though the same sorts of prejudices that permeate the rest of society have served to discourage certain groups from contributing to science as fully as they might, enough white, middle-class males have possessed sufficient talent and drive to fulfill the goals of science."[44]

The conclusion, for Hull, then, seems to be this: modern, Western science, though masculine, and hence unfair ("biased"), has worked extremely well, and tampering with it is extremely risky, with no clear gain in sight. So why not just leave it alone? But this conclusion is completely unacceptable. For one thing, modern Western science has *not* worked "extremely well." It certainly has not worked extremely well for women, who, remember, have been excluded from the most important activities in it, left invisible or represented in negative terms in it, and as a consequence, have been robbed of adequate education, medical care, employment opportunities, and the rest. Nor, on balance—remember the tainted food supply, the polluted air and water, the depleted ozone layer, the mountains of garbage, the strokes and heart disease and cancers, the dwindling resources and enormous stockpiles of nuclear wastes, etc., etc.—nor, on balance, has science worked extremely well for any of us, as I have already pointed out. And even if science *has* worked extremely well, it does not follow that a different science, a nonmasculine science, would not *also* work extremely well, or at least well enough for our purposes. Indeed, such a science would serve to open up science to the *whole* pool of talented, motivated young people, rather than just a part of that pool, and should thereby benefit science. It should also ameliorate the problems for women that have been described here, and possibly the other problems as well.

But what would a successful nonmasculine science be like, one more hospitable to women and others excluded from positions of authority in our present scientific establishment? Unfortunately, Hull and other traditionally trained philosophers of science have never investigated the question, but others have. Consider, for example, Evelyn Fox Keller's investigation of Nobel Prize–winning scientist Barbara McClintock's way of doing science.[45] According to Keller, McClintock did not aim, in her conceptualizations of the objects of her research, to reduce nature to simplicity in an effort to *master* it, to predict and control its behavior.

> Her recurrent remark, "Anything you can think of you will find," is a statement about the capacities not of mind but of nature. It is meant not as a description of our own ingenuity as discoverers but as a comment on the resourcefulness of natural order; in the sense not so much of adaptability as of largesse and prodigality. Organisms have a life and an order of their own that scientists can only begin to fathom. "Misrepresented, not appreciated, . . . [they] are beyond our wildest

expectations. . . . They do everything we [can think of], they do it better, more efficiently, more marvelously." In comparison with the ingenuity of nature, our scientific intelligence seems pallid.[46]

McClintock aimed not to master nature but to "listen to" it, to know its living forms in minute detail so as to understand and appreciate their complexity and diversity. Accordingly, McClintock chose maize for her research, a far more complex, slower-reproducing, and more environment-responsive organism than the bacteria studied by most of her colleagues in molecular genetics; she focused on the peculiarities of individual organisms, while her colleagues focused on repeatable properties of large groups; and she proceeded by a kind of global, integrative intuition, while her colleagues worked, step-by-step, in the reductionistic mode, trying to establish simple, linear chains of cause and effect on the molecular level and trying to explain everything else in their terms. And all this "listening to" nature, this concern with complexity and diversity, this desire to know in detail and firsthand, took time. No thought of competition here, no race to a common goal, no rush to publish, to "scoop" opponents, to convince others: "Barbara McClintock has lived most of her life alone—physically, emotionally, and intellectually. . . . Perhaps the word that best describes her stance is 'autonomy.' Autonomy, with its attendant indifference to conventional expectations, is her trademark."[47] And far from taking a detached, unemotional, disinterested stance toward the objects of her research, McClintock identified with them, merged with them; "her vocabulary is consistently a vocabulary of affection, of kinship, of empathy."[48] Thus, McClintock reported: "No two plants are exactly alike. They're all different, and as a consequence, you have to know that difference. I start with the seedling, and I don't want to leave it. I don't feel I really know the story if I don't watch the plant all the way along. So I know every plant in the field. I know them intimately, and I find it a great pleasure to know them."[49] And again: "I found that the more I worked with [the chromosomes], the bigger and bigger [they] got, and when I was really working with them I wasn't outside, I was down there. I was part of the system. I was right down there with them, and everything got big. I even was able to see the internal parts of the chromosomes—actually everything was there. It surprised me because I actually felt as if I was right down there and these were my friends. . . . As you look at these things, they become part of you. And you forget yourself."[50] Indeed, it was McClintock's intimate personal relationship with the objects of her research, according to Keller, that enabled her to make her revolutionary scientific discoveries, discoveries that were different in kind from those made using more traditional methods:

> To a large degree, both the kinds of questions one asks and the explanations that one finds satisfying depend on one's a priori relation to the objects of study. In particular, I am suggesting that questions asked about objects with which one feels

kinship are likely to differ from questions asked about objects one sees as unalterably alien. Similarly, explanations that satisfy us about a natural world that is seen as "blind, simple and dumb," ontologically inferior, may seem less self-evidently satisfying for a natural world seen as complex and, itself, resourceful. I suggest that individual and communal conceptions of nature need to be examined for their role in the history of science, not as causal determinants but as frameworks upon which all scientific programs are developed.[51]

Consider another example of a nonmasculine way of doing science, Ann Oakley's sociological research with new mothers.[52] According to Oakley, the traditional aim of interviewing, as of other survey methods in social research, is to gather data about people, data that are both amenable to statistical treatment and relevant to social theory. As a consequence, the interviews that are part of a research project are supposed to be conducted in such a way that the personalities, beliefs, and values of the various interviewers, as well as other "local features" of the interview situations, do not affect—do not "bias"—the data obtained. To be sure, interviewers are supposed to show no reactions to interviewees' comments, are supposed to dodge interviewees' questions about themselves (the interviewers) and their views, are supposed to refrain from emotional involvement with interviewees and their problems—are supposed to be, in short, detached, unemotional, disinterested, and objective. An interviewer, in fact (in the words of one author), is to function like "a combined phonograph and recording system," or like a psychoanalyst using nondirective comments and probes as a catalyst for the sought-after responses. Indeed, Oakley suggests that a power hierarchy is set up as an essential part of such a research process: "It is important to note that while the interviewer must treat the interviewee as an object or data-producing machine which, when handled correctly, will function properly, the interviewer herself/himself has the same status from the point of view of the person/people, institution or corporation conducting the research. Both interviewer and interviewee are thus depersonalized participants in the research process," and both are used to achieve the personal goals of researchers.[53]

As a feminist sociologist interviewing women during their transition to motherhood, however, Oakley found herself unable to engage in this objectifying, exploitative mode of research. Indeed, as a feminist sociologist Oakley aimed to document women's own accounts of their lives in an effort to give the subjective situation of women greater visibility both in sociology and in society. This meant that Oakley had to become, in her interviews, a data-gathering instrument for those whose lives were being researched, women, rather than a data-gathering instrument for the theoretical concerns of herself and other researchers. And it meant that she had to gather her data not in a hierarchical way but in a way that engaged her subjects and herself in a joint and mutually beneficial enterprise. Thus, Oakley followed such procedures as answering her subjects' questions as honestly and fully as she could ("I was faced, typically, with a woman who was quite anxious about the fate of herself and her baby, who found it either impossible or extremely difficult to ask questions and receive satisfactory answers from the medical staff with whom she came into contact, and who saw me as someone who could not only reassure but inform"), and she refrained from exploiting either her subjects or the information they gave her ("For instance, if the interview clashed with the demands of housework and motherhood I offered to, and often did, help with the work that had to be done").[54] As a result, nearly three-quarters of the women interviewed felt that being interviewed had affected them in a positive way—had led them to reflect on their experiences more than they would otherwise have done, for example, or had reduced the level of their anxiety or reassured them of their normality—and no one felt that being interviewed had affected her in a negative way. And far from Oakley's feminist mode of interviewing yielding biased data, it yielded better results, in terms of the quality and depth of information gathered, than the traditional mode of interviewing.[55] Indeed, interviewees showed a sincere interest in Oakley and her research, just as Oakley, in her research, showed a sincere interest in them and their experiences. Concludes Oakley: "In most cases, the goal of finding out about people through interviewing is best achieved when the relationship of interviewer and interviewee is non-hierarchical and when the interviewer is prepared to invest his or her own personal identity in the relationship."[56]

The nonmasculine ways of doing science of McClintock and Oakley are important additions to the picture of science portrayed by Hull. But are they more than simply interesting curiosities? Might they be superior to the masculine ways of doing science Hull has described; that is, might they be suitable models of scientific work for scientists in general, for men scientists as well as women scientists, physical scientists as well as biological and social scientists? Justifying a positive response here would involve showing, for example, that such nonmasculine ways of doing science, in addition to yielding excellent results, are gender-neutral, since persons raised in a gendered society can be alienated by and, as we have seen in the case of our current masculine science, excluded from and mistreated within a science gendered in a way opposite to the way they are gendered. (In a gender-free society, on the other hand, what we would now call "feminine" ways of doing science *would* be acceptable, so long as they were adequate in other ways. What we would now call "masculine" ways of doing science—that *is*, the masculine science with which we have been concerned—would *not* be acceptable, however, since, as we have seen, these ways of doing science have been linked with unconcern for the environment, exploitation of research subjects, and the like.) Justifying a positive response here would involve, as well, showing that such nonmasculine ways of doing science are applicable to all the various sciences, physical sciences as well as biological and social sciences, else we would be in danger of maintaining some version of the current division between "hard" (masculine, or more masculine) sciences—that is, *real* science—and "soft" (less masculine, more feminine) sciences. In these connections note that, though McClintock's method of identifying with the objects of her research and forming intimate personal relations with them can in some ways be described as feminine, McClintock explicitly denied that her way of doing science was feminine, claiming that in her work "the matter of gender drops away." And, though Oakley's method of investing in personal relationships with her subjects can in some ways, as well, be described as feminine, Oakley explicitly contrasted traditional "masculine" aims and methods of interviewing in sociology with her own "feminist," not "feminine," approach. In addition, though quite a number of studies have disclosed women engaged in nonmasculine ways of doing science like McClintock's and Oakley's,[57] men have engaged in these ways of doing science as well. For example, Stephen Jay Gould has claimed that he and male colleagues in evolutionary and taxonomic biology do science in a way similar to McClintock's.[58] And Oakley has drawn parallels between her feminist way of interviewing women and the approach to interviewing minority and working-class men adopted by some male (minority as well as majority) sociologists.[59] Note, finally, that what is common to McClintock's and Oakley's nonmasculine ways of doing science—their concern to "listen to" their subjects and appreciate those subjects' complexity and diversity, their identification with and feelings of affection for, and kinship with, their subjects, and the like—is not necessarily related to the fact that McClintock's and Oakley's subjects are living: there should be no great difference, after all, between feelings of affection for, and kinship with, chromosomes, and feelings of affection for, and kinship with, say, atoms or molecules. Indeed, at least some of this nonmasculine common core has been suggested as an appropriate stance to take toward physical nature by quantum physics.[60]

In short, McClintock's and Oakley's nonmasculine ways of doing science *may* be suitable models of scientific work for scientists in general, for men scientists as well as women scientists, physical scientists as well as biological and social scientists. But it may also turn out that other ways of doing science than theirs, or a variety of ways drawn from the various sciences, will be the models that should be argued for. Additional research will be needed to decide. In the case of McClintock's way of doing science, we will need to have a better understanding of such things as McClintock's affectionate relationship with her experimental subjects, its connection, if any, to gender, and how this relationship enabled her to make her novel scientific discoveries.[61] In the case of Oakley's way of doing science, we will need to have a fuller analysis of her relationship with her interviewees (Did the relationship constitute a feminine response to those interviewees as well as a feminist one? How, if at all, would the relationship have differed with a male feminist interviewer or with a research question not specially oriented to women?). We will also need to determine whether problems can arise from Oakley's method of interviewing comparable to the problems that arise from the traditional masculine interview methods (For example, did the personal relationship between Oakley and her interviewees, and the personal nature of the information that was shared, place the interviewees at risk of manipulation, betrayal, or exploitation by Oakley, and if so, how can such problems be avoided? And, could the relationship between Oakley and her interviewees have been genuinely nonhierarchical, collaborative, and nonexploitative when the research product was ultimately Oakley's, structured and narrated by Oakley, laced with Oakley's interpretations, evaluations, and judgments, and enhancing of Oakley's, and not her interviewees', professional reputation and financial well-being; and if it could not, what should be done about this?).[62] Finally, we will need to investigate other nonmasculine ways of doing science than McClintock's and Oakley's, and we will make a good start in this direction by looking into the work of other eminent women scientists. (It is really quite remarkable, after all, that the work of eminent women scientists is only rarely considered by philosophers of science—and then only by *women* philosophers of science!) We will need, as well, to look into the work of ordinary women scientists as well as that of the extraordinary ones—but ordinary women scientists who have been relatively free of men scientists' domination. This would include, for example, the work of women actively excluded from men's scientific communities (e.g., the researches and practices of women midwives of the past, as compared with the researches and practices of the men gynecologists who excluded them). It would include, as well, the research done by women in scientific fields after the influx of sizable numbers of women researchers (e.g., investigation of the theoretical and methodological changes in primatology that occurred starting in the 1960s).[63] It would include, finally, the recent gender critiques of men's research provided by women researchers in fields like psychology and biology. Investigating the work of women scientists in this way, along with the work of the *men* scientists that *is* regularly considered by philosophers of science, will have the added benefit of helping us to see science as a possible and appropriate activity for women as well as men, and one to which women have already made significant contributions.

MORE OF THE NEW SOCIALLY CONSCIOUS PHILOSOPHY OF SCIENCE

David Hull is not the only philosopher of science to make the masculinity of Western science visible in his account of science, and the aggression and competitiveness he describes—along with disinterestedness and emotional detachment, and the desire to dominate a nature conceived of as feminine—are only one way (the first way) in which I claimed Western science is masculine. Another philosopher of science who has integrated the social dimensions of science, and gender in particular, into a general account of science is Helen Longino, also a philosopher of biology. In her book *Science as Social Knowledge: Values and Objectivity in Scientific Inquiry,*[64] Longino distinguishes between two kinds of values relevant to science, *constitutive values* and *contextual values*. Constitutive values—like truth, accuracy, simplicity, predictability, and breadth—are the source of the rules or norms (the requirement of repeatability of experiments, for example) governing scientific practice or scientific method. Such values stem from the goals of science—for example, the goal to explain natural phenomena. Contextual values, on the other hand, are scientists' individual or group preferences regarding what ought to be, or what is best. Such values stem from the social and cultural environment in which science is practiced. Longino argues that contextual values no less than constitutive values shape scientific research and its results. More specifically, contextual values can and do determine which questions are investigated and which ignored, can and do influence the selection of observational or experimental data and the way those data are expressed, can and do motivate the acceptance of global assumptions operating within an entire scientific field, or particular background assumptions facilitating inferences in specific areas of that field, or entire research programs within a field, and the like.

Consider, for example, the contextual values embedded in the assumption of sexual dimorphism, the assumption that there are certain behaviors (e.g., lively activity) appropriate to males and quite other behaviors (e.g., quiet, domestically oriented activity) appropriate to females. Here males and females are assigned distinctive roles paralleling contemporary Western stereotypes of masculinity and femininity, with the sexism and heterosexism these stereotypes involve. Longino points out that this assumption of sexual dimorphism makes certain features of the behaviors studied in behavioral neuroendocrinology (e.g., the level of expenditure of physical energy) more salient than others (e.g., the level of hand-eye coordination) and thus makes the behaviors appear suitable as evidence for hypotheses linking gender-role behavior to prenatal exposure to sex hormones. This assumption also makes the clustering of individuals around certain behavioral poles more significant than the amount of individual variation that is as much a feature of the data as the clustering. And it influences the way those data are described. For example, girls with congenital adrenocortical hyperplasia (CAH), which involves prenatal exposure to greater than normal quantities of androgens, are "described as exhibiting 'tomboyism,' characterized as a behavioral syndrome involving preference for active outdoor play (over less active indoor play), greater preference for male over female playmates, greater interest in a public career than in domestic housewifery, less interest in small infants, and less play rehearsal of motherhood roles than that exhibited by 'normal' young females."[65] As a consequence, the contextual values embedded in the assumption of sexual dimorphism shape the questions thought worth asking in behavioral neuroendocrinology, as well as the answers given to those questions.

Scientific knowledge, then, is shaped by social ("contextual") values as well as cognitive ("constitutive") ones. But, Longino continues, it can be objective nonetheless. Indeed, in an important sense, scientific objectivity has to do with limiting the intrusion of individual subjective preferences into scientific knowledge, and hence depends on the extent to which community criticism of individuals' scientific work, and responses to that criticism, are possible. More specifically, a science will be objective to the degree that the community which practices it satisfies a number of conditions. First, the members of the community must have recognized avenues—for example, journals, conferences, and the like—for the criticism of evidence, methods, assumptions, and reasoning. Second, the members of the community must share standards—substantive principles as well as constitutive values and contextual values—that critics can invoke. Third, the community as a whole must be responsive to the criticism. That is, the beliefs of the scientific community as a whole and over time—as measured by such public phenomena as the content of textbooks, the distribution of grants and awards, and the flexibility of dominant worldviews—must change in response to the critical discussion taking place within it. Fourth, intellectual authority must be shared equally among qualified members. And fifth,[66] alternative points of view that can serve as sources of criticism must be represented in the community, the more numerously the better. A science will be objective, then, to the degree that it satisfies these conditions—to the degree that it permits what Longino calls "transformative criticism."

This view of scientific knowledge as social knowledge, as knowledge that integrates the experiences of a society with its needs and interests, is called by Longino *contextual empiricism*. How helpful is it in dealing with the masculinity of science? Obviously, Longino's view needs more clarification and argument to give a definite answer. Thus, do contextual values shape *all* scientific research and its results? Do they shape, for example, the physical sciences as well as the biological and social sciences? And do they shape the most established parts of these sciences, or are they, rather, a sign of immaturity, gradually sifted out by continuing research and the application of constitutive values, and hence not of lasting importance?[67] On the other hand, do contextual values shape even constitutive values? Longino has recently pointed out, for example, that feminist contextual values have led at least some feminist scientists to reject certain constitutive values—for example, (external) consistency with accepted (sexist and androcentric) knowledge—and suggests that the distinction between contextual and constitutive values may not be very sharp after all.[68] Again, are the conditions specified for scientific objectivity really (jointly) *sufficient* for scientific objectivity, and is each of the conditions really *necessary*? For example, the second condition stipulates that the members of a scientific community must share standards—substantive principles as well as constitutive and contextual values—that critics can invoke, but will *any* shared standards ensure scientific objectivity, or do we need to specify further conditions on the kind of shared standards that will be necessary? And the fifth condition stipulates that alternative points of view that can serve as sources of criticism must be represented in the community, the more numerously the better, but will this always be necessary? For example, in a thoroughly reformed, nonsexist and nonracist science, will scientific objectivity demand the presence of sexist and racist points of view, and hence the hiring, funding, promotion, and so forth, of blatantly sexist and racist scientists?

Contextual empiricism in its present form, then, needs more clarification and argument. But even in its present form it allows us to understand the significance of men's control of Western science—Western science's masculinity in the second sense I previously distinguished. And even in its present form it allows us to explain why Western science has tended to leave women largely invisible in its knowledge and research, and why Western science has often portrayed women, and things feminine, in negative terms when it *has* considered us—Western science's masculinity in the third and fourth senses I distinguished. Indeed, since (upper- and middle-class white) men have controlled Western science right from the start, contextual empiricism's fourth condition for scientific objectivity has never been satisfied. That is to say, when women have been permitted to engage in science at all, or when they have simply done so on their own, they usually have not been granted intellectual authority commensurate with their abilities and achievements. Nor have most of the other conditions for scientific objectivity been fully satisfied. Thus, regarding the fifth and first conditions, though women in science have frequently brought with them alternative points of view, at least regarding issues related to women and the feminine, in the past they were allowed little or no access, and still typically are allowed unequal access, to conferences, journals, information networks, and other avenues for publicizing their points of view and criticizing the dominant points of view. And regarding the third condition, when women have managed to present their views and criticisms nonetheless, in the past they were most frequently simply dismissed or ignored, and frequently still are not taken as seriously as they should be.[69]

According to contextual empiricism, then, men's control of Western science has deeply compromised the objectivity of that enterprise at least with regard to issues related to women and the feminine. It is no surprise for contextual empiricism, then, that Western science, practiced in sexist and androcentric societies as it has been, and deeply compromised in objectivity at least with regard to issues related to women and the feminine, has reflected sexism and androcentrism as contextual values in its knowledge and research in just the kinds of ways described previously. What is a surprise for contextual empiricism, or at least what lacks an explanation, is why *women* scientists have so frequently imported into their scientific work *nonsexist* and *nonandrocentric* contextual values, while men scientists have imported into their scientific work society's sexist and androcentric values, so that men's control of science has yielded the supremacy of the latter values. If it be said that feminism accounts for the difference here, that feminism has affected women scientists far more than men, then the question again arises as to why there should be this difference relating to feminism between women and men scientists. In either case, some of the ideas of *feminist stand-point theory* might prove helpful for an explanation.

For example, Sandra Harding reminds us that sexist and androcentric values in society directly benefit men (especially white men), whereas they oppress women. As a consequence, women in general—and women scientists in particular—are more likely than their male counterparts to be critical of such values. "They have less to lose by distancing themselves from the social order; thus, the perspective from their lives can more easily generate fresh and critical analyses."[70] In addition, the scientific knowledge that these values have helped to establish—the scientific knowledge that has tended to leave women largely invisible, and that has often portrayed women, and things feminine, in negative terms when it *has* considered us—is also more vulnerable to criticism from women scientists. Indeed, women scientists have generally been excluded from positions of authority in the community that has produced this knowledge and, being "outsiders" in this way, are in a better position than those more centrally involved to detect the limitations of this knowledge.[71] Women scientists are in a better position to detect the limitations of this knowledge in another way as well. Given the division of activities assigned to men and women in society, their male counterparts generally have little access to women's concrete life experiences, to the child care, dependent care, homemaking, community service, and the rest, that scientific knowledge ignores or distorts. Hence, their male counterparts are not in as good a position to detect such failures of fit. Women scientists, on the other hand, do have access to these life experiences and to at least many of the life experiences of the men, given that they do "men's work" as scientists as well as "women's work" in other parts of their lives. As a consequence, they can measure their fields' bodies of knowledge against a more complete and diverse set of experiences than their male counterparts, and hence are in a position to be more critical than they.[72]

This is not, of course, to say that all women scientists will be critical of sexist and androcentric values and the scientific knowledge they support, or that all men scientists will not be. It is only to say that these women will be in a better position, and the men in a worse position, to be so critical. But there may be other important epistemically relevant differences between men and women scientists as well. Indeed, as Eve Browning Cole points out, "It would be hard to argue against the claim that experience importantly structures our cognitive capacities, determining which ones we will work hard to develop and which we will ignore."[73] She elaborates: "Women . . . in many if not most contemporary cultures depend for their livelihood or even survival on being sensitive to the moods and dispositions of those for whom they care and those they serve. This causes them to develop perceptual capacities, communication skills, a facility for emotional management, conflict resolution, discretion, acting skill, and many other behaviors it is the privilege of the ruling class and gender to neglect."[74] All of these skills give women a special ability to engage in, and contribute to, collaborative enterprises, including collaborative scientific enterprises. In addition, "feminist awareness of the consequences of oppression, our knowledge of what it feels like to be erased, ignored, patronized, and brushed off as a potential knowledge-maker, cannot but encourage the development of nonoppressive, and more inclusive, knowledge-making practices."[75] In short, women scientists may bring special social skills and dispositions, as well as special critical perspectives, to their practice of science, ones that make them especially valuable to the scientific enterprise.

With contextual empiricism, along with some of the ideas of feminist standpoint theory, then, we are able to understand the significance of men's control of Western science, and why Western science has tended to leave women largely invisible in its knowledge and research, and why Western science has often portrayed women, and things feminine, in negative terms when it *has* considered us. And with contextual empiricism, along with some of the ideas of feminist standpoint theory, we are able to understand the intractability of these problems. After all, it follows from these ideas that science will not give adequate treatment to women in its knowledge and research until society is purged of its sexism and androcentrism, or at least until scientists, whether by recruitment or training, no longer reflect the sexism and androcentricism of society in their contextual values, or at least until women scientists, with their more critical perspectives, are granted a much more powerful voice in the scientific community. And such changes are difficult ones to achieve while men are still in control of science and society.

A NEW PROGRAM FOR PHILOSOPHY OF SCIENCE

Contextual empiricism, along with some of the ideas of feminist standpoint theory, however, do more than just illuminate the masculinity of science in the second, third, and fourth senses distinguished at the outset of this essay. Indeed, in important places these ideas change the basic issues of philosophy of science. Thus, for example, if social values, including gender-related values, shape scientific research and its results, then philosophers of science who seek to analyze, say, the structure and functions of scientific theories, or their validation, will have to deal with the analysis and justification of such values, including their origins and consequences in the society in which the science is pursued. And philosophers of science who seek to make epistemological sense of actual episodes in the history of science will have to situate those episodes in their social settings as an essential part of the analysis. And philosophers of science who seek to determine whether scientific theories are literally true representations of the world, or merely useful, will have to define a theory's truth so as to include the objectivity of its underlying values, and a theory's usefulness so as to include the purposes for which it is useful, and the values underlying those purposes, and their status. Similar

results follow from Keller's and Oakley's work. Their work, as we have
seen, along with Hull's, illuminates the masculinity of science in the first
sense distinguished earlier—that Western science has sought from the start
to dominate a nature conceived of as feminine, with a method characterized
by disinterestedness and emotional detachment, aggression and competitiveness. But Keller's and Oakley's work also changes the basic issues of philosophy of science in important places. Thus, for example, if scientists' conceptions of nature (including gendered conceptions) affect the kinds of
questions scientists raise, and the kinds of explanations they find acceptable,
then philosophers of science who study scientific explanation will have to
analyze these conceptions of nature, and their connections with scientific
theorizing. And if women, or at least some women, have done science in
different ways than men, then philosophers of science will have to investigate such different ways of doing science and how they have been excluded
from, or integrated within, scientific development, if philosophers of science
aspire to produce a comprehensive picture of science and its development.
And philosophers of science will have to investigate whether any of these
ways of doing science can be deemed both gender-neutral and successful
enough to claim the allegiance of the scientific community without excluding
or marginalizing any of its members. And the list goes on and on.

Contextual empiricism and the ideas from feminist standpoint theory,
Keller's work and Oakley's work, and related work by other writers change
philosophy of science in a still deeper way. For whereas the primary aim of
logical empiricism was to *prescribe* to science, and the primary aim of the
"new" descriptive philosophy of science has been to *describe* science, the
primary aim of this new kind of philosophy of science is, as we have seen,
equally descriptive and prescriptive. What's more, its prescriptions are
grounded not simply in descriptions of great science (which is part of the
"new" descriptive philosophy of science) nor simply in logic and epistemology (which is part of logical empiricism) but in a complicated mix of these
sources with moral and political philosophy, and especially feminist philosophy, as well. Such a descriptive/prescriptive kind of philosophy of science
is thus not morally and politically neutral; but neither are the old prescriptive and the "new" descriptive philosophies of science morally and politically neutral, the programs that have kept the gendered nature of Western
science, and its damaging effects on women (and men, and the environment,
etc.), invisible and intact. And what of its lack of moral and political neutrality?! Moral and political neutrality is not an asset in an immoral world, and
in any case, the descriptive/prescriptive kind of philosophy of science exhibited here aims to do what philosophy has *traditionally* aimed to do—capture
and clarify the established order, question it, and suggest alternatives to it.
And such a descriptive/prescriptive kind of philosophy of science might actually do some good—might actually get scientists (and others) to view their
research in as informed, as systematic, and as critical a way as the objects of
that research, so that scientists no longer see science and themselves as "fast

guns for hire," "institutions and individuals that are, insofar as they are scientific, . . . studiously unconcerned with the origins or consequences of their activities or with the values and interests that these activities advance."[76] At least the descriptive/prescriptive philosophy of science will do more of this than its two predecessor programs in philosophy of science. It should thus be an important and needed addition to the various (descriptive) social studies of science, something that cannot clearly be said of the current descriptive program in the philosophy of science.

But the descriptive/prescriptive program in philosophy of science will not do a bit of good if it is not pursued, and thus far it has been almost universally ignored by philosophers of science. Indeed, much of the work of the program has been done by scientists themselves (witness Keller and Oakley as examples), and almost all of it has been done by women. It is the aim of the present essay to change this unfortunate situation.

ACKNOWLEDGMENTS

I would like to thank audiences at Notre Dame (especially Phil Quinn and Ernan McMullin), the University of Oregon (especially Maxine Sheets-Johnstone), the North American Society for Social Philosophy (especially William Aiken), Northwestern University, and the University of Utah for helpful comments on earlier versions of this essay.

NOTES

1. See Genevieve Lloyd, *The Man of Reason* (Minneapolis: University of Minnesota Press, 1984), for more details.

2. See Evelyn Fox Keller, *Reflections on Gender and Science* (New Haven, Conn.: Yale University Press, 1985), p. 38.

3. Quoted in ibid., p. 52.

4. Quoted in Carolyn Merchant, *The Death of Nature* (San Francisco: Harper and Row, 1980), pp. 168–70, 188–89.

5. Quoted in Lloyd, *The Man of Reason*, pp. 11–12.

6. See Londa Schiebinger, *The Mind Has No Sex?* (Cambridge, Mass.: Harvard University Press, 1989).

7. Note that American sciences—especially the "hard" (i.e., more masculine) physical sciences—receive much of their budget from the military, that bastion of masculinity and power, and pursue research programs that support the objectives of U.S. military supremacy. See, for example, Paul Forman, "Behind Quantum Electronics: National Security as Basis for Physical Research in the United States, 1940–1960," and Stuart Leslie, "Playing the Education Game to Win: The Military and Interdisciplinary Research at Stanford," *Historical Studies in the Physical and Biological Sciences* 18, no. 1 (1987). And much of the funding for American sciences also comes from industry, which, of course, seeks its own brand of economic supremacy.

8. See, for example, Sharon Traweek, "High-Energy Physics: A Male Preserve," *Technology Review* 87 (1984): 42–43, and Traweek, *Beamtimes and Lifetimes: The World of High Energy Physicists* (Cambridge, Mass.: Harvard University Press, 1988).

9. See, for example, David Hull, *Science as a Process* (Chicago: University of Chicago Press, 1988).

10. Schiebinger, *The Mind Has No Sex?*; Margaret Rossiter, *Women Scientists in America* (Baltimore, Md.: Johns Hopkins University Press, 1982); H. J. Mozans, *Woman in Science* (Notre Dame, Ind.: Notre Dame University Press, 1991).

11. B. Vetter, "Women in Science," in S. Rix (ed.), *The American Woman 1987–88* (New York: Norton, 1987); H. Zuckerman, J. Cole, and J. Bruer (eds.), *The Outer Circle* (New York: Norton, 1991); L. Dix (ed.), *Women: Their Underrepresentation and Career Differentials in Science and Engineering* (Washington, D.C.: National Academy Press, 1987); Committee on Women in Science and Engineering, National Research Council, *Women in Science and Engineering: Increasing Their Numbers in the 1990s* (Washington, D.C.: National Academy Press, 1991); Vivian Gornick, *Women in Science*, rev. ed. (New York: Simon and Schuster, 1990); L. Hornig, H. Hynes, S. Traweek, E. Keller, S. Turkle, and S. Florman, "Women in Technology," *Technology Review* 87 (1984): 29–52; Naomi Weisstein, "'How can a little girl like you teach a great big class of men?' the Chairman Said, and Other Adventures of a Woman in Science," and Evelyn Fox Keller, "The Anomaly of a Woman in Physics," in S. Ruddick and P. Daniels (eds.), *Working It Out* (New York: Pantheon, 1977).

12. Natalie Angier, "Women Join the Ranks of Science but Remain Invisible at the Top," *New York Times*, May 21, 1991.

13. Sue Rosser, "Re-visioning Clinical Research—Gender and the Ethics of Experimental Design," *Hypatia* 4, no. 2 (1989): 125–39.

14. Dorothy Smith, "A Sociology for Women," in her *The Everyday World as Problematic* (Boston: Northeastern University Press, 1987); see, as well, her "Women's Perspective as a Radical Critique of Sociology," in Sandra Harding (ed.), *Feminism and Methodology* (Bloomington: Indiana University Press, 1987).

15. Jean Elshtain, "Methodological Sophistication and Conceptual Confusion: A Critique of Mainstream Political Science," in J. Sherman and E. Beck (eds.), *The Prism of Sex: Essays in the Sociology of Knowledge* (Madison: University of Wisconsin Press, 1979).

16. Joan Tronto, "Politics and Revision: The Feminist Project to Change the Boundaries of American Political Science," in S. Rosenberg Zalk and J. Gordon-Kelter (eds.), *Revolutions in Knowledge: Feminism in the Social Sciences* (Boulder, Colo.: Westview Press, 1992), p. 95.

17. Beverly Walker, "Psychology and Feminism—If You Can't Beat Them, Join Them," in Dale Spender (ed.), *Men's Studies Modified* (Oxford: Pergamon Press, 1981).

18. Marcia Millman and Rosabeth Kanter, "Introduction to *Another Voice: Feminist Perspectives on Social Life and Social Science*," in Sandra Harding (ed.), *Feminism and Methodology* .

19. See Schiebinger, *The Mind Has No Sex?*

20. See, for example, Ruth Hubbard and Elijah Wald, *Exploding the Gene Myth: How Genetic Information Is Produced and Manipulated by Scientists, Physicians, Employers, Insurance Companies, Educators, and Law Enforcers* (Boston: Beacon

Press, 1993); and Philip Kitcher, "Implications of the Human Genome Project," Diane Paul, "'Informed Consent' in Mass Genetic Screening," and Alexander Rosenberg, "The Political Economy of the Human Genome Project," all in D. Hull, M. Forbes, and R. M. Burian (eds.), *PSA 1994*, vol. 2 (East Lansing, Mich.: Philosophy of Science Association, 1995).

21. See, for example, Thomas Kuhn, *The Structure of Scientific Revolutions* (Chicago: University of Chicago Press, 1962); Paul Feyerabend, "Explanation, Reduction, and Empiricism," in H. Feigl and G. Maxwell (eds.), *Scientific Explanation, Space, and Time* (Minneapolis: University of Minnesota Press, 1962); and Stephen Toulmin, *Foresight and Understanding* (New York: Harper and Row, 1961).

22. Kuhn, *The Structure of Scientific Revolutions* , p. 6.

23. See, for example, ibid., p. 15.

24. See, for example, Dudley Shapere, "Meaning and Scientific Change," in Robert Colodny (ed.), *Mind and Cosmos* (Pittsburgh: University of Pittsburgh Press, 1966); and Imre Lakatos and Alan Musgrave (eds.), *Criticism and the Growth of Knowledge* (Cambridge: Cambridge University Press, 1970).

25. An exception was geology. See the papers for the symposium "Philosophical Consequences of the Recent Revolution in Geology" in Peter Asquith and Ian Hacking (eds.), *PSA 1978*, vol. 2 (East Lansing, Mich.: Philosophy of Science Association, 1981). But see also Michael Ruse's comment in one of them ("What Kind of Revolution Occurred in Geology?"): "Given the fact that the major topic of debate amongst philosophers of science in the past fifteen years has been over the exact nature of a scientific 'revolution,' one might think that so dramatic a revolution so close at hand, in a science which is really not *that* technical (at least is not as incomprehensible to the outsider as modern particle physics), would have attracted immediate and detailed attention by the philosophical fraternity. . . . The revolution in geology has been greeted by philosophers of science with absolutely crashing silence," (p. 240). Meanwhile, geologists themselves, as well as psychologists, sociologists, and practitioners of other ignored sciences, struggled to apply Kuhn's account of science to their own fields. See, for example, the papers in the above-mentioned symposium as well as the social science papers in Gary Gutting (ed.), *Paradigms and Revolutions* (Notre Dame, Ind.: University of Notre Dame Press, 1980).

26. See Imre Lakatos, "History of Science and Its Rational Reconstructions," in C. Howson (ed.), *Method and Appraisal in the Physical Sciences* (Cambridge: Cambridge University Press, 1976); see also, alas, Janet Kourany, "Towards an Empirically Adequate Theory of Science," *Philosophy of Science* 49 (1982): 526–48, which fit right into this trend!

27. Carolyn Sherif, "Bias in Psychology," in Sandra Harding (ed.), *Feminism and Methodology* .

28. Mary Brown Parlee, "Feminism and Psychology," in Zalk and Gordon-Kelter (eds.), *Revolutions in Knowledge: Feminism in the Social Sciences*, p. 35.

29. This holds, of course, only for "normal science," the usual goings-on of science for Kuhn. It has never been quite clear what determines or explains "scientific revolutions" for Kuhn, or in what way scientific revolutions can constitute "scientific progress," but certainly Kuhn does not rule out the social or psychological in his treatment of scientific revolutions; see, for example, Thomas Kuhn, "Objectivity, Value Judgment, and Theory Choice," in his *The Essential Tension: Selected Studies in Scientific Tradition and Change* (Chicago: University of Chicago Press, 1977), and *The Structure of Scientific Revolutions*.

30. See, for example, Imre Lakatos, "Falsification and the Methodology of Scientific Research Programmes," in Imre Lakatos and Alan Musgrave (eds.), *Criticism and the Growth of Knowledge*; Larry Laudan, *Progress and Its Problems* (Berkeley and Los Angeles: University of California Press, 1977); William Newton-Smith, *The Rationality of Science* (Oxford: Routledge and Kegan Paul, 1981); Dudley Shapere, *Reason and the Search for Knowledge* (Dordrecht: D. Reidel, 1984). (But also see, for important exceptions, Mary Hesse, *Revolutions and Reconstructions in the Philosophy of Science* (Brighton: Harvester Press, 1980); and Ernan McMullin, "Values in Science," in Peter Asquith and Tom Nickles (eds.), *PSA 1982*, vol. 2 (East Lansing, Mich.: Philosophy of Science Association, 1983), and McMullin, "The Rational and the Social in the History of Science," in James Brown (ed.), *Scientific Rationality: The Sociological Turn* (Dordrecht: D. Reidel, 1984).) The social *can*, and on occasion *does*, intervene in science according to these analyses, of course, but when it does, the science is "irrational," that is to say, contrary to the rationality defined by the analyses: "The sociology of knowledge [i.e., explanation in terms of social factors] may step in to explain beliefs if and only if those beliefs cannot be explained in terms of their rational merits" (Laudan, *Progress and Its Problems*, p. 202).

31. See, for example, Kuhn, *The Structure of Scientific Revolutions*, p. 37.

32. See note 30.

33. Of course, this is not to suggest that the practitioners of the old and "new" philosophies of science *intended* to keep the masculinity of science invisible and intact. Doubtless they did *not*--doubtless they were not even *aware* of it. But that is a completely separate issue.

34. For an indication of how diverse, see, for example, Nancy Nersessian (ed.), *The Process of Science: Contemporary Philosophical Approaches to Understanding Scientific Practice* (Hingham, Mass.: Martinus Nijhoff, 1987); and Werner Callebaut, moderator, *Taking the Naturalistic Turn or How Real Philosophy of Science Is Done* (Chicago: University of Chicago Press, 1993).

35. That is, as more than just "irrational" lapses; see note 30.

36. See, especially, Joseph Rouse, *Knowledge and Power* (Ithaca, N.Y.: Cornell University Press, 1987); David Hull, *Science as a Process* (Chicago: University of Chicago Press, 1988); Steve Fuller, *Philosophy of Science and Its Discontents* (Boulder, Colo.: Westview Press, 1989); Helen Longino, *Science as Social Knowledge* (Princeton, N.J.: Princeton University Press, 1990); Philip Kitcher, *The Advancement of Science* (New York: Oxford University Press, 1993).

37. *Science as a Process*, p. 12.

38. Ibid., p. 159.

39. Ibid., p. 365.

40. Ibid., p. 311.

41. Ibid., p. 390 n. 4.

42. Ibid., pp. 355–56.

43. David Hull, "A Mechanism and Its Metaphysics: An Evolutionary Account of the Social and Conceptual Development of Science," *Biology and Philosophy* 3 (1988): 154.

44. Hull, *Science as a Process*, p. 389.

45. In her *A Feeling for the Organism* (San Francisco: W. H. Freeman, 1983), and *Reflections on Gender and Science*.

46. Keller, *Reflections on Gender and Science*, p. 162.

47. Keller, *A Feeling for the Organism*, p. 17.

48. Keller, *Reflections on Gender and Science*, p. 164

49. Quoted in Keller, *A Feeling for the Organism*, p. 198.

50. Quoted in Keller, *Reflections on Gender and Science*, p. 165.

51. Ibid., p. 167.

52. Reported in her *Becoming a Mother* (Oxford: Martin Robertson, 1979), and "Interviewing Women: A Contradiction in Terms," in H. Roberts (ed.), *Doing Feminist Research* (New York: Routledge and Kegan Paul, 1981).

53. Oakley, "Interviewing Women," p. 37.

54. Ibid., pp. 43, 47.

55. See Oakley, *Becoming a Mother*.

56. Oakley, "Interviewing Women," p. 41.

57. See, for example, June Goodfield's study of "Anna Brito" in *An Imagined World* (New York: Harper and Row, 1981), and the many studies surveyed in Judith Stacey, "Can There Be a Feminist Ethnography?" *Women's Studies International Forum* 11, no. 1 (1988): 21–27.

58. Stephen Jay Gould, "Triumph of a Naturalist," *New York Review of Books*, March 29, 1984.

59. See Oakley, "Interviewing Women," pp. 52–55; again, see Stacey, "Can There Be a Feminist Ethnography?"

60. See, for example, Karen Barad, "Meeting the Universe Half-Way: Ambiguities, Discontinuities, Quantum Subjects, and Multiple Positionings in Feminism and Physics," in Lynn Hankinson Nelson and Jack Nelson (eds.), *Feminism, Science, and the Philosophy of Science* (Boston: Kluwer Academic Publishers, 1997).

61. See Jane Roland Martin, "Science in a Different Style," *American Philosophical Quarterly* 25, no. 2 (1988): 129–40, for other questions.

62. See Stacey, "Can There Be a Feminist Ethnography?" for a discussion of these and other problems as they arise in ethnography, and a survey of the relevant anthropological and sociological literature concerning them; and see, as well, Alison Wylie, "Reasoning about Ourselves: Feminist Methodology in the Social Sciences," in Elizabeth Harvey and Kathleen Okruhlik (eds.), *Women and Reason* (Ann Arbor: University of Michigan Press, 1992).

63. See, for example, Sarah Blaffer Hrdy, "Empathy, Polyandry, and the Myth of the Coy Female," in Ruth Bleier (ed.), *Feminist Approaches to Science* (New York: Pergamon Press, 1986); and Donna Haraway, "The Contest for Primate Nature: Daughters of Man-the-Hunter in the Field, 1960–1980," in Mark Kann (ed.), *The Future of American Democracy: Views from the Left* (Philadelphia: Temple University Press, 1983). And see the Biology and Gender Study Group, "The Importance of Feminist Critique for Contemporary Cell Biology," *Hypatia* 3, no. 1 (1988): 61–76, for possible examples of other changes that women scientists have brought.

64. Helen Longino, *Science as Social Knowledge: Values and Objectivity in Scientific Inquiry* (Princeton: Princeton University Press, 1990).

65. Ibid., p. 118.

66. Longino cites only four conditions for objectivity in *Science as Social Knowledge* (see p. 76), but makes clear in her surrounding discussion that a fifth is also needed.

67. This latter possibility is the position, for example, of Ernan McMullin. See his stimulating 1982 presidential address to the Philosophy of Science Association, "Values in Science." But also see Michael Ruse's equally stimulating discussion of and response to this position in his 1984 symposium presentation to the Philosophy

of Science Association, "Biological Science and Feminist Values," in Peter Asquith and Philip Kitcher (eds.), *PSA 1984*, vol. 2 (East Lansing, Mich.: Philosophy of Science Association, 1985).

68. Helen Longino, "Gender, Politics, and the Theoretical Virtues," *Synthese* 104, no. 3 (1995): 383–97; and "In Search of Feminist Epistemology," *The Monist* 77, no. 4 (1994): 472–85.

69. See for the latter, for example, Sue Rosser, "Good Science: Can It Ever Be Gender Free?" *Women's Studies International Forum* 11, no. 1 (1988): 13–19.

70. Sandra Harding, *Whose Science? Whose Knowledge?* (Ithaca, N.Y.: Cornell University Press, 1991), p. 126. See chapter 5 for a helpful discussion of feminist standpoint epistemology.

71. See ibid., p. 124, for a further discussion of this point.

72. This more critical perspective may extend to areas other than those directly related to women. See, for example, Hrdy, "Empathy, Polyandry, and the Myth of the Coy Female."

73. Eve Browning Cole, *Philosophy and Feminist Criticism* (New York: Paragon House, 1993), p. 92.

74. Ibid., p. 91.

75. Ibid.

76. Harding, *Whose Science? Whose Knowledge?* pp. 158–59.

Semantics in a New Key

ANDREA NYE

> To see how unlikely it is that we could break into the alien hermeneutical
> circle *merely* on the basis of "platitudes," imagine next that *we* are the cul-
> ture being interpreted and that the interpreter is a member of a primitive
> culture. He could learn to understand English by coming to appreciate a large
> number of new facts, beliefs, ways of thinking. . . . But his understanding . . .
> would by no means be an application of platitudes that everyone in his tribe
> knows; for learning is not merely a matter of applying what one already
> knows to additional cases, but of making conceptual leaps, of
> projecting oneself imaginatively into new ways of thinking.
>
> —*Hilary Putnam*, Reason, Truth, and History[1]

> To use an illustration (suggested by Nozick), suppose half of us (the females
> perhaps) use "cat" to mean "cat*", "mat" to mean "mat*", "look" to mean
> "look*", "tells" to mean "tells*", and so on. How could we ever know? . . .
> A female might answer that the supposition that she is referring to cats*
> when she says "cat" is *incoherent* (because *within* her language whatever she
> refers to as a "cat" *is* a cat). This answer is small comfort, it does not exclude
> the possibility that what *she* calls a cat is what males call a *cat*,
> and vice versa; and this is Nozick's point.
>
> —*Hilary Putnam*, Reason, Truth, and History[2]

WORKING BACK TO THE ISSUE IN COMMON

If few feminist, African, Asian, or Hispanic philosophers have undertaken
the conceptual leaps and imaginative projections necessary to enter the
"alien hermeneutical circle" of contemporary English-speaking philosophy
of language, only the most recalcitrant of male or white chauvinists would
now claim, at least in public, that the reason is lack of intellectual ability.

The failure of women or nonwhite male philosophers to take an interest in semantics would most likely be explained by disinclination: disinclination to take on the rigorous, brain-bending conceptual work of a properly scientific philosophy of language. In what follows, I will argue that this explanation does not go to the heart of the matter, heart in the literal sense of the desires and purposes that motivate philosophical inquiry. I will argue that there is disinclination on the other side, disinclination of establishment philosophy to address fear of radical misunderstanding, shock at the increasing inaccessibility of science to common judgment, and imperialist yearnings for universal truth.

Although critical theories of sexism or ethnocentricity in language have recently been developed in sociolinguistics, literary criticism, and poststructural linguistics, the impulse of these critiques has not been seen to be consistent with the project of Anglo-American philosophy of language. At its most intimate, the relation between feminism and English-speaking philosophy of language has been opportunist as feminist philosophers, with limited success, attempt to use analytic techniques derived from logicist interpretations of language to discredit sexist arguments.[3] The philosophical theories that are the basis for those techniques—truth-functional logic, truth- or game-theoretic semantics, naturalized epistemology, modal logic, speech-act theory—have for the most part escaped feminist critique and feminist interpretation.

Feminist theorizing about language has tended to draw instead on linguistics, in which there has been some, not necessarily feminist, history of interest in the question of women and language. Feminist theorists, for example, have focused on pragmatics—the branch of linguistics that studies language use. One of the founders of modern linguistics, Otto Jesperson, in his classic *Language, Its Nature, Development and Origin*, devoted a chapter to the pragmatics of women's speech, arguing that women do not innovate in language, produce half-finished sentences, and use fewer clauses and logical connectives.[4] Empirical studies in the 1970s confirmed these and other differences in women's and men's conversational and writing styles.[5] From ethnolinguistics came additional evidence that in some cultures the differentiation between women's and men's speech is institutionalized[6] or that women use a different dialect or phonetics from men.[7] From studies of "muted" or stigmatized economic or social groups came evidence that linguistic and logical "deficiencies" can be related more broadly to class or social status.[8] These studies, including the feminist work of linguists like Deborah Cameron and Robin Lakoff, went some way toward ratifying abstention of women from logical inquiries into reference, meaning, and inference. If women are less rational than men, if they do not utilize the powerful inferential structures of truth-assertive science but are more likely to express emotions and tell stories, then it might seem a matter of course that they have little interest in philosophies that map logical structures. The same might also be true of non-Western races or cultures whose languages are not scientific or "rational."

One solution was to turn the negative to a positive and to valorize a specifically feminine style of speaking or writing as a remedial alternative to masculine logic.[9] There were immediate difficulties with this approach as with other forms of feminist essentialism. Which are the women who will determine correct "feminine" writing or speaking style? Educated academics? White intellectuals? Avant-garde writers? Can any one feminine speaking or writing style be specified when women are diverse in race, sexual preference, culture, and economic situation? Wouldn't women be better advised to devote themselves to learning the rational speech styles of those in power? Inherent in these questions are fundamental issues having to do with the nature of language. Is language a transparent instrument for the expression of beliefs and intentions? Do different languages construct different conceptual schemes?[10] Is it possible to establish a common reference between diverse speakers so that they can be said to disagree?

But English-speaking philosophy of language showed virtually no interest in gender, and feminist theorists turned again to linguistics to locate grammatical and semantic structures that carry the contagion of sexism regardless of use. If the head of a committee is called a chairman, does this mean that a woman is not appropriate for the job? Doesn't the marked term "poetess" imply that a woman poet is a diminutive male poet?[11] The solution, many argued, to women's disabilities in language is neither assertiveness training nor avant-garde separatist writing styles but reform of language. Teachers, editors, ministers, and journalists were encouraged, even forced, to change the ways they referred to women; publisher's guidelines were drawn up; corrections made in grammar texts; nonsexist inclusive language mandated in official documents, church services, newspaper articles, and classrooms.[12]

Forced linguistic revision had mixed success. If it was no longer politically correct to say "chairman" and "poetess," the masculinity of authority often lingered so that a world of chairs and poets became a world of men without the women previously marked by "chairwoman" and "poetess." Conservative backlash invested "Ms.," the nonsexist title coined to replace the old "Miss/Mrs.," with a negative connotation of aggressive feminism so that in some circles "Ms." indicated a new group of obnoxious feminists to be added to the old unmarried "girls" and married "ladies." Said one leading analyst of sexism in language about nonsexist language guidelines: they "legislate on the form of words without being able to alter the meaning. They are a purely cosmetic measure which enables us to see justice being done without really doing us justice."[13] The problem of gender and language, it seemed, goes deeper than changeable speaking styles and deeper than revisable grammar or vocabulary. Where to turn for more powerful theory was a problem.

Meanwhile, a highly technical and professionalized English-speaking philosophy of language was addressing problems of the possibility of "radical" translation from one language community to another, of alternate and incommensurable conceptual schemes, of the difficulty of establishing singular reference across "different worlds," but with virtually no reference to actual failure of communication or problems of gender. Given this disinterest, many feminist theorists turned to Continental lines of thought. The forefather of these traditions was not the German logician Gottlob Frege, founder of contemporary mathematical logic, but Frege's contemporary, Ferdinand de Saussure. There, too, results were not always consistent with feminist aims.

Looking for a way to free the study of language from the mythical claims of nineteenth-century philology and comparative linguistics,[14] Saussure proposed to make the study of language scientific by taking as its subject not diverse and changing spoken "language" but a stable linguistic "competence" or system of classification that he took as the basis of any language. The new structuralist linguist would look not at the history of language families or changing ways in which people use words but at form and structure, relations between "signifiers" and "signifieds," or words and concepts, that are internal to language and relatively invariable over time.[15] Meaning, said Saussure, is internally generated: a word has meaning in relation to other words, and speaking meaningfully requires that existing linguistic relations be respected. Language, to use Saussure's analogy, is like a game of chess; if you do not play by the rules you are out of the game. Some variety of surface structure is possible (grammatical and rhetorical choices can be made between passive and active forms, for example, or less offensive euphemisms chosen), but core meaning is determined by semantic relations between words at a level of deep semantic structure.[16] As a consequence, substantive language change is inaccessible to individual choice.[17]

Perhaps the most influential and final pronouncement of structuralist doom for feminist language reform came from the French poststructuralist psychoanalyst Jacques Lacan. The presence and absence of opposed semantic features—male/female (not male), light/dark (not light), and so on—and the derivative law of noncontradiction, said Lacan, are the organizing principles of language. The primal presence/absence is male/female difference, with the result that the "name of the father" and gender hierarchy are at the very core of linguistic meaning.

Poststructuralist philosophies took gender seriously; but even with the intervention of Jacques Derrida, also popular among feminist philosophers, significant limits were placed on feminist reform of language. Lacan's "name of the father" might be vulnerable to Derrida's textual "deconstruction," but any expectation that feminists could permanently change the language in which laws, science, politics, and philosophy are expressed or that they might develop concepts that refer to real experiences of oppression or speak from real feminine agency seemed, on either the structuralist or the poststructuralist view, misplaced. Feminist philosophers would have to re-sign themselves to acknowledging the unstable origins of the rational mascu-line self with Lacan or engaging in ongoing, never completely successful, disruption of logically ordered discourse with Derrida.

Still unchallenged by recognition of sexism or ethnocentrism, unruffled by fashions in Continental thought, a prolific and institutionally powerful "philosophy of language" in Britain and the United States continued to pay no attention to textual studies of French feminists or to any other politically motivated protest. If Saussure's signifiers left an opening for a disruptive feminine voice, Frege, the founding father of English-speaking philosophy of language, seemed to have rendered it mute.

Nevertheless, both linguistic and logicist approaches to language have common roots in nineteenth-century European experience. Both Saussure and Frege were concerned with objectivity, Saussure against anecdotal and unsystematic theories of language that in the nineteenth century opened the door to unfounded theories of ethnic origin and racial identity, Frege against the excesses of formalistic or relativistic invention in mathematics and sci-ence. Two related shocks inspired both structural linguistics and Frege's mathematicized logic: first, the shock of racial chauvinism that swept Eu-rope in the late nineteenth century and that eventually resulted in fascism; second, the shock of finding Descartes's and Liebniz's dream of a universal science in jeopardy as the necessary truths of geometry and the stability of Newtonian space and time were called into question. As long as science could be assumed to be grounded in necessary and universal truth, the prob-lem of linguistic relativity did not arise. When that truth no longer has au-thority, when different logics are possible, different assumptions from which to begin to understand the world, different strings of signifying relations, radical and unresolvable misunderstanding becomes possible. "They," the others, as Putnam put it, may mean cat* and not cat, and we will never know it. As long as "cat" reflects a fact in the world, cat*s whether they are conceived by women, inferior cultures, or renegade philosophers can be safely ignored. If different conceptual schemes create different realities, there is no standing from which what others say can be denied. In Putnam's wor-ries about reference echo the disorienting and often violent confrontations between seemingly irreconcilable races, cultures, sciences, and sexes that trouble nineteenth- and twentieth-century thought.

How is someone of a "superior tribe" to understand "jungle natives"? What relations are to be established between British and Dutch settlers in South Africa and indigenous peoples? How are "smart natives" to adapt to scientific culture? How are native aides and officials to be trained so that they will perform efficiently at the lower tiers of colonial administration? How can the anomaly of the different texture of Jewish life be assimilated or eliminated in imperialist Europe? How can rational Fascists be proved wrong? How can pseudosciences be disproved? How can the cacophony of religions, cultures, and races in Eastern Europe be translated into stable nation-states? How can what women say—women whose voices had been silenced in Western politics but who now demand to be heard—be accommodated?

Saussure responded to the philological and linguistic theories these questions inspired with an apolitical "science" of language that abstracts the structural relations supposedly universal to any language. Frege ruled out racial or personal variation in meaning by devising a logical idiom that gives to scientific language the unified authority of mathematics and to mathematics the conceptual content of language.[18] Those in actual painful contact with radical otherness were not slow to learn. The young Lévi-Strauss, brooding on his first anxious and disorienting encounters with Amazon Indians in Brazil, used the model of linguistics to invent structural anthropology, a method that represents native customs and beliefs as patterns of internal abstract relations, avoiding confrontation with the problem of the destruction and exploitation of traditional societies.[19] In England and North America, where many German philosophers took refuge from Fascism, Frege's vision of structure as logical form took on the mystical architecture of Wittgenstein's *Tractatus logico-philosophicus*, written in despair of the world from the trenches of World War I. Faced with a rising tide of fanatic nationalism and romantic racism in Nazi Germany, logical positivists, precursors of present-day English-speaking philosophers of language, embraced Frege's logic and Wittgenstein's vision as canonical idioms that could defeat falsehood and myth and leave a "science" of observable facts connected by indubitable laws of logic. Although structuralist elision of material confrontations with "the other," and the subsequent poststructuralist abandonment of truth as authoritarian, might seem preferable to a positivist or neopositivist logic that rejects ethics and political philosophy as meaningless, neither structuralism nor positivist or postpositivist analysis came to terms with questions at the heart of nineteenth-century language theory: how, in a divided and hostile world, are common meaning, shared reference, and understanding between diverse others possible?

The purpose in what follows is to initiate a discussion where up to now there has been none. Restated and given substance, questions of reference, meaning, and truth are, I believe, of vital interest to feminists. What is the relation between beliefs and attitudes and the structure of vocabularies and syntax? How can truth be defined? What is the nature of meaning and reference? To these questions, abstractly formulated, establishment analytic philosophers of language such as Quine, Davidson, Putnam, and Fodor have given elaborate and categorical answers. So radical has been the schism between feminist philosophy and philosophies of language that few feminists have shown any interest. Nevertheless, on these matters rest the prospects for feminist reform of language, as well as the possibility of a widely based feminist movement inclusive of diversity. While theoretical elaboration in philosophy of language on questions relating to translation and conflicting conceptual schemes has achieved baroque complexity, painful discussions between women have often ended in stalemate as assumptions about the nature of language go unexamined.

On the other side, philosophy of language has become increasingly technical and professionalized, accessible only to a small coterie of experts, without substantive reference to human experience or human problems. Questions of gender and cross-cultural understanding surface in philosophy of language only in contrived and symptomatic examples such as Nozick's cats, or Putnam's primitive tribes. At worst, philosophy of language is a sterile formalism producing loop after loop of reflexive reference to its own theories; at best, it is an extension and ratification of current methods in computer programming or cognitive psychology. Although this professionalization of philosophy has its own deeply rooted institutional and intellectual history—in the secularization of the university, the expansion of the sciences, the founding of the American Philosophical Association—like some other moments in the history of philosophy, it may prove self-defeating, as the purposes and designs of higher education which is philosophy's institutional base change.

Between a resolutely practical feminist philosophy and an equally resolutely theoretical philosophy of language, however, there are matters of common interest that might revitalize philosophy, as Susanne Langer put it, in a new key. Can a woman express the wisdom of her "tribe" in the language of current philosophy? Should she be willing to "leap" into the alien hermeneutical circle of a profession dominated by men? Is it possible that when lesbian women or women of color say "cat" they mean "cat*" and so are continually misunderstood and silenced by straight or white women, as well as by men? The benefits, as I see it, of an attempt to repair the schisms between feminist philosophy and analytic philosophy of language are on both sides. On the one hand, in discussion with feminist philosophers, energized by real perplexities in personal, intellectual, and political practice, philosophy of language might formulate more clearly what it is about and recover reference to human life that renews its contribution to university curricula. On the other hand, feminists might begin to develop theoretically adequate concepts of truth and meaning coherent with feminist practice.

What follows is not an exhaustive or definitive analysis of contemporary philosophy of language, an exercise designed to make further conversation unnecessary. I do not "prove" that the representative philosophies of language of Quine, or Fodor, or Putnam are wrong, a strategy aimed at silencing rather than furthering talk. Instead, the readings and extensions of philosophy of language that follow are attempts at an understanding that may not be comfortably in the same terms as the self-understanding of those understood, but which, for that very reason, might elicit a circulation of meaning that, in my view, is the key to the power of language to establish common reference and truth.

Jungle Natives, Talking Heads, Twin Earths

In W. V. Quine's influential work in theory of meaning and reference, through many volumes and many papers, one scene, one primal drama, recurs again and again. A man whom Quine calls the "linguist," a Western man proud of the extraordinary success of Western science, is in a "jungle," confronted by "natives" who speak no word of English or any other European language. His job is "radical translation," the deciphering of an unknown native language. He is to produce a "translation manual" or dictionary as an aid to "negotiation with the native community." As Quine put it in a recent book synthesizing his philosophy, the manual or dictionary will be judged according to how it contributes to "success in communication . . . judged by smoothness of conversation, by frequent predictability of verbal and nonverbal reactions, and by coherence and plausibility of native testimony" (*The Pursuit of Truth*, 43).[20] What is to be negotiated, what deals are to be made, is not specified, but reference to smoothness and predictability suggests a business relation, perhaps a negotiation for native labor or for the sale of raw materials to a Western client.

In order to accomplish his task, the linguist sets up an experimental situation. He and a native informant (also male) sit down together—how he is able to persuade the native to do this or how the native views the procedure is not clear. They wait. A rabbit goes by. The linguist turns to the native. "Gavagai?" he asks. The native makes either an affirmative or a negative response. In this way, the linguist determines what Quine calls the "stimulus meanings" of words like "gavagai"—Quine's famous jungle word for rabbit—and constructs a "theory" of the native "Jungle" language, "mapping" strings of words onto patterns of native response to "stimuli."

The drama in the story, as well as the central insight of Quine's philosophy of language, comes from a surprising realization on the part of the linguist: he can never really know to what the native is referring. He can record and map the native's affirmative and negative responses to various sentences, he can calibrate those records with linguistic schema with which he himself is familiar, he can construct a manual for negotiation purposes, but he will never know for certain what the natives are talking about when they talk about a gavagai: they might be talking about a discrete physical object, a space/time wave function, or "undetached rabbit parts."[21] More than one translation scheme is possible; more than one algorithm may be consistent with all of the evidence of native affirmation and dissent and so map native sentences differently onto English sentences.[22]

The moral of Quine's story is not that there is a failure of understanding on the part of the linguist. It is the linguist's realization that failed understanding does not matter. Whatever may be going on in the native informant's head, whatever ideas he may have, whatever objects the native might be interested in are inscrutable and irrelevant to the linguist's translation manual. All the linguist has to go on, as Quine puts it, is words, his own words, as well as native behavior and native "utterances" mapped onto those words. The linguist knows, of course, that it is not enough to observe and theorize regularities in native behavior as if the natives were animals he was interested in tracking or training. He recognizes native behavior as human behavior that, like his own, is mediated by beliefs and intentions. This is what requires him to construct a workable "theory" of native language, and thereby native belief, so that communication and negotiation can go smoothly. There is, however, no reason to think, Quine insists, that the linguist correctly identifies the objects in which natives are interested. There is no way of his knowing, nor is there any need for him to know, that the "stimulations" of natives are like his own or those of his patrons.

The linguist can "do without" any presumption of "intersubjective likeness" by "empathy." "The linguist observes natives assenting to 'Gavagai' when he, in their position, would have assented to 'Rabbit.' So he tries assigning *his* stimulus meaning of 'Rabbit' to 'Gavagai' and bandying 'Gavagai' on subsequent occasions for his informant's approval" (*PT*, 43). The linguist's concern as he constructs his dictionary is not, in fact, meaning at all.[23] It is to help a nonnative client or reader "profit from the sentences he sees or hears, and to help him react to them in expected ways, and to help him emit sentences usefully" (*PT*, 57). His goal is "understanding" but understanding in the sense that he, and presumably other foreigners, will no longer be "surprised" by the circumstances in which natives say "gavagai" or by their reactions to hearing "gavagai" (*PT*, 58).

Around this central and illustrative example, Quine constructed what is perhaps the most influential philosophy of language of the postwar era. There are a number of things of note. One is the unshakable certainty on the part of Quine's philosopher/linguist and presumably his clients that Western science has been miraculously successful. Iteration of this fact, taken as self-evident and needing no argument, is prominent in virtually all contemporary establishment philosophy of language. In Quine's view, the success of science comes from its ability to predict "stimulations," impacts on sensory surfaces and sets of "triggered exteroceptors" that are the data for the linguist's understanding or lack of understanding of the natives. The philosopher/linguist is not a scientist himself. He is a user of science or, more likely, he serves those who use science in furthering the profitable or strategic activities that make necessary the negotiations for which translation manuals for native languages are required. It is because of those purposes, and not because of the logical necessity that is a function of those purposes, that metaphysical scruples about minds or beliefs are needless impediments.

The problem is not just that Quine's philosopher/linguist can never know whether the native is having the same "stimulations" as he himself is. Even the linguist's stimulations are indeterminate. Quine is famous for exposing the "dogmas" of empiricism. There is no way to firmly anchor theory in anyone's sense data or observation sentences. Science must be taken as a whole, which makes it impossible to distinguish between possibly revisable theory statements and incorrigible reports of sensation. If a sensation or stimulation does not cohere with established theory, it and not the theory may be mistaken. If sensations seem contrary—if someone thinks she feels pain when theory says she should have felt pleasure—it may be sensation that is aberrant. If the linguist has no sure footing in his own sensations or experience, all the more reason he can only guess at what the native is noticing or feeling; all the more reason he can only project the "stimulations" that he thinks he has or should have had under similar circumstances.[24] Quine's linguist is not Conrad's Marlowe, ambivalently and painfully testing his own reactions as he approaches the "heart of darkness"; Quine's linguist is a man unequivocally sure, if not of his feelings at least of his mission and his aim.

If confident "radical" translation of the languages of "jungle natives," along with the collapsing of the terms of any unscientific natural language or archaic or primitive science into the terms of current Western science, is at the heart of Quine's philosophy of language, at the heart of Jerry Fodor's equally influential *Language of Thought*[25] is one currently popular and "successful" scientific discovery and its uses. Fodor attributes the discovery to Alan Turing, the pioneer in computer science, who, according to Fodor, had "the most important idea about how the mind works that anyone has ever had," perhaps even "the only important idea anyone has ever had" (*LOT*, 26). He brought us to the "verge of solving a great mystery about the mind: *How can its causal processes be semantically coherent?*" (Fodor's emphases) (*Psychosemantics*, 20).[26]

The obvious problem with behaviorist accounts of language and meaning like Quine's, Fodor and other cognitivists argue, is that they bypass what anyone, including jungle natives, is thinking as irrelevant to what they mean. Since Ryle's *Concept of Mind*, English-speaking philosophers have agreed that Cartesian dualism is untenable and idealist introspection unreliable. How, then, can a linguist take account of what goes on in another's "head"? Turing's landmark 1950 paper on artificial intelligence, "Computing Machinery and Intelligence" provided the fortuitous solution.[27] After the war, in an effort to convert the war's computer technology to peacetime uses, programmers used the devices of mathematical logic to work bridges or translation manuals between natural language and machine functions. By mapping computer patterns of off-on switches or "machine language" onto a mathematical language, and then, in turn, onto second-level computer languages and eventually English words, anyone who spoke English could use a computer. The result was a remarkable prediction: by the end of the century, machines could duplicate anything that human minds can do. Given the possibility of programming a computer to simulate any rational process, it would be impossible to tell a computer from a human respondent. A computer's intelligence, Turing argued, is potentially "universal," not restricted to one task or problem, but programmable to imitate any "rational" function formalizable in mathematical logic.

If a computer can respond rationally, is it not intelligent? What other fair test for intelligence can there be but a functional test? Cleverly, Turing exploited the emergent postwar drive for women's equality: put a man in one room and a woman in another; if, without being able to see either of them but only hearing their answers to questions, it is not possible to tell the difference between them, then the two must be equal in intelligence. Women had long complained about the unfairness of essentialist definitions that linked intelligence to physical characteristics such as sex. It seemed only a small step to a further inference. If machines can do everything that humans can do that is expressible in quantitative terms, then the operations of the human mind can be understood as a quasi-machine function. An explosion in computer use and marketing stimulated the postwar economy of industrialized countries. Turing's universal cognitive function supported the expectation that computerization and the spread of information technology would dominate world markets.

But Turing also solved a problem internal to philosophy. He had given analytic philosophers, stalled in unresolvable debate about the existence of mysterious mental objects to which language seemed to refer, a way of giving specificity to beliefs and intentions that does not leave philosophy open to charges of unscientific mysticism. Instead of beliefs and desires being interpretable through fictional empathy or ad hoc principles of charity, using computer models of mental processing, science could identify what an "organism" thinks and means. If brain surgery is unlikely to reveal beliefs and desires, in the same way one does not open up a computer to determine what programs it runs.[28] Instead, thinking is a functional relation. Specific inputs (instructions, problem situations) are isolated and correlated with specific outputs (what the machine or human subject says or prints out) to determine the "meaning" of what an organism does or says. A rat sees a door; because it "believes" there is food behind the door and "wants" that food, it pushes open the door. Or to use one of Fodor's examples, the male stickleback fish attacks the researcher's red scarf because it "wants" to defend its territory and "believes" that anything red is a rival male sticklefish.[29] Native behavior, children's behavior, and deviant women's behavior can be studied in the same way.

Using cognitive science, Fodor, along with many other philosophers, now claimed to be able to answer the "fundamental question" in philosophy of language: How can two persons communicate? (*LOT*, 103). As Fodor put it, a certain "model of communicative exchange" is "not just natural but inevitable" (*LOT*, 106). One person wants to send a message to another. This means that he must try to get the same pattern going in the other's head as is in his own head. Because he is a human organism, and not a stickleback, he has the device of grammatical language. Conventional sequences of signals or "wave forms" are connected to the same machine sequence in another head, so that when one man says certain words he brings about a belief or functionally equivalent machine sequence in another man's brain. In this way, human males may be able to avoid the stickleback's embarrassing mistake of taking a bit of red cloth as a male rival for a female's attention. Linguistic ability consists in the fact that a person is able to "produce the linguistic form that (speakers of a given language) standardly use to communicate (the message)" (*LOT*, 106). A properly scientific philosophy of language is a "theory of messages," messages coded onto neural circuits, remapped onto surface structures of language, sent out by way of wave forms and received. If words are not enough, if the targets of communication do not get the message, the communicator can always revert back to "nonlinguistic forms of communication" (*LOT*, 106). There just is no other way, Fodor explains, that a "sensible" philosopher/linguist can now understand the mind.

Just as computers can be reprogrammed when they malfunction, human minds understood on the cognitive model can be retaught. The key to understanding of the higher-level intelligent functioning of information-processing machines, as Turing saw it, is the realization that behavioral training with rewards and punishments is limited. If, on the other hand, you institute higher-level programs that "reward" compliance with instructions in a certain language, you can teach that "everything the teacher says is true" ("Computing Machinery," 458). Machines, whether computer-guided smart bombs, personal computers, students, native employees, or disturbed patients, can be made to "function" efficiently and predictably on their own, the number of "tasks" they can be made to do infinite. Some of the programming of human organisms may be wired in, as Chomsky's structural grammar was meant to show, but human brains, which, like computers, are more flexible "devices" than the brains of male sticklebacks, can be reprogrammed or further programmed almost indefinitely. Dysfunctional subjects, like dysfunctional computers, can monitor their own cognitive functions by installing second-level executive programs (*LOT*, viii–ix).

The practices that give substance to cognitive science are in learning theory and psychotherapy. A textbook example is used by four leading theorists of therapeutic application of cognitive psychology in their standard text, *The Cognitive Theory of Depression*.[30] They describe the case of a woman, a married homemaker and mother confined to the home, suicidally depressed by her failure to be a "good" wife and mother. The successful model therapy for her "cognitive errors" and dysfunctional beliefs focuses on changing the "content and pattern of her thinking" (*Cognitive Therapy*, 104). In the course of her therapy, she is persuaded to stop undervaluing her husband's occasional invitations out, to value her accomplishments as wife and mother, to improve as wife and mother where necessary, and—the highlight of the model therapy—to learn to take satisfaction in part-time work in a shop. Just as Turing projected: higher-level programming laid over a "faulty" belief formation allows her to revise, correct, and reprogram her dysfunctional beliefs. The technique can be used in many cases, with dysfunctional learners, untrained native workers, or recalcitrant employees.

Once the practices that give the cognitive theory on which Fodor based his theory of language are understood, the import of the "language of thought" becomes clearer. The woman's depression may ease, she may be a more functional mother and wife, but she has become a "talking head." Her new beliefs and talk have little reference to the painful and frustrating reality of her life and other women's lives—to housework, child care, and low-status, part-time jobs. In the place of that reference are functional schemas, intermediaries between determinate input and output. Again an image is at the heart of philosophy of language. No longer Quine's confident advance team of Western commercial and military development bringing science to the natives, Fodor's cognitive scientists are administrators at a safe distance from their "dysfunctional" subjects.

These are men tempered and changed by the unprecedented experience and technology of World War II. Wartime computing machines were smart scanners that looked for enemy aircraft and reported back, smart bombs that adjusted course according to the range of the target, smart coding devices that scrambled and rescrambled messages. If computer scientists turned these devices into calculating machines useful in colder wars and peacetime commerce, Fodor's "language of thought," or internal machine language, performs a further function. It places functional devices in the human brain.[31] In organisms—whether rat, pigeon, man, woman, or child—are placed the same mechanical scanning of beliefs, assignment of preference orders, and representation of action outputs. An organism learns to predict future stimulations by way of monitorable internal processes of inductive extrapolation (*LOT*, 35–41). Its senses become "devices" that associate inputs with physical descriptions that are infinitely controllable.[32]

If a scene from imperialist history and a postwar confidence in the peacetime uses of military technology are at the heart of Quine's and Fodor's philosophies of language, a troubling counterfactual conjecture is at the heart of another influential contemporary philosophy of language. What if we (we scientists, we Westerners, we men, we reprogrammed learners and housewives) are only "brains in a vat" churning out senseless printouts controlled by evil teacher/programmers or therapist/brainwashers? Even worse, what if what we think we experience is due only to cosmic molecular games of chance? What if modern science (quantum mechanics, relativity theory, genetic engineering) is wrong and matter is not what science says it is after all? On an imaginary "twin earth," everything might be just as we experience but have a different chemical structure. It might have been, might still be.

So Hilary Putnam relived Descartes's nightmare of radical doubt, the doubt that inspired the dream of a unified mathematical science. This dream, now ungrounded in any validating proof of God's existence, lacks, as Fodor puts it, "epistemic immediacy." All that remains is a "passionate but incoherent yearning" (*LOT*, 204). Automated sequences of thought, functional relations between input and output may be predictable, but are they reliable? Can they have reference to changing social and natural conditions? Do they take notice of environmental stress, violent crime in the streets, despair, consciousness of frustration and injustice? Can they address the rising tide of terrorism as cultures and family networks clash and are destroyed?

So Putnam addressed the troubling lack of reference to reality in both computational and holistic philosophies of language in his *Reason, Truth, and History* (*RTH*), the source for the quotes that introduce this essay. Initially endorsing a cognitive theory of mind, in this later work Putnam proposed against the eternal universality of Fodor's "language of thought" a revised theory of meaning. Reference can be fixed but only within a historical context, as also would any basis for discussion and debate between "cat*"-speaking women and "cat"-speaking men, between Quine's "jungle"-speaking native and sophisticated Westerners, between Putnam the radical turned liberal and his conservative philosopher/friend Nozick (*RTH*, 164–65).

If it is the world that we want to speak about we must get into contact with the world, reasoned Putnam. This cannot be by way of internal circuitry that does not refer to anything, or by way of a "web of belief" not pinned down to identifiable objects. The fact is that people go on referring even though they have no adequate scientific idea of what they are referring to. They may have false ideas of what they talk about, or radically change their ideas and beliefs about what they talk about. They say *this* is not what I thought it was; they say I don't know what *this* is, they say you are wrong about *that*. When they do, the "that's" and the "this's" must stay still so they can talk and disagree. But when "this's" and "that's" are written onto the syntax of brain thought, or become the objects over which the quantifiers of a given linguistic schema range, real objects disappear.

There can be no regression to old mentalist ideas. Instead, Putnam urged, the answer is faith. We must accept a "division of linguistic labor." We must consult and trust scientific experts who are in a position to know what things are. We can go on talking about neutrinos, dysfunctional families, and clinical depression, even though we ourselves do not understand what they are, even though we can imagine "other worlds" in which they are neither existent or desirable. We can reassure ourselves that, at least within our own culture, there are binding "internal" constraints of rationality, adequacy of evidence, and appropriate judgment. Most important, we must not think that if there is conflict or a suspected falsity, "platitudes" from any jungle world or any weird universe of female cats* can help.

What of science gone wrong: the Nazi's racist science (*RTH*, 203) or Putnam's conservative friend, Nozick's, logically argued disregard for the suffering of the poor? (*RTH*, 164–65). Or feminist "cats*"? Or native magic? We can only say that such opponents have put themselves beyond our morality. If theirs is better, great; if it is worse, it is "repulsive" (*RTH*, 212). In any case, the recourse we have in judging can only be to our own tradition, which might for all that still be wrong, the tradition of "the Greek agora, of Newton, and so on" (*RTH*, 216).

The main problem, as Putnam sees it, is with postmoderns like Foucault: "What is troubling about Foucault's account is that the determinants he and other French thinkers point to are *irrational by our present lights*. If our present ideology is the product of forces that are irrational *by its own lights*, then it is internally incoherent. The French thinkers are not *just* cultural relativists; they are attacking our present notion of rationality from within, and this is what the reader feels and is troubled by" (*RTH*, 160–61). Putnam's emphases indicate how strongly he himself is troubled. The suggestion, he comments, that the point Foucault and others are making is political—that we have no right to destroy native cultures other than our own—is "very confused." What is right may be relative to a culture, but that cannot, must not, mean that a native "jungle" culture is as good as ours. We have our own standard of scientific judgment; we make a judgment. If everything is relative, there can be no judgment and everything is worthless. Reference is necessary if what we say is to have meaning and truth. If it cannot be achieved in a coherent web of belief into which other languages are translated arbitrarily, if it cannot be achieved by positing functional relations between perceptual input and output, then it must be achieved by fiat. We must accept the dictates of science. What is, is what science says there is.

On the authority of science, Putnam, Quine, and Fodor, as well as virtually all current establishment philosophers of language, agree. No philosopher, or anyone else, has standing to question the substantive findings of science. Only a few right-minded philosophers, from within, as Quine put it, might work to "improve our understanding and control of the scientific edifice."[33] All "sensible" people, says Fodor, must accept the findings of cognitive science. Philosophers can look at psychology and point out, "Here is what you guys are saying is the mind." Psychologists, in turn, may more clearly structure their experiments according to that clearer understanding. If and when cognitive science decides it has been wrong, right-minded sensible philosophers will accept the verdict; what they are doing will have been wrong too (*LOT*, viii). If much of human linguistic behavior is left out of cognitive science—noncomputative associations, emotions, creative problem solving—that only means that from now on philosophers and cognitivists will have to work in a "small vineyard." Perhaps the rest can be made the provenance of other sciences such as biology (*LOT*, 203).

Philosophy of language has become the philosophy of a particular idiom, not English or any other language spoken or written by natives, philosophers, feminists, politicians, not even the actual language spoken by scientists as they devise, set up, and explain their experiments.[34] The subject of Fodor's, Quine's, and Putnam's philosophy of language is the language of science as it should or must be if truth, or a certain version of truth, is to be possible. The subject of philosophy of language is the idiom of Quine's linguist confronting irrational inscrutable natives, Fodor's cognitive psychologist mapping and correcting the dysfunctional inputs and outputs of unhappy wives, Putnam's civilized apologist for a threatened Western tradition. It is an idiom that claims to represent truth independently of what anyone believes or desires.

Truth Without Truth

Much of current work in analytic philosophy of language has roots in Frege's struggle to devise a "conceptual notation" suited to modern science and purged of the inadequacies of natural language. Science uses the exact quantitative notation of mathematics, but if science's representations are to have content, if they are not to be empty formalities, they have to "mean" something. It has to mean something that two numerical expressions different in "sense"—for example, "2" and "1 × 2"—are equal. It has to mean something that $E = mc^2$. Otherwise, it is hard to see how either mathematics or science has any reliable use or application. But, insisted Frege, the senses that differentiate ways of referring to objects cannot be "psychological," cannot be mere ideas. The foundations of science cannot be dependent on changing and diverse ideas, beliefs, desires, or judgments. Frege's final unsatisfactory solution was "thoughts," not the thoughts of living diverse people but thoughts as objective entities existing independently of the ideas of any individual.[35]

The theory that would finally seem to solve the problem and free philosophy of language from interpersonal sense and meaning was a technical breakthrough that in the 1930s was hailed as a stroke of genius that put philosophy of language, and even philosophy itself, on a properly scientific basis. It is possible, the logician and mathematician Alfred Tarski argued, to construct a theory of truth that makes no reference to semantic concepts like sense or meaning at all. You can list the elementary truths of a language "disquotationally" ("it is snowing" is true if and only if it is snowing). Then, after defining logical connectives ("and," "or," and "not"), you can specify what truth is in a given language, as the infinite number of truths which are compounds of elementary truths.

The hard part, of course, was to account for the truth of the elementary sentences that had seemed to make Fregean senses necessary. Saying *something* about something can hardly be eliminated. A "sentence" or a string of words (the part of Tarski's formula that is in quotes) can be given force by fiat or by convention, but predication (saying something about something that does not simply identify an object as itself but characterizes it "as something") is the locus of truth if there is any. It was Tarski's genius to explain how both the truth of singular predications and statements of relations between concepts can be handled without reference to meaning. A predication is true if the subject "satisfies" the predicate, said Tarski, that is, if the object to which the subject refers is one of the objects that make up the "value-range" of the concept to which the predicate refers—the set of objects of which the concept is true. In this way, he deals with the troublesome generality of concepts, their application to a variety of objects, independently of sense or meaning.

Whether this "semantic" theory of truth is applicable to natural languages spoken or written by women and men was of little interest to Tarski. Truth- theoretic formal languages, he argued, are needed for science. People will talk as they will. Nevertheless, it seemed to many philosophers that Tarskian formal languages with defined primitive terms and rules of inference required links to natural language if they were to be more than games with symbols. The work of clearing away the barriers that block truth-theoretic semantics for natural language became one of the major tasks of analytic philosophy of language. Donald Davidson circumvented the problem of the seeming infinity of predicates in natural language by deriving infinite series of predications as modifications of a finite stock of predicates. Quine tried to circumvent the difficulty of accounting for the singular reference of names by proposing to do away with names altogether.[36] These were taken as solid successes that proved philosophy of language as a professional discipline. With more work, the problem of conceptual relativity might be completely solved, at least with speakers of English: "men" can mean men "whatever *they* are," as Quine put it succinctly (*PT*, 52).

One problem, however, with the truth-theoretic approach to natural language was less manageable. Tarksi had argued that what makes a truth theory for natural language impossible is the "universality" of natural language's predications. The universe of discourse of natural language is closed in the sense that it operates in one world; there is no metadomain of objects not subject to natural language's predicates.[37] Consequently, it is always possible to make an object out of a predicate, always possible to describe what is said in the same language in which it is said. This critical reflection back on its own terms is not a reinterpretable grammatical convention like naming but the very essence of natural language. However, it generates the paradoxes that were the ruin of Frege's attempt to reduce mathematics to logic, and is the nemesis of attempts to bring science "into harmony with the postulates of the unity of science and of physicalism."[38]

Tarski's solution for formal languages was simple. The predicative power of language must be segregated into semantic levels so that it cannot be used against itself. Science has no need of a closed universal language, he argued; its language must be made "open" to different semantic levels. Talk about science's terms and its logic, talk about truth-in-science, can go on safely only in a metalanguage. If required, talk about that metalanguage—about first-order logic, for example—can go on in another meta-metalanguage. In none of these languages need predicates be predicated of themselves. Talk about the truth of science's sentences is sequestered from the grasp of those same sentences in universes of metadiscourse not subject to either the judgments of the languages they are about or the judgments they, themselves, are in the process of making. To ask about the truth of science is to engage in a metadiscourse about science; to ask about the truth of the truth about science is to ascend to a next level of theoretical discourse.

The inaccessible technicality of semantic theories that attempted to articulate this hierarchy of linguistic levels in the "open" world of truth-theoretic semantics was, indeed, a formidable barrier to anyone theoretically fainthearted, but there is another reason truth-theoretic semantics might be of limited interest to feminists or others interested in questioning established authority. Truth in truth-theoretic semantics is laid out in structured, leveled equivalences that are truth by definition. To ensure that truth does not call itself into question, talk *about* truth is removed to a higher level, where truths about truth can in turn be laid out one by one in additional strata of structured equivalences. In Tarski's technical breakthrough, the saving paradox of any authority—is it subject to itself?—is circumvented in a hierarchy of authorities, a hierarchy that has no logical closure and so can only end in fiat. Safely "open" to different levels of discourse, language is now, in theory, automated without fear of paradox or anomaly. Just as Frege projected, logic and science become mechanical hands. Truth is a function of preestablished value ranges; talk about truth is not destabilizing talk about the sense of science's predicates, but a theory about a theory.

There are reasons why the confidence and trust in science that generate such a line of thought might not be shared by either feminists or non-Western peoples. They have been in a position to experience not only the advances of science but also the harmfulness of "good" science when it is designed to implement social values such as sexual segregation or racial purity. But only one feminist paper, to my knowledge, engaged the formidable machinery of logical semantics after Tarski. In their 1983 "How Can Language Be Sexist?"[39] Merrill and Jaakko Hintikka argued that truth-theoretic semantics deals with the "structural system" of language and takes the "referential system" for granted. The result, the Hintikkas argued, is that relations between language and the world, which are the input for the structural system, go unexamined along with "tacit evaluations or interests" on which those inputs or meanings depend. Also unexamined, they argued, are ways in which individual things are identified, which may differ between men and women.[40]

The Hintikkas' claim that reference to reality is elided in truth-theoretic semantics has implications beyond the announced aim of their paper: to prove that Jaakko Hintikka's game-theoretic semantics is preferable to truth-theoretic semantics. How are the objects of science or of any truth-telling language determined? How are thoughtful nonscientists, concerned about the state of the world, to understand a science that constructs its own objects—atoms, neutrinos, quarks, neural brain links—if those objects are identifiable only in terms of scientific theory? Must we sensible moderns accept, as Putnam says, a "division of linguistic labor," trusting to scientists to establish references? Must we accept the truths of cognitive science, along with its learning theory and therapeutic techniques, until cognitivists themselves inform us they have been wrong? Must we be Quine's user of science, give up wondering about inscrutable objects and simply interpret our "stimulations" and those of others in the light of current theory?

These questions are not only technical; they have a direct bearing on postmodern life, and they are answered in contemporary analytic semantics in the affirmative. If science is to be true, it must be expressed in the language of truth functions and value ranges; if its predicates are to be questioned, they can be questioned only at a removed metalevel of discourse in metalanguages devised to reflect the logic of the "object language." It is senseless to try to identify what science is about; rather, we should map science's truth. Science is a web of belief constantly reformed by scientists in response to stimulations, stimulations recorded by those who do or command science. "Platitudes" from the ordinary lives of Africans, workers, natives, farmers, and women cannot provide a foothold from which to understand or criticize either science or the metascientific semantics that is the professional expertise of Western philosophers. The most "aliens" can do is attempt Putnam's "leap." If few will succeed, it is because philosophy, like science, is hard and demanding.

But the "truth-in-science" theorized in truth-theoretic semantics is not the only truth or the only science. Feminist epistemologists like Sandra Harding have called for a strongly objective feminist, non-Eurocentric science that not only uses impartial procedures and methods but also is critically aware of its own voice and presuppositions.[41] This is the strong objectivity that establishment philosophy of language, rooted in truth-theoretic semantics, rules out. A strongly objective liberatory science, as Harding and other feminist epistemologists have conceived it, cannot be carried on in a language semantically open to levels of discourse that allow theory to insulate itself within hierarchical webs of belief, removing metapredicates to higher and higher levels of theoretical discourse out of the reach of critical judgment. Only a language whose predicates are universal, a language that is semantically closed, can take its own concepts, methods, and categories critically into account.

A scientific language "open" to metalevels of discourse and so immune to paradoxes of self-reference is only the latest version of an old dream—that philosophers might escape to another world from which they can look down on this imperfect world and make judgments not tainted by the ambiguities and paradoxes of temporal existence. In this irrevocably one world, Tarskian formulas for what objects satisfy what functions cannot stand intact as canonical kernels of the "whole" truth of which truth is a function. It is not only a matter of taking moral responsibility for the uses of science or the sources of science's funding. Nor does rejection of a semantic theory of truth imply reversion to competing relativistic conceptual schemes, each with its validating metalevels of discourse. Instead, what is in question, as Harding and other feminist epistemologists have argued, is the internal logic of a science in the service of a common but always revisable truth. In a science that has reference and truth, objects cannot be formally or internally defined. If they are, the essential nexus of theory with reality is lost and theory is self-generating and holistic, a web of belief in which objects are defined as what is covered by concepts, and concepts by the specified objects that fall under them. In contrast, the concepts of a science that is strongly objective in Harding's sense have reference to real objects of interest. Are there really dichotomous sexual differences, or does the human brain have a selectional and creative ability to institute novel and fluid forms of behavior?[42] Is there in physical reality a natural equilibrium of material forces or a mechanics of nuclear reaction?[43] Is syphilis a "sexual scourge" or a complex of diseases that respond to treatment with mercury? Insofar as the objects studied are real objects of interest and not the artificial objects of a theory, they emerge in administrative and funding discussions and laboratory practices conducted in natural language's "closed" predicates, predicates that have meaning "open" to revision and adjustment to the reality of shared human interests.

Fortunately, science does not always, or even perhaps often, approximate the truth-theoretic ideal. Within the "open" universe of contemporary semantics this observation is irrelevant: it is not inevitably "imperfect" science or logic as it exists that is in question but the imprecision and ambiguity of natural language and a contrasting ideal of what science must be. But by treating the "structural system" of language as independent, by taking the referential system for granted, philosophers of language succeed in creating a dangerous illusion of autonomy.

Science computes and calculates, but what it computes and calculates can be reliably determined only in natural language. To refuse to acknowledge that fact, to have ascribed to science the independence of truth-theoretic semantics, was to have made invisible the circle of those who direct scientific research in natural language. It was to have created the illusion that no native "platitudes," no woman's "cat*," no non-Western irrationality can intervene in that hermeneutical circle. It was to obscure the fact that stable objects about which truths can be told are created not by fiat but in open discussion between diverse persons that establishes the objectivity of commonality. For the objectivity of Harding's, Evelyn Fox Keller's, and Helen Longino's strongly objective feminist science, a different semantics and a different philosophy of language are needed.

The Circulation of Meaning

Since Descartes, Western philosophy of language has oscillated between two poles. On the one hand, there have been various revisions of Descartes's rationalism currently understood in the nontheological idioms of theoretical linguistics and logic. On the other hand, empiricist views of language have made meaning essentially private, a matching up of words with inner experiences currently understood on the model of computer processing. On neither of these views is Harding's ideal of a strongly objective science from the standpoint of diverse and multiple agents, women and men speaking for others as well as themselves, intelligible. On neither of these views is the power of natural language to establish common meanings, express truths, define and refer to common objects of interest, reinterpret the past, and envision the future captured. On neither view is a feminist science in the service of human needs possible. When language is seen as a code for internal events as in cognitive or empiricist theories of language, or as a system of classification as in structuralism, or as an adaptation of logical form as in truth-theoretic semantics, what is distinctively linguistic is ignored. The conceptual revision, the resaying, reapplying, respeaking of words—including the word "language" itself—that allows people to refer to changing realities and to understand others with differing experiences is lost.

It is this *linguistic* process of speaking together about objects of common interest that might be taken as the subject of semantics in a new feminist key. Cognitive, structuralist, or truth-theoretic theories of meaning may be descriptive of some or even most of existing discourse, including that of some science and politics. A feminist philosophy of language, even as it may use those theories, as I have here, to better understand uses of language, might also inquire into what language could and should be if it is to produce understanding and knowledge, knowledge that serves Africans as well as Europeans, women as well as men, non-Western cultures as well as Western.

In contrast, the project of logical semantics has been to purge language of the very linguistic elements that give language referential and communicative power. One casualty is the very possibility of the critical readings that feminist philosophers have been giving to traditional philosophy, including my own reading here and elsewhere of logic and philosophy of language. Philosophy of language has been allowed to frame debate about the value of those readings. Are feminists reading philosophy to detect private feelings or ideas of male philosophers, which are irrelevant to their philosophical assertions? Or are they looking for textual or structural motifs, symbolic patterns irrelevant to the hard core of propositional content? Neither question, in my view, addresses the ability of feminist criticism to make clear what philosophers have said and to press philosophical inquiry forward to new engagement with reality. Feelings can be declared irrelevant to truth and only identifiable by way of suspect empathy or disempathy. Deconstruction can be indicted for failing to engage the historical reality of women's and men's experiences and the ways in which philosophy reflects and rationalizes those experiences.

The key, I believe, to understanding the value of feminist readings of past and contemporary philosophy is a facet of language that has been a continuing embarrassment and stumbling block for logical semantics: intension. In spoken languages, perhaps in any conceivable language, one person can report what another person believes, desires, or fears in her or his own words. This stubborn, seemingly ineradicable intensionality, or more properly interintensionality, has been a major technical problem in logical semantics since Frege. If language is to be truth-functional, the substitution of words that denote the same object or objects must be truth-preserving. But in contexts in which beliefs and desires of others are reported, for example, "James believes that Cross's wife wrote great novels" and "James believes that George Eliot wrote great novels," it is not. Although "Cross's wife" is coextensional with "George Eliot," James may believe the first without believing the second and vice versa. In these cases, although an equivalent is substituted, truth is not preserved. This is the cog in the wheels of smooth truth-functioning that forced Frege to include, along with the reference of words, the "senses" of words.[44]

A great deal of effort, after Frege, has gone to trying to be rid of intensionality or at least to reduce it to manageable truth-functional terms. As Quine put it, intension can have no place in a science that has pretensions to be a "global theory of the world." At most one might quote, simply repeating sequences of words or letters that others have uttered or are likely to utter in given instances. If meaning in any more personal sense intrudes, there is an impermissible "break in the causal chain," in the "crystalline purity of extensionality" (*PT*, 72). Indeed it is with intension that the limits of Quine's empathy and Davidson's principle of charity are most apparent. To report what another believes, you cannot just make the assumption that she believes or reacts as you do, or even the assumption that she is in disagreement with you. This may do among a homogeneous group, like a homogeneous group of professional male philosophers; it may even do when that group of philosophers is separated into rival camps. It will hardly work for a woman or non-Western male philosopher who comes to philosophy with very different commitments and interests. Nor is the specificity given to mental states by cognitive science, a specificity that itself is nonintensional and truth-functional, likely to be of much use. Women or Third World men attempting to engage Western philosophy in a discussion with reference to experiences of oppression may not process information in the same way as a professional establishment.

Instead feminists have tried to understand what it is that the men who have been influential philosophers fear, desire, and believe. They have been interested not in quoting, affirming, or denying but in explaining what philosophers say in their own words so that inquiry may move forward and discussion between men and women can go on—discussion that might change the terms in which we think about language and other subjects of mutual interest, such as justice, race, gender, and knowledge. The point of feminist readings of philosophy, as I see it, is not that the functional state of women's minds be duplicated in men's minds or theirs in ours, nor is it to destabilize rational structures of discourse. It is to attempt to bring what women and men say back to reality.

In semantics in another key, intension—the ascription of beliefs and desires to others in one's own words and further ascriptions of belief about the beliefs of others to them or to oneself—far from being a troublesome element that must be removed so that language can refer and tell the truth, might be studied as a linguistic phenomenon that allows reference to something other than personal incommensurable mental events or alienated linguistic structures. Intension makes it possible to refer to a real object about which it is possible to say something true. It does so precisely by maintaining the universality of predicates, by refusing to cordon off critique in a protected level of semantic discourse; it does so by committing the semantic sin of blending talk about language with talk about things. As Quine puts it, "The voice of the ascriber of a propositional attitude sometimes blends with that of the man in the attitude causing *de re* intrusions and consequent ambiguities" (*PT*, 68). The effect of these intrusions and ambiguities as "things" are spoken of both as things (*de re*) and as objects of belief (*de dicto*) is that concepts and references begin to intersubjectively circulate.

The puzzle of reference to interpersonal reality is an old one. To state a truth it is necessary to both refer to something and say something true about it. But if that truth is to be determinate it seems that there must be names that are "rigid designators" and predicates which the things those names refer to "satisfy" in an incontrovertible way. When disputes arise about what a thing is—for example, what sex is, what femininity is, as well as what reason or democracy is—designations seem to slip. The fact that different qualities are now ascribed to femininity or sex seems to indicate that a different object is in question, that men and women, Westerners and non-Westerners are not speaking of the same thing and so cannot contradict each other. Classically, the problem is dealt with by making a distinction between necessary and contingent qualities: some qualities are essential, and these fix reference rigidly; about the other contingent qualities there can be dispute. But the problem is to make even supposed necessary characteristics stay fixed.

"That is an insult," a woman might say when her male supervisor once again comments favorably on her appearance when she arrives at work. She might even so testify in a sexual harassment suit. He is bewildered. How can she say such a thing? How can she be so irrational, so illogical? How can a compliment be insulting? How can there be any truth at all when not only what is talked about but also what we say about it is not defined? "That compliment is an insult" has all the dangerous paradox of the self-referential statements that have threatened the downfall of semantic theory, recalling Frege's failed attempt to logicize mathematics and Gödel's incompleteness theorem. If it is true, it is false; if it is false, it is true. What you are saying, the woman explains, is that all that is important about me is my pleasing appearance, and that is an insult. It is, as Quine notes, in just such cases that *de re* talk about things intrudes in what might have been a simple *de dicto* quote of words. It is in just such cases that Russell's theory of types is violated. It is also in such cases that the conceptual revision that brings words closer to reality is possible.

How is it possible that we continue to talk about the same things even as we dispute what they are? There are various semantic solutions. One can think of objects as rigidly designated by current theories in science or in some primitive act of ostension of an object described by science. Like Quine, one can give up on objects altogether. Like Donald Davidson, one can see objects as what are designated objects in a "theory" of one's own language. Again, the element of language that accounts for the maintenance of reference through changing predications has been eliminated. The common reference in all the complex and shifting references and concepts in human discourse, whether in science, politics, or personal disputes, is neither in the truth-functional structures of language nor in individual minds but in reality, in the actual complexity of human interaction in and with the world.

More specifically, the linguistic device that gives stability to reference in intensional contexts is not the word marker of a given fixed value range but the extrasemantic topography of indexicals that build into speakable languages flexible patterns of interaction and response that allow talk about the same things among people who disagree. "I" hear what "you" say about "our" interaction; and "I" am aware that "you" would describe "it" differently. "Then"—in the past—"this" may have been appropriate, "now" and from "here," "we" see things differently. In such linguistic exchanges, the positioning of indexicals operates as a complex of vectors that focus on a common object of interest seen and understood from different perspectives. These patterns allow a concept to form around an object in time and space without displacing it but successively describing it. What emerges is an object of interest not dependent on anyone's private stimulations or on any alienated linguistic, logical, or cognitive structure, but an object "between" people, product of a transit of meaning from one person to another.

In logical semantics, the smooth "functioning" of truth requires that interpersonal reference based on intensionality be eliminated or subdued; it also requires that indexicals, whether explicit or implicit, be suppressed. If there is to be the global Western science that Quine projects, references to specific times, places, and persons have to be eliminated. The successes of logical semantics have been innovative techniques to attempt to achieve this end. But in the process of eliminating from language terms that position speakers in time and place and in relation to each other, the very possibility of the "standpoint logic" that Harding and other feminist epistemologists see as essential for a referential and liberatory science is ruled out. The indexicality of language ensures that the speaking subject is multiple and diverse; it ensures that concepts have reference not just for one group but for others also. It ensures that a feminist science or philosophy will have generality and not be for or about only one group or interest.[45]

A language in which there is a circulation of meaning is a "language of thought," but it is a thought unlike the information processing of Fodor's talking heads. In the *Life of the Mind*, Hannah Arendt described the dialogic thinking that she believed might protect against future Holocausts. For an "I" who talks to "you's" and who therefore talks about something, solitary thought is necessary, retreat to the privacy of the mind to attempt to bring some order to contradictory shifting references and meanings that are the substance of public truth-telling. In this way and only in this way, in Arendt's view, can a person achieve a viable self that is not the illusion of a self that relies on truth without indexicals. The consistency and simplicity achieved in private thought are energized by discussions that have gone on in speaking life; back in public life, "I's" and their beliefs are again put into relation with conflicting beliefs of "you's" and "they's."[46]

The current practitioners of philosophy of language might be willing to concede this reliance on diversity of opinion in political talk or even in the "soft" social sciences. In those areas, they might argue, it is not really truth that is in question but rather values, which are a matter of personal choice and compromise. In physics, in hard science, truth-theory must rule. But if the objects and concepts of physics and chemistry are not the subject of public interpersonal debate—not to be circulated—that may only be because the interests of military and commercial powers in these areas are so implacably resolute. When once those interests are called into question, it may be clear that discussion between diverse persons is necessary to secure reliable reference to objects of human interest even in physics. Statistical correlations, mechanical formulas cannot provide reference. What gives substance to science is that it tells the truth about things that people care about. If these are atomic power, energy sources, nuclear bombs, psychosedating drugs, and genetically engineered substances,[47] this is reliably determined only in the "closed" universe of natural language. In the open universe of truth-theoretic semantics, energy can be taken as simply what is counted as energy without attention to what that energy actually is and its effects in this world, which can be devastating. There are no possible worlds or twin earths in which to escape the effects of a science that in the end must operate in this world, no way to escape the fact of what would have happened or not happened if we had done things differently.

If in natural language we have the power to say what *is* in the world, we also can say what the world has been and might yet be. This power to tell truths about past and future, also antithetical to the semantic project, might be another subject of study in a feminist philosophy of language. As with intension, much energy has been spent trying to eliminate tenses: making sentences eternal by substituting for "now" or "then" a formula specifying a date and time and place or giving tenses referential meaning by adopting some canonical geography or time measurement that further removes language from its referential matrix in human intercourse. Questions of what science or philosophy of language "might be" or "was" cause embarrassment and problems for truth-functional logic because they draw on complex temporal resources in languages that allow not only talk as an "I" to and for others but talk as an "I" or "we" from a location now about a time that has passed and about a time in the future. Again the reference is not absolute but relational, not to a canonical succession of points in time but to a moving relation between two times. In such relations, the present does not stay still, any more than the past does. As the past is reinterpreted and reread, the sense of the present changes, giving depth to an understanding of existing reality that atemporal unidimensional description cannot achieve.

For understanding the past of philosophy, including the past of philosophy of language, as well as for envisioning its future, no expression is more central than the counterfactual conditional, the management of which has so exercised contemporary semantics and inspired a thicket of dense and impenetrable theorizing about possible worlds. "If Rosa Luxemburg had been taken as the intellectual leader of European socialism instead of either Lenin or Bernstein, socialism might be alive today." For truth functions to function, sentences like this must be reinterpreted. A sentence must be either true or false. Certainly, if it is not one or the other it can hardly be of much use as a truth function. The problem is to know how the truth of a past or future counterfactual can be determined. Amid a flurry of theorizing about how objects can be identified in other worlds, much of it drawing on imaginative and often bizarre science fiction examples like twin earths and robotized cats, the answer has been that such a sentence has truth-theoretic reference not in this world but in other possible worlds, for example, worlds in which somehow Rosa Luxemburg is herself, but enough else is different so that she becomes head of the Social Democratic party and socialism is triumphant.

But this interpretation, which makes of the counterfactual a kind of mental experiment aimed at getting at the necessary or the contingent qualities of things, robs the counterfactual of its actual contribution to truth in this world. It is important to know whether Luxemburg would have led a different socialist movement not because of any possible worlds but because in *this world* there are relations between certain kinds of alienated political theorizing and the moral and practical collapse of communism, because there are relations between the present bankruptcy of social theory and the suppression of women's voices in the past. These relations between the past and present of one real world are negotiated in the counterfactual.

The same applies to conditional future statements that, since Aristotle, have provoked intense philosophical concern about statements whose truth is indeterminate and therefore seem to violate the logical "law of the excluded middle." "If we continue to leave philosophy of language to male-dominated logical semantics, feminists will lack a theory of truth." Again possible worlds provide convenient interpretations: a possible world in which philosophy of language is neglected by feminists; a possible world in which all else is the same but women become semanticists. In one world, feminist epistemology lacks vitality and logical semantics flourishes; in the other, feminist philosophers have made Putnam's conceptual leaps. But this is to miss the sense and the reference of the statement. There is only one world, this world, in which future conditionals mark out paths, paths that may be pursued or not pursued by real people. A feminist philosophy of language is not the imaginative projection of a possible world but a real, present possibility in this world that feminist philosophers might pursue.

I have only managed to indicate very roughly some paths a feminist philosophy of language might take. Out of discussion among and between philosophers of language and feminist philosophers, highlighting rather than explaining away distinctively linguistic devices of intension, indexicals, and counterfactuals, new views of the nature of language, meaning, and truth might be developed. In many feminist circles, discussions about truth have come to have a bad name. As it is theorized in professional philosophy of language, truth deserves that bad name. Truth-theoretic semantics has been the study of assertion and representation. As the prerogative and the ruse of those in authority, neither invites response but only accepts acceptance or refusal. Whatever semantics is appropriate for a language of assertion and representation, it is unlikely to be a semantics that accounts for the truths that feminists would like to explore. Assertions and representations are made in order to cover up truth rather than determine it; the logical coherence and closed "openness" that cordon off comment on assertions and representations in official metalanguages are consistent with that project.

The possible feminist philosophy of language that I have very tentatively envisioned would take as its subject matter elements that are essential to the achievement of reference and truth between diverse people with diverse interests. Such a linguistics is feminist not because it is a study of a feminine language that only women speak or a "primitive" language that "jungle" natives speak. Nor is it feminist because it criticizes masculine language that men or philosophers or Westerners speak. It is feminist because it locates in language resources that facilitate a circulation of meaning and desire that fixes the points of equilibrium between material reality and diverse human aspiration which are the necessary form of shared objectivity. Finding such common objects, I would argue, is in the interest of everyone, men and women, Continental and analytic philosophers, Westerners and non-Westerners, white people and people of color.

NOTES

1. Hilary Putnam, *Reason, Truth, and History* (Cambridge: Cambridge University Press, 1982), p. 102. In this passage, Putnam addresses the problem of translatability as it relates to the thesis of cognitive psychology that humans share a common specifiable computational mental function.

2. P. 36. Putnam is referring to Nozick's version of a much debated and discussed puzzle first proposed by Nelson Goodman. How could we tell that a person meant by "cat" not cat but a perverse "cat*," for example, cherries when there are cats around, cats when there are cherries around, and cherries when neither are around. Both "cat" and "cat*" have the same "truth-value"—come out true or false in the same circumstances in all possible worlds—so the difference of meaning supposedly would be undetectable.

3. See, for example, Judith Jarvis Thomson's much-anthologized use of counter-example in "A Defense of Abortion," *Philosophy and Public Affairs* 1, no. 1 (1971): 47–66, or Marilyn Frye's early conceptual analysis in "Male Chauvinism: A Conceptual Analysis," both reprinted in R. Baker and F. Elliston, eds., *Philosophy and Sex* (Buffalo, N.Y.: Prometheus Books, 1975); or Janice Moulton's study of equivocation in "The Myth of the Neutral Man," in M. Vetterling-Braggin, F. Elliston, and J. English, eds., *Feminism and Philosophy* (Totowa, N.J.: Rowman and Allanheld, 1977). See Janet Radcliffe Richards's, *The Sceptical Feminist* (London: Routledge and Kegan Paul, 1980) for condemnation of any attempt by feminist philosophers to go beyond logical analysis and refutation, but compare the argument of Janice Moulton in "A Paradigm of Philosophy: The Adversary Method," in S. Harding and M. B. Hintikka, eds., *Discovering Reality* (Dordrecht: D. Reidel, 1983).

4. See the chapter on "The Woman" in Otto Jesperson, *Language, Its Nature, Development and Origin* (London: George Allen and Unwin, 1922).

5. See the papers collected in D. Butteroff and E. L. Epstein, eds., *Women's Language and Style* (Akron, Ohio: University of Akron Department of English, 1978); B. Thorne and N. Henley, eds., *Language and Sex: Difference and Dominance* (Rowley, Mass.: Newbury House, 1975); B. Thorne, N. Henley, and C. Kramarae, eds., *Language, Gender and Society* (Rowley, Mass.: Newbury House, 1983); and Mary Hiatt, *The Way Women Write* (New York: Teacher's College Press, 1977); and Mary Ritchie Key, *Male/Female Language* (Metuchen, N.J.: Scarecrow Press, 1975). For a recent summary of the research, see also Jennifer Coates, *Women, Men and Language* (London: Longman, 1986).

6. Edward Sapir, "Abnormal Types of Speech in Nootka," in David Mandlebaum, ed., *Selected Writings of Edward Sapir on Language* (Berkeley and Los Angeles: University of California Press, 1968); see also Ann Bodine's summary of male-female linguistic differences in other cultures, "Sex Differentiation in Language," in Thorne and Henley, *Language and Sex*, p. 130.

7. For an example, see Key, *Male/Female Language*, pp. 68–69.

8. For example, Peter Trudgill, "Sex, Covert Prestige and Linguistic Changes in the British English of Norwich," in Thorne and Henley, *Language and Sex*; see also a bibliography of related articles in Thorne, Henley, and Kramarae, *Language, Gender and Society*, p. 327. Robin Lakoff, in *Language and Women's Speech* (San Francisco: Harper and Row, 1975), argued that women's speaking style also reflected powerlessness. Similarly, Dale Spender, in *Man Made Language* (London: Routledge and Kegan Paul, 1979), argued that men have the power to determine what words mean. Anthropologists Shirley and Edwin Ardener proposed the general thesis that the ideas of less dominant social groups are "muted" and suppressed; see Shirley Ardener and Edwin Ardener, eds., *Perceiving Women* (London: Malaby Press, 1975).

9. French feminists were particularly influential here. Julia Kristeva warned against any psychotic attempt to leave symbolic structure behind but approved a

continuing "maternal" disruption and derailing of linguistic categories that prevented too rigid a structuring of conventions. Hélène Cixous called for an *écriture féminine*, an expressive "language of the body." For a more detailed study of a very complex intellectual history, see my *Feminist Theory and the Philosophies of Man* (New York: Routledge, Chapman, Hall, 1990), pp. 172–228 (chapter 6, "A Woman's Language."

10. The ongoing dispute in linguistics is between the so-called Sapir/Whorf thesis that the grammars of different languages create different worlds (in Whorf's studies, the grammar of Native American languages) and the current view that universal theories of grammar account for translatability. Dale Spender, in *Man Made Language*, popularized application of the Whorf hypothesis to sexual difference, arguing that men, who had shaped the grammar and semantics of languages like English, created a man's world. A Whorfian linguistic relativity was also adapted by theorists such as the Ardeners and Cheris Kramarae to account for the "different realities" of "dominant" and "muted" social groups.

11. Feminist linguists found many examples of asymmetry in English vocabulary. Pairs of words are asymmetrically coded for sex so that the female is always of lesser power as in "master/mistress." Diminutive endings mark the inferior status of feminine counterparts. Euphemisms like "lady" are substituted for the distasteful "woman." Titles such as Mrs./Miss/Mr. mark the marital status of women but not of men. Adjectives and nouns are sexually coded so that "strong woman" has a negative connotation and "male nurse" is anomalous. Generic masculine forms such as the singular pronoun "he" and nouns like "man" map onto the very grammar of English the superior and primal humanity of masculinity and an ambiguous supplement of femininity. See detailed studies in A. P. Nilsen et al., eds., *Sexism and Language* (Urbana, Ill.: National Council of Teachers, 1977); Thorne and Henley, *Language and Sex*; Spender, *Man Made Language*; and G. Kress and R. Hodge, *Language and Ideology* (London: Routledge and Kegan Paul, 1979). For a general treatment of the connotations of asymmetrical language, see Carolyn Korsmeyer, "The Hidden Joke: Generic Uses of Masculine Terminology," in Vetterling-Braggin, Elliston, and English, *Feminism and Philosophy*.

12. A summary of proposed revisions can be found in Casey Miller and Kate Swift, *Words and Women* (New York: Doubleday, 1975).

13. Deborah Cameron, *Feminism and Linguistic Theory* (New York: Macmillan, 1985), p. 86.

14. For an account of the complex strands of scholarly myth in nineteenth-century linguistic theory, see Maurice Olender, *The Languages of Paradise: Race, Religion, and Philology in the Nineteenth Century*, trans. Arthur Goldhammer (Cambridge, Mass.: Harvard University Press, 1992).

15. The internal relations between words that in structural linguistics create meaning were modeled after the new science of phonetics. Bypassing unreliable interpretation, linguists recorded the presence or absence of sound features to isolate the acoustic atoms of speech. Analogously, the smallest atoms of meaning were "objectively" determined by isolating the least elements that create changes in meaning. These "morphemes" were then combined as presences or absences to make composite meanings of words.

16. This was the assumption of Chomsky's transformational grammar. From deep grammatical structure could be generated different surface structures that are the individual choice of speakers.

17. This, for Saussure, was a necessary consequence of the arbitrary nature of the linguistic sign. Law, fashion, and customs can be changed to better fit what is "natural," but there is no natural meaning in language. For this reason, language blends with society and becomes a "prime conservative force." See *Course in General Linguistics*, trans. Wade Baskin (New York: McGraw-Hill, 1966), p. 74.

18. For a feminist reading of Frege see part III, "Reading Frege," in my *Words of Power: Feminist Readings in the History of Logic* (New York and London: Routledge, 1990).

19. See the early autobiographical *Tristes Tropiques*, trans. John Weightman and Doreen Weightman (London: Cape, 1973).

20. The citations are to Quine's summing up of his position, *The Pursuit of Truth* (Cambridge, Mass.: Harvard University Press, 1990); hereafter *PT*.

21. This is Quine's famous "ontological relativity." The alternatives reflect the restricted context in which the question of reference is typically raised: preserving reference through changes in scientific theory. The first two possibilities, I take it, are analogues of the indeterminacy in quantum mechanics between particle theory and wave theory; "rabbit parts" I have only been able to make sense of as the packaged supermarket version somehow reassembled back into a rabbit and animated. How the natives might have this conception I am not sure. Quine's moral, however, is that there is no way we could know whether they did or not.

22. This is the equally famous "indeterminacy of translation." In practice, Quine says, it is seldom a problem because the linguist "imposes his own ontology and linguistic patterns on the native" (*PT*, 48). Initially Quine pointed out that examples might be used to show that indeterminacy also occurs within English because "given the rival manuals of translation between Jungle and English, we can translate English perversely into English by translating it into Jungle by one manual and then back by the other" (as reported at *PT*, 48). By the writing of *The Pursuit of Truth*, however, Quine has decided that relativity can be avoided when a truth-theoretic analysis is adopted (*PT*, 52). For how that might be done see Donald Davidson's "The Inscrutability of Reference," in *Inquiries into Truth and Interpretation* (Oxford: Oxford University Press, 1984, 227–42). In Davidson's version, stimulus meaning drops out and is replaced by "objective features of the world" as formulated in the linguist's language, which are then correlated with the native's assent and dissent and also first-order logic and quantification theory assumed as the structure of any meaningful language. The rationale from *Truth and Interpretation*: "If we cannot find a way to interpret the utterances and other behaviors of a creature as revealing a set of beliefs largely consistent and true by our own standards, we have no reason to count that creature as rational, as having beliefs, or as saying anything" (p. 136n).

23. In *The Pursuit of Truth*, Quine is willing to admit the possibility that this "territory" might be "reclaimed" in neurobiology or cognitive science, which would be an example, as he puts it, of science's strategy of "divide and conquer" in order to eventually account for all events (*PT*, 72).

24. For a contrasting account of translation, see Carol Spindel's memoir of fieldwork in East Africa, *In the Shadow of the Sacred Grove* (New York: Vintage Books, 1989): "Everyday I went out into the village and stuck out my well-trained antennae, but the information that came back was garbled as if some very important organ in my body no longer functioned. I, who had always known what unspoken words meant, now did not understand spoken ones. Even gestures confounded me. . . . As soon as I had acquired a limited vocabulary, I began to try to express

complex ideas using only simple means. I never tried to translate my thoughts directly into Dyula; that led only to frustration. Instead, I had to be content to distill my ideas down to their most basic and childlike form. . . . The obsession with words and how they fit together is a prerequisite for learning any language quickly. But it is not the only requirement. The state of being not quite articulate is a childlike state. To learn a language well and quickly, one must be willing to play the child" (pp. 42–43, 158–59, 221). Spindel learned to speak Dyula. Her husband, who was conducting studies of native agricultural practices in the style of Quine's linguist, did not. He depends on a native interpreter who cheats him, lies to him, and compromises his study.

25. Jerry Fodor, *The Language of Thought* (Cambridge, Mass.: Harvard University Press, 1990); hereafter *LOT*.

26. Jerry Fodor, *Psychosemantics* (Cambridge, Mass.: MIT Press, 1988); hereafter *PSY*.

27. Turing's paper "On Computable Numbers," *Proceedings of the London Mathematical Society* (2)42 (1936–37): 230–65, explored the possibility of mechanical computing devices that would facilitate radar, range finding, and code breaking. The suggestion that computing can be equated with intelligence came in the postwar "Computing Machinery and Intelligence," *Mind* 59 (1950): 433–60. Equally important, but not mentioned by Fodor, was John von Neumann's postwar "theory of automata." After pioneering work in military applications of computing during the war, in the 1950s von Neumann developed a theory of "automata" to be applied to both natural organisms and machines. He argued for a direct analogy between Turing's universal computing machine and the human brain, arguing that the neural activity of the brain is carried on in a machine language of partially preprogrammed digital and analog operations that can be further programmed by second-level input codes of mathematics and natural languages. See A. W. Burks, ed., *Theory of Self-Reproducing Automata* (Urbana: University of Illinois Press, 1966); see also *The Computer and the Brain* (New Haven, Conn.: Yale University Press, 1958).

28. The problems with reductive materialism were much rehearsed by philosophers in the 1950s and 1960s. It is not clear how a specific bundle of nerve cells can ever represent anything or mean anything. Turing's "great discovery" that machines can simulate any rationally ordered process or computation made it possible to explain meaning without falling back into unscientific idealism. In the brain of a speaking organism is microcircuitry whose syntax or internal construction allows semantic elements to be defined by function, just as the computer's off-on switches are wired or programmed to fire in certain sequences.

29. Fodor, *Psychosemantics*, p. 131. Fodor uses the example to illustrate the difference between wired-in programming and humans' more efficient, learned linguistic programming amenable to adjustments and not limited to genetic inheritance. Human males presumably can more efficiently process information about rivals and territories via language.

30. Aaron Beck, A. John Rush, Brian Shaw, and Gary Emery, *The Cognitive Theory of Depression* (New York: Guilford Press, 1979), 104–16.

31. Cognitive psychology was embraced by many philosophers, but Fodor's distinctive innovation was the "language of thought" that he believed was necessary if the mind was understood correctly as an information processor analogous to a computer. For cognitive functions to be possible, he argued, there has to be an internal machine language onto which the coded language of communication is mapped.

32. Representations must be recorded so as to be confirmable, but this is only the same problem, Fodor says, that occurs in philosophy of science. There are no raw data of perception. Sensory input itself must be translated into the representational language of thought.

33. W. V. Quine, "Words Are All We Have to Go On," *Times Literary Supplement* (Special Issue on the State of Philosophy), July 3, 1992. Specifically, philosophers can analyze bundles of scientific theory, perhaps isolating "tautologies," "hypotheses" that can be dropped. Quine's own contribution, he points out, was to show that objects are eliminatable from science as only the "neutral nodes" of theory that successfully predicts stimulations: "Words are all that we have to go on."

34. In contrast, see a number of detailed studies of actual scientific research that show the inapplicability of positivist or postpositivist logic to actual science. The distinguished microbiologist Ludwik Fleck, in *Genesis and Development of a Scientific Fact* (Chicago: University of Chicago Press, 1979) (first published in Switzerland in 1935), shows scientific facts emerging in an ongoing repertoire of skills and procedures, in complex matrixes of social, mythical, and cultural meanings, in creative and often disordered experimentation. More recently, in a study of quantum mechanics, Nancy Cartwright (*How the Laws of Physics Lie* [Oxford: Oxford University Press, 1983]) shows that "model-theoretic" laws are only true of objects in logical models not of real objects. Physics describes reality by way of specific phenomenological laws that are revisable modes of understanding and operating with phenomena fundamental in science. Recent feminist studies of specific branches of science—Helen Longino (studies of sex differences), Donna Haraway (primatology), Sharon Traweek (particle physics), to mention just a few—and major theoretical works by Sandra Harding, Lorraine Code, and Evelyn Fox Keller have been the basis for an increasingly rich feminist epistemology of science that critiques the view of science as truth in a logicized "God's-eye view."

35. See my account of Frege's "thoughts" as meaning something after all, in "Frege's Thoughts," Chapter 7, *Words of Power*.

36. Donald Davidson, "Theories of Meaning and Learnable Languages," in *Inquiries into Truth and Interpretation*; W. V. Quine, *Philosophy of Logic* (Englewood Cliffs, N.J.: Prentice-Hall, 1970), p. 25.

37. "Closed" might seem to be the wrong word here. What is meant is that the universe of discourse of natural language is one: there is only one world to talk about. Linguistic elements and what we say about them are part of one closed world, in contrast to formal languages, which remain open by instituting levels of discourse and separate metadomains of objects.

38. The quote is from Tarksi's explanation of the purpose behind truth- theoretic semantics, "The Establishment of Scientific Semantics," in *Logic, Semantics, Metamathematics*, trans. J. H. Woodger (Indianapolis: Hackett, 1983). The stumbling block was that if predicates are allowed to be applied to themselves, paradox results and there are sentences that are not determinable as either true or false. Two of the other solutions: Russell's theory of types laid down the rule that a set cannot be a member of itself—the predicate that defines the set cannot be predicated of itself. Kripke rejected Tarksi's metalevel approach but denied that a sentence has to be either true or false. See "Outline of a Theory of Truth," *Journal of Philosophy* 72 (1975): 690–716.

39. Sandra Harding and Merrill Hintikka, eds., *Discovering Reality* (Dordrecht: Reidel, 1983), pp. 139–48.

40. The Hintikkas' specific example was "a good man," where the meaning of good changes according to whether man is meant generically or as referring to men. They argued that this is not a question of "emotive" sexist uses of language that are of no interest in semantics but of the fit between language and the world. Even deeper, they said, is the problem of individuation. In semantic's assumption of discrete individuals identifiable across possible worlds is male bias; a "feminine ontology" might be different.

41. See Sandra Harding, *Whose Science? Whose Knowledge?* (Ithaca, N.Y.: Cornell University Press, 1991), esp. pp. 284–86. A strongly objective science would be critical not only of its surface logic but also of the conceptual framework that gives content to that logic. Such a science would give attention to the social organization of research facilities, the sources of funding, the social meaning of metaphors that shape its core concepts, and the way the objects that it quantifies are identified. Harding's "strong objectivity" might be contrasted with Putnam's "internal realism." Truth for Putnam demands that one accept the values and methods of one's community; truth for Harding demands that one call those values into question.

42. See Helen Longino, *Science as Social Knowledge* (Princeton, N.J., Princeton University Press, 1990), pp. 133–161.

43. See Paul Forman, "Behind Quantum Mechanics: National Security as Basis of Physical Research in the U.S. 1940–1960," *Historical Studies in the Physical and Biological Sciences* 18, pt. 1 (1987): 149–229.

44. See "Sense and Reference," in *Translations from the Philosophical Works of Gottlob Frege*, ed. Peter Geach and Max Black (Oxford: Basil Blackwell, 1970). In order to solve the problem of interchangeability, Frege posited a duality of meaning. A word has both a reference identified with its extension (the set of objects to which it refers) and a sense that picks out the same referent in different ways and so accounts for the failure of substitutivity.

45. See Harding, *Whose Science? Whose Knowledge*: "the subject of liberatory feminist knowledge must also be the subject of every other liberatory knowledge project" (p. 285); "women cannot be the unique generators of feminist knowledge" (p. 286).

46. I owe much to Hannah Arendt, who, in *Thinking*, argued for a phenomenal and not metaphysical reality in which the objectivity of objects is relational and interpersonal. More elemental than objects, which may be only the adumbrations of concepts abstracted from their reference in experience, are relations in which objects come into being: relations between sensations and appearances, between the private spaces and public spaces, between persons. Traditional metaphysics, she thought, takes only the end product of this complex reality, objects, and treats it as given (*Thinking*, pt. 1, pp. 19–67). In contrast, Arendt "points to the infinite plurality which is the law of the earth" (p. 187). See my *Philosophia: The Thought of Rosa Luxemburg, Simone Weil, and Hannah Arendt* (New York: Routledge, 1993) for a detailed account of Arendt's philosophy of mind and knowledge.

47. See Sandra Harding's recent edited collection *The "Racial" Economy of Science* (Bloomington: Indiana University Press, 1993), with papers on various aspects of ethnocentrism in biology, physics, other sciences, and related applied sciences.

The Feminist as Other

SUSAN BORDO

> The terms *masculine* and *feminine* are used symmetrically only as a matter of form, as on legal papers. In actuality, the relation of the two sexes is not quite like that of two electrical poles, for man represents both the positive and the neutral, as is indicated by the common use of *man* to designate human beings in general; whereas woman represents only the negative, defined by limiting criteria, without reciprocity. In the midst of an abstract discussion it is vexing to hear a man say: "You think thus and so because you are a woman"; but I know that my only defense is to reply: "I think thus and so because it is true," thereby removing my subjective self from the argument. It would be out of the question to reply: "And you think the contrary because you are a man," for it is understood that the fact of being a man is no peculiarity. . . . [T]here is an absolute human type, the masculine. Woman has ovaries, a uterus; these peculiarities imprison her in her subjectivity, circumscribe her within the limits of her own nature. It is often said that she thinks with her glands. Man superbly ignores the fact that his anatomy also includes glands, such as the testicles, and that they secrete hormones. He thinks of his body as a direct and normal connection with the world, which he believes he apprehends objectively, whereas he regards the body of woman as a hindrance, a prison, weighed down by everything peculiar to it.
>
> —*Simone de Beauvoir,* The Second Sex

FEMINISM AT THE MARGINS OF CULTURE

As cultural critics, feminist theorists have produced powerful challenges: to dominant conceptions of human nature and political affiliation, to norms of scientific, philosophical, and moral reason, to ideals of spirituality, to prevailing disciplinary identities and boundaries, to established historical narratives. Yet how often do we see feminist theorists listed alongside Foucault, Derrida, Rorty, Taylor, Kuhn, or Fish as critics and reshapers of "The Disciplines," "Science," "Philosophy," "Culture"? The answer is: rarely. More often we encounter a version of Edward Said's formulation: "There are cer-

tainly new critical trends . . . great advances made in . . . humanistic interpretation. . . . We *do* know more about the way cultures operate thanks to
Raymond Williams, Roland Barthes, Michel Foucault, and Stuart Hall; we
know about how to examine a text in ways that Jacques Derrida, Hay-
den White, Frederic Jameson, and Stanley Fish have significantly expanded
and altered; and thanks to feminists like Elaine Showalter, Germaine Greer,
Hélène Cixous, Sandra Gilbert, Susan Gubar, and Gayatri Spivak it is impossible to avoid or ignore the gender issues in the production and interpretation of art."[1]

So: Because of Barthes, Derrida et al., we "know more" about culture and
texts; "thanks to feminists," we are unable to "avoid" or "ignore" gender.
For my purposes in this essay, I do not want to make too much of the construction of the European, male contribution as that of increasing *knowledge*, while feminists apparently have simply harangued and harassed to the
point where they cannot be "avoided" or "ignored." I know that Said did
not *really* mean to suggest that unfortunately reverberant contrast. Nor do
I wish to emphasize, although I would point out, the inaccuracy of Said's
description of Gayatri Spivak, who is as much concerned with issues of race
and class as with gender. What I *do* want to insist on is the importance of
Said's juxtaposition of "gender"—what all feminists are concerned with, in
his description—and the general interrogation of "culture" and "text" attributed to the men. The juxtaposition construes feminists as engaging in a
specialized critique, one that cannot be ignored, perhaps, but one whose
implications are contained, self-limiting, and of insufficient general consequence to amount to a new knowledge of "the way culture operates." One
does "gender" *or* one engages in criticism of broad significance; pick one.

In this essay, I will argue that this construction is not merely an annoying
bit of residual sexism but a powerful conceptual map that keeps feminist
scholarship, no matter how broad its concerns, located in the region of what
Simone de Beauvoir called the "Other." De Beauvoir argued that within the
social world, there are those who occupy the unmarked position of the "essential," the universal, the human, and those who are defined, reduced, and
marked by their (sexual, racial, religious) difference from that norm. The
accomplishments of those who are so marked—of the *Other*—may not always be disdained; often, they will be appreciated, but always in their special
and peripheral place, the place of their difference. Thus, there is "History"
and then there is "*Women's* History," and women's history—unlike military history, for example—is located outside what is imagined as history
proper. There are the poststructuralist critiques of reason, which are of
"general" interest, and then there are the feminist critiques, of interest to
those concerned with gender. Said's juxtaposition of those writers who
teach us "about the way cultures operate" and those who make it "impossible to avoid or ignore the gender issues" applauds the feminist—as Other.

As de Beauvoir recognized, gender is not the only cultural form of Otherness. I had a non-Jewish colleague who, having found out that I am Jew-

ish, became unable to have a conversation with me that did not revolve around the brilliance, historical suffering, or sense of humor of "the Jewish People." On one occasion, the conversation turned to our mutual love of Broadway show tunes. For a moment, I thought I would be spared; but then he piped: "And what did you think about *Fiddler on the Roof*? I bet you loved that one!" Every time black authors are quoted only for their views on race—expertise about "general" topics being reserved for white males, who are imagined to be without race and gender—the Otherness of the black is perpetuated. On college campuses, the specter of Otherness has dogged efforts to establish multicultural curricula, efforts that continually get represented *not* as an attempt to bring greater historical accuracy and breadth to a Eurocentric curriculum but as subordinating "general" educational ideals to the special needs and demands of particular groups.[2]

Otherness thus has many faces. De Beauvoir's insight, indeed, is probably the single most broadly, deeply, and enduringly applicable insight of contemporary feminism. It has shaped numerous critical discourses—on race, colonialism, anti-Semitism, and heterosexism, for example. Yet ironically (although perhaps predictably), de Beauvoir's profound philosophical contribution itself fell victim to the dynamic that she describes. To begin with, a zoologist (rather than a philosopher) was chosen to do the English translation of *The Second Sex*. *L'Experience vecue*—lived experience, a central category of phenomenological philosophy—was rendered as "woman's life today." Only men do philosophy; women are fit to write, if at all, about the facts of our own condition. This construction of *The Second Sex* pursued the book throughout the press's marketing and the book's subsequent critical reception. *Time* even headlined its review with the birth announcement: "Weight: 2¾ Lbs,"[3] in one brilliant, if unconscious, stroke associating the book with the materiality of the body, the heavy immanence that is woman—"weighed down by everything peculiar to [her]," as de Beauvoir puts it—and woman's "natural" role of child bearer. And so de Beauvoir, that most unnatural of creatures, a woman philosopher, was put in her rightful place. Today, admittedly, we are more apt to see *The Second Sex* as having theoretical and philosophical import, but only for feminism; its more general cultural influence remains unacknowledged. Thus, *The Second Sex*, generally remembered as a book "about women," is consigned to play the role of gendered Other in our narratives of philosophical history. The truth of de Beauvoir's insight is borne out ironically by the marginalization of de Beauvoir herself.

De Beauvoir was not the last feminist to suffer such marginalization. Said's construction of the contemporary feminist as engaged in gender critique *rather* than general cultural critique, far from being anomalous, is typical of the role assigned feminism in our collective narratives of intellectual challenge and change. Consider, for example, the twentieth-century conception of the body as socially constructed. Such notions, as I argue in *Unbearable Weight*,[4] owe much to feminism—not only to the scholarly writings of academic feminists but to the more public challenge to biological determinism and essentialism that was raised by the activist feminism of the late 1960s and early 1970s—the demonstrations, the manifestos, the consciousness-raising sessions, the early popular writings. At the center of "personal politics" was the conception of the body as profoundly shaped, both materially and representationally, by cultural ideology and "disciplinary" practice. It is Foucault, however, who is generally credited (perhaps with a backward nod to Marx) as the father of "the politics of the body."

Feminist theorists, too, have exalted the philosophical contribution of the father and imagined our feminist mothers as in a more primitive, naive association with the body. Linda Zerilli, for example, while crediting Foucault for having shown us "how the body has been historically disciplined," describes Anglo-American feminism as holding an "essentialist" view of the body as an "archaic natural."[5] In my own 1980 review of *History of Sexuality Vol. 1*, I pointed out that Foucault's notion of a power that works not through negative prohibition but proliferatively, producing bodies and their materiality, was not itself new.[6] But I had in mind here Marcuse's notion, in *One-Dimensional Man*, of the "mobilization and administration of libido." Not for a moment did I consider the relevance of the extensive feminist literature on the social construction and "deployment" of female sexuality, beauty, and "femininity"—for example, in the early work of Andrea Dworkin:

> Standards of beauty describe in precise terms the relationship that an individual will have to her own body. They prescribe her motility, spontaneity, posture, gait, the uses to which she can put her body. *They define precisely the dimensions of her physical freedom.* And of course, the relationship between physical freedom and psychological development, intellectual possibility, and creative potential is an umbilical one.
>
> In our culture, not one part of a woman's body is left untouched, unaltered. No feature or extremity is spared the art, or pain, of improvement. . . . From head to toe, every feature of a woman's face, every section of her body, is subject to modification, alteration. This alteration is an ongoing, repetitive process. It is vital to the economy, the major substance of male-female differentiation, the most immediate physical and psychological reality of being a woman. From the age of 11 or 12 until she dies, a woman will spend a large part of her time, money, and energy on binding, plucking, painting and deodorizing herself. It is commonly and wrongly said that male transvestites through the use of makeup and costuming caricature the women they would become, but any real knowledge of the romantic ethos makes clear that these men have penetrated to the core experience of being a woman, a romanticized construct. (emphasis in original)[7]

Is this "essentialism"? A view of the body as an "archaic natural"? Or is the collapsing of Dworkin *on* female bodies with Dworkin *as* a female body responsible for our inability to read her as the sophisticated theorist that she is? When I wrote my review of Foucault, I was working on a dissertation historically critiquing the duality of male mind/female body. Yet, like the zoologist who translated *The Second Sex*, I expected "theory" only from men. Moreover—and here my inability to move beyond these dualisms reveals itself more subtly—I was unable to recognize *embodied* theory when it was staring me in the face. For in Dworkin's work, as in feminist writing of the sixties and seventies more generally, theory was rarely abstracted and elaborated, adorned with power jargon, and made into an object of fascination in itself; rather, theory made its appearance as it shaped the "matter" of the argument. Works that perform such abstraction and elaboration get taken much more seriously than works that do not. Dworkin, to make matters worse for herself, has consistently refused to tame and trim her own materiality, to enact the cultural control of the flesh—through normalizing diet, dress, and gestures—that would align her with disciplined "mind" rather than unruly body.

But, as de Beauvoir argues, no matter how we dress ourselves or our insights, we will almost always be mapped into the region of the Other. Thus, when feminists such as Dworkin talk about the discipline of the body required by the "art" of femininity, their work is read as having implications only for women and the "peculiarities" of their bodies. But when Foucault talks about the discipline of the body involved in the training of a soldier, it is read as gender-neutral and broadly applicable. The soldier-body is no less gendered a norm, of course, than the body-as-decorative-object. But this is obscured because we view the woman's body under the sign of her Otherness while regarding the male body—as de Beauvoir puts it—as in "direct and normal relation to the world." The ironies engendered by this asymmetry are dizzying. The male body becomes "The Body" proper (as in: "Foucault altered our understanding of the body"), while the female body remains marked by its difference (as in: "Feminism showed us the oppressiveness of femininity"). At the same time, however, the male body *as* male body disappears completely, *its* concrete specificity submerged in its collapse into the universal.[8] Thus, while men are the cultural theorists *of* the body, only women *have* bodies. Meanwhile, of course, the absent male body continues to operate illicitly as the (scientific, philosophical, medical) norm for all.

Reading and Misreading Feminist Philosophy

When we turn to cultural narratives about philosophical modernity and "postmodernity," the ghettoization of feminist insight is even more striking. From de Beauvoir herself—the *first* philosopher to challenge the notion that there *is* one "human condition" that all persons share—to feminist critiques of modern science, to contemporary feminist skepticism over the continuity and unity of identity, feminist theorists have been at the forefront in challenging the presumed universality, neutrality, and unity of the modern "subject." The challenge began with the specific exposure of gender, as feminists pointed out that Man really *is* man, albeit covertly. And *as* an embodied, en-gendered being, he could no longer be imagined to have an elevated, disinterested "God's-eye view" of reality. Thus began the widespread questioning, throughout the disciplines, of the established paradigms of truth and method that had set the standards for philosophical and ethical reasoning, scientific rigor, literary and artistic values, historical narrative, and so on.

This questioning has hardly been the canon-bashing "assault on reason" that contemporary polemics make it out to be. With few exceptions, the point has been to reveal what dominant models have *excluded* rather than to attack the value of what they *have* offered. Yet a sort of cultural castration anxiety continually converts any criticism of canonical thought into the specter of Lorena Bobbit–like academic feminists, wildly lopping off reason, logic, and Shakespeare–right at the quick. For those who suffer from this anxiety—and this includes women as well as men—there appear to be only two choices: phallocentrism or emasculation. But for many feminist critics of modernity (and I include myself here), dethroning the king is *not* equivalent to cutting off his head. Rather, sharing power is what it's all about.

Is it really, as Martha Nussbaum has charged,[9] a wholesale "assault on reason" to suggest that Western notions of rationality have developed around the exclusion of qualities associated with the feminine, or with "ways of knowing" developed by women in the domains allotted to them? Or is the elaboration and reconstruction of reason, engaged in by male philosophers from Aristotle and Hegel to James, Dewey, and Whitehead, off-limits to women? Perhaps the problem is that feminist philosophers, unlike these male reformers of reason, have invoked a suppressed or unacknowledged *feminine* alterity as a way into criticism and reconstruction of dominant forms. So, for example, Iris Young's study of pregnant embodiment suggests that pregnancy may make uniquely available (although it does not guarantee) a very different experience of the relationship between mind and body, inner and outer, self and other than that presumed by Descartes, Hobbes, Locke, and other architects of the modernist subject.[10] Young's point, it should be emphasized, is not to glorify pregnancy but to interrogate the modernist model, to force it to confront its particularity and its limitations. Similarly, Sara Ruddick develops the notion of "maternal thinking"[11] not in celebration of a distinctively and exclusively female mode of rationality *or* in order to "assault" and abandon traditional concepts of reason but to diagnose and remedy what the latter lack.

There is no denying, however, that feminism has contributed to— although it hardly is solely responsible for—a generalized cultural skepticism about claims to knowledge and truth, particularly when they stake out applicability to the whole of human history and experience. This is not the place to sort out the insights and excesses of this skepticism, which takes many forms and is the product of many forces. Clearly, however, it was historically inevitable that centuries of universalizing talk about "human beings" and "human nature" would eventually become suspect, and that new questions would begin to be asked. Just *who* is being described? Who does not fit in? What elements of human experience are foregrounded? Which neglected? Set in motion by gender critique, the "subject" had in fact begun a shattering "great fall," and many now believe that it can never be put together again.

Some contemporary feminist philosophers, in the tradition of both Hume and various Eastern conceptions, question even the unity and stability of identity in the individual. In distinction to Humean and Eastern conceptions, however, recent feminist conceptions complicate the question of personal identity with a new understanding of the diverse and mutable elements that make up our *social* identity, as in Maria Lugones's influential piece on the "world-traveling" subject:

> I think that most of us who are outside the mainstream of, for example, the U.S. dominant construction or organization of life, are "world-travelers" as a matter of necessity and of survival. It seems to me that inhabiting more than one "world" at the same time and "traveling" between "worlds" is part and parcel of our experience and our situation. One can be at the same time in a "world" that constructs one as stereotypically Latin, for example, and in a "world" that constructs one as Latin. Being stereotypically Latin and being simply Latin are different simultaneous constructions of person that are part of different "worlds.". . .
>
> The shift from being one person to being a different person is what I call "travel." This shift may not be willful or even conscious. . . . [I]t is not a matter of acting. One does not pose as someone else, one does not pretend to be, for example, someone of a different personality or character or someone who uses space or language differently than the other person. Rather one is someone who has that personality or character or uses space and language in that particular way. The "one" here does not refer to some underlying 'I.' One does not *experience* any underlying "I."[12]

I will refer to these ideas again later in this essay. For now, I only want to point out how rarely Lugones's and other feminist critiques of personhood and identity are represented as originary "postmodern" moments. No, it is Derrida who "deconstructs the 'I'"; Lugones represents the Other who stands outside the "I," the "difference" of the Latina living in Western culture. And when "the end of the regime of Man," "the death of the Subject," and so forth, are described as constituting a turning point, crisis, or "postmodern moment" of general cultural significance, feminism is constructed—even by feminists such as Pamela McCallum—as a grateful "little sister" rather than generative "mother" of the transformation: "There can be no doubt that the theorizing of those writers who have defined the postmodern movement—Jacques Derrida, Michel Foucault, Jean Baudrillard, Jean-François Lyotard, and Richard Rorty, among others—has produced a number of arguments which offer a substantial challenge to the assumptions of traditional Western philosophy . . . [e.g.,] that human reason is homogeneous and universal, unaffected by the specific experiences of the individual knower; . . . that knowledge is generated from a free play of the intelligence and is not bound up with or implicated in forms of power and systems of domination."[13] Concerning feminism's relation to these challenges, McCallum suggests that feminists would surely "give assent" to them because they support a critique of male bias in philosophy; she then raises the question of whether feminists should "appropriate" postmodernism. Here we have yet another cultural reworking of the "Adam gave birth to Eve" fantasy, in which the questioning of the universality and neutrality of philosophical reason *precedes* rather than is *produced* by feminism. McCallum does not seem to recognize that feminist epistemologists such as Sandra Harding were questioning the presumptions of Western philosophy before Richard Rorty's *Philosophy and the Mirror of Nature* appeared, or that numerous feminists were exploring knowledge as "implicated in forms of power and systems of domination" at the same time as Foucault was developing his ideas. In McCallum's characterization, the broad, general, theoretical challenges to culture originate with Rorty and Foucault; feminism "gives assent." The originary contribution of feminism is constructed as the more limited critique of exposing sexism and masculinism in philosophical traditions.

Sometimes, this construction will involve serious misreadings of feminist work. My own book on Descartes, for example, discusses the "masculine" nature of seventeenth-century science only in the last of its six chapters and mentions Nancy Chodorow's ideas about gender difference just twice, once precisely in order to *distinguish* my use of developmental categories from Chodorow's. Yet the book is frequently read, by critics and sympathizers alike, as an application of Chodorow. It is worth quoting a description from the introduction to my book, and then a recent characterization, to illuminate more sharply just what is involved in the kinds of misreadings feminist work is prey to:

> My use of developmental theory focuses, not on gender difference, but on very general categories—individuation, separation anxiety, object permanence—in an attempt to explore their relevance to existential and epistemological changes brought about by the dissolution of the organic, finite, maternal universe of the Middle Ages and Renaissance. In an important sense the separate self, conscious of itself and of its own distinctness from a world "outside" it, is born in the Cartesian era. It is a psychological birth—of "inwardness," of "subjectivity," of "locatedness" in time and space—generating new anxieties and, ultimately, new strategies for maintaining equilibrium in an utterly changed and alien world.[14]

The Flight to Objectivity, then, attempts to locate the work of Descartes and the Cartesian view of the self in the context of a general cultural transformation, the "birth of modernity." As to Chodorow's ideas about gender difference, I indicate in *Flight* that I consider her work suggestive, and potentially applicable to understanding changes that took place during the Enlightenment. But I stress that such historical application has yet to be made and is certainly not attempted in the pages of my own book. Yet here is how my argument was recently described by Margaret Atherton: "*The Flight to Objectivity* makes *heavy* use of categories of contemporary feminist theory, especially those provided by Evelyn Fox Keller and Nancy Chodorow, to illuminate Descartes' theory, *as [Bordo] believes it affects women*" (emphasis added).[15]

Elsewhere, Atherton repeats the idea; the point of my argument, she insists, is to show how Descartes's arguments have "given rise to a decline in the status of women."[16] Now to suggest, as I do, that the birth of modernity has a significant gender dimension—in separation of the self from the maternal universe of the Middle Ages and the Renaissance—is hardly equivalent to an argument about the effects of Cartesianism "on women." To read the text in this way is, rather, to view it through the template of gender duality. Under that template, the name "Chodorow" (whose work focuses on developmental differences between males and females, and has been charged with "essentializing" those differences) claims the imagination of the reader and simply will not let go. The result, unfortunately, is that "women's difference" becomes identified as a concern of the text, which becomes stamped as a work about the exclusion of women rather than about a transformation in the philosophical conception of self and world.

The feminist whose work perhaps has suffered most from such inscriptions is Carol Gilligan. Now, Gilligan appears on the face of it, of all contemporary feminists, to have most been given her due, to have achieved a central place on the intellectual landscape, even to have been recognized and celebrated outside the boundaries of academia. It might seem, moreover, as though any marking of *In a Different Voice* as about "women's difference" is the fault (or intent) of the work itself, as the title alone might suggest. This reading of Gilligan is only partially accurate, however. To be sure, the book's contrast between two modes of moral reasoning is articulated in terms of gender difference. Thus, according to Gilligan, the preference for abstract argument over assessments of particular, concrete situations is grounded in a "blueprint" of human interaction that is more characteristic of males than females. Because the "male" blueprint is atomistic, collisions between individuals are viewed as invitations to disaster and must be rigorously guarded against—by abstract notions of "personhood" and "rights," among other things, which define clear boundaries around the individual and protect against collision. Women's blueprint, in contrast, as Gilligan argued, is relational. Here the chief danger (what "disturbs the universe," if you will) is the fracturing of attachment, and the moral imperative is to restore human connection by a careful assessment of how to responsibly mend the fractures occurring in particular, concrete situations.

You will notice that I have not mentioned the word "care" in the foregoing description, a deliberate omission that will become clearer shortly. For now, I would emphasize that while Gilligan's critique is articulated in terms of gender difference, it would be a serious mistake to see its implications as "only" involving gender. In the introduction to *In a Different Voice*, she writes that the chief aim of the book is to "highlight a distinction between two modes of thought . . . rather than to represent a generalization about either sex." She stresses that the articulation of women's perspective is not an end in itself but a propaedeutic to recognition of "a limitation in the conception of human condition."[17] For "once women are inserted into the picture," as Seyla Benhabib astutely points out, ". . . be it as objects of social-scientific research or as subjects conducting the inquiry, established paradigms are unsettled. The definition of the *object domain* of a research paradigm, its units of measurement, its method of verification, the alleged neutrality of its theoretical terminology, and the claims to universality of its models and metaphors are all thrown into question."[18]

Gilligan's work has been extensively criticized by other feminists for "essentializing" a historically located, class- and race-biased construction of female "difference." And it is true that the book fails to raise questions about the generalizability of her findings, which were based on a limited and fairly homogeneous sample. The limits of her sample might have been taken, as Jane Martin points out, as calling for further research into the wider applicability of her hypothesis; instead, she was charged with racism and classism, and it was implied—without argument or demonstration—that the "different voice" was uniquely white and middle-class.[19] Arguably, the point here was not so much to challenge Gilligan's findings as to expose and protest (and not only in Gilligan's work, of course) the unself-conscious slippage from white feminist experiences to universalizing talk about "women's ways of knowing." But, whatever their justice vis-à-vis Gilligan's empirical generalizations or white bias in feminist research, such criticisms miss an important dimension of her work.

What such criticisms overlook is Gilligan's heuristic use of gender alterity to expose the universalist pretensions of dominant norms and to envision alternatives. In terms of this aim, whether or not the proposed gender difference derives from biology or from socially constructed roles, whether it adequately reflects the situations of all women or an ethnically or class-specific construction of gender—these are not key issues. What gender difference here affords (as ethnic and other cultural differences can afford, as well) is a "way into" cultural critique. In terms of this potential, it is not surprising that a number of important feminist theorists, Benhabib among them, have used Gilligan's insights to mount a critique of the possessive individualism of liberalism, the autonomous, "unencumbered self" presumed in the ontological blueprint identified by Gilligan as the dominant (rather than "different") mode.

These cultural applications of Gilligan's work may be well known to feminist philosophers. But when a recent article in the *Chronicle of Higher Education* surveyed academic work arguing for more relational, less "rights"-

dominated models of the person and the state,[20] neither Gilligan herself nor Carole Pateman, Susan Moller Okin, Virginia Held, Iris Young, Nancy Fraser, Drucilla Cornell, or Seyla Benhabib was mentioned. This effacement of the general, cultural critique implicit in Gilligan's work and explicitly carried out in the work of numerous feminist political theorists is manifest, as well, in philosophy textbooks. A revised, 1994 edition of *Philosophy: Contemporary Perspectives on Perennial Issues*,[21] for example, features a section on "State and Society," in which feminist political theory is represented by a piece by Alison Jaggar on "Political Philosophies of *Women's* Liberation" (emphasis added). "State and Society" *could* have included, in addition to Jaggar's very valuable piece, one of the many excellent feminist critiques of political liberalism. But the section was not conceptualized to allow for a feminist perspective on government or political theory. The presentation and argumentation regarding general political categories—"democracy," "libertarianism," "socialism," and "liberalism"—are reserved in the section for the "gender-neutral" (as it is presumed) scrutiny of four (male) nonfeminists; the role of the feminist philosopher, is only to represent the "difference" of women's situation.

What Gilligan's work *has* been publicly associated with, not surprisingly, is precisely that "difference"—the so-called ethic of care. To some degree, this association has been facilitated by Gilligan herself. She tries to make it clear that she is *not* arguing that women are moral angels while men are unconcerned with helping others; her argument, rather (as I noted earlier), is that women and men have different ways of conceiving of "help," based on their different conceptions of what constitutes danger. But Gilligan's efforts to avoid promoting a new version of the nineteenth-century vision of woman-as-ministering-angel were hampered by her unfortunate choice of the term "ethic of care" to describe the female moral imperative. The suggestion that men do *not* "care" as much as women is immediately (and inaccurately) evoked. Moreover, the obvious and important connections to be made to the critique of the classical liberal model of the person become obscured. Unfortunately, the "ethic of care" swiftly became *the* category through which Gilligan's work was socially defined, reducing the transformative potential of women's "difference" to the familiar notion that we need more women to provide warmth and nurture in the workplace. (For this reason, I never use the term "care" when I teach Gilligan.)

The fault, however, is not entirely Gilligan's—as I hope this paper is helping to make clear. In a culture shaped by gender dualities, there is a powerful inclination to "read" feminist work as reinforcing those dualities. So, for example, Sara Ruddick's concept of "maternal thinking," despite Ruddick's strong and clear underscoring that she is describing an ideal suggested by a particular kind of parenting *practice* (it is thus not a contradiction in terms for a man to be a "maternal thinker"), continually gets read as "essentializing" a distinctively female perspective. More subtly and pervasively, and as I have been arguing throughout this essay, feminist theory swims upstream against powerful currents whenever it threatens to assume the mantle of *general* cultural critique rather than simply advocate for the greater inclusion or representation of women and their "differences."

WHO SPEAKS FOR PHILOSOPHY?

In *Fire with Fire*, Naomi Wolf argues that in recent years a massive "gender-quake" has occurred, sinking patriarchy into "deeper and deeper eclipse."[22] In the wake of this quake, she argues, it is time for women to stop complaining and start exercising our newly developed muscle. In the words of the Nike ad that she offers as a symbol of what she calls "power feminism," women need to stop whining and *"just do it."*

But Wolf is mistaken if she believes that the ability of women to "just do it" is itself evidence that patriarchy is in eclipse. Feminist philosophy is a case in point, and a particularly powerful and troubling one. As critics of Western culture, feminist philosophers have been "just doing it" for some time. Yet, as I have argued, we remain the Other in the self-conception of our discipline, in intellectual history generally, and even in narratives about the very changes that we have brought about. To point this out is not to "whine" about how feminists have been "victimized" by their marginalization in cultural narratives, or to make feminists into the heroines of a revised, "feminized" cultural history. Frequently nowadays, feminist criticism is presented in such terms—by the popular media and by "power feminists" like Wolf, Roiphe, and Sommers. But the depiction of feminist criticism as "victim feminism" assumes, as Freud assumed in asking his famous question, that if women want something, it can only be for their sex, it can only be as the Other. This has been especially frustrating for those of us who have been drawn to feminist philosophy precisely for the vantage point it provides from which to analyze, evaluate, and participate in the transformation of *culture*.

Given this aim, it is imperative that we resist the ghettoization of feminist insight—for example, at conferences, in anthologies, in the curriculum—and insist that feminist philosophy be read *as* cultural critique. More precisely, we need to insist that "gender theory" be read *for* the cultural critique that it offers. This is no easy task. It demands vigilance—precisely because the struggle is not over *inclusion* (the liberal measure of female "power," assumed by Wolf, Sommers, and others) but over the cultural *meaning* of that inclusion. To make this distinction clear, let me provide an example. Several years ago, I attended a national working conference on "The Responsibilities of Philosophers." The only feminist philosopher in my small-group session, I had talked at length about the history of philosophy, about how inadequate was any understanding of the Western philosophical tradition that did not examine the racism and sexism that have been elements in many philosophical conceptions of human nature and reason. To do so, I emphasized, does not mean trashing Western philosophical traditions but rather bringing the study of philosophy down from the timeless heavens and into the bodies of historical human beings. Later, at the plenary session, my participation was reported as consisting of the suggestion that "we need to pay much more attention to hiring women and minorities."

The salient point here is not that I was not listened to but that what was "heard" had been converted from cultural critique to simple advocacy for the rights of the Other. Constructed as advocacy for the rights of the Other, my remarks no longer impinged on the philosophical methods or identities of the men in my group. They could continue to exalt (and teach) the "Man of Reason" as the disembodied Subject of philosophical history, while presumably letting the women and minorities whom they would hire take care of "gender and race." Thus, the insights of feminist philosophy are kept "in their place," where they make no claim on "philosophy proper." The voices of "difference" are permitted to speak, and business goes on as usual. So, for example, it becomes perfectly possible for a philosopher to assign Gilligan for a special class session on "Women and Morality," while continuing unself-consciously and without remark to organize discussion around highly abstract and uncontextualized case studies.

In the case of more "postmodern" critiques, it has made an enormous philosophical difference that contemporary intellectuals have largely learned their lessons from the poststructuralist fathers rather than the feminist mothers. Freud's allegory of the primal tribe, which murders the patriarch only to nostalgically institutionalize and reproduce the conditions of his reign, is interesting to think about here. The "fathers" of postmodernism are, after all, also the *sons* of Enlightenment Man, the inheritors of both his privileges and his blind spots. They may be eager to prove their own manhood through rebellion against his rule. But do they know a different way of being?

Thus, while Man has been officially declared "dead," like Freddy Kruger, he just keeps bouncing back. His pretensions and fantasies—the transcendence of the body, the drive toward separation from and domination over nature, the ambition to create an authoritative scientific or philosophical discourse, all of which have been extensively critiqued by feminist theory—have simply been recycled. The modern, Cartesian erasure of the body ("the view from nowhere") has been traded, as I argue in *Unbearable Weight*, for a postmodern, Derridean version (the dream of being "everywhere"). The old model of man's mind as the pinnacle of God's creation has been replaced by the poststructuralist equivalent: human language as the ultimate architect and arbiter of reality. The analytic overseer of argument has been supplanted by the master of authoritative "theory." And old forms of dominating and excluding others through professional jargon and obscurantism have merely been replaced by new forms of discursive elitism.

Thus, we see the unconscious reproduction of the "sins" of the (philosophical) fathers by poststructuralist sons not much closer than their fathers were to truly hearing the voice of woman's (or any other human) "differ-ence." As Jane Flax has put it:

> Despite the rhetoric of 'reading like a woman' or displacing 'phallocentrism,' post-modernists are unaware of the deeply gendered nature of their own recounting and interpretations of the Western Story and the strategies they oppose to its mas-ter narratives. Postmodernists still honor Man as the sole author and principal character in these stories, even if this Man is dying, his time running out. They retell the contemporary history of the West in and through the stories of the three deaths—of Man, (his) History, and (his) metaphysics. Whatever women have done with and in all this (becoming past) time is 'outside' by definition and accord-ing to the conventions of (their) story line. . . . [T]his absence or disappearance of concrete women and gender relations suggests the possibility that postmodernism is not only or simply opposed to phallocentrism but also may be 'its latest ruse.'[23]

Contemporary feminists have not been immune to the recyclings of phallo-centrism. Many of us may want to prove *our* manhood, too; this is, after all, where academic "power" (and of course not only *academic* power) resides. Ignoring, dismissing, or denouncing whole generations of ambitious and imaginative feminist work (while remaining remarkably tolerant of the mis-takes and omissions of male philosophers),[24] some feminists have colluded in "the disappearance of women" of which Flax speaks.[25] In response, other feminists participate in their *own* disappearance. Sensing that general cul-tural critique is too risky, fearing charges of "essentialism," racism, canon bashing, and white-male trashing, we may try to protect ourselves by keeping ourselves small, tidy, and specific (or by not saying much of anything at all).

For some feminists, too, it appears as though any identification with women's historical "differences" is equivalent to identification with vic-timhood and disempowerment.[26] For others, however, the "differences" of women's experiences, racial and ethnic as well as gendered, remain a well-spring from which to draw cultural and philosophical critique, to imagine alternatives that are unavailable or muted in the histories that men have told about their experience. Consider, for example, two distinctive approaches to the cultural deconstruction of the "subject" represented by Derrida and Lugones. Derrida's position is abstract and impersonal. "*I* do not select," he has written. "The interpretations select themselves." Here, while renouncing Cartesianism, Derrida perpetuates its controlling fiction that a person can negate the accidents of individual biography and speak with a purely philo-sophical voice.

In Maria Lugones's critique, by contrast, the personal (and cultural) as-pects of identity remain fully present, even as the unity and permanence of the self are challenged. Like Minnie Bruce Pratt's "autobiography" of her constantly evolving identities of "skin, blood, heart," Lugones's account is vividly grounded in personal, often visceral experience. It stresses the con-crete, social multiplicity rather than the abstract "disappearance" of the sub-ject. The self is fractured because our social experience requires it of us—

more from some than others; the experience of "unity" of identity is nothing more than the privilege of being at home in the dominant culture, of feeling integrated within it. Nonetheless, the fractured self, which has been *forced* to learn to be a shape-shifter in foreign worlds, "as a matter of necessity and survival," can teach important lessons about how to be a subject in playful, adaptable, nonimperialist modes.

My point here is not to insist that every philosopher adopt a more personal or anecdotal style. Rather, it is to insist that there is a philosophical issue at stake in the difference between Derrida and Lugones—two competing views of "the death of the subject," if you will, reflecting the different "subjects" of history that each identifies with. This issue is effaced as long as Derrida alone is viewed as speaking for "philosophy" and "culture," while Lugones is taken to represent the voice of the Latina Other. If the rebellious sons had truly been listening to feminist voices—if they had been able to recognize feminist theory as representing not merely the "different" voice of Otherness but the authority of modes of being and knowing as historically pervasive if not as culturally dominant as their own—they might have been able to achieve a deeper understanding of phallocentrism and the subtle ways that it reproduces itself. If they had looked to a human history broader than their own, they might have been less ready to project the death of their own philosophical traditions onto all of culture. Within those traditions, the "self," "man," the author, and subjectivity took very particular forms by virtue of the experiences excluded from them. Those forms may indeed now be standing on rockier, less elevated ground than they once did. Nevertheless, other forms of being and knowing have been and continue to be available, waiting to be brought from the region of the Other, to join them on the central terrains of our culture.

Acknowledgments

I am grateful to several people who assisted me in the research, conceptualization, and final preparation of this piece. First, I would like to thank Janet Kourany for inviting me to write a piece for this volume surveying contemporary feminist philosophy's contribution to contemporary reconstructions of the "self." As I worked on this assignment, I realized that feminists had contributed to the contemporary concept of the self in myriad ways, yet no one except other feminists—and sometimes not even they—seemed to realize this! So, instead of fulfilling my original assignment, I wound up writing the present essay, which Janet graciously accepted for her volume, despite the transformation in topic. Rachel Hertel, my research assistant at LeMoyne College, helped me compile the resources and discussed the project with me in its early stages. Edward Lee read and commented on the first, meandering and confused, drafts, and helped me to see the ideas about feminism and Otherness at the center of it. As I was writing the next draft, I heard Anna Antonopoulos speak at LeMoyne College; her talk was the source of several wonderful details, previously unknown to me, about the reception of *The Second Sex*. Lynne Arnault read a later version, as I was about to deliver it at the 1994 Eastern SWIP Conference in Binghamton, New York; her astute comments, as always, helped focus and clarify the argument considerably. For the final version, I thank Leslie Heywood for several keen observations and suggestions.

Notes

1. Edward Said, *Musical Elaborations* (New York: Columbia University Press, 1991), pp. xiv–xv.
2. See "P.C., O.J., and Truth: Teaching in the Real World," in my *Twilight Zones: The Hidden Life of Cultural Images from Plato to O.J.* (Berkeley and Los Angeles: University of California Press, 1997) for discussion and analysis of the "culture wars" on college campuses.
3. Anna Antonopoulos, "Simone de Beauvoir and the Differance of Translation," *Institut Simone de Beauvoir Bulletin* 14 (1994): 99–101.
4. Susan Bordo, *Unbearable Weight* (Berkeley and Los Angeles: University of California Press, 1993), esp. pp. 15–42.
5. Linda Zerilli, "Rememoration or War? French Feminist Narrative and the Politics of Self-Representation," *Differences* 3, no. 1 (1991): 2–3.
6. Susan Bordo, "Organized Sex," *Cross Currents* 30, no. 3 (1980): 194–98.
7. Andrea Dworkin, *Woman-Hating* (New York: Dutton, 1974), pp. 113–14.
8. I want to thank Leslie Heywood for this last point, made to me in personal communication.
9. Martha Nussbaum, "Feminists and Philosophy," *New York Review of Books*, October 20, 1994, pp. 59–63.
10. Iris Young, "Pregnant Embodiment: Subjectivity and Alienation," *Journal of Medicine and Philosophy* (January 1984): 45–62.
11. Sara Ruddick, *Maternal Thinking* (Boston: Beacon Press, 1989).
12. Maria Lugones, "Playfulness, 'World'-Traveling, and Loving Perception," *Hypatia* 2, no. 2 (Summer 1987): 3–20; quotation on pages 11–12.
13. Pamela McCallum, "The Construction of Knowledge and Epistemologies of Marked Subjectivities," *University of Toronto Quarterly* 61, no. 4 (Summer 1992): quotation on page 431.
14. Susan Bordo, *The Flight to Objectivity: Essays on Cartesianism and Culture* (Buffalo: State University of New York Press, 1987), pp. 6–7.
15. Margaret Atherton, *APA Newsletter on Feminism and Philosophy* 92, no. 2 (Fall 1993): quotation on page 45 (emphasis added).
16. Margaret Atherton, "Cartesian Reason and Gendered Reason," in Louise Antony and Carlotte Witt, ed., *A Mind of One's Own* (Boulder, Colo.: Westview Press, 1993), pp. 19–34; quotation on page 20.
17. Carol Gilligan, *In a Different Voice* (Cambridge, Mass.: Harvard University Press, 1982), p. 2.
18. Seyla Benhabib, *The Situated Self: Gender, Community, and Postmodernism in Contemporary Ethics* (New York: Routledge, 1992), p. 178.
19. Jane Roland Martin, "Methodological Essentialism, False Difference, and Other Dangerous Traps," *Signs* 19, no. 3 (Spring 1994): 630–57; quotation on page 652.

20. "Point of View: Clinton and the Promise of Communitarianism," *Chronicle of Higher Education*, December 2, 1992, p. A52.

21. E. D. Klemke, A. David Kline, and Robert Holinger, eds., *Philosophy: Contemporary Perspectives on Perennial Issues* (New York: St. Martin's Press, 1994).

22. Naomi Wolf, *Fire with Fire: The New Female Power and How It Will Change the Twenty-first Century* (New York: Random House, 1993), p. 11.

23. Jane Flax, *Thinking Fragments: Psychoanalysis, Feminism and Postmodernism in the Contemporary West* (Berkeley and Los Angeles: University of California Press, 1990), pp. 214, 216.

24. See Martin for an insightful discussion of this "discrepancy between our cordial treatment of the men's theories and our punitive approach to the women's" ("Methodological Essentialism," p. 651.

25. See, for example, Nussbaum ("Feminists and Philosophy"), as well as the many discrediting attacks on feminist "essentialism" (see Martin, "Methodological Essentialism," for an excellent discussion of this). On the more popular front, Naomi Wolf gushes ecstatically about "the drama of women's capturing male authority and power," symbolized for her in the depiction, in commercial advertisements, of phallic objects "emerging . . . from *women's* groins" (*Fire with Fires* p. 29). Yet at the same time as she celebrates the cultural sprouting of the female phallus, she has no qualms about dismissing—without attending concretely to any of it—several decades of feminist writing.

26. See my "Feminism, Postmodernism and Gender Scepticism," in *Unbearable Weight*, for elaboration of this idea.